The Road to Joy

THE
ROAD TO JOY

The Letters of
THOMAS MERTON
to New and Old Friends
Selected and edited by
Robert E. Daggy

Farrar · Straus · Giroux

NEW YORK

Contents

Preface

As the general editor of the Letters of Thomas Merton, I have had the unique privilege of reading all the letters stored in the archives of the Thomas Merton Center at Bellarmine College in Louisville, Kentucky. The more I have read the letters—and my total reading time in going through them would probably amount to several months at eight hours a day—the more I have felt they should be made available to as wide a reading public as possible.

Like his books and essays, Merton's letters articulated his desire, growing through the years, to be in touch with contemporary men and women as they struggled with questions of truth and meaning and the responsibilities that continually trouble the human spirit. There is a particularity about a letter that it is not possible to achieve in a book: letters are one-on-one; they exist for dialogue and call for reaction. Yet if they are good—and Merton was a good letter writer—their particularity spills over into issues that touch our common human situation. When they are deeply personal, one can put oneself in the place of the correspondent and experience the letter as if directly addressed. Because the letters often touch on perennial human questions, one can also share in their insights.

Though Merton's letters do come to grips with substantive issues, they are not ponderous or prosaic. The impish smile that lights up so many of his photographs seems to look out through the letters, too—perhaps in a special way in this volume, which bears the title *The Road to Joy*. The ready wit and the bright phrase that characterize his writing are present here in abundance.

Thomas Merton's letters, like most good letters, are not polished essays on the topics they deal with. More often there are flashes of intuition on a subject that is left open-ended. This sense of incompleteness—mildly frustrating at times, one might want to say—prods both writer and reader to follow paths that have been opened but not yet fully explored.

The Road to Joy points to many such paths. The readers of this volume are fortunate to have Dr. Robert Daggy, director of the Thomas Merton Center, as guide along the way.

WILLIAM H. SHANNON
General Editor

Introduction

If a man does not make new acquaintances as he advances
through life, he will soon find himself alone. A man
should keep his friendships in constant repair.
DR. SAMUEL JOHNSON
QUOTED BY JAMES BOSWELL

One enjoys contacts more when the letters are from one's
real friends, and not just a pile of ill-assorted business
and other nonsense from complete strangers.
THOMAS MERTON
TO SISTER THERESE LENTFOEHR

I hope you and I together will secretly travel our own
road to joy, which is mysteriously revealed to us.
THOMAS MERTON TO GRACE SISSON

The second volume of Merton letters contains correspondence with relatives and special friends. It follows the first volume, *The Hidden Ground
of Love*, which was devoted to letters on religious experience and social
concerns. Other projected volumes will present Merton's letters on religious life and renewal, edited by Brother Patrick Hart; those on writing,
edited by David D. Cooper; and a concluding collection, edited by William H. Shannon. It is obvious that these categories are loose and many
of Merton's letters may fall into more than one category. Certainly Merton
discussed his family in letters not included here, and just as certainly he
considered most of his correspondents to be his special friends. Relatives
are of course a defined category, though in this case the meaning has
been widened to include people who can be described, for one reason
or another, as "family friends." The term "special friends" presented some
problems. Merton not only had a knack for making people feel special,

but he built up his later friendships through correspondence—a necessary means, since he had so little direct contact with people outside the monastery. Yet it is true that we all have some special friends in our lifetime, people to whom we feel particularly close, people who stand outside the normal routines of our lives and our occupations, people with whom we have shared a point in time and space and with whom our rapport lingers on. Thomas Merton was no exception. He enjoyed such special friendships, connected only tangentially (if at all) to his "business" of writing and his vocation as a monk, friendships which gave continuity to his journey.

The volume begins with his letters to one of those special friends, Mark Van Doren. Teacher and mentor, colleague and chum, fellow writer and fellow traveler, Van Doren occupied a unique place in Merton's life and in his affections. They had a continuous relationship, which extended from Merton's student days at Columbia College until his death in 1968. The final connection between these longtime friends is an ironic and suggestive one: Van Doren died on December 10, 1972, four years to the day after his friend Merton. It is neither the largest nor the longest set of letters in the volume, but it is a steady one, with a letter from Merton nearly every year. Van Doren carefully kept his letters from Merton (now deposited in Butler Library at Columbia), including the handwritten ones and the ones which Merton failed to carbon. This care has left us one of the most complete sets of Merton letters we possess and one in which we can trace Merton's consistent, even deepening, fondness and respect for Van Doren.

The second section contains Merton's surviving (perhaps it is better to say "discovered") letters to and about his family, beginning with a letter written to his father's art teacher, Percyval Tudor-Hart, on the day of his father's funeral in 1931. It is the earliest Merton letter which we have. Undoubtedly, as a child, he wrote notes to his New Zealand grandparents and to his American grandparents, but all inquiries and searches have revealed no surviving letters to family members other than those included here. One tantalizing possibility emerged in a letter written in 1971 by Merton's "Aunt Ka," Beatrice Katharine Merton, to the late John Howard Griffin. She told Griffin that the family members in New Zealand had turned over all their Thomas Merton materials to the Canterbury Public Library in Christchurch, but added that theirs was a family that did not keep letters, so she was unsure whether or not any letters were among those materials. Investigation showed that her instinct was correct: the materials given to the library in Christchurch consist of signed copies of Merton's books, a few photographs, and some memorabilia—but no letters. Merton himself admitted that he wrote very little to surviving members of his family after entering the monastery in 1941. Carbons of those written in the 1960s are preserved in the Thomas Merton Studies Center.

From the 1940s on, Merton complained that he received too much mail, that he had too many letters to answer, that he did not have enough time to answer them adequately, that correspondence at times was oppressive to him. Despite this, he carried on a volume of correspondence which is staggering. He frequently wrote letters the style and polish of which are astonishing. Yet there is no doubt that he felt the pressure of an ever-increasing correspondence from all sorts of people with all sorts of requests and questions. In the 1960s he began to solve this problem in part by composing form letters to be mimeographed and mailed to his "new and old friends." These, he felt, would give his old friends news about him and his writing and would alleviate the need to write full-scale answers to new correspondents. The letter written and mimeographed in 1963 was largely intended for students who asked for information on Merton and on other topics. The Christmas 1965 letter marked the start of his growing reliance on this form as a means of answering a great deal of his mail. In the next three years he wrote more and more of these "circular letters"—three in 1966, six in 1967, and seven in 1968. These letters have been gathered together and are published for the first time as a series in this volume.

The section of letters to special friends needs further explanation. Some special friends (Catherine de Hueck Doherty, Dorothy Day, James Forest, W. H. Ferry, and so on) were included in the first volume. Friends in religion or friends whom Merton knew through his monastic experience (such as Dom Jean Leclercq, Jacques Maritain, Sister Mary Luke Tobin, Brother Patrick Hart, and Ernesto Cardenal) and friends connected with the business of writing and publishing (Naomi Burton Stone, James Laughlin, Robert Giroux, Victor and Carolyn Hammer), while often quite close and special to Merton, seemed more appropriately assigned to other volumes.

Significantly, all the special friends I have included have visited Merton at Gethsemani, some on several occasions. Ten of them were "old" friends whom he knew before he entered the monastery, whose friendship he consistently repaired. Six were chums from his Columbia days: Robert Lax (perhaps, as Merton himself reveals, the friend to whom he felt the closest), Mahanambrata Brahmachari, Seymour Freedgood, Ad Reinhardt, Edward Rice, and John H. Slate. A further comment on the Lax letters is necessary, not only because they comprise one of the longest sets in this volume but because of the significance of the early letters written before Merton entered the monastery in December 1941. These letters demonstrate, as Merton tells us himself in other places, that he was an uncertain young man, drifting, chauvinistic, foulmouthed, sexually interested if not active, even racist, and they graphically show some of the things for which he later felt he had to atone. The seventh friend, Dan Walsh, an instructor at Columbia, was the man who first told Merton about Gethsemani, and a teacher who eventually followed his pupil there.

The letters to friends he made when he taught at Saint Bonaventure University include correspondence with Father Joseph Vann, O.F.M.; Father Thomas Plassman, O.F.M. (president of Saint Bonaventure during Merton's teaching stint there); and Father Irenaeus Herscher, O.F.M., who remained, as Merton put it, his "link with St. Bonas." The other four were friends he made after he entered Gethsemani. Tommie O'Callaghan became something of a social secretary to Merton in the 1960s, meeting and greeting, lodging and driving his visitors, arranging picnics and other events, sharing her home and her family with him, eventually agreeing to serve as a member of the literary trust he set up. Beatrice Olmstead was a friend whose letters and friendship provided Merton with access to another "adopted" family. John Howard Griffin, who was first chosen to write the authorized biography (due to illness, it was never completed), described their relationship as one of *les grandes amitiés* and coached Merton in his growing interest in photography. Finally, the most unusual friend in Merton's catalogue of correspondents is Sister Therese Lentfoehr. His letters to her are the largest set of letters included in this volume, important because of the twenty-year relationship which they kept in constant repair. From 1948 to 1968 Merton wrote to her probably more, and more consistently, than to any other of his correspondents. He was permitted to write to her even in the periods when his letter writing was severely restricted (even when he could receive and write only four letters a month, hers were among them). He was allowed to write her, in part, because she did typing for him, and hence for the Abbey, and there is no doubt that Merton used this permission from Dom James Fox as an outlet for letters he was not otherwise vouchsafed to write. Another factor in their long and voluminous correspondence may be that Merton was aware that these letters would be preserved. He may not have been sure that other correspondents kept or would keep his letters, but he *knew* that Sister Therese kept every page, every sheet, every scrap that issued from his hand or typewriter. These letters in fact became an alternate form of journal keeping for Merton, another facet of the autobiographical exercise in which he was continually engaged. They provide a twenty-year record in which one can find, as William Shannon said of Merton's letters in general, "a kind of latter-day *Seven Storey Mountain*."

The fifth section is a significant group of Merton's letters to and about young people. Despite his frequent complaints about the volume of correspondence in general and students' inquiries in particular, there was something good-natured about his grumblings. He may have felt put-upon, he may have felt pressures, but he conscientiously answered the majority of letters which young people wrote to him. Merton felt a special closeness to young people and these letters show the empathy which he and they both felt.

* * *

It has been pointed out that Merton was the first editor of his letters. He compiled a series of 110 letters written in 1961 and 1962 as the Cold War Letters. Several of these were published in *Seeds of Destruction* (1964); thirty-seven were included in *The Hidden Ground of Love* (1985); and ten more are included here, as follows: No. 16, December 1961 (Robert Lax); No. 20, January 11, 1962 (Sister Therese Lentfoehr); No. 33, February 10, 1962 (Edward Rice); No. 40, February 1962 (Robert Lax); No. 43, February 1962 (Tashi Tshering); No. 45, February 1962 (Ad Reinhardt); No. 57, March 1962 (Thomas J. Liang); No. 78, June 4, 1962 (Robert Lax); No. 94, August 2, 1962 (Elbert R. Sisson); No. 99, August 9, 1962 (Mark Van Doren).

The editorial procedures followed in this volume are similar, though not identical, to those followed in the first volume. Letters are arranged chronologically within each group. Salutations and closings have been omitted, except where Merton addressed a person or signed himself differently than normal (this is particularly true in the letters to Robert Lax, where many salutations and closings have been left intact). Some portions of letters have been omitted where material was of slight interest or repetitious. The great majority of Merton's letters were written at the Abbey of Gethsemani at Trappist, Kentucky. The location has been given for letters written elsewhere; if no city or place is indicated, the letter was written at the monastery. Footnotes have not been used. Identification of people, places, events, dates, books, articles, and so forth, has been placed within brackets in the text. Finally, every attempt has been made to preserve Merton's language and his typography, particularly in those letters where he deliberately misspelled words, used odd keys on his typewriter, and toyed with English.

The Road to Joy has been planned as a celebration of friendship, showing a lighter and more playful Merton, though he discusses serious topics in many of the letters. His tone varies from stern or respectful to chatty and "with-it" to zany, yet he is always Merton. The theme of joy (a word Merton uses frequently) runs through the letters—joy found in new and old friendships, the enjoyment of being in contact with one's friends, the rejoicing together when friendships are kept in repair. The title is taken from a phrase which Merton appropriated from one of his young correspondents, Grace Sisson. In 1962, when Grace was five, her father, Elbert R. Sisson, sent Merton a drawing she had done of a house. Merton was so enchanted with the drawing that it inspired him to write a poem, "Grace's House," in which he meticulously described everything which she had drawn, ending by regretting that "Alas, there is no road to Grace's house!" Five years later, Grace sent Merton another drawing, this time of a road which she dubbed "The Road to Joy." Merton adopted the phrase in his answer to her, using it to describe the unfathomable grace of friendship. He might well have invited all his friends to join him in traveling the "road to joy, which is mysteriously revealed to us without our exactly realizing."

ROBERT E. DAGGY
Thomas Merton Studies Center

Acknowledgments

I wish to express my gratitude first of all to William H. Shannon, the General Editor of the Merton Letters, for appointing me to select and edit the second volume of those letters. It has been a rare opportunity and what has been particularly pleasing about it is that I have experienced an even rarer friendship with a remarkable person, who has been a "working" General Editor and an unobtrusive force in the preparation of this volume. He has been available for overall planning, for suggestions and insights, for establishing certain editorial guidelines, yet he has not intruded himself into the selection or editing of the letters in the volume. Any faults or problems with it are due to me, the editor.

I would also like to express my thanks to the Trustees of the Merton Legacy Trust, Naomi Burton Stone [emeritus], James Laughlin, Tommie O'Callaghan, and Robert Giroux, for having given me the chance, since my appointment to the Thomas Merton Studies Center at Bellarmine College in 1974, to become familiar with Merton's correspondence and for allowing me to be their "Chief of Research." I am especially grateful to Tommie O'Callaghan, another remarkable person and a good friend, not only for her consistent help with the letters to her included in this volume, but simply because without her I would never have come to the Merton Center and I would never have edited this volume.

Several people have provided specific help in the preparation of this volume and I wish to express my appreciation to them: Bernard K. Crystal, assistant librarian for manuscripts at Butler Library, Columbia University, for the letters to Mark Van Doren; the Reverend Paul Dinter and his assistant, Ms. Suki Scott, of the Merton Center at Columbia University for the letters to Sister Therese Lentfoehr, and for processing the drawing "Grace's House" and other items; Father Felix Donahue, O.C.S.O., of the Abbey of Gethsemani, for translating letters to Cecilia Corsanego and Silvana Ranzoli Cuccolini from the Italian; Ms. Madeleine Juchau of the Social Sciences and Humanities Division of the Canterbury Public Library in Christchurch, New Zealand, for information about Merton family materials; Sister Marialein Lorenz, O.P., who provided complete copies of Merton's letters to her and to her students; Michael Mott for letters to Percyval Tudor-Hart, which he gathered in his research for the authorized biography; Abbot Joseph Murphy, O.C.S.O., of Southern Star Abbey in Hawke's Bay, New Zealand, for information about the Merton family; Mrs. Beatrice Olmstead for responding to my inquiries despite her feeling that no one would want to read Merton's letters to her; Edward Rice for assistance with Merton's letters to him and for providing an early letter to Robert Lax; Gregory J. Ryan of Wall Township, New Jersey, for being a most helpful, earnest, and interested "research assistant"; Father William H. Shannon (again) for translating the letters to Professor Jean Hering from the French; John Stanley of New York City for sharing his genealogical research on the Merton and Jenkins families; Dr. Decherd Turner, director, and Ms. Cathy Henderson, research librarian, at the Harry Ransom Humanities Research Center at the University of Texas at Austin for help with Merton family correspondence; Dr. Malcolm V. T. Wallace, archivist, and his assistant, Mrs. Lorraine Welsh, of the Friedsam Memorial Library at Saint Bonaventure University, for early letters to Robert Lax and other materials.

One person must be named, a person who is always of good spirit and cheerful help with any Merton project, Brother Patrick Hart of the Abbey of Gethsemani. I am grateful to him not only for his help and support with this volume but also and mostly for his tireless and generous assistance with every project. In this I can speak for everyone connected with Merton studies.

I want to acknowledge the help, support, and assistance of my two good friends, Marquita Breit (my fellow Merton bibliographer), technical services librarian at Bellarmine College, and Rosalind Parnes, reference librarian at Bellarmine College. Both willingly, and even at times interestedly, searched out obscure and vague references to people and books in the text of the letters. Other friends who offered succor (and I use the word advisedly) in various ways included Gus Coin, David D. Cooper, Michael J. Drury, David R. Finkle, Thomas J. Kemme, Michael G. Krukones, Don R. Osborn, and Joan E. Wettig.

Finally I would like to express my appreciation to and admiration for my mother, Louise Linn Daggy, who has patiently forgone visits, letters, and even telephone calls during this and other "Merton projects." She may not always have understood these demands but she has acted as if she did and she has been a constant and sustaining support throughout my life.

R.E.D.

The Road to Joy

I.

To Mark Van Doren

You are certainly one of the joys of life for all who have
ever come within a mile of you.
MERTON TO VAN DOREN
JUNE 6, 1959

Mark Van Doren (1894–1972), as Merton wrote in Monks Pond, *"needs no in-troduction. He is one of the major American poets of the century." A professor of English at Columbia College from 1920 to 1959, he was Merton's teacher and figured largely in* The Seven Storey Mountain. *In 1939 he was awarded the Pulitzer Prize for poetry. They corresponded until Merton's death in 1968. Van Doren exerted great influence on Merton's writing and publishing, first in teaching and later in promoting his first published book,* Thirty Poems (1944). *Van Doren selected the poems, persuaded James Laughlin at New Directions to publish them, and signed the contract for Merton. He later selected and wrote an introduction for Merton's* Selected Poems (1959). *Merton had known Van Doren's wife, Dor-othy (Graffe) Van Doren, and his sons, Charles and John, before he entered Gethsemani. Mark and Dorothy Van Doren, to whom Merton dedicated* The Strange Islands, *visited Merton at Gethsemani in March 1954 and September 1957. Van Doren also lunched alone with Merton in Louisville in June 1956 and visited him at the Abbey in December 1961. The Van Doren side of their cor-respondence may be consulted in* The Selected Letters of Mark Van Doren, *edited by George Hendrick (Baton Rouge: Louisiana State University Press, 1987). The first four letters that follow were written to Van Doren from Greenwich Village.*

35 Perry Street, New York
March 24, 1939

Well here is this Joyceish thing. It is a dialogue between a master
& pupil. What is not clear is that the pupil is asking the questions of the
master, replying, teaches him myths. In the end the master berates him

for not knowing the difference between art & idolatry—just briefly that is.

I would like to make quite a long thing, starting from this, & going on, maybe as a masque.

March 30, 1939

Surprised Mr ffinDaruian,

and daylighted for your brief letture right in these stole of James' Joys. That glose so fain "Can Grande Latians" grace is! (Gracious!) And so to thank these pencils draw to a close.

Now were to unweight the agurbite of bitterbeer and "Herbies" shall be roarly down in black & wit: but black for line, not (just my gist has) art. And O'Neill as right I did a chief the art-heckle of Rickard Huge ["The Art of Richard Hughes"], and so far wall

Those Mervin

Pastcrit: An M. A. Theseus!

August 18, 1939

Thanks for your letter. No, I hadn't known about the mermaids with fishes heads! People who won't allow Dali to use his good idea deserve to go flat broke, I say [the Dali Exhibit at the 1939 World's Fair].

I went back up to Olean after writing to you & stayed another month & a half. Did I tell you I was writing a novel? Anyway I finished it. 160,000 words. Weighs five & a half pounds. These are about the only things I can say about it that are not completely misleading.

I sent it to Farrar & Rinehart because I heard Farrar was a friendly guy and I saw a picture of him in which he looked as if he had some humor. There again it would be misleading to say the novel is in any ordinary sense funny. And by the way I'm glad you saw that other short novel & told me it was no good because in this (even though it was entirely different to begin with) I tried to keep as far as possible away from the tone of "Marion & Winona", as well as all the private language of [Bob] Lax's & my *Jester* & so on.

The novel is called *The Night Before the Battle* but I would not be prepared to defend that title with my life. Its basis is intellectual autobiography. It goes from 1929 to the present year. Of course a lot of it has to do with my going into the church. If I were to be writing the advertising blurb I would say it was about what the generation born during the war has been worrying about & a lot of tra-la-la like that. I just mean that the jacket blurb might safely bait a hook for suckers with this inferior meat, but that is certainly not what I was trying to write or what I wrote. On this foundation is built a novel about a lot of fictional characters & a complex business with no little parody & burlesque in it. I don't know how to start explaining how it goes.

But one character has four love affairs which all burlesque one another, because they all have a similar pattern. A whole lot of things happen in the book & it reads fast I think & everyone who has seen it has liked it fine.

I judge from a note from Farrar that he is himself reading it, but don't know if that means much or even if it is true. To be clear: I sent him a letter giving a vague idea what the book was & got a letter back saying "I look forward to reading it." He has had it about a week. I don't know how it will turn out at all, but I am sure it is a good book, although I will want to rewrite parts of it.

It is not without commercial appeal since it is about English schools & Cambridge & Paris & Cannes & Rome & New York & every place I ever went to, practically, &, as I say, a lot of things happen in it.

By the way, you are in it, I hope you don't mind: that is your Shakespeare class is talked about & I say some things I learned from you, & say I am glad I learned them from you. Is that all right? It all has to do with poetry. By the way, I invented a great fool in the book & made him one of the editors of *The New Yorker*.

The Dali poem came back from *Harpers Bazaar* with one of their most flattering rejection slips. This time they were more than sorry, they were "exceedingly sorry" to send back one of my poems. I didn't even try *The New Yorker*. Now *Southern Review* has it, along with some others.

[James] Laughlin sent the pastoral back & didn't even say anything about it. I haven't done any more work on it since I have been too busy on the novel.

John Crowe Ransom sent a friendly letter back saying he couldn't use that old Washaw article & this completes this summer's rejections. I think it's about time somebody took *something* of mine, & I hope it will be the novel! But, as I say, I never sent a novel to a publisher before, & I don't know what to expect. Maybe I was silly to send it to Farrar, because they only seem to publish *Anthony Adverse* & Mary Roberts Rinehart.

I had a fine summer: now it is hot here, though; but I am finding out a lot of good things. One is that I can read Provencal fairly easily, & I have been finding out Provencal poetry is just as fine as they all say! A lot of it is amazingly fine religious poetry. And where the Latin poetry of the same time is all naive, more or less, this stuff is of much more stature. The sound of the language itself is wonderful, —adjectives & participles ending in -etz & -atz. Take this:

> *Senher Sant John Baptista*
> *Que fust per Dieu marturiatz*
> *La tieu testa fou requista*
> *El tieu sanc fou escaupatz*
>
> *(Lord St. John the Baptist*
> *Who was martyred for God*
> *They claimed your head*
> *They shed your blood . . .)*

Some endings for lines! Some beat, too. The way I found out I could read Provencal was from the lines about Arnaut Daniel in the *Purgatory of Daniel.*

October 24, 1939

. . . They gave me a teaching job in extension: composition at night for business folk. It is quite dull and harder than I had expected to find it: much harder. But anyway I have got them so that they all like Thurber, except one brute who thinks it's monotonous to laugh so much as Thurber makes you laugh. I keep telling them if they want to write, why don't they first read something besides *Time* magazine and second do a *little* writing at least.

I guess they are all very willing, and some of them write a lot of extra things and bring them too. What I mean by that is, they write a lot of essays about real estate, for practice sake: but that's all right. I don't mind that at all.

I was scared I wouldn't have enough to say in my classes, and would find myself stuck after the first fifteen minutes, trying to think up ideas to talk about: but that isn't so, rather, I talk so much that I really never get around to actually discussing their themes in class.

I was in Olean all summer, and wrote a novel: I suppose I told you. Well, Farrar and Rinehart kept the novel a long time, but not so much because they were interested in it as because the reader kept getting colds or something. They gave it back saying they didn't quite follow it, and why did the plot have to be so complicated? On the other hand, they *did* say it was dull, and I was afraid it might be that to someone besides friends. I sent the pastoral to *Southern Review,* but I don't know what they have been doing. I think they lost five of my poems, too, in August. On the other hand I am not caring so much about not getting published, because I am less convinced that what I have been writing is any good.

Did you ever get to see all the good pictures in the Old Masters exhibit at the fair? Coming back to New York I found they had done a fine job of messing up Dali's dream of Venus with a lot of rubber turtles the publicity agent thought up out of his hollow head. Also they finally came around to putting mermaid pants on the mermaids, which made them very awkward and silly, swimming about unhappily with their feet tied together in a sack made to look like a fish's tail made out of a sack. The whole amusement area has been pretty sick, I suppose, ever since the first week, but then parts of it were surprisingly good. Nobody believes that any more. [Bob] Lax came to New York for a minute, but he was only here long enough to refuse a job writing a kids' poetry program for the radio. Now he is back in Olean.

I am not paying any attention to my dissertation now. In fact I am more interested in medieval Latin courses and medieval philosophy courses than in English courses, which I have not gone to much yet. I may start finding out a lot about the language of analogy in Bonaventure and Hugo of St. Victor and write some paper explaining that you can't make a literal statement about anything that is worth while talking about . . .

During his visit to Cuba in the spring of 1940, Merton wrote a poem called "Song for Our Lady of Cobre," which he sent Van Doren with the following note.

Santiago, Cuba

Here is a poem I wrote. Cobre is a place in the mountains of Cuba near Santiago & the Virgin of Cobre is miraculous. I am in Santiago now, it is a fine place with a fine harbor & a lot of mountains around it but very hot so tomorrow I expect to start back to Havana.

When I get back to America I hope to go into a monastery to be a Franciscan. Back in October & November some angels told me it would be a good thing. My novitiate begins in August. Will you be in Connecticut in May, June or July & if so may I come up and see you? I suppose I will run out of money & come back to America in about 2 weeks.

Olean, New York
June 16, 1940

You see I am back here living in [Bob] Lax's hut. I got back from Cuba a month or so ago. It was fine there, it is fine here. I wrote some stuff called a travel book there and I am not bothering to write anything here, as there is no necessity for me to write anything just now. Everybody else here is writing a lot though and I think Lax's big page of masque for his girl was the best thing they ever printed in *New Yorker*: I never knew they were so smart.

You remember about that Joyce pastoral of mine? Well some little crazy magazine in Woodstock is going to print it, and I am happy that it is going to be printed, even if only by this little magazine I've never even heard of. The way they got hold of it is, I figured *Phoenix* might be the sort of magazine would think my pastoral was just the thing for their crazy pages, so I sent it to *Phoenix*, and *Phoenix* gave it to the fellow next door who has a magazine called *Ritual* which says it is "devoted to the revelations of idiocy and insanity, both simulated and pathological" which is their way of being funny. But I don't care; as long as they are going to print this pastoral I am glad.

Lax said you were surprised a little that I was leaving the world and that surprised me a bit, too, as I hadn't thought of it in negative terms, but only that I was going to become a Franciscan. If it comes to that, a fellow is supposed to leave the world as soon as he is baptized: that is part of the baptismal vows, but then of course I will take the added vows of poverty, chastity, and obedience giving up all the world has to offer of property, wives and personal independence. But on the other hand a Friar is perhaps in the world more than I have ever been in the sense that he leads a more active life than I have ever led, what with preaching and teaching and hearing confessions and possibly in my own case writing if I am told to write anything. But of course I will have an opportunity to lead a more contemplative life also than I have ever led, by reason of being part of a religious community and because of those same three vows which take away a false kind of freedom and replace it with a real one.

I will begin my novitiate early in August. I am not only doing this because it is the easiest way of saving my soul, but because that is the kind of life that seems to me to be the best, because a priest's way of life is supposed to be patterned more closely than any other on Christ's own life. To be a priest does not mean that you are necessarily perfect but that you are solemnly bound to a manner of life in which you observe all those things pertaining to perfection.

Meanwhile I sit in the sun and look at the trees and wear a white tennis hat and wait for it to be August. I haven't even been reading anything much except a few snatches of *The City of God* and the Vulgate and Lorca's poetry. But anyway, that reminds me, I did write a couple of poems this month. I send them, along with a couple of others, and along with my best regards to your whole family.

Olean, N.Y.

August 25, 1940

It turns out I had to give up my plans about the monastery: my mind was changed for me, not by me. If I had gone in I would now be busy with the things novices are busy with and not letters. As it is I have been writing a lot of things, another novel, poetry. I don't think, though, I have enough good things to give to Laughlin III. Here is some for you to look at, I mean for your pleasure, not for business thoughts, unless they happen to be the only thoughts possible about such poems.

I am still in [Bob] Lax's house. I was in Virginia for a while and Virginia is very different from this. It is a fierce sort of a place and sometimes I like it a lot. What I am doing now is hunting for a place to work, teaching English. I thought for two seconds of asking you if you thought it would be worth while my trying to get something at St. John's, but I don't ask you that at all, because I think it is perhaps the last place in the world I ought to be at, after Columbia. I don't want to go back to Columbia because I am tired of the place, and I would be scared of St. John's because I'm not smart enough, or don't think I would feel smart enough, if I am, to teach there. Then again I am scared of getting into a round of 'unusual' places and spending my life shuttling between St. John's and Bennington and other places that get written up in *Life*. My instinct now is to be teaching all the guys at Notre Dame, and taking my chance with the fellows who never heard of a book, because I think I would like to tell them about books and everything else important, than talk about

Donne to people who had already gathered three opinions about him from the Sunday book reviews.

Anyway, what I am doing is asking the Catholic colleges for jobs and no one else. They seem to know exactly what I mean by a job: a place to eat and sleep and a typewriter to write on and a couple of classes to talk in and whatever money they can spare for the movies, and not much talk of seething ambition. But I don't know where I'll end up, except I am confident one of them at least will take me in.

My old novel is with an agent [Naomi Burton] who likes it. Pretty soon it will have been to every publisher in the world, and then my new one will be finished, and so on until they put an ersatz rifle in my hand and send me to sleep on the ground at Plattsburg some hard winter, waiting for them to order me a tent.

Thank you for naming my name to New Directions. I wish I liked enough poems to send them, but maybe by Christmas I'll have some more. As to the [Joyce] Pastoral that was to have come out in June, I guess the little fellows in Woodstock broke their mimeograph and lost their stencils, because I haven't seen anything of it . . .

St. Bonaventure, New York
January 28, 1941

. . . I have just corrected eighty-six English exams in one of which I read: "Chaucer's ABC was a dirty character in one of the *Canterbury Tales*." There is a lot of snow here, and it is mostly very nice. I am not bothering to go further than Olean between terms because I have a lot of good things to do here. I have been reading St. Anselm's *Proslogion*, and St. Bonaventure's *Itinerarium* with this Franciscan philosopher from Germany, and I am finding out all sorts of good things about scholastic philosophy, and, incidentally, learning to be critical of St. Thomas, which is a good thing for a Catholic to be, I find—and a rare one.

The novel course has not yet started but it should be fun.

[Bob] Lax, I suppose you know, has a job on *The New Yorker*, which could be a very good thing. Anyway that is the sort of job he wants, not because it is on *The New Yorker*, but because it leaves him free a lot of the time, and that is the most important thing.

He only just got the job, and so I haven't heard from him about it. His relatives told me. Another thing that has been keeping me busy is making speeches on the radio, some against our trying to fight the Germans by butting them with our hard heads (since big thick skulls seem to be all we have to use) and some about "Literature and Life" i.e. anything that comes into my head. They have been mostly about the Middle Ages.

I said I rewrote the novel. Well, more than that I don't know myself, except I got a very friendly letter from the Little Brown people (sounds like a race of rabbits) saying they had heard the book was changed and would be happy to read it over again. That was their idea. I did not write to taunt them, or anything. Of course the agent was the one who told them I had rewritten the thing.

I was very sad that Joyce died, and I hope he gets to heaven. His death was the same kind of news as that of the fall of Paris, to me.

I have been wondering if there ever was such a thing as a great novel, a *Hamlet* among novels. Of course there must be: perhaps in Russian or French. The nearest bet in English is *Ulysses*. Everything else is good healthy amateur amusement, and nothing more.

> [St. Bonaventure, New York
> Lent 1941]

Thanks for the letter, I was happy you liked the poem. Some time ago I became a Franciscan Tertiary, which is an order for people in the world (Dante was one), and a good thing because it has a rule of prayer and relative penance etc. that has made many saints. Well anyway I have been writing a great rush of poems ever since, some good some bad, but nothing I am terribly ashamed of and some that I am happy about.

Most of them have gone to this bird Charles Henri Ford who just happened to write and say he had seen a song from the Joyce Pastoral (as much as has so far been printed by the crazy magazine in Woodstock) and liked it and wanted some of my stuff for an anthology of what he called "View" poets for a Press of one James Decker. I don't know what "view" poets are, or who Decker is, or anything about Ford except he is in New Directions anthologies, which I have never read at all anyway. But I sent him a lot of these new poems.

As for most of those you have seen, *Southern Review* has had them for at least five months. What does one do in a case like that? Do they get sore if you ask for them back, I mean does that finally decide them one way or the other, concerning the poems? Is that all they are waiting for to refuse them?

I have spent most of this evening writing out my reasons to tell the draft board why I don't want to shoot people. It took me some time to make up my mind to object, but about a month or six weeks ago I finally came around to this way of thinking: there is no doubt that I can't see killing people with flame throwers as any form of Christian perfection. If the law just said flatly that everybody had to fight, I would have to go, because that's what Catholics have to do. But if the law asks you to express the reactions of your own conscience to this business, I certainly would be wrong in not saying what I believe, and trying to get out of combatant service. I have made it very clear, then, that I think Christians are supposed to try and imitate Christ, who didn't kill people but healed the sick and told Peter to put down his sword, in Gethsemane. There have been saints who were soldiers and saints who were killed for being pacifists, so there is no absolute position on war one way or the other, except the war has to be "just", as if anybody knew! My aim is to get put in ambulance or hospital work if there is a war, and if there isn't I'd just as soon stay a poet, thanks, and not sour my happy disposition in Fort Jiggs.

They sent me my questionnaire, and it got here Feb. 28th and was due there Feb. 28th. I am not supposed to send my objections with the q. but put a mark in the right place and then they will send me a blank to fill in. I have written a whole little pamphlet already, and by the time the blank gets here I will probably have four chapters of a monumental book. The other day, though, I heard [Bob] Gibney had put in a kick and they had exempted him, whether altogether or just from combatant duty I don't know. He said they complimented him on his knowledge of French, Spanish and Italian, also. I can't figure out what part of the blank he slipped that information into. I got it wedged in where it said "What past jobs have you had" and I said "interpreter, French etc, etc". My friend the Franciscan philosopher has read my reasons and found no holes in them except he laughed a lot at the quotations from St. Thomas Aquinas. I suppose he's the wrong one to consult, seeing he's a German and had the G-men trailing him around all summer: for he is a botanist, and spends a lot of time poking around in abandoned parts of the woods and marshes with cameras, compasses, magnifying glasses and all kinds of suspicious objects, like books . . .

There is a story floating around Olean that Lax received one thousand manuscripts for *The New Yorker*, of which he only passed on, to the next man, ten. If that is true, he certainly threw out all the ones the guys on the board would have been interested in, and wanted to print. What would they want with those ten good poems? I haven't been reading *The New Yorker*, but only because it's Lent. Secretly I am convinced that it is the only good magazine in New York anyway, but still, I've been in the habit of complaining about it for six years.

The novel is going the rounds and I am sure I don't know what's happening to it. I have discovered that the agent [Naomi Burton] doesn't really like the second one, but is sending it around out of respect for the first one, which in turn is completely non-commercial, according to the man at Little Brown: except he's at the *Atlantic Monthly*. Also the agent says the second ms. isn't changed enough to go back to *Atl. Monthly*.

I think of going before Easter to a great Trappist monastery in Kentucky and making a retreat. It is apparently a wonderful place; after that I will be in New York, the week after Easter, and will probably call you up . . .

St. Bonaventure, New York
November 10, 1941

This is the carbon of a book [*Journal of My Escape*] I am trying to sell—that same agent is working on it. I thought you might enjoy it, and that is why I am sending it to you. You will see right away why I am having trouble selling it: it contains some Joyce talk, here and there and only has a mock plot. I am afraid the first part is incomplete: it begins at the beginning, and then there are gaps. But from the time Madame Gongora sings the song in Spanish, it goes on straight through, complete. You will be perplexed about the character B. because some stuff on her is lacking, but it doesn't matter. The book is confusing anyway, except as a Journal, which is what it is.

If you like it, perhaps you might have some ideas about what I might be able to do with it. It has been, as far as I know, to Harcourt Brace, where [Robert] Giroux, who is undoubtedly the best friend the book is likely to meet among publishers, regretted that it was not commercial.

I have given up trying to figure out what "commercial" means, and simply write what I write.

Here it snows, and I work, but hope to come to New York for Thanksgiving. I was here all summer except for a month or so, during which time I got up an anthology of poems of religious experience, from metaphysical poets, Hopkins, Blake, etc. etc. and it makes a rather unusual book, because it is more selective than the other anthologies of religious verse I have seen. I don't know very well how to go about getting rid of this either: tentatively I am sending it to the man at Atlantic Monthly books in Boston who seemed slightly interested: that is, at least he didn't give a flat "No" as soon as I mentioned the idea.

I sent [James] Laughlin some poems which I thought good, and he seemed to like them, but then he decided to make his anthology a Russian anthology this year and I was forced out by the Soviets and the Commissars. I believe I am the most unpublished man in seven kingdoms.

Now that *The New Yorker* finally did buy one of my poems, they have put it away in a drawer without printing it. They took it in May, and it is a summer poem, and now it is winter . . .

Are you going to be in New York between November 20 and 23? I hope I can get a chance to see you then. If not, perhaps you might turn over the Journal to Lax at *The New Yorker*, or at his place on 114th St— he is easily contacted (wow! where did that word come from?) anyway, and he wants to pass the thing on to a friend of ours, with the idea that this man (a very funny actor) might make the book into something for radio without too much changing around.

Anyway, I hope I get a chance to see you.

St. Bonaventure, New York
November 14, 1941

Thank you for the letter, & I am very happy you liked the Journal, & want to send it to [William] Sloane. I think it would be better for the book if you showed it to him, don't you? After all, he may not know my agent very well. And he can always talk business with her if it comes to talking business: meanwhile I would be happy if you would pass on the copy you have to him. In the complete copy there are another 35 pages or so, all of which are very straightforward & perhaps the most "commercial" writing in the book. Perhaps he would want to know this, & that *Miss [Naomi] Burton at Curtis Brown* (347 Madison) has it. I will write to her at once & tell her I have asked you to show Sloane this carbon.

I will look forward to seeing you Friday or Saturday of next week. I leave here Wednesday, says our schedule; & am eager to talk about the Journal & everything else. I am really very happy you like it, because I like it a lot too & it makes me sad to think the average publisher doesn't.

St. Bonaventure N.Y.
November 28, 1941

Thanks very much for sending [William] Sloane's opinion on the *Journal*. I was rather pleased that he said it was, in its psychology, old fashioned, although that was not meant as any compliment. There were a couple of things that will probably continue to grieve me as long as I try to sell the Ms. The first was that he insisted on taking it as a novel and being surprised that it was 'like poetry.' The second was that nobody seems ready to publish anything that is 'merely good writing.'

So perhaps the only thing is to try New Directions with it. What do you think?

Meanwhile, if you have the carbon (you speak as if you did) of the Journal, will you hand it over to [Bob] Lax? As for *News*, perhaps I will change my mind and ask you to send it back to me, express collect, if it is not too much trouble. Then I will type out some more of the stuff which is all in longhand in a ledger, and add to this.

Perhaps all I can say is that nothing surprises me less than to have something I have written, which I myself like, rejected. So I enclose a poem, which I hope you will like.

Apart from this, writing is not what I think about most at this moment. There is still this very big open question about what I am to do. When I first started teaching, I tried to convince myself there was no more question: but that didn't work. Then I tried to act as if what question there was was only some kind of a temptation—a temptation to desire something you haven't got merely because you haven't got it and not because you really need it. That has eventually worked itself out to be wrong, too.

Probably everybody who reads the New Testament is curious about stories like that of the rich young man who asked what he should do and, when he was told, turned away sad "for he had great possessions." I clearly remember the polite and academic interest I used to take in such a story. And I can compare it with what the story means to me now: it half kills me to read it. I can't think about it and sit still.

And I am not absolutely sure, either, that Harlem answers the question for me: so much of the work in Harlem seems to me to be, from the point of view of whatever it is I want, so much wasted effort: standing around for several hours just so that your presence may keep order among some children playing ping-pong, or maybe arguing about how to mimeograph something or other, with a couple of girls from some college, doing social work. It isn't the spending of time in doing nothing apparently important (because simply watching over a bunch of kids is also immensely good and important) that seems fruitless—none of this, in itself, is fruitless at all. But it all seems ordered in some scheme of references that would be more significant to somebody else than to me: and the same standing around, the same apparently wasted time, could be very fruitful for me in some other context. In other words, I have to seriously consider whether my vocation is not contemplative rather than active. I hope you will say a prayer for me—and let me know if you have any good ideas!

St. Bonaventure
December 9, 1941

Many thanks for the letter, which I am in too much of a hurry to answer now. I am sending these [manuscripts] not only for you to look at when you feel like it, but principally for you to hold for me until you next hear from me, when I hope to explain more than I can now. The miscellaneous stuff in the binder represents fragments of a novel, items collected for an anthology, and practically all of my poems, with that pastoral, you remember. [Bob] Lax has another binder full of more miscellaneous stuff you might have fun reading sometime—although I am really not trying to promise you anything. Rather I am asking you to do me the favor of keeping these for me, for a while.

On St. Lucy's Day, December 13, 1941, Merton sent his first circular letter, a poem, "Letter to My Friends / Explaining that I am entering the Trappists in Kentucky." He penned the following note at the bottom of the poem sent to Van Doren.

I have been tentatively accepted & will enter the community within the next few days. I still don't know what, about all those books I sent you, but will let you know soon. Possibly I might ask you to send the handwritten notebooks down sometime—& the poems. As to *Journal of My Escape from the Nazis*, & all rights connected with it—I make you a present of it. Pray for me.

April 14, 1942

We are allowed to write letters very seldom, but I got special permission to send you some of my poems. I have been writing here. Also, I enclose a page or two of a Journal I have been keeping: it is completely to do with religious experience—& so are the poems, & so is my life, naturally.

And what a life! It is tremendous. Not because of any acts we perform, any penance, any single feature of the liturgy or the chant, not because we sleep on boards & straw mattresses & fast & work & sweat & sing & keep silence. These things are all utterly simple acts that have no importance whatever in themselves. But the whole unity of the life is tremendous. That is because the life *is* a real unity, because the foundation of its unity is God's unity: the ontological basis of our life is the simplicity & the purity of God. His simplicity *is* our life. We *live* His oneness: we *live* His singleness of concentration on His own immense purity and goodness. No wonder it is wonderful. The life is God: it is Christ, in the sense that Christ is the principle & end of absolutely everything that a Trappist does, right down to breathing. Really, I have only one reason for living at all and that is the love, the glory, the good pleasure of Christ. Therefore, since this is the sort of thing men were created to do (not necessarily all as Trappists, of course) I am very happy. I never was really unhappy in my life except perhaps for a while when I was most mixed up—the year I was registered at Columbia but hardly ever came to school, although I was supposed to be doing everything there was to do on campus besides classes too.

Now I am here, it already seems quite clear how the whole of my life until I came here is at last intelligible. All that chaos, France & England & everywhere else I lived, straightens itself out & points to our cloister & our fields . . .

Here the silence does away with almost all the troubles arising from people being bores or cranks or political guys, or joke lovers or whatever you get to drive you crazy where people live together.

It is wonderful to see a postulant arrive—just an average guy in a suit you might see on the subway or in an office or at Columbia, maybe a little preoccupied, or on some kind of a defensive—& watch him turn into a splendid, happy, holy, gentle, self-possessed monk in a very short time. That is, outwardly. Underneath a lot still goes on: but in peace & not in a chaos of dilemmas, as it did in the world. The silence does this.

It is wonderful to live with people who are absolutely concentrated on being good & gentle & becoming saints. The Franciscans I know were all very embarrassed with the notion of sanctity. Only here and at Friendship House in Harlem have I found people who really wanted to be saints, and knew they could be, too, because God will make anyone live for Him who wants to, and when you live for love alone, you become filled with love, & that is to be a saint.

At the same time, I never loved God so much as now, & I never so clearly realized how much I am *not* a saint. Here in this peace I see so clearly the Iscariot in me, that the knowledge of the kind of baseness I could be capable of—& have been—would be terrible, & drive me to some sin of self-hatred or despair if I were not completely dependent on God as I am here. But He is all peace & all joy, & I have learned a very necessary truth—that there isn't any evil to which I wouldn't be drawn, if I were without God altogether, but with Him, there is no good which I cannot do, if I let Him do it in me . . .

Did my ex-agent [Naomi Burton] get in touch with you? I would be interested to hear if the *Journal of My Escape* (which I definitely make you a present of lock stock and barrel, since you liked it) aroused any interest at New Directions, or did it ever get there?

Also, if [James] Laughlin is not, like everybody else in the army, he might still want to do something with some poems. The poems are yours too. However, all *rights* over these I send belong to the monastery, as they were written here. Perhaps [Bob] Lax would like to see them. I haven't a chance to write to him now—we have to get special permission to write to any but our own relatives.

I would be interested & glad to hear from you when you get time. I have forgotten what New York must be like & don't want to remember, but hope everybody I know is all right, & happy. I pray for everybody. We don't pray for ourselves very much. We live for God & for the world— to live for God's glory we have to desire that others shall come to Him & glorify Him more & more as well as ourselves. So I desire that for you, too, & your family & Lax & everybody, & may God bless you & fill you with joy & peace & give you eternal life. How good it is to be a monk, & therefore in a position where I can say such things straight, officially, & without apology or disguising or excuses!

May 12, 1943

Let these poems serve for news of my religious life. My only activity is to remain motionless (as to the will: the body may be breaking rock with a sledge hammer) attentive to God. Any movement that interferes with this motionlessly simple & perfect act instantly causes the torments of purgatory: consequently it is hard for me to write anything, except it be something commanded by the superior (I translate pages & pages of French without a qualm). Excuse the pencil. I am waiting to get shaved (We don't shave ourselves. No mirrors thank God).

What I am writing for is this. Will you please send, express collect, the typescript of *The News* etc.? The Abbot wants to consider whether it would be of any use here. He is also showing the poems I have here to someone, but I don't know what will come of it. I find it painful to write poems too—but not *so* painful. Besides: if I had tried *not* to write these it would have killed me dead. Will you please pass them on to [Bob] Lax? Last I heard of him he was at Olean—that will always reach him.

Please pray for me: my purgatory is very excellent, but also very fierce in its joys & terrors. God does not always let you be motionless— (but it is always my own fault). Pray for yourself too & for peace. And that we may all love God very much. My regards to all your family.

Merton wrote to Van Doren about a projected volume of poetry to be published by New Directions. The volume, Thirty Poems, *published in 1944, was Merton's first book and the beginning of a long association with James Laughlin. Van Doren selected the poems and signed the contract on Merton's behalf.*

February 22, 1944

Tomorrow it will be Lent & I won't be able to write any letters so I am writing this in haste now. I do not yet know if the poems are approved, but I assume they will be, & am giving this to the Abbot so that if they are approved he can simply drop this in the mail. Consequently, if you receive this, it means that everything you have of mine, plus this one I enclose, is all right, & may be published. Nothing I wrote before coming here needs censorship (except maybe parts of "News" which isn't worth publishing yet—or ever—anyway) . . .

April 16, 1944

Day by day in this monastery I realize more & more how far I have failed to show gratitude to all the people who have been kind to me—& realize also how inadequate my thanks really are! Not the least of these good friends is yourself. A series of cryptic messages from [Bob] Lax tells me that [James] Laughlin has taken the poems and is printing them. So I thank you—and the poems thank you. And if my thanks are, as they are, far short of adequate, let me add that Jesus said that anyone who gave a cup of cold water to one of His little ones would not be without his reward. And that you have done this good thing for the poems—which are Christ's poems & not mine, in so far as there is any good in them— you have begun to have your reward. "Love is repaid by love alone" says St. John of the Cross. So what can I give you by way of thanks? I offer you your own charity, which is in you from Christ, through the Holy Spirit—and which is, in so far as it is of & from Him—my charity also, & everybody's charity, & is the same infinite & simple & eternal act of Love, in Whom we are all one, uttering Himself in one of His multitudinous utterances in time. For every good work we do speaks the Name of Christ, in Whom is all Truth, Love & Reality, & Who is the actuality of everything that is . . .

I can bless you now as a monk, for I have made profession, & my novitiate is over, I am a Cistercian monk, I have a cowl. This cowl—I wear it, or rather I dwell in it. It is the most beautiful of garments. It is like the cloud that protected the children of Israel in the desert. It is as voluminous as a house. It hides & embraces my mortality like the Immortal Soul of Christ, & is the symbol of His humanity, in which I live, & for which I live: which is also, the "Whole Christ—the Head & the Members"—the Church.

If I could only say how dead I was and how alive I am. Only our Easter liturgy can say it for me. Someday I hope you will come & visit us. Our house is full of love & peace . . .

December 26, 1944

Since we cannot write during Advent this is my first chance to thank you for the *Thirty Poems*. I never saw anything so well done, I think. Also you did a fine job of selecting: I was very glad the Lorca poem got in & "St. Agnes" too & the one about the Greek acropoli, & "Our Lady of Cobre" & "Ariadne at the L[abyrinth]." I was pleased to see "Evening" & "Death" fitting in, although I had not thought of them, as I remember.

Best of all—I looked at one poem (I forget which & had no copy at hand to look) & was surprised at one line being so much better than I remembered having written [it]—because of one word. It turned out there were a few more like this & I attribute the changes to you: they are all big improvements, & thank you very much.

I think Fr. Abbot [Frederic Dunne] is quite pleased with the book. Thank you for giving us the copyright, although there was no need for it, of course. But anyway, in a word, thank you for taking so much trouble: I can only pay you with prayers, but then I don't think I need say "only" to you, since you know what prayers are & what they do.

Bob [Lax] is here & I saw him for a moment yesterday. I think he is very happy & pretty much at peace but it does not sound as if this could be said of most of our friends like [Bob] Gibney etc. . . .

I write a lot, all of it business for the monastery, lives of our saints, etc. Would like to write a book all about the Contemplative life, prayer, etc.—& have in mind for an anthology of things from the Liturgy (hymns, sequences etc.) Latin on one page & English on the other, like Helen Waddell only better material. Do you think New Directions might conceivably be interested? . . .

On May 22, 1945, a group of friends and former students (including John Berryman and Robert Giroux) gave Van Doren a "surprise dinner" at the Algonquin Hotel in New York. Clifton Fadiman acted as master of ceremonies, dividing the program of tributes between speeches by those present and letters from those who could not attend. Van Doren says in The Autobiography of Mark Van Doren *(Harcourt, Brace & Company, 1958): "Thomas Merton sent a letter from Gethsemani so long that [Fadiman] could not read it all." He quotes one of the letter's paragraphs, which follows.*

This is not the time for me to be writing a spiritual autobiography; but in 1935 it was an especially good thing that I came in contact with you . . . With you it was never a matter of trying to use poetry and all that is called English literature as a means to make people admire your gifts; on the contrary you always used your gifts to make people admire and understand poetry and good writing and truth.

July 20, 1945

Here are some more [poems]. The others are not yet censored. One censor in Rhode Island is very busy & very slow. These have not even begun the process. We do not need to wait if you think it opportune to approach [James] Laughlin (or anyone else) with the idea of another book. With these, there should be twenty or twenty-five imprinted Gethsemani poems, and besides there remains another (I hope) twenty written before I came here. Since these new ones are longer, they would all make a regular book. Or what do you think? If Laughlin is interested, send me the ms. you have & I will get the whole business together, but don't go to the bother of sending anything down here until there is something definite. Did you ever hear from [Raymond] Larsson? I did not. I was thinking of some of the pre-Gethsemani things like "Oracle", "House of Caiphas"—"Dirge for Town in France," etc. Any chance of interesting Laughlin in *Journal of My Escape from Nazis*—did he ever see it? I began work on the liturgical book but had to drop it again, being extremely busy. Hope I am not breaking in on your vacation. I mean spoiling it— with this business! Glad at least half the war is over & praying hard the other will be soon. I hope your airman will be sent to Europe & kept there in some nice place like, say, Rome.

August 8, 1945

. . . If N[aomi] Burton asks again, try her perhaps on the *Journal of My Escape from the Nazis*. Anyway, thanks for everything, and I am praying hard to get rid of everything phoney and make the new book good. For a title I thought: "The Habit of Wonder." But now I don't know.

September 27, 1945

I thought to have sent all the poems long ago to [James] Laughlin but they are still held up by the censors—for no reason except they have no time. Right now I am very busy rewriting & doing footnotes on the lives of our saints, & feel as if I don't want to write poetry but rather history, on account of reasons like St. Augustine's. Because when you penetrate to the meaning of historical events & movements—like the growth of the Cistercian Order—you come in pretty intimate contact with God in his providential effects. So it is very interesting. I hope I am not too interested in it. Please tell Laughlin the poems are held up, if he asks.

November 7, 1945

. . . All those fat ms. books, longhand: if they are in your way, you could send them here as I now have a place to put them, and a mousetrap to catch the mice before they eat them.

On All Saints' day we went to fight a forest fire, which some brothers had been fighting since four that morning, so that it was well in hand, and it turned out to be more of a picnic for us. It was very far in our hills farther than I had ever been. We saw a man who ran away from the monastery twenty years ago and became a hermit. I thought he was a Negro, but he used to be some sort of a German. I don't think there was even a path to his house.

Tell Bob [Lax] I liked Bob Lowell's review of *Thirty Poems* and think he is right about most of his criticisms, but not about the poem called "The Regret". Also thank Bob for his letter and tell him I am bursting with great health, which is true.

I read much Duns Scotus, who when it comes to psychology, at any rate, fills in certain big gaps that leave you unsatisfied with St. Thomas. You would like very much John Ruysbroeck, "the admirable"—and if you see any extra copies floating around a bookstore, tell them to send them here, with a bill, and we will give them its weight in gold, as we have practically nothing.

Laughlin said you were tired or unwell. I hope you are refreshed and very well, and I pray for you to have all sorts of spiritual and temporal benefit.

Oh, please warn Laughlin about our not being able to get letters in Advent (Dec. 1st about to Christmas) but if there is something urgent in the way of proof he would undoubtedly write "urgent" all over it, and seek to explain it to Fr. Abbot, and it would be, I think, okay.

September 19, 1946

Maybe by now the ms. of the *Journal of Escape from the Nazis* has got back to you. It went from [Raymond] Larsson to a publisher in Chicago who liked it a lot and wanted me to rewrite it. But I can't rewrite a thing like that here—where would I get the proper sort of ideas? I might make some small changes of style etc. Now Larsson still thinks it ought to get published as it is and he wants to see it some more, and write an article he says, about it and the poems and everything. For my own part, that is okay with me: but first, has [James] Laughlin ever seen it? I think he should see it before anything else is done, don't you? Therefore will you pass it on to him with my compliments and tell him that it is the nearest thing to the kind of autobiography I first promised to him last spring but that I am unable to do a complete recasting of it, even though that may be needed.

Incidentally, since I have never seen Larsson, how did he strike you, anyway? Or don't you remember? He claims he is the victim of anti-

Catholic persecutions and that somebody is writing him anonymous letters full of threats. Maybe—but I haven't heard of anybody else getting that kind of letter for that kind of reason outside of Alabama for a long time. But he seems like a good fellow by his letter, and he is certainly all in favor of the journal and the poems, and a fervent Catholic all right. I wish Lax or somebody knew him, because it might turn out after all that he really needed some help—which might for instance take the form of his getting out of N.Y. to somewhere like St. Bonaventure or here. I just remembered that when I was wondering what had happened to the ms. I thought of writing him somewhat to this effect: "What has become of you anyway? Are you dead?" It is just as well I didn't, I guess.

Incidentally, remember that this ms. is your property—or does that give you a headache? . . .

I am just about finishing a straight autobiography called *The Seven Storey Mountain*—a title which is literally, physically accurate. I don't suppose Laughlin would want such a book, although he seems to be asking for it . . . It will run some seven hundred pages long . . .

November 5, 1947

For a long time I have meant to write and haven't had the chance. I don't even know if I thanked you for your letter of sometime last year with comments on the poems I sent. I meant to do so because criticism is a most rare commodity here—above all *good* criticism and I want to show my appreciation of it so as to get more if possible. [James] Laughlin is bringing out another book [*Figures for an Apocalypse*] so I haven't much new and in fact I want to lie fallow for a bit—and try & get into some different rut, as I am thoroughly tired of the old one! The book will show plenty to be tired of, I am afraid.

It is such a long time since I wrote to you that I am in another age of the monastic life and definitely feel it, too. I made my solemn vows last March (and re-make them in my heart every day!) and am going on towards the priesthood which is about two years away. When I say I feel it—I mean this. I can see all the big responsibilities beginning to creep up on me: material offices and cares, jobs in the community etc. Just where I least expected it I can see that I will have to confront the problem of not becoming that middle aged professional man whose shadow I thought I was escaping.

I am tremendously busy with writing. Magazines are beginning to be after me and I have to do a lot of judicious refusing. I can only write for magazines on condition that I keep myself in one field & on one plane—and the nearer it is to mystical theology the better. My superiors have more or less let me go off on my own & make all my own decisions as far as writing is concerned with the one exception—they won't let me give it up.

What grows on me most is the desire for solitude—to vanish completely and go off into some desert and never be heard of again—& pray, & keep still. Sometimes this desire is a temptation (whenever it takes some concrete form and presents itself with a map of Arizona in its hand) but otherwise it is a grace—and all I know about it is that I must have it undefined for the moment & that God will make the details & circumstances of it take shape in His own good time: and it probably won't be a desert but something better. My vows of course always allow me to look for something *higher*—if I can persuade Rome that it is higher.

Laughlin was down here and I liked him very much. He is helping us put out a booklet about the monastery which I shall send you. Harcourt Brace is bringing out the autobiography next Spring. It still needs a lot of cutting and incidentally I hope it is all right if you appear in it—at any rate I refuse to allow you to refuse to appear in it.

You still have a standing invitation to Gethsemani . . .

March 30, 1948

Easter gives me a chance to acknowledge your beautiful letter about *Figures for an Apocalypse*. Thank you very much for your kindness & deep understanding. In the year that has gone by since that essay ["Poetry and the Contemplative Life"] was written I have found out many things.

The problem is a fearful one in itself, and as it stands on paper—and *in the abstract*. But on the other hand God is *God*. I still hold to everything I said in the article about the nature of the problem itself but I am beginning to see everything in a strangely different light.

I can no longer see the ultimate meaning of a man's life in terms of either "being a poet" or "being a contemplative" or even in a certain sense in "being a saint" (although that is the only thing to be). It must be something much more immediate than that. I—and every other person in the world—*must* say: "I have my own special, peculiar destiny which no one else ever has had or ever will have. There exists for me a particular goal, a fulfillment which must be all my own—nobody else's—& it does not really identify that destiny to put it under some category—"poet," "monk," "hermit." Because my own individual destiny is a meeting, an encounter with God that He has destined for me alone. His glory in me will be to receive from me something He can never receive from anyone else—because it is a gift of His to me which He has never given to anyone else & never will. My whole life is only that—to establish that particular constant with God which is the one He has planned for my eternity!"

Once that contact is established—I feel it in my bones & it sets me on fire—the possibilities are *without end*. Unlimited fruitfulness, life, productivity, vision, peace. Yet I have no way of saying just what it will be. I don't think it will be merely writing & I don't think it will be anything I have ever yet known as contemplation & in fact I don't think it will be anything that anyone on earth can see or understand—especially myself.

In the light of all that it doesn't make so much sense any more to be planning to either renounce or to adopt whole "blocks" of activity—cutting out "all" writing or "going into solitude for good" (as I would like to)—the thing is to take a new line & let everything be determined by immediate circumstances that manifest God's will & His action here & now. No matter where it may seem to lead, because I don't really know anyway & I don't have to know provided that God is doing the leading . . .

April 8, 1949

I write to you although it is Lent because my correspondence is now completely out of hand and I have to write when I can. The object of this letter is something that ought to be taken care of soon.

It is to invite you, officially, to come down here if you possibly can on the 16th of May when I hope to be ordained to the priesthood. The date is not absolutely certain, and I know it is not a good one for university people. Anyway, Bob Giroux said something about having spoken to you about it already. Do keep it in mind, and I will let everyone know definitely when the date is really settled. I am asking Bob Giroux and of course Bob Lax and [Ed] Rice and all of them who can come, and Jay Laughlin also. Jay has been down here a couple of times now.

Tomorrow is Palm Sunday. I am a deacon now and that gives me some special things to sing in the Easter Liturgy—a closer participation, materially and spiritually, in everything that is going on. It really does have a considerable effect on a person to take part in these things. I know the priesthood is going to be something tremendous. A kind of death, to begin with. But that is good. The whole business about Orders has been striking me as something much more important than religious vows. The question of sacramental character comes in, for one thing. Then you become public property. At the same time you are mystically more isolated in God. The combination is quite baffling.

Anyway, the priesthood will end up by giving me a completely social function. Perhaps that was what I was always trying to escape. Actually, having run into it at this end of the circle, it is making me what I was always meant to be and I am about to exist.

As soon as I put on the vestments of a subdeacon and stood in the sanctuary I was bowled over by the awareness that this was what I was always supposed to wear, and everything else, so far, had been something of a disguise.

Abbot James Fox had written at the bottom of Merton's letter: "May 26 is the definite day of fr. Louis ordination," and Van Doren recorded that he was unable to attend because he had to be present at Donald Keene's doctoral examination at Columbia.

[December 20, 1949]

I liked very much the poem on your card. Do you know we do not have any of your books here? And did Jay [Laughlin] send you my *Tears of the Blind Lions*? . . .

April 7, 1953

It was wonderful to get the letter and the book [*Spring Birth and Other Poems*], which both arrived long enough before Lent for me to have answered them long ago, if I had not been busy. I know you understand what "busy" means, because I think I am closer to people working in the woods than I would be writing them letters. But now that Easter has come I can at least tell you how happy the letter made me. It made the writing of [*The Sign of*] *Jonas* seem completely justified. I had a little trouble with the book within the Order, and it does not appear that I will be writing another one like it quite soon. But that does not matter very much and I do not regard it as strange that Trappists should be surprised that a Trappist should publish a journal! *Spring Birth* is wonderful. I still think I like the sonnets best of all—I saw them before in the pamphlet. But this time I discovered all the Old Testament pieces, and after reading about your visit to Uncle Mark I was sorry you didn't stay with him for a couple of weeks. Since I have been down here, I have developed almost a veneration for people like that: they live all around us. I ran into one when we were fighting a forest fire last October. They call him Gringsby Collins, and he lives out in the woods with a couple of acres of corn, with his two kids and his old mother. The fire was all around his place, and I never saw anybody less excited. The monks were running around wildly, and here he was standing there in the trees like St. Benedict and he isn't even a Catholic. For my own part I nearly got burned up in a thicket of young oaks—ten year old saplings with the dead leaves all over them: no place to fight a fire. It seems that I save up all the forest fires to tell you about in the rare letters I write. Remember the hermit [Herman Hanekamp]? He and I are great friends now, and when I was over at his place a month ago he was showing me the letters from his niece Thekla back in the old country (Oldenburg). And a picture of his terrible father now long dead. Maybe that is the reason why he is a hermit: that his father lived, I mean, not that he is dead. *Spring Birth* will be useful for my scholastics: I will give them the book for the Old Testament poems in it especially. They read the Bible backwards and forwards and can't get to know too much about the people in it. In a place like this you can eventually get so that you live with Abraham at one elbow and Elias at the other: you go around with them all day, and the old brothers look just like them. I had a Frater David, a big kid from Missouri, who was just like David. But the place busted him and he went home and he is doing all right. So anyway I was very very happy with the book and the letter. Write again when you can and don't forget that you are always invited to stop by here when you are in this part of the country.

August 11, 1953

In case I do not get a chance to write again before next March, I am doing so now in order to tell you that by all means you must come and visit Gethsemani, Lent or no Lent. I have the permission. Besides I think the country around here says a lot about Lincoln. It is angular and honest and poor. For my own part I love it more and more. I am glad too that you have a sabbatical and I hope you will be enriched by your solitude. Its poverty is a great enrichment. I was glad to have news of the boys. I have sons in the army too—some of the scholastics who left here for one reason or another have been drafted, and they write to me. And I think of them and pray for them. Johnny too.

I have also adopted a terribly tough kid who is in the penitentiary waiting to be executed for murder. In Missouri. But he writes wonderful letters. Meditates on fire. Prays when he hears the rain running down the walls. Writes poems. Desperately writes hundreds and hundreds of short poems, as if to stave off death. He is not a Catholic. I am flattered that I am one of the only two priests he will have anything to do with. He says all the other "squares" are crooks.

Our cow barn burned down in little over twenty minutes or half an hour—like a pile of brush. We could do nothing to put it out. Everybody thought it was a really beautiful fire, and it was. I am sending a poem about it ["An Elegy for the Monastery Barn"].

One of the amusing things I have found out how to do is to use Paul Hindemith's record of the *Four Temperaments* in spiritual direction. I play it to them and get them to figure out what temperament they are. Do you know it? I think it is wonderful. Although I am not at all phlegmatic I find that the part I respond to most, myself, is the fast part of the phlegmatic movement which practically makes me fly out the window.

Hindemith was down here in Lent, so I don't see why you should be abashed at coming then.

In the spring of 1954 Van Doren and his wife, Dorothy, traveled from Hodgenville, Kentucky, where they visited Lincoln's birthplace, to Gethsemani where Merton had permission to see them. They met and talked on March 5, 1954. Van Doren recalls that he remarked that Merton had not changed much and that Merton replied: "Why should I? Here our duty is to be more ourselves, not less."

June 3, 1954

. . . I was sitting out there in the hermitage, or to be exact in front of the hermitage, when I heard a shot and simultaneously a bullet whistling past like in the movies. I always thought that twang in the movies was meant to indicate the bullets ricocheting off rocks, but I guess this one just made that noise going past my ear, unless it had bounced off a tree. A few days later one of the brothers was proclaimed for "shooting off a high powered rifle in the bottoms, and one bullet landed fifty feet from where a couple of novices were working" . . .

Again, I am so glad you and Dorothy were able to come, and I insist that you make every effort to come again, when you can. When you had left I remembered that I had omitted to ask you to tell [Joseph Wood] Krutch "hello" from me, but I am sure you did. Meanwhile I am sending a draft of the "[Tower of] Babel" poem, which has somewhat changed since this stage, but this will give you an idea of it. I keep being interested in your Scripture talks, and hope you will let me have them if they get published.

God bless you both, and the boys. Everything is wonderful here, because we have had a lot of rain. And the other night a couple of the young monks got lost in the woods and I had to go out to look for them in the evening, and visited all my friends, [Herman] Hanekamp the hermit (who was reading a German book called the pilgrimage) and Grigsby (not Collins) Cauldwil, who had just come back from town and hadn't seen anybody (though as a matter of fact they got lost around his farm, where the forest fire had been).

October 16, 1954

At last it is raining and I not only have the time to write a letter but am more or less in a mood for one. So after a long delay I thank you for *Selected Poems* which was a very pleasant surprise. I was really happy to have it. Fr. Matthew [McGunigle] and I had been cooking up a plot to ask you for some books of verse of yours, and then this came. Now he has it, but before he took it I had time to dig into *Winter Diary*, which I had never read, and to re-read so many other favorites. I still like your sonnets best. And I want to use one of the later short pieces ("If they could speak") in a book I have been writing this fall, which is all about man being in the image and likeness of God. It is largely about Adam, and the poem would come in where I talk about him naming the animals. The book is called (so far) "Existential Communion" [eventually published as *The New Man*]. It is about the business of "coming to oneself" and "awakening" out of the inexistential torpor that most people live in, and finding one's real identity—in God. Which is possible because we are His image and likeness, and by our charity we are identified with Him. Thus our knowledge of Him is no longer merely as though it were the knowledge of an "object"! (Who could bear such a thing: and yet religious people do it: just as if the world contained here a chair, there a house, there a hill, and then again God. As though the identity of all were not hidden in Him Who has no name.)

I talk about rain, at the top of this page, as if it were something unfamiliar. It has been, here. We have hardly had four good showers all summer, and everything is half dead. (Except we irrigated our tobacco, with the lake you saw, and got a tremendous crop of two kinds of burley.)

September was busy, with writing the book and cutting tobacco and canning things. But now, as I say, it has rained, and we are back in cold fall weather (which was a long time coming). I like the woods best when there are a lot of black clouds streaming along the hills.

Are you still on your sabbatical? Or did it end in September? I had a monosyllabic card from [Bob] Lax in France, and he sent a lot of people a mimeographed letter which was very funny and was signed "Noah Webster" . . .

December 30, 1955

Your wonderful letter from Beaune [Côte d'Or, France] was a happy surprise. Thank you for thinking of me at the Grande Chartreuse. Even to be thought of there is something. Thanks for telling me about Bob [Lax], and above all thanks for the poem, which is so true to him. I even put it up in the novitiate so that all could ponder on a poem about a spiritual subject. You don't know, do you, that I am now master of the novices—a much more responsible and occupying job than the other one. I have practically a small kingdom of my own, a wing of the monastery in which Canon Law says I am the boss. The young ones entering live there and depend on the broken reed they have received as their support. The best of it is that the place is quiet, and we have our own garden and chapel, and the job is not too plaguing. In fact I find that if I overcome a little of my selfishness, it is quite pleasant.

Imagine if you can what led up to it. Again the old wrestling, more awful than before, about solitude. This last year I really plunged into the fight for true. I found a couple of people who told me "Yes, you should leave, you should go off and live alone—or enter another order etc. etc." Armed with this I even got as far as Rome (I mean with pestering letters) and finally the highest Superiors under the Pope calmed me down and told me to stay here. It sounds silly but I had to go through it. Having done so I feel pretty well cleaned out. I mean washed of everything. There is very little I seem to want at all—or so it seems, until I turn around and realize that I still cling to this bodily life, for instance. It would be too impossible of me if I suddenly turned out to be detached from that. Actually, I think the only valid step that has come out of the whole thing is that I am detached from detachment. And from ideals, I no longer want to know, or to think, what I am or what I've got or where I'm going . . .

In December 1955, after having visited Merton at Gethsemani the previous year, Van Doren wrote a poem called "Once in Kentucky (To Thomas Merton)," which he sent him in January 1956. He included the poem in The Autobiography of Mark

Van Doren (1958), pp. 331–32. He wrote below the poem when he sent it to Merton: "This is your poem if you want it . . . I am terribly interested in what you tell me about your wrestling over solitude again. I don't pretend to understand it all, but with your sufferings I have, believe me, the fullest and tenderest sympathy. And I can doubt that you are washed literally of everything. You couldn't be, and I dare to say shouldn't be. For instance of your created person. Which is why I send the poem—to show that someone saw that person."

February 11, 1956

We want to love in the minds of other people and we are surprised when we find ourselves there, as if it were after all not possible. And it is not the "we" that we think of as ourselves, because the person each man thinks he is does not exist. What an existential problem your poem suggests! You have met in Kentucky a person that I have been acquainted with for some time, but whom I have not yet learned to understand. In the poem (about the men you met in their cages) are mixed the sorrow of the cage and the joy of liberty, and I am glad you think my joy is thin enough to survive, for I hope it will. And yours too. And it is true that the fat joys that sit in the world's door try to be implacable. But you know they are dead. And I would be glad if there were none on my doorstep. Let us be happy then in the *ver sacrum*, the Lent which is the doorway to the victory of Easter . . .

For the rest I lecture the novices on Cassian and on the customs of twelfth century monks and on the behavior of twentieth century novices and secretly I pry into the psychoanalysts. These are the occupations which God has given to Masters of Novices in Cistercian monasteries. I have no other, except the felling of trees, and the praying of prayers. In the distance, on top of the hill, I can see the fire tower when I look out the windows of the novitiate. In the evening it is surrounded with seraphim.

. . . Come to Kentucky some more.

In the summer of 1956, Van Doren visited Louisville, where he lectured at the University of Louisville on June 25. Merton obtained permission to meet and talk with his former teacher in Louisville.

The Courier-Journal *reported that Van Doren had lunch with "Trappist monk Thomas Merton" at the Arts Club in the old Henry Clay Hotel, at which newswriter William Habich and Julius John Oppenheimer, dean of the University's College of Arts and Sciences, were also present.*

July 3, 1956

. . . The Louisville session was wonderful. I can't get over it. I know you are more used to being treated as a celebrity than I am, in fact I am never treated as one face to face in real-life-flesh-and-blood adulation. This once was I thought very funny, right down to the good old type with his comments on the demise of De la Mare. It was all wonderful. And I did think the Dean was a good egg, and will go and see him some time. When I say funny, I mean "humorous" in the Johnsonian sense (and I suppose that too has to do with my own rather unorthodox interest in analysis, which I hope did not sadden you). All people are funny because they are at the same time real and false, and that is what is so good about it. Original sin is serious enough for it to be blasphemy to find a joke in it, and yet since from the first a Redeemer was promised, and since He is sent, and is in the midst of us, the mixture of reality and serious falsity that is everywhere becomes very funny if we see that in the midst of everything is the Christ, the Real One, Who does not mind our caricatures as much as we would if we were in His exact position. He sees it all in another way, through the lens of a mercy which does the same thing to everything as does Zen to whatever it looks at. (Zen can only do things to what it looks at for, of course, it redeems nothing.)

I am still so dazed that I have not remembered half the things I forgot to say, or I would say some of them here. But of course they were never meant to be said, I suppose. They have been uttered in the Word and we can understand them all in His silence. Once a Zen master reproved a disciple saying: "You are all right, except that you talk about Zen." Yet of course they would immediately agree that an agreement *not* to talk about it would not be Zen either.

The next letter was written at St. John's Abbey in Collegeville, Minnesota, where Merton was attending a series of lectures on psychiatry for priests given by psychoanalyst Dr. Gregory Zilboorg—his first extensive trip outside Gethsemani since entering in 1941.

> St. John's Abbey
> Collegeville, Minn.
> July 30, 1956

I was deeply moved by your last letter. Certainly there is little one can do about being a celebrity except bear with it, and I was not really disturbed by the business at the club, except that it could have been much more pleasant if we could have gone on talking alone as we did up in the room. It was well worth it, if it was the price of seeing you again and, as you say, talking about the things we did not really say but conveyed. So the club can be forgotten, it was nothing. The substance remains.

Here incidentally everything has been fine. First of all it is so good to be received in all simplicity by a community of other monks, as a monk, no questions asked, no incitements to act famous. Then there has been the short summer school.

I think I told you I would be here for some lectures on psychiatry for priests. You have no idea how good and how right the approach has so far been. Far from trying to teach us jargon, they have not hesitated to purge those of us who brought a little with us. They have been sternly opposed to tendencies to diagnose and pry, to "peep and analyze" on the grave of a human value. They have made us want *not* to have technical means of manipulating people. On the contrary they have kept up a magnificent emphasis on human values, on getting in real contact with a person who is in trouble and needs your help, and on really giving him the help he needs instead of something he does not need from you. Zilboorg, the dominant spirit, who has a tremendous mission in this regard, made a statement which has set the tone for the whole business: that the priest cannot be the accomplice of formalists and legalists who use their techniques to destroy human values in the sick individual, or the criminal, or the man in trouble—or the person they do not like. We are being taught that we cannot and must not attempt the kind of thing I think you most object to when psychoanalysis corrupts literary judgment. So you see I am gaining much . . .

April 9, 1957

As I prepare to tell you that I have dedicated my last book of poems [*The Strange Islands*] to you and Dorothy, I reflect that since things move so slowly down here, you have probably already received the book from New Directions before I have had any to send you. My copies arrived last evening, however, and I am inscribing one and sending it off right now. As I say, I am sure New Directions must have sent you one, or some. I hope you will like it, anyway. I know you have seen most of the poems before, and liked them, and I thought you would not mind the dedication. It is twenty years since I have dedicated a book to you, so I thought it was about time to do it again.

It is probably also the anniversary, or nearly the anniversary, of that wonderful day when you and Dorothy stopped by at the monastery, after being at Hodgenville. It is just the same kind of day, bright and dazzling with all sorts of promises. We have had a lot of rain, and I have planted hundreds of pine seedlings and yellow poplars and it looks as if they are going to do well if we can keep the hermit's goats away from them. So, on a sunny spring day with a new book of poems dedicated to you, I have every reason to think especially of you and Dorothy and to pray for you especially and do whatever else a monk can do to bring good to his friends.

The way things are with me at the moment is: no writing at all. The weather-vane is pointing that way, this time. It is just as well, for I am busy with the novices and have written so much that it is time to slow down and rest. So I am reading a lot instead, all sorts of things, whatever I can lay hands on, especially some interesting Greek Fathers, though not as much in the original as I would desire. Maybe after I am no longer novice master, I will write again.

I had another occasion to think of you, when news of Charlie's exploits on TV filtered through. I was given to understand that he had become the king of Persia as a result of being very smart, but that it was the tax people who actually wore the crown. It must have been harrowing, and if, after it all, he feels like entering a Trappist monastery, well, the novitiate is wide open.

We are just finishing Genesis, after all these months. I'd love to see a Russian Ballet of the Joseph story, which has in it unending depths of wonder and of goodness: for it is at once the Gospel and the Last Judgment. One of the things that has not yet worked out is the ultimate destiny of the Jews: but it is all there in Joseph, for Joseph is the Christ of the Last Day. Isn't it tremendous? Not only for the Jews, but for all of us, brethren of various shapes and sizes.

The Van Dorens visited Merton at Gethsemani again on September 28, 1957. In his letter to Merton planning the trip, Van Doren cautioned: "Don't go to Nicaragua before the 28th."

September 17, 1957

By all means come in the afternoon of the 28th. I will be expecting you about two. That will give us a couple of hours and more to talk—do you want to stay overnight? Or for supper? You are very welcome if you do. Why not stay for Vespers & supper & then go to Louisville for the night? We will see anyway . . .

November 20, 1958

Well, they are hammering again, and I am sitting down to another letter. This time it is Father Joseph with the hammer. A few days [ago] I got a note from Fr. Benedict asserting that he intended to "scrap the walls" by which, as I discovered, he meant to scrape them. Which he did. Fall is a season of special monastic madness. But also the monastery being old is constantly getting fixed and re-modelled as they say. They pull out whole floors and put in new ones (as is being done now with the novices' dormitory). It goes without saying that they scrap the walls.

What I really want to do in this letter is thank you for the book on *Liberal Education*. I am sorry I never read it before, it is a wonderful book. It is not at all like the books professors write about colleges today, but much more like the books of the people you quote, people who have actually had a liberal education. And the best argument of your book for liberal education is the way it is written: finely. I am constantly being brought up short by the fact that every sentence has something important to say. There is never any waste of time or paper on what claims to be inevitable nonsense. So true is it that people who write books in which large patches of nonsense "have to" appear to get them from one "point" to another, do not have anything to say in the first place. All that I have ever said about the seriousness with which you take truth, I repeat in connection with the *Liberal Education*. I am going to make sure that a lot of the monks and novices read this. There is so much in it, and it is about all of life and not just a department of life. This too is another argument for the book's excellence, and the author's.

All this being so, then there is nothing for it: we must have the book on *Don Quixote*. I am sorry to be so grasping, but we are in a predicament here getting ready to supply for the education which many of the young people never got in their high schools and colleges, and they will surely need this. Will you let me bother you for it? In return I will begin pulling wires to have them send you a Trappist cheese of some sort which, by the time it reaches you, may be strong enough to walk by itself.

(Father Joseph just broke a window.)

I think the new Pope [John XXIII] is a wonder, a fine simple old man, who would not let anybody kiss his foot, and whose first thought was to go back to his native village and have a fine fiesta with his brothers and cousins. (Though it turns out he probably can't go.) Whose first public statement, or one of the first, was that the Pope doesn't have to know everything and be able to do everything, and that all he has to be is the Pope. I have written at once to say that he is my favorite Pope.

We have an old farmhand working here, who has been here for over fifty years, and his father was here before him. He often walks up to the monks and tells them what he has heard over the radio (frowned on but tolerated). He came up to me the other day full of wonderment and said "Father, the Pope has just chosen Spellman a cardinal." He was disappointed that I didn't seem amazed, and when I made him signs that I thought Spellman was already a cardinal, he went off and checked, and the next person he told, he gave them a paper with the names written down so he wouldn't get them wrong. He meant Cushing, of course.

He's the same one who, if a bear gets loose somewhere in Wyoming, gives out the news in such a way that everyone believes the bear to be in New Haven [Kentucky]. On one such occasion I got the cellarer to issue me a big hunting knife, before going out into the forest.

Once again, many thanks for the *Liberal Education* which I like the way I like Thoreau—it is that kind of a book.

December 18, 1958

Quixote is here, where he belongs, among so many others like himself, and most welcome. I quite agree with you that "he had his own reasons" for behaving as he did, and I think that sums him up. His only fault, if it be a fault, was that he played too seriously. And that was the fault of the Renaissance all over, I think, though they would all with one voice deny it. The Middle Ages just played without reflection. Don Quixote and his age perhaps reflected too much. And we—what on earth does our age do? I do not have words to describe it: certainly the very thought of "play" is something we have forgotten, but that we are eternally self-conscious about trying to do it, or watch it done professionally by somebody else.

Thank you in any case for giving me the pleasure of reading such a book and of having it here for the novices. We are all grateful.

Sometime a fruitcake soaked in Bourbon should reach you from here, with our love, for Christmas. Which I wish you and Dorothy and all very Merry.

In 1959 Van Doren received the Alexander Hamilton Medal given by Columbia University for meritorious accomplishment. Merton was asked to write a letter of tribute and wrote several drafts for a humorous "message," the first of which is given here. Subsequent drafts were titled "Message to Marx Van Doorway for the Alphabet Medal" and "A Message to be Inscribed on Mark Van Doren's Alphabet Medal." The final version, called more sedately "Message to be Inscribed on Mark Van Doren's Hamilton Medal," is included in The Collected Poems of Thomas Merton *(New Directions, 1977, pp. 800–1).*

Oh Mark:

Whooping up the side of the house in a fast storm come messengers with ice on their whiskers and great lolling heads of snow. Me they find in lenten emaciation meditating various meats. They wipe their eyes, and have me in focus. One makes a hole in his stuffed blizzard and out of this, in words reminiscent of language, he speaks: Marx Van Doorway has fallen upon the Hamilton muddle. What, I cry, is this some country treat? No they reply in fat gusts, he's a metropolitan winner. Winner of what I lean, as a matter of question, winner of a race? Has he outfooted champions and presidents and won himself a cup? No, but rather for personal eminence he is decked with muddles, in the middle of a city banquet. Grand, I cry, and is everybody at the banquet rich? He is filled with muddles on all sides by millionaire poets, for singular worth, particularly worth of letters. You mean I say that people are writing him letters? Not only people, but even you. Fine, I say, I too will praise my friend Max Van Dusen. I will praise him for the twenty-four letters of his alphabet. Of all the writers I ever heard about, he uses the best alphabet.

June 6, 1959

I have not yet written you the "Dear Mark" letter I should have written for the "feast" of your retirement. For you a feast, and for Columbia an occasion of mourning. Of course, all the public celebration of the Hamilton Medal put me a bit out of my stride and I could not begin to say anything I really wanted to say. So I was merely facetious and cryptic, knowing you would know all that was behind it. As Tate remarked in the collection of letters written to you, it was you who honored the medal by receiving it.

As for you and Columbia: I tried to say a little of what I meant before. But since then I have gone on piling up a debt to you and there is no way of paying it. That is the best thing of all, because if it were a "debt" in the sense of something that could be paid, where would be the joy? Love's debts have this in them that they are too great to be paid, and that therefore one loves to remain in debt. I hope that I will owe you more and more that I can never repay, and I fully expect to. You are certainly one of the joys of life for all who have ever come within a mile of you. And everybody knows it and says it. So you have become a kind of sacrament, which is what every man should be. You are certainly one of the most Christian people I have ever seen, for this is what it is to be a Christian: simply to be Christ and not to realize it. In this there is nothing but reasons for humility, because everybody is Christ. But not everybody is able to work out, in his life, the meaning of who he is. Most people manage to obscure it and even deface it, sad to say. If this bewilders you, that is fine. It should. Anybody who understands such things has not understood. Let us just settle for the fact that you are a most Christian person, and perhaps all the more so for not having acquired some institutionally Christian "form" (which would only limit you to the Christianity of a certain age, time or place.)

Of course these things might shock some people, but I am not saying them to the people who would be shocked, only to those who will understand (without understanding).

And now I maneuver myself into greater debt.

J. Laughlin was here for two days and we had a fine time riding to Lexington and back, as it happened I have a novice in the hospital there and we both have a friend there, a printer, an old Austrian [Victor Hammer]. That is not what I wanted to tell you. J. is bringing out a volume of my selected poems, and at first they wanted me to write a preface. But the other day we agreed it would be much better to have someone else: who else but you? You are the one who started the whole thing going. They will be, I hope, the best of the poems, and an essay, for a ND paperback. I would be so happy if you could find time to do it, and could think up something to say about the poems (which you already have so well and so generously!) I gave J [Bob] Lax's poems too and he seems very interested in them. I think he will want to publish them, or some of them. Lax was here too, but he told you. It has been gay all summer.

July 24, 1959

. . . Mark, thank you for taking on the preface. It will give some point to the book, I hope. Not that I think the poems are all bad. But the fact that you like them will enable people to see them rightly, and find whatever good is there. I forget whether or not I had included "The Barn" on the original list, perhaps I was shy about it. As a matter of fact it is for me subjectively an important poem, because when I was a kid on a farm in Maryland (yes, even that, for a while) a barn burned down in the middle of the night and it is one of the earliest things I can remember. So burning barns are for me great mysteries that are important. They turn out to be the whole world, and it is the Last Judgment. New Directions say they have sent you the bits and pieces of poems in any case. I am very glad . . .

America means to me Mark, Dot, the boys, Lax, and all the fellows, and Krutch and Thurber and then back further Thoreau and— It is not a very long list. So it seems that only a very small sector of the country really means a lot to me. But I think it is a very important one, and essential enough so that I have no apologies to make to any of those committees, do I? They, the committees, are about the last thing in the world I ask for America and for their sakes I would gladly part company with the whole business: them, and *Time* and Coca Cola (this is heresy, don't tell Lax, but I have suddenly gone manichaean on Coca Cola. Not that I drink any, but I have just come to detest the very idea of the stuff because of some ads that I saw going in to Louisville. I mean the uggsome pictures of healthy, optimistic, empty-headed, crew-cutted, sweatered, American youth swilling that damn stuff in order to bear witness to our incomparable national IDEAL.) (There, now I've said it.) There are some other things too, but I forget them, happily . . .

In 1959 Merton learned of the television scandal which involved Van Doren's son Charles, to whose appearance on a TV quiz show he referred in his letter to Van Doren of April 9, 1957. Charles Van Doren's appearances on the show made him a popular celebrity and won him $129,000. But in October 1959 a nation-wide scandal broke when it was learned that participants had been given in advance answers to questions. The public which had adulated Charles Van Doren turned on him and he bore the brunt of the antipathy and embarrassment that followed. Merton's letter to Charles Van Doren is included in the final section of this book.

> St. Anthony Hospital
> Louisville, Kentucky
> October 17, 1959

Do not be surprised at the letterhead. I am just in here for a minor operation.

But while here I have seen the papers and all the nasty fuss about Charlie. I am so sorry to hear that everything has turned out so disagreeably & I want to express my sympathy for him & for all of you. I hope it will not be too unpleasant & that you will not have to bear too much unnecessary publicity & trouble, but that soon everything will be cleaned up satisfactorily.

This whole affair, in its foolishness & sordid cheapness, is something I cannot help regarding as symptomatic. I for one do *not* believe that all is right with America. On the contrary I think this is a sick and deluded nation (along with all the others, of course). And this proves it in some sense. Why? Charlie, precisely because he is in most ways just what so many Americans want themselves to be—clear-headed, frank, & ingenuous—has to pay for it by becoming a victim of advertisers, manipulated & sold by them. To me, this is just another indication that few people with any influence care, any more, about anything except how the best things look & how they sell. And the pity is that *everything* is reduced to that level, including all the things that can neither be seen or sold.

That Charlie should, in all innocence, be the victim of sick manipulation is a sad & terrible thing. At least he has his innocence. But that does not spare him from the insane gestures and exhibitions of the inquisitors who are bent on staging their own kind of show: the great, stupid bluff of governmental zeal & integrity!

So I want you all to know that I am very angry & very sick & very fed up with what has happened to you all, and that I have considerable difficulty in keeping the anger within ordinate bounds.

But you can have the consolation of knowing that if such things happen to you, it is because you form part of the honest & civilized remnant for whom such attentions are reserved . . .

October 31, 1959

My last letter to you from the hospital was a little inadequate, especially as I was peeved about the whole affair that poor Charlie is going through. Now that I have slightly more perspective on it, and it is growing more unpleasant I really want to write to you about it in a more detached way (I hope) and say some of the things I think ought to be said about it. And of course the first thing I want to say above all is that I do hope you are not all of you too distressed and shattered by it. Please do not be, because there is really no reason for that. Actually in many ways this can be seen as a very good thing, though I know I sound like Eliphas the Themanite when I dare to say it. But before I launch into some Job's-comforting of my own, I offer, as the only apology for words, my love for all of you which, if possible, has become very much greater as a result of all this. And I am sure that with all your friends it is and will be the same.

First of all let me say this: my respect for Charlie is immeasurably greater than it was when he was winning all the money and getting all the favorable publicity. Then, one could not help feeling a little uncomfortable about it, because it was basically false like everything else on that level of being—like everything else that people seem to cling to most blindly for support in this poor benighted country we live in. Now, brutally but perhaps mercifully, suffering and humiliation have entered into the picture to add a note of reality for which one has reason to be thankful. Forgive me, even all of you have reason to be thankful for it, and I think very much so. It certainly gives Charlie a "tragic" stature which is much more human than the nice optimistic role of a year ago. And, too, this is not a role. Isn't that after all a blessing? I mean, even when everything was going so well, Charlie was still, without doubt, seduced into impersonating himself, in order to please and comfort this foolish, and pitifully foolish nation, with a daydream of itself.

So America grabbed Charlie and set him up in the middle of its dream, so that he could be the dream image for a while. And the people who were making money out of it could see that it had evident possibilities. And after all, America continually and stupidly pays people like that millions of dollars all the time precisely in order to suffer this kind of deception. America *wants* to be kidded and the only crime is letting the people know, realize, the falsity. We are such babies that we want our unrealities to be real and the only thing we resent is the reminder that they are not.

What one of us has not been coaxed into doing things of which he is terribly ashamed? Certainly there are things in my past that I do not want to have known all over the country, and you know, they still might be. When one person out of all the rest is picked out to have *his* shame known by everybody, then perhaps it may be because he is very much more of a person than the rest, and is capable of growing because of it. But the rest of us have to grow by it too. I do not know what the reactions have been, but if people have just deserted him (which is possible) then I don't think much of this country. But if they have stood by him, even in his shame, then I think perhaps there is some hope for us. Perhaps we are able to realize that we are *all equally guilty*. Lao Tse has said wisely that the man who praises virtue by that very fact leads someone into vice, and it is the narcissism of the whole blind lot of us that has got Charlie into trouble because he is such an image of frankness, honesty etc. We had better be very careful how we praise honesty in this day, and when there are such instruments as TV around.

The thing that is so appalling in this whole affair is the frightful eruption of guilt that it represents. The boundless, bottomless guilt that this country cannot help feeling and cannot bear. Does it really make such a difference that this brainwashing process has arisen spontaneously among us, while in totalitarian states it is cynically planned? Are we still so blind that we cannot see that we do the same thing to our own people as they do in Russia and China, but not yet on so great a scale? And still, as it were, with our right hand not knowing what the left is doing? It is the same all over the world, and yet we have this abominable illusion that we are shining, candid people and they are all the rest of them dark and base. Good God, we are all base and black, who the blazes do we think we are? That is the first step in being human, to recognize that. We can't. Instead, we push people out on to stages, and before cameras, to impersonate the white image of ourselves, and when we find a speck on him we kill him. It is dreadful, and because of this we are a very sick country.

The reason why I feel this so strongly is that it is to a great extent my own problem, and in a way it is also yours. We are all of us comforting images. That which is nice in us, and is admired, is perhaps now what we have to be most afraid of. I know that I for one have become part of a very big false front of which I am ashamed and by which I am often very much upset. But one of the fortunate advantages of monastic community life is that, in it, no one is very prodigal with compliments and admiration. That has been a corrective, but not much of one, when the whole thing gets shot through with falsity. I don't know if you ever see anything of our particular brand of phoniness, but it is certainly quite humiliating.

Not to prolong this beyond measure: forgive one last platitude. Certainly there is nothing in this that cannot be used as a great good, and it can perhaps turn out to be the one thing that has saved Charlie from becoming just another one of those people whose faces are everywhere. Just another big smile. If it gets him back into the woods, and out of the limelight, and gets him back to what he really knows as himself instead of what other people want him to be, then what could be better? It can be a liberation, and I hope that is what it is. That is my prayer for him, and for all of you, and for all of us. And I do not mean to say that I think he has been much hurt by success, or anything like that. I know he must have been strong enough to take it well, but this requires even greater strength. And no one can be a success without suffering from it in some way. This is the only way of suffering from success that really amounts to anything. The other ways are poison. One is infected without knowing it. This way you know what is hitting you.

But I do hope you realize that all your friends are very much with you, and that we all love all of you more and more. Such is the point of this whole sermon, which I trust your love to forgive and understand.

November 12, 1959

Charlie sent me his "confession" signed, "with love from Babylon" which immediately reassured me. I am now more or less straight about what happened and wrote to him as soon as I got the statement. I don't take back anything I may have said that applied to the case, and regret only having bothered you with letters that were more or less off the target. It would have been more sensible to write just one that was directly to the point. But of course you understand. I am no longer mad, but still smouldering no doubt. With resentment against the whole country, in so far as they have tried to make Charlie a scapegoat for a national sin. How stupid it all is. Just suppose he had taken an enormous sum of money to have his picture printed in a magazine over a statement that he thought that product was utterly superb—whatever it was. Nobody would have accused him of lying. It is perfectly respectable to tell that kind of a lie. Of course I understand that they got mad when the point of the other business was its supposed genuineness. Still, the difference is very artificial. *Omnis homo mendax.* It is about time this was admitted.

Enough of that whole business.

I have read your preface [*Selected Poems*] and it made me feel warm all over on a cold day. There is no way of saying how happy I am to have such good things said by someone who knows what he is talking about. It will add immensely to the book and be one of the best things in it. Of course I do not mind letting you use the letters. Why not? In fact I had forgotten all about them and was interested in them myself. I think it was a very good way of starting. But I am really happy to think, finally, that some of my poems really make sense, and that as a whole it is poetry. That is comforting, because for a while I was disgusted with the whole lot of it, since the middle book (*Figures for an Apocalypse*) was so bad in many ways. The last book didn't seem to get anywhere but I am still glad about it, and have learned that if critics (with a capital K) don't like it, it still makes no difference. Really no difference at all. It is a relief to wake up and see clearly that these people seldom know what they are talking about . . .

[P.S.] I take seriously the last lines of your preface, and will write verse when and if I can.

September 17, 1960

Thank you for your card about the little book on Solitude. I knew you would like it and understand it. Now I am sending you a bigger book of so-called *Disputed Questions* in which the same material on solitude is in fact done at slightly greater length. The censors brought it about that I became even more explicit than I had been before. The beauties of censorship. This is often not realized outside the Church. Censors have, as one of their unintentional effects, the power to make one more ardent, more explicit, more indignant, more succinct and in the end they force one to come right out and say many things that would otherwise have remained hidden. I don't know what "good it will do" but I did not write this in order to do good, but simply in order to speak the truth and the truth can take care of itself and do its own good.

You might also like the essay on the power of love and for the rest of the book I don't know. It has a mixture of strange things in it.

Charlie [Van Doren] wrote me last year that in my Pasternak article my attitude toward politics was undeveloped and naive and this is true. I didn't develop anything since then, at least in the article. But someday I will, and I hope I can do it outside of a concentration camp.

Bob [Lax] is coming down in October or at least he says he is and I think he will. I am looking forward to it anyway. This has been a busy year. I hope this winter I can sit more in the woods or wander around in them. We are not cutting trees much anymore, everything is cheese. We are cursed with business even here. Sell cheese, buy wood. What kind of a life is that? However, there it is.

February 16, 1961

It is a very long time since I have written. The pretext is this mimeographed thing, a deadpan thing, a simple chaining together of clichés that are frightening ["Original Child Bomb"]. I think the same words were used by the human race when the things happened, and I have just picked up what was said by the human race. Its pitiful and sudden attempts to exorcise the horror with cheap symbols. Bob Lax probably wants to print this in *Pax* and it is the first thing almost that he had had in a long time especially about pax. But I like [Ad] Reinhardt's dogmatic definitions about abstract art . . .

Here it rains. In the pine woods I have a little house. It is on the point of being approved or reproved and I don't know which. I have a house hanging by a thread. The most beautiful little house in the world, mostly for conversations with protestant ministers who come here to find a little peace and quiet and some agreement. We actually get along very well.

I hope it is coming around time for you to be out this way so that you can stop by and see the house and sit on its porch. I don't live there, though my heart probably does. I don't even have a typewriter there. There is no electric light and of course no telephone even to the monastery, and there is no road only a path through the woods. If the thread holds and becomes a cable, then I hope some day we can comment on the pine trees and chickadees and the pileated woodpeckers and above all the quails which I keep tripping over all the time as they seem to recognize me as one of the few in Kentucky with whom they are safe. (They live in the area where the house is.)

Ed Rice was down here and nearly slid off all the roads in America driving back to New York. I am working on an art book, or am supposed to be.

Lax sends wonderful incoherent prophecies and scribbles, very wise.

Later will come to you more *Desert Fathers*, the same ones as before but more and in a different book. I don't know how much later, but it will be a pretty book.

As the dour meditation indicates, I want very much to say a loud "No" to missiles and polaris submarines and everything which sneaks up on a city to destroy it, no matter whose city, no matter what the supposed wickedness of it. Who is to judge cities if not even Christ came to judge the world? For the just there is probably no pardon. If you know what I mean by "just"—of course, unjust. That is one of the principal lessons of the Gospels: that the just are unjust and that those who are "justified" are so only by mercy received and given, for it is this that brings them "in line", for the line is mercy, not justice.

I hear that the business about Charlie [Van Doren] still smoulders a little and remains nasty. Can't they finish with their righteousness?

Columbia University awarded Merton the University Medal for Excellence in 1961. Because of the rules of the Cistercian Order which would not allow him to be present, the Trustees of Columbia agreed to make an exception to their "hitherto inflexible rule" and gave him the medal in absentia. *He asked that Van Doren accept at the Commencement Exercises on June 6, which Van Doren did. The citation, signed by President Grayson Kirk, read: "Gifted master of language, in poem and prose, light-hearted as you are grave, you have reached out with winged words to the world you left. In the phrase of one who was your beloved teacher in days on Morningside, you are much less lost to the world than many who insist they are still in it. To his hand, for early conveyance to you, I entrust the University Medal for Excellence as a testimonial of your Alma Mater's admiration and enduring respect."*

May 13, 1961

All I can say is that as June 6th approaches I am happy that no one but you will be going there to get the medal for me. No one but you should. Of course if I went back to Columbia today the buildings would collapse, probably. I have to sit here with my shoes off among the ants and rave at the world from a distance. But I do love Columbia and don't rave at it at all, on the contrary. I am not aware of any reason why I should have received a medal. But that is where you come in. To you it seems logical that I should be getting a medal, then to me it seems logical that you should receive it for me.

It has finally stopped raining and snowing (?) around here. The quails live all around my house, and whistle in the grass. I read Chinese philosophers and discover that this is what I am, in fact, myself. Though doubtless some other things too.

For three months I have been pounding away at a mad course in mystical theology and have enjoyed the sweating, but it is finally ending and I enjoy that more. It is always racking to talk about what should not be said. I ended up last time Beguines, beguines and beguines. They were wonderful, like the quails around my house. Everybody has forgotten them, but they were very wise and Eckhart learned all the best things he knew from them.

[Ed] Rice is worried about [Bob] Lax, says he went off in confusion to Greece. Where else should one go in confusion?

The poem ["The Moslems' Angel of Death"] I send does not come from knowing Algeria so much, but I suppose it applies.

And you: do they still heap medals upon *you*? Or is this your year to collect medals for other people who deserve them less than you do?

June 21, 1961

Here is the June solstice and I thank you for the medal in its box with its message of light and its questionable claim that I have somehow served somebody besides myself. Thank you above all for your kindness in getting it for me, and for enjoying it on my behalf (which I would not have done for myself if I had been there). I wrote Grayson Kirk a letter. The fact that his secretary wrote the kind little statement diminishes nothing of my gratitude to the President and to his university. Next year is my twenty-fifth anniversary. I mean that of my class. I don't know what is left of 1937, probably quite a bit. Really I am more '38 than '37 ([Bob] Lax and so on). I actually got my degree in February. But I was always supposed to be '37, since I edited the yearbook and other things were done which are understood to make one a member of that class forever and ever.

Anyway, thinking over the unbelievable fact that it is twenty-five years since these things happened, I am once again aware of the fact that I liked being at Columbia and that it meant a great deal to me. The place, the people, the classes, the library, the books, the things done, the noise made, the time wasted well and the time wasted badly. I would not want to appear on the campus next year with a false nose and a funny hat (if that is what one does on these saturnalia) but I would not want the year to go by without my having thought of this: and if they think of me too, so much the better. I am glad you said they felt as if I were there.

Here it is a cool summer, and the birds sing well, and the trees throw a very good shade. The flowers come up and there were millions of strawberries. I read and enjoy Chinese classics and the Lord knows what else. They (meaning Harcourt Brace) are working on a Merton Reader, and I am keeping my fingers in the selection process to make sure it does not become either too dull or too frivolous. I am not writing much at the moment and not intending to write much except for doing chores like an Encyclopedia article (*New Catholic Encyclopedia*, which will probably be stuffy).

Guess what I have on the table in a little phial of water: a gardenia. We grew it in the garden, the plants were sent to us from our monastery in South Carolina. They have to be taken in for the winter. There have been a lot of small blooms this summer. This is the second I have sur-reptitiously picked (I am novice master and I can do what I like with the novices' garden, but I wouldn't want to be seen picking gardenias) and have this placed before the little Mexican image of Our Lady of Solitude. The scent is very pure: when I was in the world I did not think this. I can now see why.

Thank you for your good letter, then. And for the medal. And if you are a ghost of mine you are obligated to haunt my house, at least for a brief interval.

Van Doren came again to Louisville in December 1961 to speak in a joint project of Louisville colleges called the "Book of the Semester" program. He actually spoke at the University of Louisville and Ursuline College, though Bellarmine College was his official host. On December 3, Van Doren paid his third visit to Merton at Gethsemani. He wrote later: "I shall never forget that day, at the retreat, in your class, and on the Abbey walks . . . It was wonderful to have lunch with the Abbot [James Fox], whom I'm afraid I didn't thank eloquently enough . . . I'll be thinking of you in your little house—but not so little either. I was impressed."

September 20, 1961

It was good to get your letter and I am very happy that you can come. Sunday is not the best of days, but since this is exceptional we can certainly make the most of it. There will at least be a bit of time in the afternoon for you to see the hermitage: probably a little chilly, enough for a nice wood fire. So let us by all means plan on December 3rd. Probably the best thing would be for someone of the Bellarmine people to drive you out Saturday evening. Sunday morning there is Mass about 10. You would get a little time to think and breathe. We can get you back to Louisville whenever you need to get your plane, but I hope you don't have to leave us before 3 in the afternoon.

[Bob] Lax sends me all kinds of cryptic cards from some non-existent place in Pennsylvania saying "Isaacs for Prothonotary" and other such incitements to civic zeal.

J. [Laughlin] has published a poet called Denise Levertov I think you would like. Have you seen her book? It starts with a wonderful version of a Toltec poem about what an artist ought to do . . .

November 22, 1961

Thank you for the latest letter: I was deeply touched that the Thurbers wanted a copy of the poem about Jim ["Elegy for James Thurber"] and of course I would want them to have it with all my heart, if they like it. Everything today is at the same time sad and full of irony: one can be humorous because behind it all is the mercy of God, and the ponderous cruelties and stupidities of men are not the last word about anything.

About December 3rd, the first Sunday of Advent, and your Advent: I shall make sure that someone in Louisville drives you out Sunday morning, the earlier the better, but of course you have to sleep: don't think I am urging Cistercian hours on you, much as I would like to. But at least I hope we can have most or all of the afternoon. Then I can promise, I think, the wood fire, unless we have one of those summer days that sometimes come in December and of which there is, at the moment, no threat . . .

January 15, 1962

I hear indirectly that this awful business about Charlie [Van Doren] is starting up again. I hope that it is not true, or that I have not understood it. Once again this frenzy of justice which fixes itself relentlessly on one who does not have the conventional defenses of the big lawbreakers. It cannot hurt Charlie, because he has outlived whatever was wrong in it for him, and has got far beyond that. And yet I hope he will be spared very much, and that he will be able to rise above whatever he is not spared. You too. I wish this did not have to be, but in any case I will remember it in prayer often, and will get the novices to do this also. And meanwhile, this remains a grim sorrow, along with all the other grim ones.

January 18, 1962

J. [Laughlin] was here and left yesterday. I asked him if there was anything new about Charlie [Van Doren] and it seemed that I had been misled by a rumor. Thank heaven that there was nothing to it. I am sorry I wrote so excited a letter. I had better be careful about that in the future.

We have pretty well planned the peace book [*Peace in the Post-Christian Era*], with a lot of good things in it, and I think it will be a persuasive book. Certainly I like it myself and think it says many things that need to be said. Thanks to the folly of people, a situation has arisen in which they had to be said, so therefore there is some good in all the nonsense. I still keep hoping that the air will be to some extent cleared, and that we will be able to go ahead with at least a little of the light of reason, and find our way patiently into some new dimension where war will be a thing of the past. It seems unlikely, though . . .

On February 4, 1962, Van Doren sent Merton a poem entitled "Prophet." In his note Van Doren said: "It has taken me years to finish. I send it to you because I know now whom it fits. You."

March 29, 1962

If I have not written sooner about the Prophet poem it is probably because I am too busy with the prophet business, & when one gets that way he is probably more of a fool than a prophet. Sometimes I think the grave I am digging is for everybody's soul. A great grave of absurdity for everything. Surely I am not entitled to take my disillusionment that seriously!

And I do not intend to with such nice weather, so many birds, such a smell of new grass growing, such a coming of different freights!

The Bishops do not like my war songs about peace, which is natural no doubt. They are in the bishop business, & that has more to do with being a manager than I am able to understand. They would be more at home around the Pentagon than I, and no doubt I would be & am more at home in the pine trees. They can let me talk out loud to myself, & if they don't like what I say they can be just a little more patient & shall soon find out who was right . . .

Merton sent Van Doren a copy of his poem "Grace's House," inspired by Grace Sisson's drawing of a house with no access. Later she provided "The Road to Joy," as Merton dubbed her second drawing.

[*Cold War Letter* 99]

August 9, 1962

Here, a poem. That is all. I have no other pretext for writing, but glad to have this one. It is a poem about a drawing of a house by a five-year-old child. What a drawing, what a house, what suns and birds. It is true that we do not know where we are.

That there are circles within circles, and that if we choose we can let loose in the circle of paradise the very wrath of God: this is said by Boehme in his confessions. We are trying to bear him out, but children can, if they still will, give us the lie and show us our folly. But we are now more and more persistent in refusing to see any such thing. All we will see is the image, the image, the absurd image, the mask over our own emptiness. And we will beat on the box to make the voice come out. And it will speak numbers to us, oracular numbers, delphic billions this way and that way.

I have read a little of Thoreau and know enough to lament that such good sense died so long ago. But it could still be ours if only we wanted it. We do not, we want the image, the consuming image, the dead one into which we pour soft drinks. The smiles of the image. All the girls are laughing because the image has a soft drink. He will, with the power of the drink, explode a moon.

The book on peace [*Peace in the Post-Christian Era*], did I say it? was finished and told to stop. Stop they said this book about peace. It must not. It is opposite to the image. It says the soft drink is an untruth, and that exploding moons is not the hopeful kind of sign we have pretended. Or claimed. But let the moons explode and the books be silent. Let the captains whirl in the sky, let the monkeys in the heavens move levers with hands and feet, and with their big toe explode cities, for a soft drink.

I know this is the wrong kind of image. I have rebelled against an image. This is not safe, is it? Well, alas, so I must reconcile myself to the unsafe, because the safe I can no longer stomach.

Let them beat on the box while the voice comes out in a stream of lighted numbers. I have resigned from all numbers.

August 18, 1963

Thanks for the letter and above all for the book [Van Doren's *Collected and New Poems, 1924–1963*]. THE book in every way: yours, ours, the year's, the world's and the time's. As it should be, a world in itself, and a century in itself, an era, an Eden, full of Bible, full of world, full of America, full of farms and people and animals. In every way the best book ever . . .

This fall I have *Emblems in a Season of Fury* coming out, of which you have seen most, I think, in bits and flakes. You will see it, but it is only small, and mad. Better I think than some of the others though.

Yes, I hear always from [Bob] Lax, marooned on purpose on the very best of islands. Why isn't every sane man doing the same? You and I, I suppose, have our islands in the woods. That is good enough. They don't have to be Greek. If Lax stays there, though, he will be wise.

Sly villains report there will not be a war right away and that it is time for the Russkys to befriend us and find out how to fight the crooked Chinee. This report is as worthy as the slyness of the reporters, and I remain, sly as sly can be, under the same rug as before. And when I look out I see portents, monsters, wens, two-headed infants, birds without wings, buildings all drunk from top to toe, urn, alarms, cinders and a general confused cloud of deceptions. Let us continue more sly than before and than the villains.

It is said that one of the monks must now go blind as a result of having looked too intently at the eclipse. Was the eclipse full in your place? Here it was only a bite out of the sun's side, like flaming zinc let into the bigger fireball. Yes, I was looking also at the eclipse but have not yet inquired if I must be blind, and don't much care. We will all eventually be eclipsed anyway . . .

Glad you was to Harvard, it does good for Harvard to get educated.

February 11, 1964

I have not been able to keep track of who owes who letters (as if there were scoresheets in these matters) but I think I owe you more than one. It is not a matter of debt but of having a moment to find joy in writing you. I have here a letter you wrote me in September and which found me in the hospital in Louisville, tied up and trussed with weights hanging from my head, all very silly and not comfortable, because the picture of my seventh vertebra seems to look something like the cover of *Emblems*. It is not a disk, just the vertebra injured. Bah. So I go out and fall in the snow. It is all right. I have got traction of my own in a little room up under the roof and they won't get me back in the hospital if I can help it. Actually it is not painful much now, but my typing is worse than it ever was . . .

Well, now, there is snow outside the window and it is Shrove Tuesday and for my Mardi Gras I have entertained the thought of caffe espresso with lemon rind and some rum in it. Not very satisfying an indulgence, in this abstract state. It would go nicely with the snow, I tell my angel, but my angel says nothing. The espresso remains a mere thought, but better than some other thoughts I could think, I imagine.

Have you read a book by a man called Walker Percy, called *The Movie Goer*? I don't read enough novels to judge, but I think this is a good one. You think at first he is making this Movie Goer a supreme dope of some sort for going to so many movies, but in the end it turns out that he is the only smart one, in a wild existentialist kind of way, and the best thing about the book is that in the end nobody says who is supposed to be right anyway. I think it is very important at this juncture that novels should not insist that somebody is right. Because when somebody is right, then someone else is wrong, and this gets us forgetting that we are all wrong, or, in some sense, right. The thing is to see that unless we know we are wrong we cannot be right, because the only thing we can successfully be right about is the fact that we are all wrong. The one incontrovertible fact of human life. When one starts from that one, however, the rest begins to make sense. Hence there is no justification for consoling religions. I mean the kind that think they can console by saying everything is all right. But I am not propounding the idea that everything is all wrong, as a source of religious consolation. It is just a fact, not consoling. Anyway, in *The Movie Goer*, besides a lot of intriguing New Orleans names, there is a Mardi Gras to which nobody goes. The author of the book has written well about Kierkegaard somewhere too.

Yes, you are right (change context from last paragraph) about going on saying that the Negroes are trying to tell us something and about the way so many people want to know how to agree. But the whole thing is like a dream, and when we all think we are finding out what to say or do next, everything gets away again and we are in a different building, a different town. In the enormous absence of certainty they turn away and put the works of Shakespeare through a computer.

Here is a message for some poets ["Message to Poets"]. It was read at a meeting of a whole lot of young poets from all over the place in all parts of Latin America. They came out of where they were and got to Mexico City and said there was a new solidarity of poets. This is good, not Communist or anything, just a lot of poets who want to say there is a new solidarity of poets, with no strings attached. I wrote a message saying there was a new solidarity of poets. I represented the poets that are in this part of Kentucky, Nelson County I believe. I don't know what other poets are in these woods but I have a new solidarity with quails against hunters. The quails live all around the hermitage, and I rush out in hunting season and tell the men get off this land it is posted. Between myself and hunters there is no solidarity whatever. They resent my attitude because it disturbs their preconceptions: they feel that they can hunt on Trappist land because Trappists can't tell them to get off. But I do. They look at me with wrath and shattered idealism. And some, if Catholic, assert that they have been given permission by the parish priest of some nearby town. Others make like they would enjoy nothing more than shooting a Papish priest.

[Bob] Lax has asked me to edit his big long book of poems and this I will do, when I get to it. Have you seen all his poems (one word a line, half a word a line) and have you any special favorites? I like them all very much but when it comes to editing them as a book I suddenly find it very hard.

Ted Andrews [Shaker expert Edward Deming Andrews] has written several times, usually mentioning you. He is doing a new book [*Religion in Wood*], as you know, and it sounds splendid. He asked me to write a preface and this will be a delight if I can measure up to it.

Deceived by my left hand I spell worse and worse and type incomprehensibly, so I had better stop . . .

August 4, 1964

Thanks for the word in the silence. I am sorry only of the occasion for it. I had as a matter of fact heard very indirectly of Ted Andrews' death, from a Benedictine down this way who is interested in Shakers because his monastery is in an old Shaker Village. Also, on the day you wrote the letter I was sending the Preface to Faith [Andrews], so everything is all right. At least I hope it is all right.

I enjoyed writing the preface and brought a lot of Blake into it. Let's hope that it serves its purpose. Ted Andrews is a loss: he had such a wonderful sense of all those things. I think his book will be great, though I have not actually seen the pictures, only the text. The list of pictures alone is exciting.

Here is heat. Much heat. The kind that makes everybody mad, and the kind that probably accounts for some of the craziness and violence of the South. In this land one sees things through a nasty mean haze in which the houses and trees are crooked and the people swim at you like spectres. And this is only Kentucky. What must it be in Mississippi? . . .

One of the novices came proudly in with a big yellow apple off a tree when I said all winter that the orchard was never going to bear fruit again. This at least bears fruit. I am glad to be wrong . . .

December 19, 1964

Yes, you bet we got winter. Your card woke me out of hibernation. Not really. But I have not been writing purposeful letters or any but daft business ones for a long time. Last night I was sleeping in the hermitage (where I sleep now, by the way). It was Zero and I had everything in the place piled on top of me, and felt like a bear. Thought of all the beasts and varmints hibernating in the woods all around. It is a pity to wake up every morning. But when I did, this morning and came down after my meditation, with everything cracking under foot and moonlight bright all over the place, a deer started up down in the hollow and bounded off. I caught sight of it momentarily in the moonlight, between cedars. There are quite a few around as the state has been stocking the woods. I am happy to have them, and to have them near. If I ever get any assurance that hunters will respect the signs I have put up all over the place, I will get a salt block for the deer and have it just across the fence for them.

Which reminds me that the *Narrative Poems* came, and I like best *The Mayfield Deer* always. Your two books together with the bright covers are very comforting, a presence and a reassurance. Someone at least has done something worth while: you. Thanks for this one too, and for the other. I am sending you my new one [*Seeds of Destruction*], it has peace talk in it and anger about race. The peace talk was nearly not published but eventually got done up better and was allowed. So there it is. And to plague you more in a season when you are deluged, here is an article ["Rain and the Rhinoceros"] I was asked for, and wrote in the hermitage. As one can easily tell.

It was a pity Ted Andrews died. I have been writing to Faith, and she has the preface. But seemingly no publisher has the sense to definitely take their book. How silly can they get? I suggested Doubleday, but naturally that is a big barracks of computers and the computers read the Shaker book, having been previously programmed only for baseball. Though I have a friend [Naomi Burton] at Doubleday and may go there from Farrar Straus, even though it is now also Giroux on the FS [Farrar Straus Giroux]. I don't know. I don't know. I am getting like [Bob] Lax now that I too have found my island. Meanwhile we send each other code messages, whom to elect, whom to defend, whom to trounce. He is for defending Lizzie Borden. I forget who I trounced in my last letter, but I have a program for rushing to the support of Baumgarten. In French.

Oh yes, and as you will see if you are patient with the article past page six, I have been reading Ionesco, and him I like. His latest play or one of his latest is beautiful in a way, like your imaginary worlds of angel transients, in fact a very lovely and haunting play about a man who suddenly discovers that he walks on air because that is man's nature anyway, and because he is happy. I don't suppose it was yet in NY or perhaps will be, since there too they are all programmed exclusively for baseball. And as a play it may even be a bad play, I don't know, but the ideas and imagination there are fine. To the novices I have been talking about poetry, no less, that old Donne again. On St. Lucy's day I read them the "Nocturnal," and it is a beautiful poem, but did his girl really die or was that just an idea he had? You would know. It makes no difference, because the real idea of the poem is about being the epitaph of everything that is nothing . . .

Once there was an invisible snake and it struck at an entire country and the country turned all in a wink to dust as if there had never been a country there at all, though the machines went on whirring for some time after. And the hairy ones danced and tromped in the machinery.

And history, if any, later declared: this was a really *unusual* snake. Who shall say, though, whether history is ever right, or ever even on the target?

Once there was a Scotchman met an Irishman met a Jew met a Scotchman and they said hello Pat and they said who the hell are you calling Pat? And they had a fight and in the end it turned out they was only one person fighting himself, wasn't that a funny thing to have happened. What is history going to have said about *that*?

September 29, 1965

How are you? I hope in good health now, though last I heard you were in a hospital. Reason for my long silence is that I now have all the time in the hermitage & see practically no one—everything is so totally peaceful that I have little or nothing to say, except when I drop a log on my foot or something serious like that . . .

Anyway, the main thing is how are you?

Here the sun is silent, there is mist in the valley, & a train whistles out there somewhere just like when the world first began.

February 24, 1966

. . . There is no need to tell you where I am. You have seen the hermitage and I am living in it—have been really for over a year, but only in the last six months have I been free of any job or obligation in the monastery, so I am here all the time. I just go down to the monastery once a day for Mass and a cooked meal. It is a serious, by no means idyllic sort of life—quite a lot of cold here in January and February, and one takes stock of, gets to grips with, a lot of things. What infinite nonsense is in the world and it turns out I am not exempt from much of it: I have to sweat it out of myself here. In a way the best thing about the life is chopping wood. And then burning it in a good lively fire, and making tea, and reading St. Thomas or the Desert Fathers or the Bible or more recently the tales about a mad Persian called Nasrudin, who seems to have been the subject of all the good jokes that ever got into anything later, from Don Quixote to the Marx Bros.

You have probably heard some of them, but here is one:

Nasrudin is about to fall in a pond, and a friend grabs him in time so that he does not fall in. Then his friend keeps reminding him, day after day, of the fact that he kept him from falling into the pond. Nasrudin finally loses patience, drags the friend down to the pond and then jumps in. "Now," he says, "will you finally leave me alone?"

Another: Nasrudin walks into a shop. The shopkeeper comes out and says: "Can I help you?" N. says "Have you ever seen me before?" "No," says the shopkeeper. "Then," says Nasrudin, "how can you help me: how do you know it's ME?"

One more. Nasrudin walks into a store and says: "Have you got leather? Have you thread? Have you some dye?" "Yes," says the shop-keeper, to all these questions. "Then," says Nasrudin, "why don't you make yourself a pair of shoes?"

These stories are so archetypal that you must have heard them in some form, but apparently Nasrudin is the original. The stories all have implications for Sufism and the mystical life. I want to get hold of some source material and do something with it (not a third book for another year however).

I have been having much company of great constellations around here on the clear nights, and right out in front of the house, when I get up at two-thirty, is scorpio raising his head out of Tennessee and it is quite impressive to see him climb up and unroll his body behind him. I am supposed to be able to see canopus, denied to the North, these nights, but there is always a bit too much haze in the early evening and by the time the haze is gone either canopus has set or I have.

All the publicity is a bit embarrassing. Ed Rice is doing a story in *Jubilee* ["Thomas Merton Today"] and then, I hope, it's all over. I have no ambition whatever to be known any more of in this society.

But I certainly do not regard news from you as an intrusion. Quite the contrary, I need more.

July 25, 1966

It is so long since I wrote to you and so much water has gone under the bridge that the bridge itself has vanished and all the water has turned to rain. But I wanted to send you this scurrilous poem ["Western Fellow Students Salute with Calypso Anthems the Movie Career of Robert Lax"] which I am sending to Lax who is, really and truly, in a movie. Ed Rice came back from Greece and said Lax was honestly acting in a movie and "making a lot of money." The last part is what I doubt. Lax himself mentioned it in a letter but I thought he was kidding. Anyway, I thought it merited this song.

As for me as per the end of my third stanza I am more in the old folks' home than in the movies. I must have told you of my mad operation, not so mad really to others but mad enough to the one who had to have it. Since then I have dug in more and more in the woods and am doing less and less. The woods certainly agree with me as nothing else does and I am no longer able to imagine another form of life. So now I think I am stabilized in Kentucky, finally. (As if there were any doubt.) But as I say I feel like old folks, what with creaking back, red hot bursitis, unpredictable knees, rubber ankles, but to all of this I thumb the nose. It means I can't cut much wood, so I will train rabbits to come and breathe on me or something. Incidentally there is a most beautiful fox that plays in the field around sunset when his colors are most attractive and his movements most worthy of praise. Such a dancing and leaping fox, and such a spirit of play. Lither than any cat. Actually there is a family of them (foxes) living barely a couple of hundred feet from the hermitage, but they stay out of my way, knowing man.

How are you and Dorothy? What is new? As if there were anything new under the sun: but it would be good to hear from you.

August 21, 1966

. . . Do you know Edwin Muir? You must have read some of his poems. I am sure you would like him very much—you have much in common. I am doing some reviews on him. But what I really wanted to say is that if you never read his *Autobiography* I think you would be delighted with it. I don't presume to recommend books usually to others, but I really think this would please you. But you probably know it well. Who knows perhaps you even recommended it to me twenty years ago. That is possible too, except I think the first edition was more recent.

Otherwise I am in the woods, and content with them. My troubles begin as soon as I am out of them and end when I am back in them.

March 12, 1968

Many thanks for the card of old big boots down in Mexico. I thought seriously of Tlaloc last night when the rain was pounding down on the roof of my place. Good rain. I have transplanted some beech and pine saplings and the rain will help them along.

Lately I have almost given up even trying to keep up with mail, so it is ages since I have written to you at all. I am content to let the mail situation be more or less hopeless and write when I get a chance or an urge.

What makes it more insane is that in my old age I decided to start a magazine (herewith) [*Monks Pond*]. I excuse and justify myself on the ground that I intend to quit after four issues. But it is also fun, in so far as one discovers good poets hiding around in the bushes. The ones in this magazine all seem to be living in the woods or trying to. So now that you have seen it, you know I am inviting, urging you to send something if you have something—prose or verse or just a shout of some sort. But I know you are pestered by everyone under the sun so . . . if you have something. I'd not want the pond to be without you.

Bob [Lax] is back and I hope he will get down here when spring is further along. And it's a long time since you have been seen down here yourself. By the way Bob and I are thinking of publishing our "letters". Neither of my two publishers has the courage to take them and I think they are both hoping the book [*A Catch of Anti-Letters*] will go, if at all, to a very small hidden publisher with no money and on the verge of despair. This does not suit Bob at all. He thinks the public needs our letters and he knows he needs the money. He may have written to you about it. I do have a small hidden (though not despairing yet) publisher that is interested. Finally, I think that old novel, from back when, you remember, the *Journal of My Escape from the Nazis*, is going to be published. I have gone through it again and find it holds up pretty well and suits our current frenzies without need of the slightest adaptation. In fact perhaps better now than ever.

All goes well here. I am busy, writing a lot, long poem or series of poems [*The Geography of Lograire*], articles: and on nice spring afternoons I run off into the woods and sit in the sun by an, of course, pond. An pond. Hm.

April 12, 1968

They can call this Friday Good: bright sun, blue hills, many birds, and the local mockingbird who as a celibate all winter chased every other damn bird out of the rose hedge has now got himself a wife and settled down and everything on wings is nesting in the same hedge with them. The Peaceable Kingdom: it is at least here.

I like the poem ["Merton's Wood"] and obviously want to use it like in the third issue [of *Monks Pond*]. May I? The only problem is one of local politics or whatever you'd call it. My name in the title would be pride like this notepaper etc. Pride pride pride all is pride. If the monks thought I was trying to own these woods (mockingbird in winter hedge) it would be bad. I thought I'd change the title (for purposes of this mag at any rate) to the official (proud of course) title of the hermitage: "Carmel Hermitage, Gethsemani" or even the full (prouder prouder) title "St. Mary of Carmel Hermitage." Get the subtle pride in "of" for instance. Pride is "of." Pride is in hyphens, asterisks, commas. Enough of that though, I would be happy to have you in the magazine before it stops. It must stop, because I am losing poems, not answering letters, putting everything backwards, sorting out the magazine all wrong, stapling it to my own thumb, etc.

[Bob] Lax is now in a camp of colleges called "Beagle" in S. Dakota. But later in the summer we are promising ourselves to gather here with cocolas.

Doubleday is being square and hedging about *Journal of My Escape* but if they finally reject it J. Laughlin says he wants it. My editor at D. likes it very much but I guess the business boys don't. As to the Letters (Lax and mine) we are still hunting around, but I think we will end by editing it with Santa Caluses I mean Clauses. (A Santa Callous:

> *O Santa Caloso*
> *Making famoso*
> *The leapyear letter of Lax.*)

I am working at guess who: Joyce and Blake again. Back in full circle to thirty years ago. Joyce all brand new! . . .

July 23, 1968

M. Pond (iii) is now in the press, which is to say it is being typed on stencils by a Jesuit scholastic [Philip Stark] who has volunteered to come here for the summer and do it. Your poem about the hermitage is in it, for we don't have antipoems only: we even print real poems. I really want it, it says just the right thing about the place—but not in such a way that anyone in the guesthouse would immediately know where it is. So I am grateful for it. And we have a pile of usuals, and an even greater pile of the unusuals, including a mad section of concrete funny sheets (I suppose you'd call it). This is being done first and I will send it separate, the rest will take a little time, our Jesuit being very careful. But after this there is only one more issue. And then . . .

And then, man, I fly to Asia. Really, that is the plan. All sorts of places I am supposed to go to if I don't faint from delight at the mere thought. Since I hop from Singapore to Darjeeling, and have a meeting there with various swamis gurus etc, I hope to sneak into Nepal. Then maybe a bit more of the top of India. Then Thailand (if not Burma, hard to get into, but may manage), then Indonesia (a monastery of ours there) then Japan, then home. Maybe. If they can get me home, I should say. This doesn't begin until October but at the moment I am itching with vaccinations and expectations and being photographed for the passprops and phonographed for the pesthouse and airlifted to the quarantine and divided up into computers. If I survive I may manage to get to a country where they don't even have roads. And where if you ride it's on an ox or not at all. Or a yak. Or an elephamp. All this because of a meeting of dull Abbots in Thailand, but who would not go to a meeting of Abbots for all those other secondary gains?

[Bob] Lax was here in June and brought me innumerable cans of tuna fish and several pints of whiskey, the latter being more practical than the former. We had great conversaziones and took a lot of pictures (mine not yet printed, will send some if any good).

Right now, as I say, I am taken up with getting shots and visas, and cleaning up my premises and finishing up all the absurd jobs I took on when I was a low creature of earth and not a prospective world traveler. I assure you I hope to make the best of it while it lasts! (Think of all the cablegrams saying "RETURN AT ONCE" being shot to Bali, Tibet, Kamchatka, Ceylon, the Maldives, the Endives, the Southern Chives, the Lesser Maundies, the Nether Freeways, the Outer Salvages.)

Darjeeling, India
November [1968]

I have been confronting this huge presence [Kanchenjunga] for about 10 days. Out of one month or more in India, most of it has been in the Himalayas. Calcutta, Delhi—& I'm off to Madras & Ceylon, then Indonesia & strange dances. This has been a marvelous trip—Lamas & all sorts . . . How are you? Monastery forwards mail to me. I will be gone another four months or so.

In a note on a Christmas card sent to Gethsemani (which Merton, of course, never saw), Van Doren said: "I rejoiced in your card from Darjeeling—unbelievable, of course—and in all the news you managed to pack in. Please now continue to have a wonderful journey through unimaginable places . . ." On December 11, Abbot Flavian Burns sent a telegram to Van Doren: "We regret to inform you of the death of Father Thomas Merton in Bangkok." Van Doren responded: "Terrible as it is, thank you for sending me tonight the news of Thomas Merton's death. He was one of the great persons of our time or of any time. I shall mourn for him as long as I live."

II.

To Family & Family Friends

*New Zealand is where my father came from and I have
lots of relatives there, it is a kind of homeland in a way.*
MERTON TO FATHER PLACID, O.C.S.O.
AUGUST 5, 1964

To Percyval Tudor-Hart

*On the day of his father's funeral, Merton wrote to Percyval Tudor-Hart, who
had been Owen Merton's art teacher, mentor, and close friend. Two years later
Merton wrote Tudor-Hart from the same London address about an exhibit of his
father's paintings.*

2, Mandeville Place, London
January 20, 1931

I must thank you and Mrs. Tudor-Hart for the kindness you showed
in coming to the funeral of my father this morning. I know from his own
words how good you had always been to him, and how you had practically
taught him all he ever knew about art. I cannot tell you how I appreciate
all you have done for him.

I naturally will feel his absence greatly, for he was always so awfully
good and kind to me, and we enjoyed life so much together in the South
of France. I cannot quite accustom myself to the knowledge that he and
I shall never visit our old haunts together anymore.

His unsold pictures, I suppose, are mine for the moment, but as of
course I know not how to deal with the situation I should be very glad
to leave it to the discretion of such people as Dr. [Thomas Izod] Bennett
and yourself, who would know how to tackle it.

December 28, 1933

I would like to thank you very much indeed for your card, letter, and generous present this Christmas, and assure you how deeply grateful I am for your kindness. It is generous of you to conceive an exhibition of my father's work and I look forward to the time when it will be possible to hold one. A number of his water-colours, which belong, I suppose, to my brother & me, are still in New York, and many are here at the Bennett's. I have no idea what has become of some of the oils painted at Canterbury during his last year, but Dr. Bennett, now in Paris, will probably know. There are also some unfinished screens about. But of course the best of his work can probably be easily found in various private collections, and there is a whole number of pictures, representing that very important period in his work—I mean the Collioure & Algerian water colours, which I should be glad to have an opportunity to see! I have only seen the two pictures in the Bennett's dining room, which are amazingly beautiful, & lead me to imagine what the rest must be like!

I wish either my brother [John Paul Merton] or myself had inherited even a small part of our father's genius. I have a great deal of his sensitivity, which unfortunately seeks expression in poetry (and that rarely!) while my brother leans away from all art & wants to be a scientist.

To Freida ["Nanny"] Hauck

After the death of Merton's mother in 1921, Elsie Hauck Holahan came to live with his grandparents to help take care of Tom and his brother. Elsie was the widow of Captain Patrick Holahan, who had died in the Easter Rebellion in Ireland in 1916, and had two children, Peter and Patricia, with whom Merton became friendly. She stayed on in the Jenkins' household as a "companion" to Merton's grandmother, "Mattie" Baldwin Jenkins. In 1938, after the death of both grandparents, she married Merton's uncle, Harold Brewster Jenkins (1889–1972), who had inherited the house. Merton also grew friendly, then and after his return to America in the 1930s, with Elsie's parents, Peter and Freida ["Nanny"] Hauck, growing especially fond of Nanny. Nanny Hauck (1874–1965) had grown up a Catholic in Kentucky and had bought a rosary at the Abbey of Gethsemani. Nanny and her daughter attended Merton's ordination in May 1949. Nanny, by report, "helped to raise" Tom and she often referred to him as her "grandchild." When Merton received the telegram informing him of her death in 1965, he was reported to have known it already, having sensed her death "in his solitude" that morning.

December 10, 1941

Well, here's some news for you: today I am entering the Trappists in Kentucky. From now on, I hope, as long as I live, I can belong entirely

& completely to God, refusing Him no sacrifice. It will be tough at first for anyone who's had it as easy as I have, but I know you'll pray for me, Nanny! I have a lot to make up for. I'll never forget you in my prayers.

January 12, 1959

It was nice to get your card. There were a lot of people I didn't hear from, but it was good to hear from you. So you are living in Great Neck now: back in the old house. It must seem like old times.

I am sorry I haven't written more. There is seldom anything new, and I don't have much time. I am still Master of the Novices and they keep me pretty busy. We have a nice novitiate, at the back of the monastery looking out over the woods, with a nice garden. It is quiet and peaceful. The novices are all good kids. We have a big husky Redemptorist priest from Brooklyn who has entered here, Fr. Geo. Bryan. I think he will do quite well. It is hard for them when they come from the active life and try to adjust to this kind of life, in the cloister. I don't write much these days. I have to keep a certain amount of time free for reading, meditation and prayer. This life wouldn't amount to much without that. After all, what is the use of doing a lot of work, if you don't keep your heart for God? That is what I try to do. That is the only way I can be of use to others. I certainly appreciate your prayers and I remember you too in my Mass. God is very good, and He knows how much we need Him. He will give you every blessing I am sure. I hope you will have a holy and happy new year. Give my love to all, to Walter and Ruth [Hauck] and the girls and all the family—I wrote to Elsie and Harold [Jenkins] the other day.

December 22, 1960

I got your nice card written by Mrs. McCaffrey. It was good to hear from you after so long. I am sorry I haven't written more often, it is just impossible to keep up with all the things that have to be done, and letters are something we are supposed to reduce to a minimum. I never manage to do so, and even then I never write as many as I should. But anyway you will know I am always thinking of you and praying for you.

This will come to you in a letter to Elsie [Jenkins], I presume you will be over at Douglaston some time during the Christmas holidays. I am sorry to hear that things are not going well in the household at Great Neck. The Lord knows what He intends to do for your soul, Nanny. Do not be discouraged. If you can bear this patiently you will do great good for yourself and for others. I know it must be awfully hard and lonely. But there is no other way to heaven than the way of hardship and loneliness. It was lonely for the Christ Child to be born in a stable. And He did not have many friends around Him when He was on the Cross. Bear with the misunderstandings that come your way. People are nervous and their nerves are sick, sometimes it is not their fault if they seem to be hard on us.

I am still in charge of the novices here. It is interesting work. Recently one made profession who was formerly a priest in the Redemptorists and his folks live at Brentwood. But we don't get many from around New York. Most of them are from the midwest or south, though they may come from anywhere. A lot from other Orders, who change over to get more of a life of prayer.

It is a long time since I last saw you. I hope you are keeping reasonably well. Trust in the Lord and be patient. Your reward will be greater than you think, just be faithful and trust. And keep praying for me, Nanny.

To Agnes Gertrude Stonehewer Merton ["Aunt Kit"]

"Kit" Merton (1889–1968), second of Owen Merton's four sisters, was the New Zealand relative whom Merton knew best in his later years. She had been a schoolteacher in New Zealand, in Australia, and, for a year, in England. She never married, making her home in Christchurch with her mother, Gertrude Hannah (Grierson) Merton (1855–1956), and her sister, Beatrice Katharine Merton ["Aunt Ka"] (1891–). She retired from the Christchurch Girls' High School in 1947. In November 1961 she surprised Merton by visiting him at Gethsemani. She died April 10, 1968, drowned when the interisland ferry Wahine *sank in Wellington Harbour.*

December 1, 1963

I am not sure I remember when I last wrote but I have an uneasy feeling, rooted perhaps in bad habit, that I have owed you a letter for a long time. Probably I wrote when I was in the hospital, and I think perhaps you replied to that, but I have been so busy that I am muddled. I was in the hospital with a bad back in September. There is some kind of injury in my spine, going back quite far, and it is something that cannot be completely fixed up, but it is all right and I can live with it if I take care. It can be painful if it acts up, but usually one can keep it behaving.

Of course the thing on everyone's mind is the terrible business about Kennedy, ten days ago. It still has an eerie effect about it, and seems quite uncanny. No one knows yet what was behind it, and the very aimlessness of it makes it seem more evil. I am inclined to think there was something more of a plot than people think, but what kind? Who can say? In any case it has really shaken and moved the whole country, and in many ways the effects have been good. Certainly it has established Kennedy as a hero for the country, and I am glad of that for his sake and for the sake of the good things he attempted to do. Of course the race question is still the great thing that hangs in the air and the south has by no means been converted by Kennedy's death. On the contrary, in some parts there has been expression of satisfaction, and even refusal to fly flags at half mast, etc. This is certainly not encouraging, is it?

Another strange thing: a person came here claiming to be a distant relative, a [daughter] of Father's cousin. That would be your cousin: do you have a cousin called Morrison, still apparently alive, in Winchester (Hants.)? The letter of this girl sounded plausible enough and I got permission to see her, but there was absolutely no evidence that she had anything to do with our family and she seemed completely American to begin with. So I don't believe a word she said. And she really had nothing very clear to say in any case except that her father was called Morrison and lived in Winchester and worked in a bank?? On the other hand maybe there were some relatives of ours in that part of the world. I wonder if you can tell me anything that makes any sense about it?

Things go along quietly here. I try to get as much time reading and working in the cottage as I can. The afternoons are quiet except that the woods are full of hunters and there seems to be no way of keeping them out. I chase them out when I get a chance but I can't spend all my time running after them, and trying to avoid getting shot into the bargain. I have a new little book of poems [*Emblems of a Season of Fury*] coming out and by now you must have got a copy of the magazine *Ramparts* [with his essay "The Black Revolution"].

Do not worry about the fact that you don't get deeply philosophical over religious things. It is better to be quite simple and have a simple faith in God and leave what you don't know to Him. I think I have a kind of obligation to say things as I say them, if I happen to be articulate on those points. But it is not a condition for being a Christian! Perhaps you are better off not having a lot of ideas about such things. In the end, we can only say that we believe and that we don't really know. Still, if I can do something to make faith intelligible, I will continue to try. That is my job, I suppose. Well, it is always good to hear from you. I hope you are getting along well in your summer there.

To Professor Jean Hering

In 1930 at Christmas Merton went for his holidays to Strasbourg. He says in The Seven Storey Mountain: *"I spent most of the holidays in Strasbourg, where Tom [Bennett] had arranged for me to go for the sake of the languages: German and French. I stayed in a big Protestant pension in the Rue Finkmatt, and was under the unofficial tutelage of a professor at the University, a friend of Tom's family and of the Protestant patriarch. Professor Hering was a kind and pleasant man with a red beard, and one of the few Protestants I have ever met who struck one as being at all holy." Merton resumed contact with Hering in 1963 (with a letter that has not survived). Hering responded: "It is good of you not to forget the grandfather of the C.E. [the pension where Merton had stayed], who also has happy memories of the visit to Strasbourg of 'Little Merton' (as Mr. and Mrs.*

Bennett called you) . . . I hope that all goes well with you and that the Trappists are no longer 'water-drinkers' . . . As for Mrs. Bennett, I have not heard from her in a long time, but her brother Gaspard Weiss teaches at the Monterey Institute for Foreign Studies (California)." Professor Hering's letters are translated from the French by William H. Shannon.

April 6, 1964

Thank you for your good letter and for all the information you included. Unfortunately we do not have your Review [*Revue d'Histoire et de Philosophie Religieuse*] in our library, but I have contacts with all the Protestant seminaries in this area and have been able to obtain several of your articles and also your commentary on First Corinthians. This has given me the opportunity of renewing our friendship on a deeper level. I was not able to appreciate your interest in [Edmund] Husserl when I visited Strasbourg in the days before the war. Now I am much closer to sharing your views and I see that phenomenologists do have some good things to say to the rest of us. I am thus a little less an "essentialist" than I was twenty years ago, when I studied theology from poorer texts than we now have.

I am very happy to hear from you and I can imagine your lodging along the banks of the Ill. I am sorry to hear about your "diplomas" and diets, but not too sorry since you are not a "water-drinker"—something which I am, though not all the time. When a priest from France comes to visit us, I have the opportunity of dining with him in a more civilized fashion.

I no longer travel, but if I did I would want to see Alsace and Strasbourg, the city of Tauler (another one I did not know about in those days there); and I would like to see you also. I hope that your two months in Menton were delightful, in the glorious sun.

For my part, I take my recreation in the woods, where I am something of a hermit, though still living in the monastery. I keep on writing books, too many, though I think I have done enough of this foolishness, and I am planning to stop, at least gradually. We shall see. But in the meantime I am sending you some things that might interest you. By the way, I very much enjoyed what you had to say about eschatology in the large collection of yours [*Phénoménologie et Philosophie Religieuse*] which I have read. We are living here in an atmosphere that is rather apocalyptic, although generally people do not think so: which is normal . . .

To Agnes Gertrude Stonehewer Merton ["Aunt Kit"]

May 27, 1964

Your letter came this morning and since I have been such an abominable correspondent I will make amends to some extent by answering it at once. And first of all, everything is all right with me. My back bothers me at times but I have learned more or less what to do to prevent it from getting bad, and my chief aim is to avoid an operation. I heard from someone who had one and he certainly does not sound too well off. And if I had it, I would still have to go on with what I am doing now, and perhaps a great deal more. So much for that.

I have been working along and have really got too involved in seeing people and doing various odd jobs like writing prefaces and articles that people ask for. I am even now writing some songs ["Eight Freedom Songs"] for a Negro singer [Robert Laurence Williams] to sing in a concert that is supposed to help the civil rights movement. I wanted to do something in this line but I am not sure if this particular project was wise, as I do not know if the "songs" are turning out to be very wonderful. Still, that is not so bad. I am hoping that I will be able to cut off some of the new contacts and not make others and so get back to a quieter life. Yet there is always the question of charity and dedication to the good of the Church etc. It is not always easy to figure out the answer. Forgive Americanisms please.

Lately I have been reading about hermits and recluses in early Celtic Christianity and in England. Wales was a very monastic and eremitical sort of a place. I think we all have some of this in our blood. What you write about religion is very understandable to me, except where you say I am "too mystical" and all that. Actually there is no question that social and communal religion tends always to be a bit formalistic. It is necessary and certainly one cannot just be completely individualistic about religion. But at the same time if one depends on the group, the parish, the monastery to do everything for one and provide all the light and inspiration and so on, then you can wait a long time before anything gets at all clear or acquires any meaning. On the other hand religion is not a matter of extraordinary spiritual experiences and that rot. The most important thing is a really simple and solid living faith. I think the thing that matters for most people is simply to live in an atmosphere of reasonable and alert faith and love for God and for other people, and in that way everything gets quite soon to have a simple religious meaning.

Did you ever read Thomas Traherne? He is one of the very best and most delightful Anglican writers. I think that part of the problem is that Anglicanism assumes a great deal and takes a lot for granted: first of all that you are able to do most of it on your own, so to speak. The Roman Church goes to the other extreme and tries to push you into everything and do it all for you, including all your thinking (and some of us don't take too kindly to this, as you may imagine). I think the best thing is to aim at the real English spirit of the *via media* with a good spirit of faith, some steady reading of the New Testament, some use of the psalms as personal prayer and some good reading and thinking about the realities of the Christian life. It is more than a matter of just getting along in a common sense pragmatic sort of way and hoping for the best, yet on the other hand we must not expect a lot of wonders and hope to see ourselves vastly improved in every way in an instant. The basic truth is our dependence on God in a realm where so terribly much is completely unknown and in a way unknowable. What we must do is to keep that fact in mind and turn frequently to God in simple faith without expecting to "see" Him or to understand too much about His ways, but anyway to follow the principles of the Gospel and to live for truth above all. And then to see that what matters is to do what is right whether or not it is satisfying at the moment, and to do this not out of moral obligation only but in a spirit of faith in Christ. This keeps alive in us the conviction that we are children of God for whom He has a deep and constant care, and we live in the belief that He loves us and will let nothing happen to us that is not for our good. As we go on we realize more and more how deeply this care of His for us extends into the minutest details of our lives so that He is in fact always with us and indeed in us, for we could not exist if He were not there. In this way we can develop a simple and wordless way of living in companionship with Him and this will help us to get a better realization of what our faith is all about.

To Professor Jean Hering

Hering wrote twice to Merton after he received the April 6 letter, in the second addressing him as: "Dear Father and dear 'Little Merton' (as Mr. Bennett used to say)."

July 28, 1964

I enjoyed very much your "Fable of Lafontaine" on peace, and I agree with your observation that the powers of the world of darkness are very much involved with us. All the more so because people do not believe in them. Yes, we have to deal with these powerful super-human powers and the worst of it is that the human powers so very easily accommodate themselves to them. This is what is so frightening. I had to write another article on the Race Question here ["Christianisme et question raciale aux Etats-Unis"], this time for a French magazine [*Frères du Monde*] (a very small one edited by a Franciscan committed to non-violence). I must tell you that I am a bit like that myself, aligned with the pacifists, the "non-violent," the radicals, the "outsiders." For I believe that that is where the priest must be, and not with the rich, the powerful, the generals, etc. Alas, it is on that other side that we all too often find ourselves, especially if we have become "monsignors." But it is still possible to keep this from happening . . .

I thought of you when I was reading a book on Rulman Merswin and the Friends of God, on Green Island, in Strasbourg. I am very fond of these movements, including Tauler, Eckhart and the rest.

To return to the whites and the blacks: yes, you are right we must make clear how they complement one another. For this to happen, the "whites" must accept the fact that they need the "Blacks." They desire only "to be good to them," but without entering into reciprocal relationships with them . . . The Black Muslims are already at odds with one another. Two huge divisions, but they will continue to be dangerous. We are going to have a situation of anarchy that will be very painful. Do pray for us!

To Beatrice Katharine Merton ["Aunt Ka"]

"Ka" Merton, born in 1891, with her twin Sybil Mary (Mrs. Tom Kempe Wreaks) the youngest of the six children of Alfred and Gertrude Merton, also, like her sister "Kit," never married. She was a nurse and lived in Christchurch, New Zealand. She visited with her brother, Owen, and his children at Douglaston, Long Island, and Cape Cod in 1922.

September 23, 1964

This summer I have been worse than usual in answering letters and I don't think I have written to New Zealand since about Easter. Or before that. I am sorry. Please tell Aunt Kit of this, and I will try to get a letter to her at least in time for Christmas!

Things have been frightfully busy for me. I have had a lot of trouble getting my new book into print (*Seeds of Destruction*, about the peace problem, war and so on). It is considered a bit outspoken by many, but I thought it was about time there was some speaking out from the Church. The situation has been confused and unhappy, and gets worse all the time. The Presidential election this year has not helped matters, since one candidate pushes the other into absurd positions. I have been especially disgusted with the awful mess in Viet Nam: but have not written about that. I really do not have access to all the information (much is not known here) and in any event I am not able to write about everything that goes wrong in the world. After this one big excursion into the more typical problems, I suppose I will be able to keep to the things that are more germane to a monastic life.

This summer has been difficult too because I got some kind of skin infection that took the skin off my hands and made it difficult to work at the typewriter. That has more or less cleared up now, as I finally got into Louisville to see a doctor about it. I am still not quite sure what caused it. At first I thought it was poison ivy, but tests on that showed up negative.

I was glad to hear you had seen one of father's pictures, just being sent off to a buyer. It sounds like one of the very early ones. I often think of the others. I wonder where they all are? It would be a very good thing to get them all together some time and have an exhibition. Have you any idea where his pictures of the last ten years or so of his life are to be found? I think they were all with Tudor-Hart, but I have lost track of TH.

Thanks for all the news and interesting details about NZ, also for the booklet. I am always very interested in these things. I regret that I never had a chance to come out there, I would love to see it.

I have been doing a bit of work on Celtic monastic history which is fascinating. Perhaps I shall be able to get a book done on this. It is a good field and has not been too well worked yet, though there are a few very good scholars in it.

Well, I must stop now and get a lot of other letters written, I am far behind with correspondence as I said at the beginning. This is my fiftieth year and I am beginning to feel a bit aged, though I am beginning to see too that fifty is not so much after all. When one thinks of Granny [Gertrude Hannah (Grierson) Merton (1855–1956)] at a hundred and two! But I can't keep up with everything as I used to . . . I do get a frightful lot of letters from all over the place, all sorts of fantastic suggestions and proposals or questions and pleas for help, for money, for God knows what. This morning a letter from a woman in Poland wondered if I could not send some pills for her nerves, especially Miltown!! Well, God bless all of you. Love to all the family.

To Nancy Hauck Boettcher

Nancy Hauck (Mrs. Kenneth Boettcher), daughter of Walter and Ruth Hauck and granddaughter of "Nanny" Hauck, wrote to Merton on September 13, 1964, about Nanny's plight: "I am half way through your book, A Thomas Merton Reader, *and find it fascinating. However, that is not why I am writing. My parents were over to my house today and told me your life history for they are Mr. & Mrs. Walter Hauck. It seems your mother was Harold Jenkins' sister and he married my father's sister Elsie . . . I am writing to tell you about Nanny (Mrs. Frieda Hauck) my grandmother. She is going to be ninety years old in November. Five years ago my Aunt Elsie and Uncle Harold literally threw her out of their house, so she is living with my folks. It has been a terrible strain on my mother (almost to the point of a nervous breakdown) and now that my father is retired there is no money to put her in a home. Aunt Elsie, Pete and Pat (her two children) have turned their back on her and my father. Nanny is so lonesome and has been praying to die . . . She still has most of her faculties and talks of you constantly as her grandchild . . . Please ask God to spare my parents and Nanny this hell on earth . . . I did want you to know what was going on in as much as Nanny can't write herself."*

September 24, 1964

I have no need of an introduction to you, as I remember you with affection as a nice little baby, back in the days when Walter and Ruth

[Hauck] were living in Little Neck Hills. So your letter was welcome. I can see however that you have grown some since then.

Thanks for telling me about Nanny. I am sorry she is having such a tough time. It is really sad how old people are not appreciated any more. Nanny made a whole lot of sacrifices to bring up her children and grand-children too, and one would think that there was a debt there that required some return, but of course it is always the in-laws that don't see the debt. On the other hand, we can't be too harsh on people today, they have grown up in a world where things are radically different from what they used to be . . .

Besides praying for Nanny, I would like to help. My idea may sound a little rough, but in the long run it is practical, if it is tactfully explored and done rightly. No one likes to send someone like that to the Little Sisters of the Poor, it looks heartless. But it is certainly more honest and more effective than just keeping her around and treating her like an awful burden. Actually, with the Little Sisters Nanny would have a good time, and also it would be easier for Walter and other members of the family to go and visit her under more cheerful and less strained conditions than would be had if there was a brooding in-law sitting at home and putting a wet blanket on the conversation. Why don't you quietly investigate this possibility? The Little Sisters, I repeat, are a very good bunch and the old people that are there are happy and have a good time together, within their limits. I know the place in Louisville, and it is inspiring. It is not just an "old folks' home", it is a real house of God and a real little Christian community. It would be wonderful for Nanny. If you like, I could write her and suggest it. I plan to write her anyway, but I will wait to hear from you before mentioning anything, and even then it would be best if I did not butt in with that right away . . .

To Nancy Hauck Boettcher

October 28, 1964

When I suggested the Little Sisters I realized that the suggestion would be a bit of a bombshell on Vista Road. Those things are hard to handle, because probably Walter [Hauck] thinks that it would mean a kind of disgrace for him, as if he were putting Nanny [Hauck] out on the street or something. It would not be that at all, but it is hard for people to see beyond the surface and the conventional social outlook on things. Well, I hope Nanny will make out all right and that everything will gradually calm down. You certainly did what you thought your conscience required and I think you were right. Don't let them upset you.

To Canon Delteil

Canon Delteil of Saint-Antonin, France, wrote to Merton, enclosing two letters of his father, Owen Merton, as well as some pictures. The letters were addressed to "Monsieur Picques."

December 5, 1964

May the Lord be with you. Thanks for your kindness in forwarding to me the two letters of my father and his pictures. The letters were written in his last sickness and the second was dictated when he was very ill in Scotland, before going to the hospital for the last time. I am grateful for them. And I would certainly very much like to have a set of cards of Saint Antonin. I see a photo of the town once in a while and it has not changed much. I wish I could see it again, but that is out of the question.

Yes, I continue to write much. Perhaps too much. But next year I will be probably writing somewhat less, and will return to a more contemplative life, though I still expect to be Master of Novices for a while. Later perhaps I can retire altogether into silence.

It is always good to hear from you and my old friends in Saint Antonin. How long ago those days seem. It was another world.

To Freida ["Nanny"] Hauck

December 28, 1964

Well, how have you been? I bet you are thinking it took an awful long time for me to get around to writing. But I am just avalanched with correspondence and can't keep up. But I think of you often and keep you in my prayers. I know that as one grows older life tends to get a little lonely sometimes, but we have to look at that in the right way: it can bring us closer to God who is our best friend. So trust in the Sacred Heart and stay with Him and the Blessed Mother. You will find they will give you much comfort and strength and prepare you to see them face to face. Pray for me, and I remember you also in my prayers.

Give my love to Walter and Ruth [Hauck] and to Elsie and Harold [Jenkins] and everyone. It is a long time since I was on L.I. I bet things must have changed.

To O. Paul Gabites

Paul Gabites, Consul General at the New Zealand Consulate in New York, wrote to Merton on January 28, 1965: "Some time ago, the National Art Gallery in Wellington began publication of a series of pamphlets illustrating their collection.

Among the latest of these to arrive in New York is one illustrating 'The Old Curiosity Shop' [the painting] by Owen Merton. I thought you might like to see a copy of the pamphlet." This pamphlet is on file in the Thomas Merton Studies Center.

March 4, 1965

The book has arrived and I find it very attractive. In fact it is something I am very glad to have. I have tried for a long time to persuade my New Zealand aunts to send me something of the sort, but without success. So I am grateful for your kindness. I will be happy to read the New Zealand poets.

Of course I have a great fondness for New Zealand, though I have never been there. There is not much chance of my going now, though our Order has a monastery in Hawkes' Bay. I have relatives in Christchurch and thereabouts, and have always had a desire to get into the forests of the South Island, where my Father used to camp out a lot . . .

To Agnes Gertrude Stonehewer Merton ["Aunt Kit"]

April 20, 1965

. . . I was certain I had answered your last letter. I wonder if something happened to it. I never know what becomes of mail. Things are always getting lost. From your letter it seems I never sent you the book [*Seeds of Destruction*]. I will see that one goes out to you today or tomorrow. It has not had a very good press in this country, probably because I am not lined up with any recognizable political group, and do not take a line that is familiar in one way or another. And I suppose that most people don't quite know what to make of it. However there has been an increasingly religious response on the civil rights issue. But the mess is so great and so confused that I do not expect anything really decisive to be settled for a long time. I am becoming more and more convinced that this country is in a bad way, though fortunately there are a great number of good and honest people around who speak up when they realize what is going on. But the press lies more and more, and important news is being suppressed or slanted so that it is difficult even for the most sincere people to make really good judgments. Hence it is very likely that through the folly of people in Washington and men with money and the so-called war hawks, this country may finally end up by starting a third world war in Asia. I know there are actually people who consider this reasonable, in order to blot out Communism. The root of the trouble is an absurd messianic notion that many Americans have that this country has a mission to protect the whole world from Communism. This unfortunately sounds very much like Hitler's big idea, though it is not quite the same.

My health has been all right except that I got a bad flu virus a couple of weeks ago and was in bed for a bit with a very upset stomach . . . The best news I have is that I have been sleeping in the hermitage and more or less living there a great deal of the time. I sleep very well here. In the monastery I was having a hard time sleeping, and in fact that had been a problem for years. But as soon as I got out here the problem vanished and I sleep very well. It is quiet and remote as you know. There are a lot of deer around, too. Everything is fine, except that they have been spraying the alfalfa fields from an aeroplane and the stuff they use is very potent. It may kill some of the birds and may even poison a deer if the creature eats some of it. In the end the insects suffer least, because they develop a resistant strain and the birds that prey on them die off. This is another of our follies.

I am sorry to hear that you are having trouble with the apartment, but I hope that soon everything will be as you desire it. Landlords are not always very accommodating. The mystery play sounds good. I am going to talk to the novices a bit about Greek drama, as it is important for them to know about this and they lack a lot of necessary background. Recently I got a nice letter out of the blue from the New Zealand Consul in NY. He spoke of some picture of father's that had been exhibited in Christchurch or somewhere, and sent me a nice book about NZ which makes me regret once again that I have never been able to get there and see it. However, as long as I have this peaceful and quiet place in the woods, I can get along without such things as travel.

Really, I must admit that mail is a bit of a problem. I imagine that I am keeping up with it but really I am getting more and more unable to do so. However, I will certainly try not to let you go too long next time without a letter . . . I will send the book and some other things. Best wishes and blessings always, and my love to you and Aunt Ka.

To Nancy Hauck Boettcher

Nancy Boettcher wrote to Merton to tell him that "Nanny" Hauck was seriously ill.

May 27, 1965

Thanks for telling me about Nanny. I did not know about her, but in the middle of Mass this morning I suddenly started thinking of her & praying for her & now I will continue. Best love to all the family.

To Agnes Gertrude Stonehewer Merton ["Aunt Kit"]

Aunt Kit had asked Merton for his sleeve measurements without telling her nephew why she wanted them.

June 9, 1965

Before I forget, here is the sleeve measurement: on the inside, from armpit to cuff, it is nineteen inches. Is that right? I mean does that sound like the right sort of number, or did you want some other measurement? I am surprised that the book [*Seeds of Destruction*] has not reached you yet, and I am having another sent in case something went wrong. Do please take good care of yourself. I am sorry to hear that you are unwell, but it is certainly a good thing that Aunt Ka is there near you. Do not be afraid to rest a bit.

The winter in the hermitage was not bad. It got quite cold but with plenty of blankets and a fire I rather enjoyed it. The only real problem is that there are no "modern conveniences" and if my stomach goes on a rampage it is rather inconvenient to rush out into the woods in the snow to the outhouse in the middle of the night. I must try to negotiate this momentous problem by next winter. Apart from that everything is fine. I have electricity now, or did I tell you this? I can cook on an electric stove, and will probably take more meals up there as time goes on and as I learn what to eat. I find that tinned stuff is mostly not too good for me, but I can get along well with rice, oatmeal, eggs and so on. With fruit, tea and the rest I do quite well. Someone gave me some very good tea, Twining's, a couple of special blends, much superior to the tea bag stuff that is floating around the monastery.

Of course I have been busy with various things. I will put a few of the recent mimeographs into an envelope, they might be of some interest. I very much like the Chinese philosopher Chuang Tzu and have been doing some renderings which cannot be called translations since obviously I don't know Chinese, but they are based on several different translations: and I observe by comparing the translations that much of it seems to be guesswork. So I just add a few guesses of my own, and my Chinese friend and advisor [John C. H. Wu] in this matter says my guesses are about as good as anyone's so far. I hope to make a regular book out of this soon, and I have a book on Gandhi [*Gandhi on Non-Violence*] coming out also.

It is always good to hear news from you. Did I tell you the NZ Consul General in New York wrote some very friendly letters and sent a book? I am happy about the flat. Take care of yourself, and now that you have winter, keep warm and dry.

To Nancy Hauck Boettcher

Nancy Boettcher sent Merton a telegram to inform him that "Nanny" Hauck had died.

June 16, 1965

Thanks very much for sending the telegram to let me know of Nanny's death. It was very thoughtful of you and of course I have been praying for her and also on Monday I offered Mass for her. May she rest in peace. She was certainly a good, honest and devoted soul, who led a long life of faith and gave herself for others. I was always very fond of her, and I am sure she will be well rewarded by God. I am glad everything worked out all right in the end. Please convey the expression of my sorrow and sympathy to Walter and Ruth [Hauck]. I am so snowed under with correspondence that I can't write to all I should write to, but I hope to get a note to Elsie [Jenkins].

The Mass I offered for Nanny Monday was a concelebrated Mass, the first Mass of one of our young priests. It was quite an occasion. But we have been having frequent concelebrations here all year. I like it for big occasions, but do not get into it on any and every feast. Anyway, if Nanny needed it, I hope she benefited by this Mass. I am sure she will pray for all of us. It is good to reflect that we may all be old some day and that being old is not easy in an age when youth gets all the appreciation.

To Elsie Hauck Holahan Jenkins

Elsie Jenkins was "Nanny" Hauck's daughter and sometime companion to Merton's grandmother, "Mattie" Jenkins. Relations between Merton and his uncle, who married Elsie, were strained before he entered Gethsemani and The Seven Storey Mountain *did little to improve the situation. Elsie is reported to have been upset by the comments on Zion Church and other Douglaston matters. As Merton himself points out in this letter, he had had little communication with his uncle and aunt in twenty-four years (Elsie had accompanied her mother to Merton's ordination in 1949).*

June 16, 1965

Nancy [Boettcher] sent me a wire about Nanny [Hauck], and I offered Mass for her Monday morning besides praying for her all along. Well, her troubles are over and she has gone to her reward. I am sure you will all miss her very much. I will never forget the old days when we used to go over to Vista Road and spend the evenings. I did not give much thought to it then, but actually I think I enjoyed those visits almost as much as anything we did at that time. And the days we went to Jones Beach together. More than thirty years have passed since then. Well, Nanny was a really good soul. She must have been pretty old, these last few years, and I understand things were not always too easy. One cannot be terribly sorry that she has gone, especially as she died peacefully. Her time came and I am sure she is not sorry herself now. I will of course keep praying for her if she needs it.

Of course a death in the family makes us all thoughtful. We will all sooner or later go ourselves. For you, Elsie, there is still that canonical problem, but as far as I am concerned I think the important thing is for you to be as simple and trusting as you can be in your conscience, directly with God. As time goes on, we are beginning to see that all these marriage problems [a reference to some irregularity in Elsie Jenkins's marriages] are not necessarily the final word on how one stands with God. The Church bureaucracy has made things much too complex. I hope that soon things will be ironed out so that such difficulties will arise more seldom. But in any case, there is a question of conscience for you, but I think it is one which you can take up in all simplicity before God and trust in Him. Try to do what is right, as best you can, and everything will work out ok, even though from the human and institutional viewpoint everything may not be quite perfect. If we all had to do things just in the way that suits the Roman Curia, I think we would find life a lot more complicated than it should be, or that Our Lord intended it to be. Of course if you do get a chance to fix things officially with the Church, take it.

I am fifty this year and that makes me feel a bit "old" in my own way. I remember when Pop [Merton's grandfather, Samuel Adams Jenkins (1862–1936)] was fifty and that seemed to be just about as old as anyone could get, when I was a child. I find that I still feel pretty young. I have had some back trouble and some stomach trouble. Had a lot of difficulty this spring with intestinal flu that I couldn't get rid of, but now I have been taking a more effective medicine and things seem to be improving. I am still with the novices but I expect to be relieved of the job at the end of this year and go into a more solitary kind of life. I will probably still write a bit. Did the publisher send you the new book I had out this year, *Seeds of Destruction*? I had trouble getting it past the censors, and it was not too well reviewed. I suppose the perspective one gets from down here may seem a bit distorted, and perhaps it is. Still, I thought I ought to say what I had on my mind. I have been very much opposed to the war in Vietnam. I think Johnson and Co. are probably sincere and well meaning, and think they have a duty to do what they are doing, but it seems to me that in fact they are consolidating Asian communism and alienating people from our own objectives. In the long run I think the war there will do more harm than good and of course there is danger that it may explode into something really serious. Let's hope not.

I think often of you and Harold and the family. I haven't heard from you in a long time. And I haven't been much good at writing letters myself . . . I have never tried to dictate letters, and think it would be foolish in a monastery (except of course the Abbot has to do that). As to monastery news, there is not much except that we are planning a foundation in Norway. I will almost certainly not be involved in it . . .

To Agnes Gertrude Stonehewer Merton [*"Aunt Kit"*]

Merton learned why his aunt had wanted his sleeve measurements when a belated Christmas package arrived with a sweater she had knitted for him, the second such sweater, obviously.

January 30, 1966

The new sweater arrived yesterday, which happened to be the coldest day of this winter so far, and I have it on now. It is fine, a bit more roomy than the other, though the other has stretched and is comfortable too. If it gets much colder I shall wear them both, though really there is no need: last night it was about five below zero on my porch thermometer, but that is sheltered. Probably the real temperature was ten or twelve below, perhaps more. It got down to freezing in parts of the house, but I was really very snug in bed I assure you. I do not mind a little cold, in fact I much prefer it to the overheated rooms of the monastery. I am in desperation when I get into that hot place—everything is about seventy there, or more. I cannot help sweating, and then when I go outside it is much more unpleasant. However everything is going very well.

There has been deep snow for about a week now, and this morning I went out in it about sunrise, found some fox tracks and saw where the fox had found a half frozen woodpecker sitting in the snow and ate it. In nature it does not do to sit down on the job. The deer tracks have been around the house too, and I can see where I have missed some pretty sights where they have jumped over the fence right in front of my window: unfortunately in the dark.

I am having someone send you a bit that was in the paper about your monkish nephew [James Morrissey, "Talks with and about Thomas Merton"]. Picture and everything, quite a long piece. I was at least glad to use it as an opportunity to say what I thought about peace. It does not seem that we can really have peace in Viet Nam. I suppose Johnson was sincere in trying to do something to that effect, but the Pentagon does not want peace and neither does Red China. Neither does Saigon. Only the poor people of Viet Nam want it, and their desires are of no account whatever. They are being "defended" by benefactors, and their job is to be killed or burned or bombed out of their homes. What a stupid world we live in. So in a sense the article represents a kind of goodbye and a good riddance to it, the world we live in. A sort of protest in its own way against the insanity of it all. I hope now I can settle down to the business of just being a real hermit, writing less, and less involved in complex affairs. Identified by silence with the people who have no say about anything and who are used by the people who have so much to say and are so sure they know all the answers.

Aunt Ka sent a nice picture of the flats. I sent some books a few days ago I think to her. I will probably alternate in sending one book to her and another to you rather than sending one to each. I forget if I sent the book on Gandhi to either of you. Will you let me know if there is at least one copy there? I sent her *Chuang Tzu,* which I think you will both like.

All the best of love. Tomorrow I can say I am fifty-one. God bless you always, and thanks again for the sweater, both you and Aunt Ka.

To Agnes Gertrude Stonehewer Merton ["Aunt Kit"]

June 1, 1966

. . . My main news (I thought I might have told you, but evidently did not) is that I had a rather complex operation on my back. That was in March. Something went wrong due to an ancient rugger injury, a broken disc had to be removed and replaced by a bone graft taken from my hip. I was rather knocked out by the operation at first, as you can imagine, and it was slow at first. But not nearly so slow as these things used to be. I got out of the hospital in a couple of weeks and convalesced slowly around the monastery for a bit. It was not long before I could get to the hermitage in the daytime, but I have been back here at night for only a couple of weeks. There is no question that it makes a difference sleeping up here. Coming up in the daytime is not enough. One has to be here all the time (except of course that I still go down for my Mass, dinner and now supper—I have a water problem and cannot carry water up here myself). They have been promising me a well but month after month goes by and nothing happens about it. This year another monk [Flavian Burns] is going to be a hermit and he was going to settle at the opposite end of my hill, but the abbot made him go elsewhere fearing no doubt that I would be a baleful influence. Or that we would fraternize or something. Pass on news and other such activities.

The winter was not bad at all, but I used up the last of my disc chopping wood. I got a good supply chopped and then came to the end of my capacity, and went to the hospital: so now I have extra wood left over for next fall but I ought to be able to chop again by October. At the moment typing is no longer painful on the back, but I have a bad elbow which sometimes acts up. My bones seem to indicate that I am growing older.

Perhaps Aunt Gwyn [Gwynned Fanny (Merton) Trier, Owen Merton's oldest sister] has by now had a visit from a neighbor of hers in East Horsley who has a brother here. He [Louis Wulff] is editor of the *London Evening News* and called her some time ago. I met him and spoke with him and suggested that he ring her up. He did not know her. She would probably be interested to hear about the place first hand.

You probably do not know that our church is being renovated. It is all torn out inside and the old steeple is coming down, as it was not safe. It will not be replaced, as far as I know, but I haven't been much informed about what they intend to do. The interior will be simpler and more modern. Less Gothic that is, and with fewer frills. More Protestant, some say. I don't mind too much either way.

I am still busy with articles and so on. Will send you a new batch— but rather I will see that your address on the list is corrected. I have to get a book [*Mystics and Zen Masters*] shaped up for publication this summer: that is, I have to prepare the ms. material for publication next year. I have one coming out this fall which is rather a general sort of shotgun approach to everything all over the lot in the form of notes and observations, called *Conjectures of a Guilty Bystander*. This ought to be palatable for the "general reader" or at least almost any reader ought to find a bit here and there that he would like. I hope so anyway. It won't be ready until November. Another paperback [*Raids on the Unspeakable*] will be out before then, but it is more obscure and arty I am afraid.

I have been writing quite a bit of poetry lately. It has been a nice spring. Glorious May weather, and now June is opening unusually cool: it was nearly down to 40 farenheit on my porch this morning. A bit chilly at night I can tell you, for you go to bed when it is still warm and while you sleep the thermometer can drop ten or twenty degrees . . .

I am not working with ecumenical groups at the moment. Since I came up to the hermitage Fr. Abbot feels I ought not to do any kind of active work with people, and I am not terribly anxious to unless it should turn out to be necessary . . . If I were in New Zealand on the other hand I would think it quite important, as I imagine there has not been very much done in this line yet. I have lots of Anglican contacts, convents in England, a good friend at Pusey House, Oxford [A. M. Allchin], some people in Boston (Cowley Fathers) and so on. All High Churchy as you might well imagine. But I am a pretty liberal bloke myself, if not radical. Actually I feel very much at home with the C. of E. except when people are awfully stuffy and insular about it. I have never been and will never be aggressively Roman, by any means. It would not be possible for a Merton to go too far with a really "popish" outlook. We are all too hard-headed and independent.

I think I told you our Irish abbot [Dom Joseph Murphy] of the New Zealand monastery [Southern Star Abbey] was here and threatened to call on you some day. Very Irish, a bit quizzical, simple and basically a good chap. *Life* magazine put out a book about Australia and NZ and I enjoyed looking at the pictures of Christchurch etc. It seems to be by far the most English place in the lot.

The hermitage is a joy to be in, now that we have lovely weather. But I like all the seasons. The only one that is slightly annoying is the autumn when you cannot keep the hunters away and they blast in all directions . . . They use high-powered rifles to get the deer and one of those could really take your head off in short order. I have deer all around the place here, though I haven't seen much of them in the warm weather . . .

To Nancy Hauck Boettcher

Nancy Boettcher wrote to Merton to tell him that her mother, Ruth Hauck, had had an accident. She also said that her brother, Frank Hauck, was thinking of visiting Merton at Gethsemani.

July 22, 1966

. . . Sorry to hear of Ruth's accident. I hope she will get well quickly, and please tell her I remember her in my prayers, as I do all the family. If Frank [Hauck] thinks of coming down, he should be sure to let me know so I can get permission to see him. I might not be able to as I have a lot of visits from ecumenical people and use up my ration that way: our visits are sort of limited. But I would be glad to see Frank if I could.

My back is as good as one can expect. I am told now by the doctors that there are other disks that may give trouble, and I can feel it. It is just that my whole back is now in rather poor shape due to injuries long ago when I used to play rugby. I don't mind much, when one gets to be my age one expects this sort of thing. But I will miss chopping wood for my fireplace in the winter. Sorry to hear your father-in-law had to have the operation *over*. I don't like the sound of that at all!!

Well, Nancy, I am always glad to hear from you and get the family news. Take care of yourself. How is the baby coming along? Send me some pictures of all of you some time.

To Iris Weiss Bennett

Iris Bennett, widow of Merton's English guardian, Dr. Thomas Izod Bennett (1887–1946), wrote to Merton on August 14, 1966, while visiting relatives in Monterey, California. Relations between Merton and the Bennetts had not been good since the 1930s and Merton apparently never acknowledged Bennett's death by writing to his widow. The publication of The Seven Storey Mountain *(Elected Silence in England), with its somewhat unflattering descriptions of the Bennetts, had obviously done little to soothe Iris. Both mention a letter of Merton's written in 1957, but this letter has not been located, nor has the one Iris mentions he wrote to Bennett in 1945, in which he told him of being in the monastery and of the death of his brother, John Paul. Iris Bennett wrote, in part: "These last few days, I read letters from your Parents—written at the time you were born, & later—(some, on our engagement!—) And found a few surviving photographs. A marvelous one of your Father—You & John Paul as Babes, etc. Also the letter you wrote to Tom, in the autumn of 1945, when you told him of your decision; and spoke of John Paul's death. That letter was a great shock and sorrow, to Tom. Though I shared his sadness, I felt that, if you found peace in a monastic life, one could only hope all would be for your ultimate happiness. Tom died some months later. And, as I never heard from you, I assumed you, perhaps, did not know. When you published* Elected Silence, *so many people were shocked, in various countries, at reading your description of Tom, & I—that I was urged to take action . . . Greatly surprised, and moved, to hear from you, after so many years (4 December 1957)—my first impulse was to cable—when I realized it was improbable you would get my message. Indeed any attempt at understanding . . . Today I read an extract from* Conjectures of a Guilty Bystander *where you say, of your own novices: 'There is in many of them a peculiar quality of truth that older people have rinsed out of themselves in hours of secure right-thinking and non-commitment.' I wonder if you will understand my reaction to this sentence of yours?"*

August 24, 1966

Your letter came to me as a complete surprise, and one that was in its own way *bouleversant* [upsetting]. I had given up all hope of ever hearing from you, and I never imagined that you would be in this country, though now I do recollect that in a letter of a couple of years ago Prof. [Jean] Hering spoke of your relatives in California. (How is he now? Have you recent news of him?)

At any rate, let me warmly thank you for the kindness of your letter. It reassures me to some extent at least. Simply to hear a few friendly words from you means a great deal to me I assure you. As in my letter of 1957 I went into the whole question of my regrets for the past, I will not dig that up again unless there is something that specifically demands further explanation, in your opinion. The news of Tom [Bennett]'s death reached me only after a very long delay and in a roundabout way via New Zealand. By that time I had no idea where to reach you.

The sentence you referred to in *Life* was aimed at *my* generation, Iris. Being fifty-one I think I am entitled to consider myself "older". I was not referring to my own elders.

I will not speak much of my life in the monastery. I am thankful God brought me here. There is no perfectly ideal life anywhere on earth and I have not found this always easy or universally rewarding. However, I am convinced that it is my own vocation and that is what matters. For the last year, having given up my job in the community, I am living alone in the forest in greater solitude. This is very good indeed and I am happy in this new arrangement, though it has some limitations too. I have had an operation on my back recently and it makes it hard for me to do the necessary manual labor.

Let me once again thank you for your letter which brings back other times and places and recalls the immense debt I owed to Tom and which, all appearances to the contrary, I have never forgotten. And the debt I owe you too. I assure you that what I wrote in the book was not intended to injure anyone, and in fact when I wrote it I thought that if Tom had seen it he would have laughed at it . . .

To Gwynned Fanny (Merton) Trier ["Aunt Gwyn"]

Gwyn Merton (b. 1885), oldest of Owen Merton's sisters, had married Erwin Julian Trier in 1915 and lived in England, at Fairlawn, West Horsley, when she wrote to Merton in the 1960s. She had two sons, Merton Trier and Richard Trier.

September 8, 1966

Thanks for your letter: I was glad to hear from you and glad to get the news that the [Louis] Wulffs had been in contact with you. He is editor of the *Evening News*, and I had a good chat with him when he was here, an interesting person. His brother [Fr. Augustine Wulff] is one of our monks—came here from Argentina.

Yes, it is true I had an operation on my back in the spring. It was quite successful and I have no complaints about that. The trouble is that more of my vertebrae are also a bit beaten up and I am afraid I may have to have other operations, and I certainly don't want any more. It is rather rough going, but one recovers quickly. Still, I hate to have them getting into my central nervous system. It knocks you out for a bit and is unpleasant. I still feel numb in one of my legs as a result. But still, one has to put up with this sort of thing. I think the source of the trouble goes back to my rugby days at school. And I am not worried about it: I have reached the age at which one has to be patched up rather frequently. It cramps my style a bit as I cannot do the wood chopping and other things that I need to do out here in the woods.

Otherwise I am very well settled. Aunt Kit must have told you about my cottage and all that. It is very good indeed, isolated and quiet, and I am here all the time now, except that to save cooking and fuss I go down to the monastery for main meals. It is ten minutes walk, and by the time I go down and come back I have spent less time than I would have had to spend if I had to cook and wash up for myself. If it is bad weather then I can always make myself a sandwich here. I am still writing a bit, but probably less than before—though perhaps more varied.

I often think of the old days, and Fairlawn and all the other places where we spent holidays, particularly Rye. I remember having such wonderful walks in the country there. I suppose Horsley is getting terribly built up now. Aunt Kit told me that a cousin from New Zealand (niece for you) is in England and may stop here on the way home: she should be sure to write to me well in advance so that I can make arrangements to see her. If one just shows up at the gate, there is no chance of seeing me. I am told someone was there recently; I hope it was not she.

Are you planning a trip to New Zealand one of these days? Be sure to come through America going or coming so that you can come here: how long is it since I have seen you? It is well over thirty years. It was over forty since I had seen Aunt Kit, but it was a memorable visit. I am glad to hear news of Merton and Dick and their families . . .

To Agnes Gertrude Stonehewer Merton ["Aunt Kit"]

Merton's "Aunt Gwyn" Trier had sent him two letters written by his father, Owen Merton, to Esmond Atkinson. This prompted a concern to locate, and possibly to collect, his father's surviving paintings.

December 12, 1966

Here is a picture of me with the sweater you knitted. I would have sent it long ago but I only just got a print of it. It was taken last winter. I hope it will reach you by Christmas . . . I have been a bit busy. Articles, proofs of another book, and people have been after me to write prefaces. This is always a nuisance and I will probably have to stop consenting to such requests. I already do to some extent. Another problem about being an author is that people who think they ought to be writers plague you with their manuscripts, usually not very good. In fact it is my impression that those who are really going to be writers do not bother other people and do their own dirty work for themselves. In any case I have to assure many people that I cannot undertake to be their literary agent.

Winter started early this year with snow right at the beginning of November. Lately it has been cold and rainy. Because of my back I have not been able to chop much wood but they put in a gas heater and there is a gas tank on wheels that can be taken away and refilled. This works very well and I have not been cold at all. I am getting good use out of the sweater.

Aunt Gwyn wrote recently and sent two letters of Father's, dating back to 1916 and 1917. They were very interesting. Once again that brings back to mind the question of his paintings. At a nearby college [Bellarmine College] here they are collecting my manuscripts and so on, and I am sure they would also want any of the paintings that have no special place of their own. Instead of someone keeping them in storage, this might be a good idea. I remember speaking to you about it, and yet we do not seem to have decided anything. Have you any idea where I might find those that were not sold and were simply left in the care of Tudor-Hart or someone like that? Do you have any better idea what might be done?

. . . This December I have been at the monastery for twenty-five years. They went by fast. I hope you are all well, and this will bring you my very best Christmas wishes and all my love. Take care of yourselves. This may cross with cards from you, and if you did not yet get my new book (*Conjectures of a Guilty Bystander*) please let me know . . .

To Gwynned Fanny (Merton) Trier ["Aunt Gwyn"]

Merton's aunt wrote to him on November 3, 1966: "The enclosed two letters were written by your father to an artist friend in New Zealand—were sent on to me recently by his wife, a very close friend of mine. She thought you might like to see them, as they give a clear picture of your father at that time. I have so appreciated reading them & re-living the past—& feel you may like to, too— We do not want them back. Your father O.M. as he was called & Esmond Atkinson were close friends with so many ties of friendship, it was sad they never met again— I liked the reference to 'little Tom.' "

December 20, 1966

Thanks so much for sending along the two ancient letters of Father. They are splendid, especially one of them which I have copied in part and have sent to a small magazine, "Sincerity in Art and Life: From a Letter of Owen Merton" [in *Good Work*]. The editor [Christopher Derrick] is in fact in England at Wallington, Surrey, and he may ring you up asking about possibilities of illustrations—reproductions of Father's paintings for example. Which reminds me that for a long time I have been thinking of looking into all that. I never got down to doing anything about it. I suppose you would be the best person to start with. Have you any notion where his paintings are? Iris Bennett was in this country and wrote me a letter, but for years I have been on such utterly bad terms with her that I cannot begin to deal with her. In fact I wrote her a rather formal reply giving every possible implication that I was living as a recluse in an underground hole or something. Since then I have not heard. She is a most nervous and sensitive person and I mortally offended her by the autobiography (for which I learned that she was almost on the point of bringing me to court). Ever since then she has had a rather neurotic attitude toward me. In fact before that she had it, because when I stayed in their flat I was not exactly a model of pious living (as a Cambridge undergraduate) and this mortally offended her too. Not to go into all that however: do you think there is any possibility of finding Father's pictures, if they survived the war, and doing something about them? Perhaps an exhibition could be arranged in this country and then those not sold could be placed somewhere where they could be seen. It would not be at all difficult to find a place for them.

The brother [Fr. Augustine Wulff] of Mr. [Louis] Wulff, who is a monk here, was making some sort of signs about his brother calling you, but our sign language is not very clear. At any rate, they brought you news that I was alive. That is the main thing. I am still having a bit of trouble with my back, but I seem to be getting off lightly: one can hear all sorts of gruesome stories of people living in casts like mummies and God knows what. At least I haven't come to that yet.

Well, it seems like a totally different world from that in which we used to spend Christmas together at Fairlawn in the old days. How utterly distant that all seems. And that Christmas at Windsor, too. That was 1929, wasn't it? Or perhaps '28. Incredible, that is almost forty years ago. One had so much fun then: children do not know how fortunate they are to be children! Then they grow up and it has got away from them before they knew it. The place I liked best of all, when we were together, was Rye. Such a heavenly little town. I remember it with awe, as though it were enchanted. You mentioned going back to Bodiam again. It does not sound a bit changed. I will send you my new book [*Conjectures of a Guilty Bystander*], all this is mentioned somewhere in passing, in some nostalgic pages. At any rate (this will probably reach you after Christmas) we can be together in spirit, and I will pray for all of you: pray for me too. All my love to all, to Merton and Dick and their families. Why not send me some snapshots some time? And best love to you above all.

To Gwynned Fanny (Merton) Trier ["Aunt Gwyn"]

Aunt Gwyn wrote to Merton in January 1967, partially to send him birthday greetings. In answer to his queries about his father's paintings, she said: "About your father's pictures I have always assumed that they did not survive the war. Since Tom Bennett's death I completely lost touch with Iris, not that we were very much in touch at any time. Would you call her très difficile!! *The aunts in Christchurch only have some of his earlier work—but the bulk of his later pictures was all at the Bennetts' flat. I am sorry I cannot be more helpful."*

February 17, 1967

. . . If more of Father's letters turn up, please send me copies or the letters themselves if you can: I think they are well worth preserving and perhaps publishing in one way or other. Really it would be a pity to let all the good things he did be forgotten. Thanks for your information about the paintings—or where they might be. We must keep them in mind, at any rate, if any have survived the war. If you learn any more about them please let me know. I remember bringing a great lot of them over with me in 1931 or 1934, for a possible exhibition. Better if they had been left in New York . . .

To Agnes Gertrude Stonehewer Merton ["Aunt Kit"]

August 14, 1967

I am finally trying to catch up with my mail. I don't dare count the letters I should answer—and in fact I have thrown out a few in despair because I know I can't answer them. Others I try to take care of by sending the mimeographed sheet (enclosed, to give you an idea). What has kept me busy this summer: I suppose I have had more than the usual requests for this or that short article, review, etc. And in many cases I have been interested enough to enjoy it. In other cases I have felt obliged in one way or other to write something. Then I have had to see people frequently. Nothing special, but the tiresome business of allergy tests and getting the right shot for the combination of things that are apparently my bane . . .

Actually, the summer has not been bad at all. The weather has been unusually cool. Of course, in Kentucky you can't expect to get through the summer without a few torrid days, but they have not been too many. We have had some very violent storms, and even floods. I suppose that has helped keep things cool and green. Storms at night are exciting in the hermitage: a real fireworks display over the valley, and some jolts when the lightning strikes nearby. Of course the house itself is protected, but the other night my lights were blown out (electric now) by a near hit. Violent crashes of thunder and trees blown down too.

Your NZ abbot [Joseph Murphy] from Hawkes Bay stopped by and I had a short chat with him. I suppose he will have been in contact with you. I have been trying to keep from getting mixed up with what goes on at the monastery. They are changing a lot of things, but that does not necessarily concern me and I am not perfectly convinced that they know what they are doing, or that it is important.

I read Laurens Van Der Post's book *The Dark Eye in A.* some years ago and was very impressed by it. He has many other good ones too, some you would like even better as they are less abstract. I have had some correspondence with him in the past . . . Some time ago I saw he had a book out about Russia. The ones on Africa are the best. By the way I am working along those lines a little myself: interested mostly in the religious-political messianic movements, native Churches and whatnot. Especially in Melanesia though. The Cargo cults etc. If you see anything on that, or especially anything good on the Maori, I hope you will let me know about it. I hope your health is all right now. Take care of yourself. Your spring will be coming soon, with our autumn. I think of you often and Aunt Ka too: my best love to all of you out there.

To Mr. and Mrs. Harold Brewster Jenkins

After years of noncommunication, Merton's uncle, his mother's brother, Harold Brewster Jenkins (1889–1972), wrote a note on a Christmas card in 1967. He said, in part: "I will be 79 yrs. old next Jan 19th & am beginning to feel my age, especially the last year or so. My main recreation is reading. Elsie sends her love. She has always been fond of you, and was of John Paul. I know it would give her great pleasure, as it has in the past, to hear from you occasionally." Merton responded with a letter to both.

December 31, 1967

Thanks for the card: I was glad to get a little news from Harold. Sorry I haven't been writing more regularly myself but it is just impossible to keep up with the enormous correspondence I have. Most of the time I manage to catch up with the business mail and that's about it. Still, I do think of you often and wonder how things are getting on. Last year I got a little news from the family indirectly via Nancy Boettcher . . .

As you know, I am living alone, apart from the community, in a cottage in the woods. For a long time I had been trying to get this permission and finally moved out here altogether between two and three years ago. I no longer have any office in the community, and am here doing my own work and living pretty much the way I want. I go down to the monastery for one cooked meal a day, though I also cook up a can of soup for supper myself, or fry some eggs, or fix up some rice. I really enjoy this kind of life. It is what I have always really wanted. The woods are beautiful, there are deer around (five went by yesterday afternoon) and now there is a snowstorm and it is very quiet. I am about ten minutes' walk from the monastery in a completely isolated spot.

I haven't seen anyone from the family for several years: Aunt Kit from NZ stopped by on her way through in 1963 or '64. I haven't had regular news from out there this Christmas and haven't yet written. I get cards regularly from Gerald Babbitt now that Faye has gone. He sounds a bit lonely. I have some friends who come out once in a while, mostly men I knew at Columbia. Several of my gang at Columbia have died, like the artist Ad Reinhardt last year. Bob Lax, one of my closest friends from school, has lived in Greece for a long time but left there and came back recently. I have kept in close touch with him, more than anyone else. Hope perhaps to see him. My publishers (J. Laughlin of New Directions especially) get down quite regularly, and I have another close friend [W. H. "Ping" Ferry] who comes by frequently, one of the men at the Center for the Study of Democratic Institutions out at Santa Barbara. Otherwise I see a lot of ministers and others on an "ecumenical" basis. My main interest in that line however is keeping up with Buddhists, especially Zen people. They are the ones for whom I seem to have the closest affinities. We get along quite well, and I did a book [*Mystics and Zen Masters*] on Zen last year: the first offer for translation came very fast from Japan, and now some of our own monks in Japan are interested in Buddhism.

Why don't you come out this way some time? In early summer the weather is nice, we have a new ladies' guesthouse where Elsie could stay. Visitors can be here a couple of days so there is no great rush to move. I'd be glad to see you again after all these years. Likelihood of my travelling is still slight, though with the new changes I may get sent out to conferences perhaps. I am not expecting it or trying to wangle it . . .

To Agnes Gertrude Stonehewer Merton ["Aunt Kit"]

January 5, 1968

I have not heard from anyone in the family this Christmas (except by surprise from Uncle Harold, who had not written to me in over twenty years—I think he was upset by my autobiography). How are you? I hope you are all right. I know that I myself have not written for some time but I still have a hazy memory of writing in the autumn. I hope I did . . .

It is very cold here now. We have had quite a lot of snow and it is freezing up: in fact it has been frozen up for some time. Pretty and brisk winter weather—the kind of thing I like. I have a gas heater and it keeps the place pretty cozy. It takes a bit of work to get it filled in bad weather as I am up on this hill and they have to come up with a tractor through the field and drag the tank down to fill it. In summer, a gas truck comes up. But I don't need it in summer.

Christmas has gone by quickly. I am always busy with writing jobs of one kind or other. A new book [Cables to the Ace] is coming out in a couple of months but I hardly dare send it—it is experimental verse and may seem incomprehensible. But I think that is what I have to do, that and some other kinds of things. I have got very interested in the Cargo Cults of Melanesia and am writing something on them. If you run across anything interesting about them, I hope you will send it along. I presume there might be articles in magazines and papers. All these strange movements are so persistent and so universal that it is time we paid a little attention and realized that they mean something. Perhaps they are not altogether logical at all times, but there is something behind it all. In any case it is strange and fascinating. At least to me . . . Things are very peaceful in the hermitage and I am always grateful to be here on my own. It is the best thing possible.

To Beatrice Katharine Merton ["Aunt Ka"]

April 28, 1968

A nun [Sister M. Nivard] in some New Zealand convent saw Aunt Kit's name in the paper among those lost in the Wahine disaster, so she informed me, sent papers and so on. I was terribly shocked and saddened, and I know you must all be very distressed. Such things are so hard to grasp and understand. One remains completely stunned by them for a long time, especially since the whole thing took on the shape of a national tragedy with homes wrecked by the storm, communications disrupted and all the rest.

One feels so helpless at the finality of such things. I know Aunt Kit was one to measure up fully to the situation, and was not surprised when someone told me that survivors said she was very courageous. I hope she did not suffer too cruelly.

In any case, on receiving the news I offered Mass for her and have continued to pray for her, with the faith that her life was well lived and that she has entered into a reward we do not understand where she is somehow united with all those we love who have gone before us. I know we will be together there, and pray that by God's mercy we may live in such a way as to deserve it. As she did. Do please convey to all the rest of the family the assurance that I share in the common sorrow, and am praying for all of us together . . . I haven't heard from anyone in the family for a long time. I do hope we will be able to keep in touch.

To Sister M. Nivard

Sister Nivard, a nun at Villa Maria Convent in Christchurch, New Zealand, sent Merton a clipping about his aunt's death and a newspaper devoted to the story of the Wahine *disaster. She wrote: "Reading through the newspaper recently I noticed in the Obituary notices the name of Miss Agnes Merton. The following day a brief summary of her life appeared which stated that she was your sister. From your writings, Father, it would appear that she is your aunt, and seeing you live so far from this country you might be interested in hearing the details of the* Wahine *disaster in which Miss Merton, R.I.P., died."*

April 28, 1968

Thanks for your letter of sympathy and above all for sending the Dominion *Times* supplement about the *Wahine*. That was the first news I had of it all, and it reached me even before your letter. It was quite a shock to see my Aunt's name in the list of dead. Really a terrible thing. I am sorry for all those who suffered in one way or other, those whose homes were destroyed or damaged as well as those lost in the shipwreck. Perhaps later when the investigation comes to some conclusion, you might send me a clipping. I wonder why more was not done to help. Another correspondent wrote that my Aunt had been quite courageous in the wreck, and that does not surprise me.

She was probably the closest to me among my surviving family, the only one with whom I regularly corresponded, so it is a real loss. But I know she was a wonderful person, and very upright, generous, kind, sweet. I am sure that God in His mercy has taken her to Himself. But we can continue to pray for her and for all the others. Certainly I will remember you in my own prayers and hope you will pray for me too.

To Elsie M. Ryan

Elsie Ryan of Blenheim, New Zealand, also wrote to tell Merton of his Aunt Kit's death. The obituary in the Christchurch Press *had erroneously stated: "Her brother is a well known religious writer, the author of* Elected Silence *and other works." Mrs. Ryan wrote: "Although I know you will find comfort in the Faith it will also console you to know your sister will ever be remembered by those who found her a tower of courage—she walked up & down through the terrified people encouraging & comforting them—A lady who is a friend of a neighbour here, was one of those saved & it is she who told of Miss Merton's outstanding fortitude." Aunt Kit had boarded the last lifeboat, which capsized.*

April 28, 1968

Your letter reached me yesterday, with the enclosed clipping. I had barely heard of the *Wahine* disaster a day or two before, and was aware that my aunt was among the victims. I had no further details. I am writing to contact the remaining members of my family there now. Miss Merton was my aunt, not my sister (the paper had it wrong). I have two other aunts in NZ besides an uncle and some cousins with whom I have never corresponded. Thanks for your kindness in informing me. My aunt was a fine person, very good, and I hope God in His mercy has brought her close to Himself.

To John James Merton

John Merton, son of Owen Merton's older brother, John Llewellyn Charles Merton ["Uncle Lyn"] (1883–), was vicar of the Parochial District of New Brighton in Christchurch, New Zealand, when he wrote Merton to inform him of their Aunt Kit's death. He apologized that tragedy should have occasioned his first letter to his cousin and spoke of the "tremendous courage" shown by their aunt in the disaster.

June 17, 1968

Thanks for writing about Aunt Kit. I was away when your letter arrived. Though we seldom travel here, I went to California to give some talks at a convent of our nuns there. I had heard the news of the *Wahine* from various sources and of course realized that the family there had gone through a lot. I have since also heard from Aunt Ka. It must have been very rough on everybody.

I was of course terribly saddened by the loss as Aunt Kit was the one I was closest to, out there, since I had recently seen her and we kept up a correspondence. There is not much that one can say in such a case, as words are not adequate. She was to me very much like Aunt Maude

[Merton's great-aunt, his grandmother's sister, Emily Maude Mary (Grierson) Pierce (1859–1933), of whom he wrote in *The Seven Storey Mountain*]. There was a special kind of calm about her even in her death, as I understand it.

I do want to keep in touch with the family in New Zealand somehow. I shall write to Aunt Ka soon. If you are interested in any books or articles or anything of the sort I can always send them. I have always stayed close to my Anglican friends, notably one [A. M. Allchin] at Pusey House, Oxford, and many others. I think of myself very much as an English Catholic, though Roman. Anyway all that is very much in evolution these days.

Though it does not seem likely, I may some day get a chance to go to the Orient and if I do I will try, if possible, to take in New Zealand and see the family. I should be interested to hear about the investigation of the *Wahine* affair. Though we are all so far apart and some of us have never met, still you are about all the family I have left—with Aunt Gwyn in England, and I do feel that the ties are there. I keep all of you in my prayers.

III.

Circular Letters to Friends

I appreciate the loyalty of so many old friends and the
interest of new ones.
THOMAS MERTON
1968 CIRCULAR LETTER

To "My Dear Friend" (ca. 1963)

Merton frequently mentions in his correspondence that he had prepared a form letter to send out to those, especially students, who wrote requesting basic facts about his life and writings. The following letter was sent to Mrs. Tommie O'Callaghan in 1963 with the notation: "This might amuse you—I send it to High School kids who want me to write essays for them."

Forgive me for answering you with a form letter, but I get so many requests like yours that this is the only way. It is either this, or no answer at all. You perhaps do not know to what extent correspondence is restricted in a monastery like ours. Even though I have to write many more letters than the Rules provide for, I would never be able to answer everything that comes in. I will put down some notes on the things about which people generally ask, and I hope your question may get answered somewhere along the line.

First: most of the factual information you may need can be found either in the usual reference books (*Who's Who in America, Catholic Authors,* etc.) or in books of my own. *The Seven Storey Mountain* and *The Sign of Jonas* are both autobiographical. More recent information may be found in the preface to a *Thomas Merton Reader* (1962). This *Reader* is probably the handiest way of getting to know what I have written and what I think. There is a *Bibliography* of materials by and about me, edited by Frank Dell'Isola. This however goes only up to 1956.

To give you a quick rundown on the facts of my life: born in France, 1915. I was educated at grade schools in New York, Bermuda, France. In high school and prep school in France and England. I went to college at Cambridge, England and Columbia University N.Y. I did graduate work at Columbia. I taught at Columbia and at St. Bonaventure University. Entered Trappist monastery of Gethsemani in 1941 and have been here since. Ordained priest in 1949. In the monastery I have been spiritual director of the monks studying for the priesthood (Master of Students) and Master of the Novices, that is to say I am supposed to guide and instruct the new ones who have just entered. I have them for three years, give them classes and so on. This takes most of my time.

People are always asking if I am still here. This is because all sorts of rumors go around to the effect that I have left. I haven't. I am still here. I have not been seen in any New York nightclubs for twenty-five years. I am not teaching at Columbia University now. Nor am I teaching at Georgetown, Purdue, Chicago, Southern Methodist, Stanford, the Sorbonne or anywhere else except Gethsemani. I am not a priest in a parish in the Bronx or even in Brooklyn. I am not traveling around Chile giving retreats to nuns, etc. If you hear anything of this sort you can assume that it is for the birds.

People often ask why I am here in the first place, and what the contemplative life means to me. It means to me the search for truth and for God. It means finding the true significance of my life, and my right place in God's creation. It means renouncing the way of life that is led in the "world" and which, to me, is a source of illusions, confusion and deceptions. However I say this only for myself, and I have no criticism of anyone who seeks truth elsewhere and by some other way of life, provided that they really seek the truth. There are all kinds of ways to God, and ours is only one of the many. But it seems to be the one for me, and it is the one I have chosen and accepted as God's will. There are three gifts I have received, for which I can never be grateful enough: first, my Catholic faith; second, my monastic vocation; third, the calling to be a writer and share my beliefs with others. I have never had the slightest desire to be anything else but a monk, since I first came here. But I have often thought I would like an even more solitary life than we have here in the monastery. I think solitude and silence are very important elements which are sadly neglected in the life of modern man, and if you want to find out more of what I think about this, there are books like *Thoughts in Solitude, New Seeds of Contemplation, The Wisdom of the Desert* and parts of *Disputed Questions.* If you want to find out about the monastic life, besides *The Sign of Jonas* you can also consult *The Silent Life, The Waters of Siloe*, and some of the pamphlets published here at the monastery, like *Monastic Peace.* I would be glad to send you one if you want it, as a present.

For those who ask what I think about poetry (I write poetry), there is an essay published in my *Selected Poems* which deals with poetry and the contemplative life. At one time I thought I ought to give up writing poetry because it might not be compatible with the life of a monk, but I don't think this any more. People ask me how I write poetry. I just write it. I get an idea and I put it down, and add to it, and take away what is useless, and try to end up with some kind of poem. A poem is for me the expression of an inner poetic experience, and what matters is the experience, more that the poem itself. Some of my favorite poets are St.-John Perse [Alexis Léger], F. García Lorca, Dylan Thomas, Gerard Manley Hopkins, Boris Pasternak, William Blake, John Donne, Dante, Shakespeare, Tu Fu, Isaias, Aeschylus, Sophocles, etc.

To those who ask what I think about art, there are a couple of essays on the subject in *Disputed Questions*. I like modern art. I have always liked such painters as Picasso, Chagall, Cézanne, Rouault, Matisse, and so on. I like expressionists and impressionists and post-impressionists and abstract expressionists and most of the other "-ists" but I don't like social realism. Nor do I like candy-box art or the illustrations in the *Saturday Evening Post*. I am not prepared to enter into an argument in defense of these preferences.

Some may want to know what I think about politics. I think that we citizens of the United States, as a nation, ought to make more serious efforts to act our age and think in proportion to our size. For this, a whole lot of people who never thought about anything serious in their lives are going to have to wake up and start thinking about their moral and political responsibilities. It is no good going on emotions and prejudices and slogans and feelings of righteous indignation. It is no good simply letting our minds become a passive reflection of a television screen. It is no good going around shouting something that someone else has suggested that we shout, no matter what it may be. If we want to become a seriously political nation, the people have got to do some thinking for themselves.

I think two issues in this country are extremely serious: one, the race issue; two, the question of nuclear war. The second one is worse than the first but both of them are pretty bad. I do not believe that people who fight for integration are all Communists. I do not think that people who are opposed to nuclear war are necessarily enemies of America and paid agents of Communism. I do not think that military might is the solution to our problems. It may defend our pocket books, but it will never defend our liberty. Liberty begins inside your own souls. Our souls cannot be free if we believe only in money and power and comfort and having a good time. I do not think that our present line of action is doing anything to keep us free.

Doubtless I could go on to explain what I think about Jazz (I like it); the movies (haven't seen one for years, don't miss them); smoking (don't miss it); TV (never watched it, don't want to); the newspapers (seldom see one); modern youth (I like them, at least the kind we've got around here—they are the only ones I know); cars (I never had one); wives (never had one, can get along without). There must be some other things about which I ought to have an opinion, but this is enough.

Once again, I am sorry I cannot answer you personally, but I think by now you understand. I will be praying for you. God bless you, pray for me too.

A Christmas Letter—1965

I hate to resort to mimeographed letters, but it has now become completely impossible for me to answer most of my mail personally. Last summer I received permission to do something I had been hoping for since my early days in the monastery. I am living in solitude and trying to do the things that I really came here for. This means that to a great extent I have to sacrifice the semi-public life of the writer, though I will continue to do some writing. Correspondence has been greatly reduced. Anyway it is pretty cold now where I am and this means I have to keep busy cutting wood, besides my other work.

Visits have been practically discontinued and I am not in a position to give spiritual direction by mail. Also, I receive scores of books, pamphlets, poems, manuscripts and other items people want me to read. I cannot possibly comment on them all.

The monastic life by its nature should open out into a greater solitude with more attention given to prayer, meditation, study and the real business of the monk which is to seek God alone. I realize that this is not something that everyone agrees with, but for some people this is a real necessity since they are called to it by God. Hence I ask your prayers that I may be able to do what He asks of me and be faithful to my vocation.

As a result of this more solitary life I am not involved in any kind of direct political action. It is true that I am still convinced, together with Pope Paul and the Council, that the Church must help man to work for the abolition of war and to overcome all the other evils which confront us. I am certainly concerned about this as a pastoral issue and do not intend to remain entirely silent on it. But I do not see where I can do any good by engaging in political controversy when I am not in a position to keep up with events and judge them objectively. However I will say that I am completely opposed to the war in Viet Nam and hope that with honest negotiation some way of ending it will soon be found.

Be sure that I appreciate your letter. I am always glad to get news of my friends and I keep you all in my prayers . . .

Statement to Friends—1966

For many years idle rumors have claimed that I had left the monastery of Gethsemani where I made my vows nearly twenty-two years ago. Recently these rumors have become more insistent. It is "positively" and "undeniably" asserted that I have left my monastery. Hence it becomes necessary for me personally to deny these rumors. I have not left Gethsemani, and I have no intention of leaving. Any reports claiming that I have been "seen" elsewhere are false. They should be dismissed as totally groundless.

In actual fact, far from abandoning the contemplative life I have received permission to live in greater retirement, for the purpose of prayer, meditation and study.

As a result of this more solitary and meditative life I have no further opportunity to engage directly or indirectly in politics. I am not keeping track of daily events and am not involved in any of the current controversies. Though my name is mentioned in connection with the peace movement I am not in a position to take an active part in it.

However, I believe in supporting any action of individuals and groups that will implement the teaching of Vatican II, and of the modern Popes on war. If Pope Paul came to New York and pleaded for peace, there was good reason for it. If my name is among the sponsors of the Catholic Peace Fellowship, this is because I believe that this dedicated group can do much to spread the teachings of the Church on war and peace and on the brotherhood of man. However, my sponsorship does not imply blanket approval of any and every particular move made by this group, still less by individual members of the group acting on their own responsibility. The Catholic Peace Fellowship does not advocate the burning of draft cards or other acts that might be interpreted as provocative. I do not personally condemn those who have felt obliged to burn their draft cards. But I do not entirely agree with them and I would prefer to see more positive and constructive action for peace. Most people are disconcerted by attacks on public authority and cannot see how provocative acts can be considered really non-violent. I favor all constructive and positive action for peace, but no one is entitled to infer that I automatically approve of a merely negative and destructive type of protest. I believe that the Catholic Peace Fellowship favors constructive action in accordance with the teachings of the Church.

Christmas Morning—1966

Sorry, I have just had to give up any hope of answering most of my Christmas mail personally. It is humanly impossible. I hope you will accept this instead: especially as it is my second attempt at a mimeograph letter this season. I junked the other because it was too full of alibis about why I could not read everybody's manuscript and so on.

Christmas night was marvelous: as you know (or don't know) I live in a hermitage on a wooded hill some distance from the monastery. I started down for midnight Mass in bright moonlight and cracking cold, stars shining brilliantly, watching a distant farm across the valley lighted up for the holiday (about the only human habitation I see from my place). I was surprised to find even more mail in the middle of the night: those who happened to be there were remembered most specially in the Con-celebration: like Jack O'Neill with the Peace Corps in Liberia, Sister Marion William and her thesis, Dick De Martino of the Eastern Buddh-ists, Margaret Von Selle of the F.O.R. [Fellowship of Reconciliation], Jaime Andrade of Quito who did the statue of the Bl. Virgin for the novitiate, and Sister Luke [Tobin] of Loretto, our Council Observer and our pride and joy. And so many others, like Fr. Alberton in Rio de Janeiro whom I will try to answer briefly in a moment, as his question is of general interest.

The Midnight Mass was beautiful of course, yet I felt the community was tired and burdened and a little depressed somehow. There had been flu there and anyway the Church is all torn up and liturgy is held in a temporary third floor chapel. There is a sort of grim desperation in the air as people wonder whether there will be real *aggiornamento* or not, and so on. The usual. It was a joy to get back into the cold starlight and trek back into the woods, with a little light snow crackling and frozen under my feet. I made some tea and ate some of the splendid new buns our baker is making, fresh and full of raisins, and sat around for a while before going back to bed. Now the sun is up and shining brilliantly, and after dinner (at the monastery) I hope to go and visit our other hermit who got permission to move into the woods last August (Fr. Flavian [Burns], the former Prior).

Fr. Alberton asked about the war in Vietnam: he does not agree with my opposition to it. The usual question: but are you going to let the Communists take everything over? I have only two thoughts to express briefly. First, I am afraid that the conduct of the war is so desperately stupid and brutal and is having such devastating effects on S. Vietnam morally and otherwise, that it does not make much difference who takes over. In any case, the U.S. seems to be driving Asia into the arms of Communism and the Vietnam war has certainly had a lot to do with the hard-line revolution in Communist China. Second: I do not see why everyone is so bent on accepting the idea of either/or, as if there were *only* Communism and the U.S., no other choice. This is the hard line view taken both in Washington and Peking and the view is to my mind fantastical. It implies a refusal to *even consider* the possibility of any other choice, and justifies every kind of violence as a "lesser evil" (than the abominable alternative—Red or Dead, Dead or Red). The Holy Father certainly seems to think that we have an obligation to do all we can to find other alternatives, and that is my view, also the view of Thich Nhat Hanh, the Buddhist monk about whom I wrote in *Jubilee* ["Nhat Hanh Is My Brother"] this summer after his visit here. I got a letter from France about that, incidentally on Christmas night. I heard from Nhat Hanh Christmas Eve: he was in Japan. He is not planning to return to Vietnam now, it would be too dangerous. He is persona non grata with *both* sides because he favors looking for "other alternatives" whereas they both want a fight to the bitter end. God help the poor people who are caught in between. Pray for them.

To the many who have written to ask me about their poetry, how to get it published and so on. As if I knew!! Some of the best poets in the country have great difficulty getting their poems published commercially in book form. Most of their stuff appears in little magazines, and a lot of it is circulated in mimeograph or other cheap processes. This is the best thing to do with your poetry, this and reading it in coffee houses and so on. The idea that anything good has to appear between hard covers is a pure myth and you should stop being obsessed by it. Do you want to be *read* or do you want to have the imagined "status" of a book publication that may or may not mean being read? If you want to be read, get your stuff into the hands of those who are likely to be interested, in any form you can. You yourself have to find out who is likely to be interested in *your* poems. I can't tell you, it is a question of your own relationships, part of your own life.

To the many who have sent in gifts, I return warm thanks. Books are always most welcome: if I cannot read them all myself, I can turn them into the monastic library where they are much appreciated. I will be very glad to say Masses for all the intentions sent in to me as soon as possible. Be sure that I keep all these needs you have mentioned in my prayers and think often of all these problems: God knows, you are by no means alone. Most of you, even with all that you have to suffer, are much better off than you realize. Yet the heart of man can be full of so much pain, even when things are exteriorly "all right." It becomes all the more difficult because today we are used to thinking that there are explanations for everything. But there is no explanation for most of what goes on in our own hearts, and we cannot account for it all. No use resorting to the kind of mental tranquillizers that even religious explanations sometimes offer. Faith must be deeper than that, rooted in the unknown and in the abyss of darkness that is the ground of our being. No use teasing the darkness to try to make answers grow out of it. But if we learn how to have a deep inner patience, things solve themselves, or God solves them if you prefer: but do not expect to see how. Just learn to wait, and do what you can and help other people. Often in helping someone else we find the best way to bear with our own trouble.

My prayers are with you in the New Year. Pray also for me. Pray for peace, because people need it and because violence will lead inevitably to the establishment of tyranny in one form or another. Pray for freedom both for those who know they are not free and especially for those who think they are free and do not realize they are prisoners of dead ideas and prejudices.

Septuagesima Sunday 1967

Several wrote that they liked my mimeographed Christmas letter and urged me to go on mimeographing more often. This has one advantage: at least I can send replies to letters which I would not otherwise be able to answer. I am once again forced to keep down letters to a minimum. First of all Lent is close—Easter is early this year. Then my publisher fondly imagines that I am working on a book for which I have signed a contract, so I had better get busy on it. For three months I have not been able to do anything with this manuscript because I have been bombarded with requests for other things—articles, statements, and so on, plus correspondence. Now I want to concentrate on my true work for a while. And of course live my life. Hence another mimeograph. I hope those who did not know about this, and who expected a personal reply, will have the kindness to understand.

It is a cloudy quiet Sunday morning, not too cold. I am hoping for some rain to fill my rain barrels and give me water to wash dishes with. I still have water from the monastery daily in a gallon bottle. I know what it means to save on water, and I guess I use only two or three gallons a day for everything, at the hermitage. (Showers I take at the monastery.)

There has been a lot of talk about Fr. Charles Davis and his farewell to the Church. Note, his problem was Church authority, not celibacy. He could conceivably have left the priesthood and got married with a dispensation. In a long statement which was front page news in England, he made some very drastic criticisms of the abuse of authority in the Church. I do not think these criticisms were altogether baseless or unjust. The present institutional structure of the Church is certainly too antiquated, too baroque, and is so often in practice unjust, inhuman, arbitrary and even absurd in its functioning. It sometimes imposes useless and intolerable burdens on the human person and demands outrageous sacrifices, often with no better result than to maintain a rigid system in its rigidity and to keep the same abuses established, one might think, until kingdom come. I certainly respect Fr. Davis's anguish—who of us does not sometimes share it? But I cannot follow him in his conclusion that the institutional Church has now reached the point where it can hardly be anything other than dishonest, tyrannical, mendacious and inhuman.

He feels he has a moral obligation to leave the Church and he offers this theological justification for his decision.

I hope most of us Catholics have learned by now that this kind of decision on the part of one of our brothers merits our compassion and understanding, not fulminations against heresy and bad faith. One can feel Fr. Davis is still a brother without coming to the same conclusions as he did.

I have in fact just been reading Romano Guardini's excellent little book on Pascal [*Pascal for Our Time*]. He analyzes the "demon of combativeness" in Pascal—a demon which is no prerogative of Jansenists. At times one wonders if a certain combativeness is not endemic in Catholicism: a "compulsion to be always right" and to prove the adversary wrong. A compulsion which easily leads to witch-hunting and which, when turned the wrong way, hunts its witches in the Church herself and finally needs to find them in Rome. There are always human failures which can be exploited for this purpose. Pascal nearly went over the falls completely but he recognized the destructiveness of his own inner demon in time, and knew enough to be silent and to believe. And to love. The story of his death is very moving.

There comes a time when it is no longer important to prove one's point, but simply to live, to surrender to God and to love. There have been bad days when I might have considered doing what Fr. Davis has done. In actual fact I have never seriously considered leaving the Church, and though the question of leaving the monastic state *has* presented itself, I was not able to take it seriously for more than five or ten minutes. It is true that if I had at one time or other left the Church, I would have found scores of friends who would have approved my action and declared it honest and courageous. I do not claim any special merit in having decided otherwise. Nor does a decision for Christian obedience imply an admission that I think authority has always been infallibly just, reasonable or human. Being a Catholic and being a monk have not always been easy. But I know that I owe too much to the Church and to Christ for me to be able to take these other things seriously. The absurdity, the prejudice, the rigidity and unreasonableness one encounters in some Catholics are nothing whatever when placed in the balance with the grace, love and infinite mercy of Christ in His Church. And after all, am I not arrogant too? Am I not unreasonable, unfair, demanding, suspicious and often quite arbitrary in my dealings with others? The point is not just "who is right?" but "judge not" and "forgive one another" and "bear one another's burdens." This by no means implies passive obsequiousness and blind obedience, but a willingness to listen, to be patient, and to keep working to help the Church change and renew herself from within. This is our task. Therefore by God's grace I remain a Catholic, a monk and a hermit. I have made commitments which are unconditional and cannot be taken back. I do not regard this position as especially courageous: it is just the ordinary stuff of life, the acceptance of limits which we must all accept in one way or another: the acceptance of a sphere in which one is called to love, trust and believe and pray—and meet those whom one is destined to meet and love.

More and more I see the meaning of my relationships with all of you, and the value of the love that unites us, usually unexpressed. This is the area in which the term "union in Christ" really means most to me, though some of you are not enrolled in the Church.

More and more since living alone I have wanted to stop fighting, and arguing, and proclaiming and criticizing. I think the points on which protest has been demanded of me and given by me are now well enough known. Obviously there may be other such situations in the future. In a world like ours—a world of war, riot, murder, racism, tyranny and established banditry, one has to be able to stand up and say NO. But there are also other things to do. I am more and more convinced of the reality of my own job which is meditation and study and prayer in silence. I do not intend to give up writing, that too is obviously my vocation. But I hope I will be able to give up controversy some day. Pray for me. When one gets older (Jan. 31 is my fifty-second birthday) one realizes the futility of a life wasted in argument when it should be given entirely to love.

God bless you. I really appreciate your letters. When there are really urgent questions and problems in them, I will always do my level best to answer. Please understand that my visits are severely limited and I cannot possibly even think of seeing more than a few people who ask to see me. But there is such a thing as being united in prayer, or even thought and desire (if you can't pray) and in our friendship. The main thing is that we desire good for each other and seek within the limits of our power to obtain for each other what we desire.

P.S. For those who have not been in touch with developments here: I have been living more or less as a hermit for several years. The dividing line between "less" and "more" came in the fall of 1964 when I began spending the night in the hermitage. Living there day and night became "official" in August 1965. My latest book: *Conjectures of a Guilty Bystander* (Doubleday, November 1966). The next one, *Mystics and Zen Masters* (Farrar, Straus and Giroux, March 1967). New Directions will publish two paperbacks of mine in 1967—a new *Selected Poems* and *Wisdom of the Desert*.

Lent 1967

The last mimeographed letter is running out and there are still more than four weeks to go before Easter. And in any case I write this one on the eve of going into the hospital for a minor operation (bursitis on the elbow) which may make typing difficult for a while. So here goes with another one, to fill the gap.

We have had some cold weather but nothing like the blizzards up north around Chicago recently. In front of my place, crocuses came up on Ash Wednesday and have persisted since, even through snow and low temperatures. They are still there (from the bulbs Eileen Curns sent last year). Speaking of Eileen, who was a papal volunteer in Brazil, I got a letter from a Holy Cross Brother in Brazil taking me to task, as many critics have done, for what seems to be a negative attitude on technology in *Conjectures [of a Guilty Bystander]*. It might be well to try to dot the i's and cross the t's on this point. Am I "against technology"?

Obviously I am not maintaining that we ought to get rid of matches and go back to making fires by rubbing sticks together (thought of this yesterday when burning brush piles, lighting matches in the wind). Nor am I maintaining that modern transportation, medicine, methods of production and so on are "bad." I am glad to have a gas heater this winter, since I can't cut wood. Yet I am not saying I am a better human being this winter, when I have more "leisure," than I was last winter when I did a lot of chopping. Nothing wrong with chopping either. What I question is the universal myth that technology infallibly makes everything in every way better for everybody. It does not.

Modern medicine is certainly a good thing. Thank God for it. Thank God for the fact that penicillin saves thousands of lives. But let's also face the fact that penicillin saves lives for people whom society then allows to starve because it is not set up to feed them. If it used its technological resources well, society certainly could feed them. In fact it doesn't. Technology comes into a "backward country" with an industrial setup that works fine in an advanced country—and depends for financial support on an advanced country and brings profits back to the advanced country. It may simply dislocate the "backward country" completely. Today twelve percent of the world's population (repeat, *twelve percent*) live in the appalling shanty towns and *poblaciones* that are seen in the outskirts of South American, African and Asian cities. What is technology doing for these people? It is not creating work for them, but is developing more and more labor-saving methods of production because technology in our society is not in the service of people but in the service of profit. What I am criticizing then is the myth that this kind of "labor-saving" technology will turn the world into a paradise. It will not. Look what technology is doing to Viet Nam!!!

On the other hand, I am quite willing to admit that the resources are there and that things *could be* quite other than they are. Technology could indeed make a much better world for millions of human beings. It not only can do this, but it must do it. We have an absolute obligation to use the means at our disposal to keep people from living in utter misery and dying like flies. Note: there has never been such abject misery on earth as that which our technological society has produced along with the fantastic plenty for very few. What I am "against" then is a complacent and naive progressivism which pays no attention to anything but the fact that wonderful things can be and are done with machinery and with electronics. Even more wonderful things might be done. But in our present setup, the chances of them getting done are not as good as these people seem to think.

We face an utterly self-defeating and even absurd situation. A critic [Michele Murray] took me to task for saying in the book that "the realm of politics is the realm of waste." It is and always has been. When a human question becomes a "political issue," unfortunately the human problem gets shoved into the background, human hopes are derided and ignored, money passes from hand to hand and a lot of noise is made in the press, and the human problem may or may not even be touched. Witness Johnson's great "war on poverty". It is a sheer insult to the people living in our Eastern Kentucky Mountains. All the attention and money are going not to help them but to exterminate innocent non-combatants in Viet Nam and to enrich the big corporations that are making higher profits now than they ever did before.

In our technological world we have wonderful methods for keeping people alive and wonderful methods for killing them off, and they both go together. We rush in and save lives from tropical diseases, then we come along with napalm and burn up the people we have saved. The net result is more murder, more suffering, more inhumanity. This I know is a caricature, but is it that far from the truth?

What is my answer? I don't have one, except to suggest that technology could be used entirely differently. But the only way it ever will be is to get it free from this inescapable hang-up with profit or power, so that it will be used for people and not for money or politics. The essential message of an encyclical like *Mater et Magistra* or the Council Constitution *Gaudium et Spes* adds up to this: technology has given us the means to alleviate human misery, but the profit system makes it practically impossible to use the means effectively. The myth of technology (as distinct from the reality) serves the religion of profit vs. people. He who swallows the myth is serving that religion.

Sorry for this long tirade, but I thought it was worthwhile to make this point clear. Obviously I have no intention whatever of turning the clock back to the Middle Ages, though there are people around who want to do that too.

And so we turn our eyes to the great feast of Christian hope: the Resurrection. Too often the Passion and Resurrection of the Lord have been used in the past to canonize earthly injustice and despair: the old business of saying "Yes, you are getting a dirty deal, but just offer it up and you will be happy in heaven." The real root of Christian hope is the presence of the Risen Lord among us and in us by His Spirit which is the Spirit and power of love. The power of the Resurrection is the power of love that is stronger than death and evil, and its promise is the promise that the power of this love is ours if we freely accept it. To accept it is not just a matter of making a wish, but of entire and total commitment to the Law of Christ which is the Law of Love. Let us realize this, and believe it, and pray for one another. Let us be one in this love, and seek to make all men one in it, even here on earth. And if technology helps to express the creative power of love, then all the better: it will give glory to God and have its own place in the Kingdom of God on earth. But technology by itself will never establish that Kingdom.

Easter 1967

It has been a beautiful warm Easter here, though the most recent news from the East Coast complains of much snow. Jim Forest wrote from his C[atholic] P[eace] F[ellowship] office in Nyack that he felt like Dr. Zhivago in Siberia, and Adrienne Mariani had some amusing suggestions about what might be done to discourage the ground hog from sticking his head out and being confronted with despair. Actually, however, it was eighty all afternoon here on Holy Saturday and sixty at one-thirty a.m. when I got back to my cell after the Easter Vigil.

Answering letters individually gets to be more and more of a problem. Not that I am pitying myself but just to give new correspondents some idea why I simply cannot answer letters most of the time: Besides my ordinary work I now have on my desk the following: One complete manuscript of a novel on which I am asked to comment by a publisher. A set of galleys of a book on Zen, ditto. Several chapters of a book on mysticism to read and criticize. A long statement on the Vietnam War I am supposed to sign (generally I don't sign any of these statements, because I can't read the papers or watch TV to keep up as others do). A list of twenty-four magazine articles which I must either read and report on myself, or get others to summarize, for the magazine of the Order. A book review article of six or seven books on Camus, in state of outline, to be written somehow in the next week or so. At least two books to review for the magazine of the Order. (I mention only the two that happen to be directly visible at the moment. There are probably others on the shelf behind me or buried under the mass of other material that confronts me.) Finally, on top of that, I have an urgent report to write on an official matter, and am requested to give this top priority. And so on. The life of a writing hermit is certainly not one of lying around in the sun or of pious navel gazing. Nevertheless there is the question of meditation which, to me, is always the first thing of all because without it the rest becomes meaningless. In such circumstances, writing letters, receiving visits and so on would simply complicate matters beyond all reasonable measure. Yet I do of course have to answer business mail, urgent requests, questions from people in a state of crisis, and all that. Carrying on an ordinary friendly correspondence is normally just out of the question. Note also that I have no secretary for correspondence, and that it is increasingly difficult to find someone in the monastery to type manuscripts. (I am most grateful to the ones who are helping me in this matter, both inside and outside the monastery.)

I recommend a very interesting and important new magazine which is being published at Cambridge (England). The first issues have just reached me. It is called *Theoria to Theory* and the purpose is to get some lively dialogue going between theologians and contemplatives on one hand and secular scientists, philosophers and humanists on the other. It is the most promising new venture of its kind that I have seen. It is edited by Anglicans and is more informal and free wheeling than the new Roman Catholic publications, which still strike me as too formal and still a bit triumphalist. (There is of course a new aggressive triumphalism of the left just as there is an old stuffy triumphalism of the right.) Part of the editorial in the first issue reads as follows: "To those who . . . still hope there might be something in Christianity or indeed in any other religion we would simply say: Things aren't as hopeless as you might think. There are more things in heaven and earth than are dreamt of in any of the philosophies currently in use. *Nil illegitime carborundum*, which is hot dog Latin for Don't let the bastards grind you down." The magazine can be obtained from 9 Marion Close, Cambridge, England.

A friend wrote quoting a line of verse [by T. S. Eliot]: "In the juvescence of the year came Christ the Tiger" and wondered if Easter was going to be like that. There is an inner strength which is "ours" yet "not ours," which can be for us or against us, depending on whether we resolve to face it and submit, or seek to evade and resist it. Easter is the season of that strength (and Easter is all year round, really). At Easter we resolve liturgically and communally to "face it" and to join this Tiger who is then our Tiger and our Lamb. (I am thinking of the two great Blake poems: "Tyger Tyger burning bright . . .") [Both called "The Tyger"] There is no joy but in the victory of Christ over death in us: and all love that is valid has something of that victory. But the power of love cannot "win" in us if we insist on opposing it with something else to which we can cling, on which we trust because we ourselves can manipulate it. It all depends [on] who is in control: our own ego, or Christ. We must learn to surrender our ego-mastery to His mastery. And this implies a certain independence even of apparently holy systems and routines, official "answers" and infallible gimmicks of every kind. Easter celebrates the victory of love over everything. *Amor vincit omnia*. If we believe it we still understand it, because belief is what opens the door to love. But to believe only in systems and *statements* and not in *people* is an evasion, a betrayal of love. When we really believe as Christians, we find ourselves trusting and accepting *people* as well as dogmas. Woe to us when we are merely orthodox, and reject human beings, flesh and blood, the aspirations, joys and needs of men. Yet there is no fruit, either, in merely sentimental gestures of communion that mean little, and seek only to flatter or placate. Love can also be tough and uncompromising in its fidelity to its own highest principles. Let us be united in joy, peace and prayer this Easter and always. "Fear not" says Jesus "It is I. I am with you all days!"

Pentecost 1967

The main news at this season is the ordination to the priesthood of my old friend Dan Walsh, formerly my professor of scholastic philosophy at Columbia. It was he who first told me that such a place as Gethsemani existed. For the past seven years he has been living here and teaching at the Abbey and at Bellarmine College (Louisville). The retiring Archbishop of Louisville, John A. Floersch, decided that Dan would make a good priest and got all the dispensations necessary to ordain him without further delay. Dan is in his sixties. The ordination took place in Louisville on Pentecost Sunday and was very moving. Dan has so many friends and students, and his ordination became for all of us a kind of providential happening that reminded us that unpredictable changes can occur. I think everyone is looking for a less systematic and less rigid kind of Church structure, something that leaves room for a more charismatic kind of religion, and this gave some of us a small glimmer of hope. I had the joy of concelebrating with Fr. Walsh at the Louisville Carmel (where he has also given some talks) and that too was a real happening. The contemplative nuns entered into it with a great deal of very authentic joy that did one good.

There is everywhere a kind of hunger for the grace and light of the Spirit in forms that can be actually *experienced.* One hears a great deal of movements that can be called in a broad sort of sense "Pentecostal" even though they do not restrict themselves simply to far-out Protestant groups by any means. I am often asked what I think about all this. I cannot really judge from hearsay, but at any rate the phenomenon represents a real spiritual hunger, just as the craze for LSD represents a real hunger for experience—I hasten to add that I don't think an LSD trip is the answer for most of us! Personally, my own life and vocation have their own peculiar dimension which is a little different from all this. I have always tended more toward a deepening of faith in solitude, a "desert" and "wilderness" existence in which one does not seek special experiences. But I concur with these others in being unable to remain satisfied with a formal and exterior kind of religion. Nor do I think that a more lively liturgy is enough. Worship and belief have become ossified and rigid, and so has the religious life in many cases. The idea that "the

Church" does all your thinking, feeling, willing, and experiencing for you is, to my mind, carried too far. It leads to alienation. After all, the Church is made up of living and loving human beings: if they all act and feel like robots, the Church can't experience and love in their behalf. The whole thing becomes an abstraction. Certainly it is fine that now the liturgy is becoming more spontaneous, more alive, and people are putting their hearts into it more. (I am not saying it was not possible to enter into the old Latin liturgy, but it was hard for many.) But we need a real deepening of life in every area, and that is why it is proper that laypeople and others who have been kept in subordinate positions are now claiming the right to make decisions in what concerns their own lives. This is also true in religious orders. As long as everything is decided at the top, and received passively by those at the bottom, the vocation crisis will continue. There is no longer any place in our life for a passive and inert religiosity in which one simply takes orders and lets someone else do all the thinking. Those who fail to accept such a situation are not rebels, most of the time, they are sensitive and intelligent human beings who protest against a real disorder and who have a right to be heard.

That brings us to the question of monastic renewal. It is a question that I do not feel competent to talk about at the moment. There is at present a General Chapter being held. Our Fr. Abbot left the other day for Rome. Most of us in the community here seem to be doubtful whether anything special will come of it: there is a sense of "wait and see". A big questionnaire was sent out to everyone in the Order—a complicated but routine affair—and most people apparently write in their answers. But most seem to have felt that this Gallup Poll approach was not too promising. At any event, a lot of "wishes" will have been tabulated. Unfortunately the tabulation of wishes is not enough to constitute renewal.

If I were to leave it at that, this letter would perhaps be a bit discouraging. It need not necessarily be that. The institutional machinery for renewal is perhaps not adequate, but that does not mean that renewal depends on the machinery alone. It will not come from the machine or the establishment but from persons. Fortunately the establishment is much more willing to relax and give special permissions to try out new ways, provided the establishment itself is absolved from responsibility for them. This is a very good thing. It provides opportunity for growth. One such experiment is under way in France now, a return to a more primitive and solitary monasticism in a wild mountain area, under the direction of one of the best men in the Order. The experiment is taking place *outside* the Order, hence it will have leeway to function and to grow. I think it has very good possibilities. I also think that the directory for hermits written by Dom Jacques Winandy (who has a group of hermits on Vancouver Island) is one of the best monastic documents to have appeared in the modern era. It is not in print, however, and does not need to be. It will reach those for whom it is intended.

As for me, the job of renewal boils down to the conversion of my own life. That is quite a job in itself. Please pray that I may finally get down to it seriously and do something about it. I am grateful to be in a situation in which I should be able to achieve all that I believe I am called to do. My best wishes always. Have a good summer.

Midsummer 1967

Recently I heard of the following strange event. Frank Sheed, in London, was awakened at four in the morning by a person-to-person telephone call from Cleveland. The caller claimed to be Thomas Merton. Frank said he did not recognize the voice as mine, and could not quite figure out the message which did not seem to make perfect sense: he wondered if it really could be I, and inquired of a mutual friend who set him straight. Moral: there are people around who are crazy enough to think that if they pretend they are Thomas Merton it means something. (As a matter of fact one such was trying to collect money on that basis.) So if you ever hear of anything of the kind, don't be taken in. And if possible, send information that might help identify the one impersonating me. (Note: in this particular case, quite by chance, a similar call from Cleveland to the monastery gave a clue to the possible identity of this person.)

The purpose of this letter is, as usual, to provide some way of answering all those I cannot answer personally. I do not intend it to be a sermon or an encyclical, and there is not much news, except that the renovation of the Abbey Church looks as though it is finally going to be finished in a month or two. I am still leading a marginal life in solitude, which I enjoy very much, and one of the effects of this is that I find I have less and less to say. When you are alone you take stock of things and see them in an entirely different perspective.

One has a choice of various attitudes toward silence and communication. The most obvious one is to assume: "I know something, and I want to tell everybody about it." There is a reversal of this, favored officially by monks, which says: "I know something very very profound, but I am not going to reveal it to anyone: instead I will surround myself with mystery and silence and keep it all a deep secret." But the trouble is that if you know something and do not share it, you lose your own knowledge of it. Perhaps though behind this attitude there is merely a pretense of knowing something: and a very real emptiness of the heart and of the head. A blank, or a private myth which is not put into words because when you externalize it, it is immediately seen to be what it is: nonsense.

I admit that I have not kept many secrets, profound or otherwise. And the risk of putting my cards on the table has been worthwhile, because

I have learned from it. More and more the cards I have been putting on the table have been saying: "I don't know the answers, but I have some questions I'd like to share with you." There is always an implication that it means something to know the questions, especially if they are common questions. But now I am beginning to wonder if I even know the questions, or if they are common to others. In such a case one eventually gets around to saying: "Since I don't know where it all begins, I'd better just shut up." Of course, it will not be that easy to shut me up: I am writing less, but still writing. No doubt the writing will tend to get further out and less popular. And I still recognize some obligation to take up a position on this or that moral issue of general urgency, not because I claim to have the answer, but because one has to take a responsible stand. Stupidity and evasion are no excuse from complicity in what goes on in the world of today. To have lived under Hitler and merely ignored the death camps is not an enviable moral position . . . I won't go into that again.

Once more I am having to refuse requests to write prefaces for this or that new book. I really ought to refuse to give "blurbs" for books too, but it is easy to find reasons for helping someone out I guess. The really hard-boiled writer is the kind who, when asked to write a preface, says: "OK, but my fee is a thousand dollars." I guess that would cut down on the requests. But it doesn't fit in with the Rule of St. Benedict. A plain "No" will have to do.

This summer I have had the sorrow of losing one of my oldest and best friends, Victor Hammer, the artist and printer, who died in Lexington on July 10. He was getting close to ninety years old. An Austrian, he grew up in Vienna and left when Hitler took over. He had been teaching and painting in this country since the thirties, and especially printing fine limited editions on his handpress at the Stamperia del Santuccio. We did several book projects together and Victor was always a wonderful person to have around. When someone like that dies, you begin to realize how a man like Camus could be so fiercely convinced that death just *should not be*. It is literally absurd that such a person should cease to exist, and as Christians we believe that they do not do so. It was significant, I thought, that the last painting on which Victor was working when he fell ill was a painting of the Resurrection. Pray for him, please.

I am embarrassed when people want to send me gifts: actually there is nothing much you can send. My needs are minimal and are well taken care of. I suggest instead that you send something to people who are in *real* need: the refugees of the Arab–Israeli war. A reliable place to send such help would be: Friends Band of Missions (Quakers), 101 Quaker Hill Drive, Richmond, Indiana. They will distribute things properly. I am trying not to appear to take either side in this senseless conflict, rooted in hate and misunderstanding and fomented by power politicians in the "big" powers. But the refugees and homeless are refugees nevertheless, regardless of the merits and demerits of their "side." Of course you can always find arguments for one side or the other. But in the long run no argument can justify the needless suffering this Near Eastern war has caused and the immense danger it still presents to the peace of the world.

Once again, to those I have not been able to answer personally, I offer my apologies. I cannot undertake direction by mail. I try to answer important questions when possible, but I have to try to keep my correspondence within reasonable limits. I wish you all a good summer, peace, contentment, and the joy you seek: or at least the courage and light to live free from care amid unavoidable trouble! The greatness of man, Camus wrote, consists in his ability to find something bigger than himself—and he added that if we cannot expect perfect happiness in this life, we *can* measure up to this kind of greatness. Don't let the system grind you down! Joy to you in the Lord Jesus, who is our peace and our hope. Pray for me.

Advent–Christmas 1967

This year has gone by fast, and not without sorrows. Besides the death of Victor Hammer last summer (see previous letter) I also lost two of my oldest friends from Columbia in August and September: Ad Reinhardt, one of the most brilliant artists of our time, and John Slate, who was not only a fine lawyer but had a fabulous sense of humor which made him legendary in New York. He also wrote a few pieces for magazines in the last few years: I had got back in touch with him when I read a very funny article of his in *The Atlantic* on hospitals, last year. Both died of heart attacks, and both were about my age. So if I suddenly follow their example I will be the last one to be surprised.

Our renovated Abbey Church has been reoccupied since September, and it is a great artistic success: with all the simplicity and clean-cut grace a true Cistercian Church should have. Much credit is due to the architect, William Schickel, who did a great job with true patience. I don't imagine it is always easy to work for a bunch of monks. At least monks themselves don't always find it so. The Church of Gethsemani is an inspiring place to worship in. The old one was that, in its own way, but the new one is a great improvement, and the community has felt the difference. The only problem that remains is the acoustics . . .

About religious renewal: obviously it is slower and more complicated than most of us would like. It is a pity that so much useless and misleading fuss is made about it in the papers: people's hopes are raised beyond measure then crushed by some conservative, then raised again by someone else. For my own part I am keeping out of all the political maneuverings that are involved, even in my own Order. I am not trying to sell anybody anything. My part in renewal, as far as this community is concerned, is to be a hermit. That too is a full-time job.

I do not have enormously sanguine hopes about what is likely to be accomplished all of a sudden in monastic renewal. I do think that a lot of the hopes are deceptive and sometimes silly: but the long term view seems to me to be quite good. A new generation is sooner or later going to take over, and I think the youngest generation in religion and elsewhere (those born about 1940–47) look very good indeed. The old guys like me have had it anyway, and as for the ones in between—well, let's hope they make out. They have a fifty fifty chance, maybe. As for the ultra-conservatives, I am afraid I gave up worrying over them long since. There is nothing to be done about them, or about people who insist on filling the air with lamentations about everything as if the Church were just about to go over the falls and as if there were ten commandments under every bed. To be frank, I think a lot of what is said and done is truly pathetic, but it is not worth paying attention to. It is God's Church, and I assume He knows what to do with it. For all I know He may be quite willing and ready to let a lot of dead wood fall off the tree without the slightest attempt to save it. Christ in the Gospel told us long ago that the branches of the vine would have to be pruned off. That may apply to some religious institutions. I can think of plenty of Catholic publications that could do the world a favor by going out of business. Others are trying hard to look alive, and I wish them luck: same way with colleges and schools.

Other opinions: I don't think the Hippies are a menace to the nation. If Lyndon Baines Johnson suddenly went into nirvana and abandoned politics, it would not be a disaster. However the "hate Johnson" trend in some quarters is repugnant and infantile. I like the Beatles (what I have heard of them). The mere mention of LSD does *NOT* make me break out in a cold sweat. Several friends of mine were in the peace march on the Pentagon in October and they say that the impression of violence given by the press was a gross distortion (several of those present were ex-monks).

In other words a great deal of noise is made about issues that are peripheral, while some other issues are so serious as to be really critical: the chief of these is the racial tension in this country. In this area the future does not look good, because there is a real failure of communication. Violence seems inevitable. About the Vietnam war, the less said the better. It is one of the greatest and most stupid blunders in American history, and the results are a disgrace.

I did not intend to reel off a litany of "controversial issues"—as if I really knew what they all were. The times are difficult. They call for courage and faith. Faith is in the end a lonely virtue. Lonely especially where a deeply authentic community of love is not an accomplished fact, but a job to be begun over and over: I am not referring to Gethsemani, where there is a respectable amount of love, but to all Christian communities in general. Love is not something we get from Mother Church as a child gets milk from the breast: it also has to be *given*. We don't get any love if we don't give any. And fear, suspicion, the sense that we have often been "had" and may well be "had" some more in the future, understandably restrain the spontaneity of love at times. So in the end we have to hope mightily in God who sent His Son into the world to bring out not just optimism and good business but the only chance of man's making it at all.

Christmas, then, is not just a sweet regression to breast-feeding and infancy. It is a serious and sometimes difficult feast. Difficult especially if, for psychological reasons, we fail to grasp the indestructible kernel of hope that is in it. If we are just looking for a little consolation—we may be disappointed. Let us pray for one another, love one another in truth, in the sobriety of earnest, Christian hope: for hope, says Paul, does not deceive. A blessed and joyous Christmas to all of you.

New Year's 1968

Christmas mail was an avalanche this year: it always is, but much more so in 1967. News from friends everywhere from Argentina to Pakistan and from Brooklyn to India and Japan. But nothing from my family (the remaining aunts) in New Zealand. To be truthful they will not have heard from me either, as I have not been able to write them yet. They at least should not have to be content with a form letter.

Besides the need to acknowledge some of the pile of mail in this way, I have another reason for this form letter. Some friends have been disturbed by a recent article on the Trappists in the *National Catholic Reporter* [Colman McCarthy, "Renewal Crisis Hits Trappists"]. The article quoted me, and I had in fact written a letter answering some queries by the writer last summer when he began preparing his story. He incorporated my answers in an article which strongly expressed his opinion, which was not exactly identical with mine. I have since written to the NCR about that, just to keep things straight ["Regain the Old Monastic Charism: Letter to the Editor"]. I do not think that the Order is about to collapse or that Gethsemani is ready to shut down. Nor was I happy to give the impression that I was in a state of tension with my Fr. Abbot [James Fox]. Or that the community here was in a state of inner conflict. Things are going reasonably well, indeed very well from a certain short term viewpoint. Though personally I feel we have long term problems that cannot be met merely by adjustments in the daily time table and in the liturgy.

Colman McCarthy who wrote the article is a former member of the Trappist community at Conyers, Georgia. His feeling is that for the monastic life to be relevant to today's needs it has to be more active and outgoing. On the other hand, the superiors are mortally afraid of getting involved in commitments to "active works" (parishes, etc.) that they could not get out of afterwards, and from their point of view they are right too. My own feeling is that there are real possibilities for development, but they must be authentically monastic, that is to say they must focus on the reality of the monastic vocation to inner freedom, to creativity, to dialogue with other contemplative traditions, and this presupposes that we have some real contemplative discipline and experience ourselves. But the problem arises from the fact that merely remaining officially locked up and out of touch does little or nothing to develop authentic contemplative possibilities. I do not have a lot of answers, and as I said before I am not promoting any form of new legislation: I believe that I am obligated however to develop my own vocation in its peculiar and personal character of solitude, dialogue and creative work. This has always struck some people as a strange, even impossible mixture. There was once a time when I could not understand it myself. Maybe I still don't understand it, but I believe it is what I am supposed to do, and believe it so strongly that I feel I could never accept election to the abbatial office.

There is to be such an election here very soon, as our Fr. James [Fox] is retiring from the abbatial office to live in solitude. This is a momentous decision, but it will be better understood if you realize that the very possibility of the hermit experiment now going on in the Order is due to Dom James' intervention. If he had not been active in taking initiative to get the experiment officially recognized, there would still be no hermits in the Order. The possibility of living as a hermit in the woods near one's own community is certainly a very simple and practical one and is probably the most secure way of doing it. We owe him thanks for his achievement in this particularly, but also in all the other ways he built up our community and provided for it over more than eighteen years as Abbot . . .

Blessings and joy in the New Year. Pray for peace at home and abroad. May the Lord bring you peace in your own hearts and joy always. God be with you.

Pre-Lent 1968

. . . January was as rough here as anywhere else. Many of us had that very unpleasant 'flu. I can sympathize. It knocked me out for nearly a week. I was fortunate not to get the second round which some people had. We had more snow than I can ever remember seeing in Kentucky.

The result of our Abbatial election was, as most of you know, the choice of Fr. Flavian [Burns], a young monk who, I would say, represents a middle position between conservatism and wild innovation. He has the confidence of the community, is open, has no special axe to grind, and gives everyone the feeling that he does not intend to exploit the community or its manpower for personal projects. We feel he has the interests of all, singly and communally, at heart. And we are all right behind him. This is a good situation and we are grateful for your prayers. Keep them up, please.

I can't go into all the many things I have on my mind, but one idea does grow on me: more and more of those who have left the monastic and religious life seem to me to have done so in the full consciousness that they were continuing the search that had originally brought them to the monastery. In fact many of them continue, in a schematic way, something of the community life they first formed in the monastery, living together in groups and trying to work out some sort of rule for themselves. This, to me, is very significant. The chances of their getting anywhere are perhaps not too good: there is great risk of their merely getting lost in the shuffle. But I think they should be considered as still forming part, however marginal, of a "Monastic Order" and someone should be interested in helping them out. In other words, the communities to which they formerly belonged should perhaps consider them as still part of the family in some way, and remain in fruitful dialogue with them. I mean by that a two-sided dialogue from which both sides might conceivably learn something useful! This is an area in which I think a great deal needs to be done, at least in the way of exploration.

Another area of importance is suggested by the relatively many nuns in cloistered orders who want lives of greater solitude and *more* contemplation (as opposed to merely "opening up" and getting more involved). Perhaps not all these aspirations are genuine calls to solitude—many may be illusory. But nevertheless there may be something developing here. What is to be done about it? I feel that this is a matter for study and concern.

Once again I am saddened by the death of an old friend. Sy Freedgood died tragically in mid-January when his house on Long Island burned down in the middle of the night. Sy had suffered from a bad case of bursitis, and was taking a lot of medicine. It is believed he was too doped to get out of the fire in time: or perhaps he had a heart attack in trying to escape. He was one of the editors of *Fortune* magazine, and in the past had published a few brilliant stories in *Harper's* about his Jewish grandmother. He was one of my oldest and best friends from Columbia days, and it was through him that I met the Hindu monk Bramachari who was so influential in my own life. Someone remarked rightly that though he seemed outwardly a sardonic and agnostic person, Sy was always obsessed with ideas of God that could never be articulated. Pray for him.

Going back to a subject I touched on above: people ask if, now that we have a new Abbot, I will be able to "get out" more. Will I be able to visit campuses and engage in conferences, dialogue, etc.? The policy of the Order has not changed in these matters. Some monks, it is true, seem to think it is very important for us to get more publicly involved in things.

For my own part, I do not think that even if it were possible for me, I would be justified in going around appearing in public, or semi-public, and giving talks. I feel it would not be consistent with my real vocation. The fact of having a "public" existence as a writer is already enough of an exception. It seems to me that travelling around, talking, and appearing before large groups of people would be playing an unreal and useless role—for me. Others have a mission to do that kind of thing. I definitely do not, and I would feel it was a dishonest sort of gimmick on my part. A man cannot do everything and one's choices are after all limited. I am committed to a life of solitude and meditation which I hope I can share with others by a certain amount of writing. And that is about it. I am less and less inclined to try to sell anybody a line, even in writing. For that reason, the book *Cables to the Ace*, which New Directions is bringing out this spring, may baffle a lot of readers. It is obscure and indirect. Perhaps some of the younger ones will intuitively pick up some of the short-hand. It does not preach. It does not have a "message". Maybe most of you better steer clear of it.

Later in the summer Notre Dame Press plans to bring out *Faith and Violence*. The title indicates that it is a tract for the times. It will make a lot of people very mad. I don't claim to have final answers to contemporary problems: just opinions, which are subject to modification. And maybe by the time the book is out I will have changed many of them myself.

I have already said more than I intended. God bless you. I appreciate your friendship and your communications. Keep well. May your understanding of life deepen, may your freedom grow strong, may you be more and more independent of the forces that try to dominate and standardize our lives in massive futility. May you grow in love, may you have joy!

Easter 1968

As I write this there is snow on the ground from a blizzard we had the other day, but the sun is bright, the birds are singing, and Easter is on the way. This letter is early. Mail has continued to pile up. More and more requests come in for me to go somewhere and talk (all of which have to be refused). More and more letters I can't answer personally.

Some of the recent questions concern the ongoing debate about the validity of the religious life. Some theologians have frankly stated that the cloistered life is not and cannot be even "Christian." Obviously, for people who have laid their lives on the line in the sense that they have sincerely "offered them to God" in monasteries and convents, and have made considerable sacrifices to be true to what they felt was a serious commitment, it might be a little upsetting to be told that they have not only wasted their efforts but have even been dishonest and unchristian.

In my opinion, when the argument is pushed that far it becomes unchristian itself. Simply to condemn and excommunicate people out of hand, without any sympathy for the fundamentally generous fidelity they have shown in a demanding situation, is not much evidence of Christian love! Much of the criticism of religious life shows not only a justifiable impatience with archaic modes of life but also an unjustifiable contempt for human beings who have identified themselves, in good faith, with those modes of life.

I have frankly said, myself, that a completely medieval style of monastic life is finished. On the other hand, when I wrote *The Waters of Siloe* twenty years ago, I was aware of certain basic values in medieval monasticism. Those values were real, even though they might not be precisely what we need to renew in the Church of the twentieth century. It is important not to repudiate them, even though we happen to be looking for something different ourselves. It would be a real impoverishment if we were to be completely insensitive to the real vitality and creativity of twelfth-century monasticism. But the impression one gets from critics today is that the *entire past* has to be repudiated *in all its aspects*. It was *all* irrelevant: more than that it was *all* "gnostic," "manichean," "jansenistic," or tainted with some other heresy. If the argument is pressed to its logical conclusion we would have to admit that the Church ceased to be Christian seventeen hundred years ago.

It would be utterly dishonest for me to claim that when I first came to Gethsemani the place was not for me a "sign of Christ." It *was*, in spite of all the shortcomings I instinctively realized. We who entered cloistered orders ten, fifteen and twenty-five years ago were certainly chilled by the sense that there was something warped and inhuman about it. We were not totally blind and stupid. We knew that we were getting into something hard, even unreasonably hard. But we also knew that this counted for very little in comparison with something else which in our case was decisive. We believed that we were really called by God to do this, to entrust ourselves to him in this peculiar form of life, to enter into it believing in His word and in His promise: that this was one way of being a completely dedicated Christian, taking up one's Cross, and living as a disciple of Christ. It is true that we were told absurd things, made to behave with a stupid and artificial formality, and put through routines that now, as we look back, seem utterly incredible. How did we ever stomach such atrocious nonsense?

It must even be admitted that the climate of Catholic spirituality, perhaps especially in contemplative orders, has been infected with a theology that is in some ways pathological, in some ways heretical. Certainly the cloistered life has proved for many to be unhealthy, both physically and mentally. We carry deep wounds which will prevent us from ever forgetting it. To this extent, we are all able to agree fully with the critics. There is something deeply unchristian about the way in which the monastic life is sometimes interpreted and "enforced." We have all seen things done which still make us shudder. Nor are we perhaps entirely through with them!

On the other hand, the injustices, the distortions, the inhumanities of the secular life are incomparably worse (so we feel) even though they may to some seem acceptably "painless" (or even enjoyable). Thus we—I speak for myself and others like me who have stayed put in spite of the fact that we have seen good reasons not to—repeatedly renewed our initial choice. Though we may have shed one illusion after another and gone deeper and deeper into the radical questioning of our life and our vocation, we have nevertheless elected to stay put with it because we have continued to believe that this was what God asked of us. We have simply not seen any alternative that seemed to us better. Admittedly I would hate to write a book extolling the monastic vocation today, and would be very slow to urge anyone else to enter it as it now is. What matters to me is not the monastic life but God and the Gospel—as exemplified by these words of St. Paul from the Easter liturgy: "Since you have been brought back to true life with Christ, you must look for the things that are in heaven, where Christ is sitting at God's right hand. Let your thoughts be on heavenly things, not on the things that are on earth, because you have died and now the life you have is hidden with Christ in God. But when Christ is revealed—and he is your life—you too will be revealed in glory with him." According to the critics I have been citing, St. Paul would seem to be a Gnostic, a Manichean, a Jansenist! . . .

May Easter bring you peace and inner strength. The world badly needs peace—and may not get it. One gets the feeling that difficult times are ahead for everyone: certain problems are so great and so complex that they seem to have no human solution. But the peace of God "which surpasses all understanding" can be the ground of unexpected solutions. Let us remain in that peace, or at least let us desire to, and try to.

Paschal Time 1968

My Easter letter was written a couple of weeks before Easter, and it is of course not much use my sending out now a letter that talks about blizzards. And there is more need than ever for a circular letter to take care of all the many letters that I am completely unable to answer. I thank all of you who have written. I try in these circular letters to take up some of the questions I am asked, but I cannot always do so.

First of all, the tragic death of Dr. Martin Luther King coincided in a significant way with Passiontide and Easter this year. I was in rather close touch with these events as Dr. King had been tentatively planning to make a retreat here before the "Poor People's March." The day before his death a friend of his and mine [June J. Yungblut] wrote from Atlanta:

"Martin is going to Memphis today; he is going cold into a hot situation, and I wish he were going to Gethsemani instead . . ." But it is evident that Dr. King was expecting something and went to meet it with his eyes open. His final speech was certainly prophetic in its way. I believe he felt the best thing he could do would be to lay down his life not only for the Black people but for the whole country. He always hoped to preserve the country from senseless violence that would be merely destructive, and may have hoped that sacrifice of his life would bring home to people the need for a fully Christian solution of the grave problems we all face. I believe the Black people understood this better than the white. Too many whites think that non-violence may be all right for Negroes but see no reason to practice it themselves. And of course non-violence has been to some extent abandoned and discredited. It should be remembered that in the rioting that has happened and will continue to happen, there is always violence on *two* sides. Few people seem to realize that most of those killed in riots are Negroes killed by whites, and not the other way round.

Since this assassination the race situation in this country is probably worse, and we do not yet know what the summer will bring: but there is no point in letting ourselves be governed by fear. If we think in terms of objective rights and wrongs, we will see that the Negroes of this country are still trying to get what is due to them, and though the mass media try to make a sensational story out of everything, and thereby distort the perspective, we still must try to look at things as they are.

I will not burden you with my views on the presidential election, it is far too early for that. Like everyone else, I heard with relief that Johnson did not intend to run—or said he didn't. I presume Humphrey is Johnson's candidate, which means I won't vote for *him*, anyhow.

Rather than waste time talking about public events, I have another personal loss to record. In New Zealand, just before Easter, one of my aunts, my father's sister [Agnes Gertrude Stonehewer Merton (1889–1968), whom Merton called "Aunt Kit"], was lost in a disastrous shipwreck. She was on the *Wahine*, which sank in a typhoon just outside Wellington harbor. Of all my remaining relatives she was perhaps the one who was in fact closest to me—the only one with whom I was able to correspond more or less regularly. She had visited me here at the Abbey, four years ago. I was told that survivors said she was very courageous in the wreck, and before the ship was abandoned, went around trying to encourage and help others. The rescue efforts and equipment were very inadequate, many life rafts capsized, and an investigation is being held to find out why more was not done about it (few ships and planes were sent to help, when it all took place in view of land). Please pray for her.

It may interest some of you to know that I have recently had a chance to write an introduction to an important book on Zen Buddhism [*The*

Last of the Patriarchs: The Recorded Sayings of Shen-Hui, edited by Richard S. Y. Chi], a series of texts of a Chinese Zen Master, Shen Hui, to be published next year by the University of Indiana Press. As you know I am very interested in dialogue between Christianity and Asian religions, especially Buddhism. Also for almost a year I have been lecturing on Sufism, the mystical side of Islam, to the monks here. It is very revealing. For a long time Christians have too readily assumed that other religions had little "depth." This is entirely wrong. I think today we need to be more aware than we are of the real depth of the other major religions and the "mystical" side of their experience. Especially is this true when in some ways it can be said that the Western trend is toward activism and lack of depth. As one who came thirty years ago to the Catholic Church because I sought something deep and substantial which was not evident in ordinary secular and academic life, I can say it is an illusion for Catholics to try to "appeal" to the world of our time by merely reflecting its own attitudes and obsessions—especially when the reflection is something like the kind you get in a fun-house mirror. The "world," unfortunately, is just not interested in this, in fact less interested than in the image of a Church that is totally "different." The more I see of certain efforts at creating a "new image" of the Church, the less I am interested. Genuine progress must take place on a much deeper level—and will doubtless do so.

As Pentecost draws near, let us reflect a little on the reality of the Spirit who is truly given to us as to a Church that is called to be in every sense prophetic and eschatological: a sign of Christ which is at once a sign of supreme hope and a sign of contradiction. We all have work to do if we are to measure up to this vocation.

Midsummer 1968

. . . Several magazines asked me to write something concerning the assassination of Robert Kennedy. I refused because I am a bit suspicious of what seems to me to be a growing ritual cycle: murder, public acts of contrition, deploring violence, gestures of appeasement, then everything goes on unchanged and presently there is another assassination. The cycle continues. The sickness seems to be so deep that ritual expressions of sorrow, horror, astonishment, etc., have just become part of a general routine. At such a time perhaps silence is more decent. Certainly the sense of shock is real. People are indeed horrified by the fact that nothing is safe, and that the *least safe* are the people, the values, that we admire, love and rely on the most. In a word we are beginning to sense in our society a tendency to harm and to destroy the very things we claim to need and admire. The Kennedys (for all that they had enemies and critics) did offer something of an image of what Americans like and approve of:

what they identify with. The fact that this is precisely what is most menaced, and menaced from *inside our society*, not outside it, is what is significant. It is not enough to say that the assassins of both Kennedys were in some sense "unamerican." They emerged from a society which made their crime easy. In the case of Dr. King, evidence seems to suggest that there was indeed a conspiracy and that the assassin was after money that had been explicitly *offered* to anyone who would get Dr. King out of the way. In any event, this is my comment: the problem of violence in our society is now critical, and it is not just a problem of a few psychopaths or rebels. The violence that threatens us to the point of possible self-destruction is endemic in the whole of society, and more especially in the establishment itself, the military, the police, the established forces of "order"—they are all infected with a mania for overkill, rooted in fear. The future promises an era of force, suspicion, terrorism with more or less futile acts of protest, violently repressed. Unless we get some really intelligent and creative leadership, our future as a democracy is not bright.

Then of course many ask me about my good friends, Fathers Dan and Phil Berrigan. To many, their acts of protest have seemed incomprehensible, wild, extreme. Well, I think they were intentionally "extreme," though they remained in essence non-violent. They were intentionally provocative. Both Dan and Phil believe that as Christians they must protest against a futile and immoral war to the point where they are jailed for protest—or else stop the war. This goes pretty far, I admit. It shocks, and is intended to shock. Perhaps the point will never get across to some people, it may be too shocking. All I'd like to say is this: I noticed very little, if any, shock at all when a Catholic bishop had the droll effrontery to speak of the Vietnam war as an act of Christian love. CHRISTIAN LOVE! It seems to me that this fantastic concept of what the New Testament is all about ought to have shocked a lot more people than it did. No, it was accepted as a bit strange, perhaps, but "normal." Well, because it has become "normal" to regard war—any war demanded by the military—as Christian duty, Christian love, Christian virtue, that a few like the Berrigans, in their desperation, try to show by extreme protest that it is not normal at all.

My own position is somewhere in between. It just seems to me that the Selective Service Law, which allows the military to demand the lives of young Americans for a dubious adventure in Asia, should not be on the books at all. It should be abolished, by the normal political means. In this I am not "far-out" at all, and I would note that there are many conservatives who share my opinion. In the atomic era (no matter what one may think of the bomb, it's there and it "deters"), we have absolutely no ground for saying that we need the draft for defense. It is being used to interfere in the affairs of other nations that we do not even understand.

I apologize for insisting on these points. If I do so, it is mainly in order to let you know where I stand myself, since a lot of people are wondering. Sooner or later I hope I can make things clear enough so that I will not have to continue "clarifying." I am against war, against violence, against violent revolution, for peaceful settlement of differences, for non-violent but nevertheless radical change. Change is needed, and violence will not really change anything: at most it will only transfer power from one set of bull-headed authorities to another . . .

But the problems of man can never be solved by political means alone. Over and over again the Church has said that the forgetfulness of God and of prayer are at the root of our trouble. This has been reduced to a cliché. But it is nevertheless true. And I realize more and more that in my own vocation what matters is not comment, not statements of opinion, not judgments, but prayer. Let us pray for one another and try in everything to do what God asks of us. My best regards to all of you.

Fall 1968 [September]

. . . I have been asked to attend two meetings in Asia, one of them a meeting of the Abbots of Catholic Monastic Orders in that area, the other an interfaith meeting with representatives of Asian religions. I will be spending some time in at least two Asian monasteries of our Order, to help out there, and will doubtless be invited to others. Considering the crucial importance of the time, the need for monastic renewal, the isolation and helplessness of our Asian monasteries, their constant appeals for help, I feel it a duty to respond. And I hope this will also enable me to get in contact with Buddhist monasticism and see something of it first hand. The length of my stay in Asia is indeterminate. Needless to say, this is not anything unusual in the monastic life. I ask your prayers for the success of this undertaking: and of course, please do not believe anything that rumor may add to this simple scenario.

I am certainly grateful to those who have contributed something toward paying my way, and especially to those who have helped me in making contacts. Outstanding among them has been Dom Aelred Graham O.S.B., who last year visited many religious centers in Asia and has been most generous and helpful in sharing with me the fruits of his experience.

By the time you receive this letter I hope to be on the way. It is understandable that I cannot undertake to answer any requests about writing articles, prefaces, or to give out statements on this or that. It will be impossible for me to think of keeping in touch with political issues, still less to comment on them or to sign various petitions, protests etc. Even though the need for them may be even greater: but will they by now have lost any usefulness? Has the signing of protests become a pointless exercise? In any case, anything I do on this trip will be absolutely non-political. I have no intention of going anywhere near Vietnam.

I have no special plans for immediate new writing, though perhaps this trip will be very significant in that regard. However, I am leaving more than one manuscript . . . and I trust they will appear in print in due course [*The Geography of Lograire, Sensation Time at the Home and Other New Poems, Day of a Stranger, A Vow of Conversation (Diary 1964–1965); and The Climate of Monastic Prayer*].

Once again, let me say I appreciate the loyalty of so many old friends and the interest of new ones. I shall continue to feel bound to all of you in the silence of prayer. Our real journey in life is interior: it is a matter of growth, deepening, and of an ever greater surrender to the creative action of love and grace in our hearts. Never was it more necessary for us to respond to that action. I pray we may all do so generously. God bless you.

Asian Letter—November 9, 1968 [*New Delhi, India*]

This newsletter is not a reply to mail because I have not been getting mail on this Asian trip . . . I have received permission to be absent from my monastery for several months, chiefly because I was invited to attend a meeting of Asian Catholic abbots in Bangkok and give a talk there. Since this gave me an opportunity to be in Asia, I have been permitted to extend the trip a little in order to learn something about Asian monasticism, especially Buddhist. I will be visiting our Cistercian monasteries in Indonesia, Hong Kong, and Japan, and giving some talks there. Apart from that, the trip is not concerned with talking but with learning and with making contact with important people in the Buddhist monastic field. I am especially interested in Tibetan Buddhism and in Japanese (possibly Chinese) Zen. (Maybe there are still some Chinese Ch'an [Zen] centers in Taiwan.) I hope to see John Wu in Taiwan.

I am writing this in New Delhi, the capital of India, an impressive city which I like very much. My first contact with India was at Calcutta, which, no matter how prepared you may be, is always a shock. The poverty and misery are overwhelming there—and even more so in rural India. Some towns are indescribable. This morning I went to put a small coin into the hands of a beggar and saw he was a leper whose fingers had been eaten away . . . It's like that. People sleep in the streets—some have never had a house to live in. People die in the streets. In Calcutta you walk out the front door of your hotel on the "best" street in the city and find a cow sleeping on the sidewalk. I rather like the cows wandering around. They make the Asian traffic more interesting.

Bangkok was the worst place for traffic I ever saw; no lights, you just step on the gas and race five hundred other cars to the crossing. The main rule of Asian driving seems to be: never use the brake, just lean on the horn. It is wildly exciting. Especially in the Himalayas, where you whiz around corners at dizzy heights and speeds and meet these huge buses coming the other way painted to look like dragons. Usually the road is just about one lane wide anyway, but somehow one manages. I am still alive.

I don't want to waste time and paper in gossip. The main point of this letter is to tell you something about my contacts with Tibetan mysticism and my meeting with the Dalai Lama in his new headquarters, high on a mountain at Dharamsala, which is an overnight train trip from Delhi, up in the Himalayas. (The Himalayas are the most beautiful mountains I have ever seen. There is something peculiar about the light there, a blue and a clarity you see nowhere else.) I spent eight days at Dharamsala making a kind of retreat, reading and meditating and meeting Tibetan masters. I had three long interviews with the Dalai Lama and spoke also with many others.

The Dalai Lama is the religious head of the Tibetan Buddhists and also in some ways their temporal leader. As you know, he had to escape from Tibet in 1959 when the Chinese Communists took over his country. There are many Tibetan refugees living in tents in the mountains, and many also forming colonies on tea plantations. I have seen monastic communities on these plantations. The Dalai Lama is much loved by his people, and they are the most prayerful people I have seen. Some of them seem to be praying constantly, and I don't mean monks, lay people. Some always have rosaries in their hands (counting out Buddhist mantras), and I have seen some with prayer wheels. It is customary in the West to laugh at prayer wheels, but the people I have seen using them looked pretty recollected to me. They were obviously deep in prayer and very devout.

The Dalai Lama is thirty-three years old, a very alert and energetic person. He is simple and outgoing and spoke with great openness and frankness. He is in no sense what you would expect of a political emigre, and the things he said about Communism seemed to me to be fair and objective. His real interests are monastic and mystical. He is a religious leader and scholar, and also a man who has obviously received a remarkable monastic formation. We spoke almost entirely about the life of meditation, about *samadhi* (concentration), which is the first stage of meditative discipline and where one systematically clarifies and recollects his mind. The Tibetans have a very acute, subtle, and scientific knowledge of "the mind" and are still experimenting with meditation. We also talked of higher forms of prayer, of Tibetan mysticism (most of which is esoteric and kept strictly secret), especially comparing Tibetan mysticism with Zen. In either case the highest mysticism is in some ways quite "simple"— but always and everywhere the Dalai Lama kept insisting on the fact that one could not attain anything in the spiritual life without total dedication, continued effort, experienced guidance, real discipline, and the combination of wisdom and method (which is stressed by Tibetan mysticism). He was very interested in our Western monasticism and the questions he asked about the Cistercian life were interesting. He wanted to know about the vows, and whether the vows meant that one became committed to a "high attainment" in the mystical life. He wanted to know if one's vows constituted an initiation into a mystical tradition and experience under a qualified master, or were they just "equivalent to an oath"—a kind of agreement to stick around. When I explained the vows, then he still wanted to know what kind of attainment the monks might achieve and if there were possibilities of a deep mystical life in our monasteries. I said well, that is what they are supposed to be for, but many monks seem to be interested in something else . . . I would note, however, that some of the monks around the Dalai Lama complain of the same things our monks do: lack of time, too much work, inability to devote enough time to meditation, etc. I don't suppose the Dalai Lama has much time on his hands, but in the long talks we had on meditation I could see that he has certainly gone very thoroughly and deeply into it and is a man of high "attainment." I have also met many other Tibetans who are very far advanced in a special type of Tibetan contemplation which is like Zen and is called *dzogchen*.

At this point in the letter I was interrupted, and went out to meet a Cambodian Buddhist monk who has been running a small monastery in India for years. He is of the Theravada (Southern or Hinayana) tradition, different from the Tibetan. Here too the emphasis is on disciplining the mind and knowing it inside out. But the methods are simpler than the Tibetan ones and go less far. He told me that the best monks in the Theravada tradition are in Burma and Thailand. In fact I did see a monastery in Bangkok and met a very interesting English Buddhist monk [Phra Khantipalo] who has a great reputation for scholarship and fervor among the Thais. He was just about to withdraw to one of the "forest wats" or small eremitical meditation monasteries in the northern jungles of Thailand where the best masters are found. These are almost completely unknown to Westerners.

One of the most interesting people I have met is a young Tibetan abbot who, since escaping from Tibet, has been trained at Oxford and has started a small monastery in Scotland. He is very successful there, apparently, and is a talented man. He has written a book called *Born in Tibet* about his experiences in escaping. I recommend it. His name is Chogyam Trungpa Rimpoche.

I have also had some contact with the Sufi tradition (Moslem), which has penetrated India in the Delhi area (which used to be capital of the Mogul empire and is still quite Moslem). I met an expert on Sufism who told me of the meetings at which the Sufis of this area use singing to induce contemplation, but I have not been to any of them. I do hope to hear some singing of this type in Urdu at a local restaurant where it is featured on weekends. The food here by the way is wild, it is a positive menace. For the most part I try to stick to Chinese food rather than Indian, which is (for me at least) lethal.

In summary: I can say that so far my contacts with Asian monks have been very fruitful and rewarding. We seem to understand one another very well indeed. I have been dealing with Buddhists mostly, and I find that the Tibetans above all are very alive and also generally well trained. They are wonderful people. Many of the monasteries, both Thai and Tibetan, seem to have a life of the same kind that was lived, for instance, at Cluny in the Middle Ages: scholarly, well trained, with much liturgy and ritual. But they are also specialists in meditation and contemplation. This is what appeals to me most. It is invaluable to have direct contact with people who have really put in a lifetime of hard work in training their minds and liberating themselves from passion and illusion. I do not say they are all saints, but certainly they are men of unusual quality and depth, very warm and wonderful people. Talking with them is a real pleasure. For instance, the other day one of the lamas, at the end of our meeting, composed a poem for me in Tibetan, so I composed one for him (in English), and we parted on this note of traditional Asian monastic courtesy. There is much more I could write about: the rich art, music, etc. But it would get too involved.

I hope you will understand why I cannot answer my mail these days. I am entirely occupied with these monastic encounters and with the study and prayer that are required to make them fruitful. I hope you will pray for me and for all those I will be meeting. I am sure the blessing of God will be upon these meetings, and I hope much mutual benefit will come from them. I also hope I can bring back to my monastery something of the Asian wisdom with which I am fortunate to be in contact—but it is something very hard to put into words.

I wish you all the peace and joy in the Lord and an increase of faith: for in my contacts with these new friends I also feel consolation in my own faith in Christ and His indwelling presence. I hope and believe He may be present in the hearts of all of us.

IV.

To Some Special Friends

To Dr. Mahanambrata Brahmachari

*Our oldest chum Bramachari, geworfen in the neun-
zehnten jahrhundert.*
MERTON TO FREEDGOOD
JULY 1, 1965

*Merton has told the story of his meeting with Brahmachari and of his influence
in his autobiography,* The Seven Storey Mountain. *They never met again, but in
1965 Merton sent Brahmachari in Calcutta, India, a copy of his book* Seeds of
Destruction. *Brahmachari responded with a thank-you letter in which he said:
"Let us meet again in old age and exchange ideas. How would you like it, Tom?"
He also asked Merton to pay his passage to the United States, where he said he
could "live in your monastery to share spiritual communion with your good self."
Merton's answer is his only surviving letter to Brahmachari. Though the correct
spelling is Brahmachari, Merton and his friends (including Michael Mott and
others) invariably spelled it "Bramachari."*

August 8, 1965

It was a delight to get your letter dated May 28th, and I am sorry
to see that so long a time has passed before my answer. I have been
thinking about some way to get you here, and have still not come up with
a practical answer. However, there are one or two possibilities. I am in
contact with a couple of people who would be able to get some university
interested in having you come. The great problem would be in paying
your passage. But there must surely be all kinds of ways and means of
obtaining this from some foundation. However, I am so out of contact
with all this that I am not able to work at it very effectively.

There is one other problem. I have finally received permission to
enter upon a kind of *vanaprastha* retirement in the forest and one of the
conditions would be that I would have only very rare visits. I have asked

my Superior to make an exception so that I could see you, but it would be only a short visit of a day or two, he said. Even this, however, would be of great worth. I would love to see you again and there are many things indeed we could talk about. There is no question that the mysterious ways of providence manifested themselves in our encounter thirty years ago, and I wonder what you have been doing since then. Last year I met someone who knew you, a journalist from Calcutta.

I have written to Seymour [Freedgood] about your project. He ought to have contact with the kind of people who would know what to do to get you over here. I will mention the idea to others. I think probably the most practical thing would be to get you involved in some lecturing. Would that interest you? There are also meetings of East–West philosophers in Hawaii, which might get you half way here. I can try to find out about them.

In any case, let us keep your project in mind and I will work on it as best I can. I am not sixty yet only fifty. I have hardly been out of the monastery at all for twenty-four years, and have very little contact with what goes on in this country, see very few people, but I still have quite a lot of correspondence, in fact more than I can adequately handle, which explains why it sometimes takes time for me to get a letter answered.

God bless you always, and I hope that perhaps next year some time we will be able to get together. It would indeed be a great grace.

To Seymour Freedgood

My thoughts naturally turn to my old chums, so utterly
geworfen.
MERTON TO FREEDGOOD
JULY 1, 1965

Seymour "Sy" Freedgood (1915–68) had been Merton's classmate at Columbia. Edward Rice says in The Man in the Sycamore Tree: *"Seymour Freedgood, one of Merton's closest friends, liked to appear mysterious and daring. He lived in a world of deep, dark secrets and undercover acts, which nobody, particularly Seymour, took at all seriously." Freedgood attended Merton's ordination in May 1949. He later became an editor of* Fortune *magazine. He and Merton thought of meeting in New York during Merton's June 1964 visit to engage in conversation with D. T. Suzuki, but Merton apparently obeyed his abbot's strict instructions to see none of his old friends. Freedgood visited Merton at Gethsemani in March 1967. He died in the fire when his home burned in January 1968.*

February 25, 1950

Father Abbot [James Fox] gave me your letter to answer. There is a statute of the General Chapter forbidding movies to be taken in our monasteries. Also, after the centenary, everybody is thoroughly fed up with pictures. So there is nothing that can be done about the idea—sorry. It is a good idea all right and it would be very good with all the fellows working on it. But—

Forgive me for waiting so long to answer. I only get a small part of the week for answering letters and therefore I am weeks behind with everything. I have a secretary who mails out the "Trappists-no-write-letters" card to the fans, but he doesn't help me make a dent in the pile of real business.

Will you thank John Fischer at *Harper's* for sending the Alexis Carrel book? I haven't read it all but I have glanced at it and want to persuade Father Abbot to have it read in the refectory. It looks quite good. There is mention of a certain Dom Alexis, abbot of Boquen, in the introduction. I'll tell you all about him some time. He has started a reform which may or may not be just an experiment in archeology.

A Sanskrit scholar in New Delhi writes to me about Panjatali's Yoga. The Carmelites in France are putting out magazines that are a lot of fun, with a lot of things about mysticism in the Greek Orthodox Church. Have you ever seen a magazine called *Dieu Vivant*? Publishes all kinds of people Jesuits and Karl Barth side by side in a way that is very encouraging. It is a very good magazine. Got an article coming out in a magazine called *Cross and Crown*, about the primacy of the contemplative life maybe you would like ["The Primacy of Contemplation"]. I'll try to get you an extra copy. And I wrote to Dan Walsh not to make speeches about me which goes more or less for everybody: I mean formal speeches at banquets. Dan Walsh has made himself tired with this type of speech.

Did you know I got a job teaching? Seventy students novices and young professed. Course for all of them called "Orientation in the Contemplative Life" and course for some of them called "Mystical Theology." Busy . . .

January 2, 1964

Got your letter in August and went to the hospital soon after it with a bad back because the pixies have chewed a piece out of one of my vertebrae. This is not comfortable to live with. I have not heard from Bramachari but will write to him some time. There is really nothing I can do but give him the address of a Catholic hospital in those parts and that is probably useless.

Shall I meet you at the old West End Cafeteria? I have been mulling this over, but I guess a conversation about Tao is not enough to warrant excommunication (for me, not for you). As for coming down here, later I will flash a signal on that one, but right now I don't know what the plans may be for the year. I have a tendency to get enmeshed in a group of Ecumenical folk from various places around here like Vanderbilt and this eats into the time that is necessary for me to tie my shoes and think and rather not think. Later when they have evaporated I can think twice about the signal. Watch for smoke, not in the shape of a mushroom cloud.

Instead of that let me put into an envelope various curiosities that emerge from the hutch here, and among them you may find something that will please you and Anne [Freedgood's second wife]. And as for her and the Doubleday Anchor books, by all means send Anchor books. You might know that I have ended by getting interested in people like Jaspers, Sartre, Merleau Ponty, Rudolf Bultmann. I do not wish to disedify you beyond measure with this, and I am not too involved. But I like them. We must take a broad view. Max Weber I liked plenty. This is the kind of thing that helps an aging monk.

I hear from [Bob] Lax who is hopping from one Greek Island writing one-word poems. I tell you what, I will send you my own poems.

This is Happy New Year of the Dragon, Dragon shall lead the dance of the New Year and shall shower pennies upon *Fortune* as well as Doubleday. But for me and the publishing business we are, to say the least, at odds.

July 1, 1965

As I gradually approach the terminus of my latest work, *The Metaphysical Footnote*, now running to 876 pages, and as I set my pen to the epilogue which is entitled "Must we now at last come to terms with Geworfenheit?" my thoughts naturally turn to my old chums, so utterly geworfen. In fact, the real reason for this letter is our oldest chum Bramachari, geworfen in the neunzehnten jahrhundert, which as we all know was a hell of a time to get geworfen or geboren or to have one's dasein gefunden in gelassenheit. But it was of course not so bad in India (father burning etc.).

Now here is the question. From Bramachari I have unexpectedly received a letter, and he proposes to come to America. But this time he does not intend to swim. The only way I can think of getting him here is to have some institution or foundation detach itself from some funds in order to pay his way in return for lectures or something. Maybe the State Department could invite him in as an agent from outer space or something. But as you know I am utterly innocent of these machinations, engrossed as I am exclusively in my metaphysical footnote and the epilogue. Or to be more exact the concluding transient eclogue postscript which has as its title "Must we not now at last etc. . . ."

You on the other hand could perhaps invite him to write an exhaustive study of the cotton gin for *Fortune*, thereby sweeping the journalistic field clean of novelties.

If you have any ideas as to how to get our old chum back into our midst (waterwings) please let me know. He speaks naturally of coming here, perhaps to join. At that time you too might join. It would do you good. Or else you might finally make that visit and we could all together put the concluding metaphysical flourish to the epilogue.

Man told me the other day a long and exhausting story of how he got a gold diviner here to find Indian gold, and set him up on every hill and down in every hollow and the gold diviner couldn't divine one damn thing excepting guess what, Fort Knox. So now this man says he is waiting until they get the gold finally out of Fort Knox (they are taking it away piece by piece he says and putting uranium in its place—fissionable of course). When they get the gold out he is going to get the gold diviner back and once again go to work on that Indian gold. That will undoubtedly provide a footnote to the flourish of the epilogue. Love to you and Anne. How are the Polish poets going?

January 10, 1967

I am writing to inquire about a subversive outfit in your building and perhaps even right under your desk. What about Time-Life Books? What about a project of a huge illustrated interfaith antifaith profaith Bible? Abraham Heschel than whom there can be no better has got me roped in to considering this fool project and writing a huge illiterate introduction to vol. 1 which in itself [is] the introduction to vols. 2–300. A man called Russell Bourne is after me about it. What is your candid opinion of this subversive outfit and its activities, especially this monster Bible illustrated with vignettes by Henry Luce? Can I participate in this without entirely losing my honor as a foe of all that is decent?

Needless to say I know nothing about the subject. I am entirely and fanatically devoted to the *Book of Mormon* alone, and to no other source of revelation. I am constructing a laborious new theology based on the *Book of Mormon* alone. My warcry will be "Polygamy for priests". You will see how I will go them all one better. As to God I shall prove that he is not dead but red, and has defected from the CIA, with portentous consequences for the ethical decisions of the faithful.

Incidentally I wish to let you know in strict confidence that the CIA is now being infiltrated by agents of the CIA, as is in a state of gendarmerial schizophrenia. This bodes well for everybody. Please let me know your opinion of TIMLIFBKS.

Who are these Julias and Reepicheeps, these filmstars [Freedgood's daughter and her horse]? Why have I not been told before about your filmstar family? With touching pictures they have made my Christmas half human, softening the awful austerities of a life devoted to flagellation.

Anne wrote about Yevtushenko who wishes to join the monks. I accept him and will duly indoctrinate him in the *Book of Mormon* alone. Should I meet Vosneszensky next year she asks? I'll think about it, when I have read a bit of him. Does Anne have anything good in Anchor Bks about this yere Bible? Also I am working madly on Faulkner: has she got anything on him?

Take care of yourselves. All the best. Maybe this year would be a good one for you and me to discuss Tao. I thought if you wanted to come down we'd better do something about it before I get all booked up. Am still ok for March and then after May. Otherwise it is all Hindus, etc.

Freedgood wrote to Merton about "a possible meeting this spring to discuss the current state of the West End Cafeteria," their old hangout at Columbia.

February 4, 1902 [i.e., 1967]

Ok, I have wiped out all the tapes and have sunk a tugboat called the *Maine* in Havana harbor. This ought to quiet things down a bit.

With regard to Time-Life Bibles, I am not yet swallowed by Leviathan but almost. I have that is to say made the mistake of saying that I felt it was within the limits of my physical capacity to produce the article they desire, "I *could* do it . . ." which they have interpreted as meaning that I am flexing my muscles and getting right down to it. Frankly, though, I am not as opposed to the idea as I was before, and it would be no skin off'n my nose as they say. Too many other cats involved in it. If you are all going to yell at me to stop and turn back, do so now. I am waiting for what Naomi Burton [Stone] will say.

In a couple of weeks I go to the hospital to have my elbows peeled off. This is very unpleasant and in March I shall be all bandages until Naomi Burton comes here about the middle and after that is Easter. April is cluttered with Anglicans, but after that is plenty Tao, wide open freeways full of Tao in all directions. End of April begins to be wide open with Tao.

With my sick elbows you will not be able to teach me much karate that the doctors will not have done on me already. Thanks for your ever more concerned missives. I got them all. Let no one ever be disturbed in Time Inc. Let universal calm prevail. Yrs. in the shadow of Henry Luce.

February 13, 1967

I am horrified to hear how [John] Slate was set upon by Hells Angels in the Metro. The Metro ought to be locked up. Slate ought to ride only in helicopters. Where is Slate? I have received from him a heartfelt telegram of congratulations on my wounds when I was hit by Hells Angels in the Metro on my birthday, Jan. 31. Nobody is allowed to get a broken jaw on my birthday. The West End Cafeteria should be locked up once for all, it is the old age home of Gertrude Stein. Slate should have kept out of the West End Cafe in the first place. It is no place for a Gentleman of the Cloth such as Slate. He ought to be ashamed.

Yes I am going to the hospitals with my arm in a slang. But it is nothing, it is nothing, merely what I copped when I beat up Hells Angels in the Metro the other day as I was passing by my friend Slate. I am having an operation for purse on the elbow, since that is the only way the Dr. can get it. No I am only fooling he is an ideal Dr. and for the purse on the elbow he has nothing but serene contempt. Me too.

Now let's get straight: when are you coming down here on the wings of Tao? I ought to be out of the hosp. by March 1 and Naomi Burton is coming down to beat me back into the hosp. on March 15. Then is Easter when I ride in the Metro. After that the Anglicans. I am always surrounded by Anglicans immediately after Easter. After that a lull. Most of April is a pure lull, except for the 11th etc. when I am again surrounded by Anglicans all of them in bad standing. I too am in bad standing. How are you getting along with your Eglise? I am for locking up Englise myself. But c'est la vie.

Consider Vietnam: what is it but "Onward Christian Soldiers" graphically enacted according to the script written personally by New York's Card. Spillway. You are unlucky to be living in New York the place will probably be hit by something unpleasant.

Tell me where I can contact old Hamp Slate I want to send him a telegram informing him just why I have the measels. The programs he is getting through these wires is the real goods and he ought to be grateful. They are authentic inspirations from our Tantric center right here in Kentucky. I get messages every day from [Bob] Lax in Greece, who wouldn't be happy in Greece? Now I go sit in the sun. Tell me Slate's address so I can send him a crate of Trappist corn pone.

Freedgood visited Merton at Gethsemani, arriving all bandaged on March 16, having driven his car into a tree on the way from Louisville. He urged Merton "to get out and see things and meet people." They spent a day in Lexington. On April 5, John Slate visited Merton to advise him on setting up his literary trust.

April 12, 1967

Many thanks for your two letters and for the transcript of the tape. Thanks also for discussing the letter with the analyst. I recognize of course that the decision rests with me. As far as I am concerned, I know very well that if I make enough fuss I can pressure my superiors into letting me out of here in one way or another. On the other hand, since I tend to let off a certain amount of steam when talking about the system here, I may create the impression that I am eager to get out. I am not. Not that I want to spend the rest of my life in a kindergarten: but with the completely unique set up that I have now, I am absolved from the kindergarten and have things just as I like them. When I said I was interested in analysis, I meant that I realized it would be very useful for me: but not at the cost of having to leave here and live in a city. I have here what I want, and in a city I would have everything I don't want. It boils down more or less to that.

If I started being analyzed, I imagine the first thing the analyst would want to know would be why the hell I was such a damn fool as to leave something I had wanted and struggled for all my life, in order to pay him twenty-five dollars an hour to listen to my reasons for having wanted it. Thus far I can do my own analysis. I have what I want and I do not experience any kind of urge to reach out for something else, when I am reasonably sure that I could never get it so good anyplace else. I can live with my anxieties, which are the usual ones I guess most people have. Though I would gladly get to the root of them, I think I stand as much chance of doing so just sitting around here and figuring out my own problems for myself. The woods seem to be the best kind of therapy I have hit so far. At any rate I have moments of conscious happiness which are unusually frequent. In this day and age, I consider myself very fortunate.

Probably the best thing for me is to be visited and upbraided by well informed friends. When are you and Anne coming down? I enclose a note for Anne, about some poets she might want to publish. Slate's visit was very lively, and we will probably leave a literary estate that will confuse all law for centuries to come. I refer of course to the estate of Victor Hugo.

Freedgood formed an "organization" in 1967 called the National Institutes of Public Scolds, NIPS for short. It was intended to complain about bureaucratic red tape, absurdity, etc. He named Merton to the "NIPS Steering Committee" and eventually devised a letterhead for his "organization." After he had returned to New York from visiting Merton, he asked "Jack Heinz of the pickle factory" to send Abbot James Fox a parcel in payment for the car rental while he was in Kentucky. A Heinz truck arrived at the monastery and unloaded seventeen cases of Heinz products, containing all "57 varieties." The abbot was flabbergasted.

May 6, 1967

Thanks for the Nips blasts. The enclosed will show that I am doing my own small part [a letter to *The New York Times* about Lewis Mumford's book *The Myth of the Machine*].

Today is Derby Day. Louisville is full of surmise. What kind of race, they all say. Will it be the Negro Race vs the horse race? Or will Negroes race the horses? Or will the horses sit down in front of the Negroes? Or will the whites race the grandstand? (To see who will get the prize for immobility?) . . .

Thanks for the pickles, and by all means send the Abbot a pickle factory whenever you feel like it. What he needs is more factories. In a few days he is off to the moon, where our superiors always meet. They will make decisions. Saturn enters the Crab. The air is filled with fumes.

May 12, 1967

Thanks for bringing to my attention the momentous decision of Judge Milton Shalleck regarding topless cellists. The decision contains what I might call a nutshell aesthetic unequalled by Irwin Edman, and it brings to light one of the most crucial problems of modern art. "In no poem, no prose respected by the test of time have I read, in no valued oil, in no statue or bust have I seen either visually described or portrayed a picture of a nude or topless cellist in the act of playing the instrument." Volumes of commentary would not exhaust the rich content of this epic statement:

1) Respected by the test of time. Ah! But what about my ten volume lyrico-analytic postscript in poetic prose which I have just dashed off precisely in honor of topless cellists and of topless cellists ONLY. Obviously since it was written yesterday and had unfortunately been mislaid it cannot be said to have been respected as yet "by the test of time". But Time is on my side and on the side of topless cellos as we shall eventually discover. Judge Shellac will be forced to eat his words.

2) No *valued* oil. But the best oils are beyond value, invaluable. Such as banana oil, for instance, in which I have just painted a monumental fresco of twenty-five topless cellists inviting Pablo Casals to perform in the state of half undress referred to by Judge Shillings.

3) In no statue OR BUST. There he gives himself completely away. The precise bust in which the portrait of the topless cellist has been visually described is the bust of Miss Charlotte Moorman. Right in front of his nose, but his nose was buried in a twenty-five page document on legalistic aesthetics and he was unable to see it.

I have many other valuable insights to offer on this occasion but I must pass over the opportunity to deepen further the questions raised by Judge Moorman, the paintless shellac of our courthouse. Yours in the unfailing dyspepsia of NIPS.

On May 16, 1967, Freedgood asked Merton to attend a reception for Andrei Voznesensky. As Freedgood put it: "The Rusky has written to say he'd like very much to meet you but, as I understand it, Father Abbot doesn't like you to take trips (except, of course, LSD trips, which I trust you are wise enough not to undertake except under competent directions)."

May 17, 1967

. . . I have recently talked to the new Archbishop of Louisville [Thomas J. McDonough], a very open-minded and good sense type of person who is interested in finding solutions for the sort of problem you and I discussed when you were here. The outlook is perhaps hopeful.

Dan Walsh was ordained priest on Sunday amid singing telegrams from James Guttman and John Randall. Thanks for the Heinz correspondence. I shall be looking with interest at incoming foods, although in a recent visit to the allergist (when poked with a needle) a bright light went on in the middle of my back saying "beware of all fifty-seven varieties."

May 22, 1967

Thanks for the interesting clipping on Voznesensky. As a matter of fact, I would like to meet him too. If there is any possibility of his getting down here during his stay in the U.S., I hope it can be arranged. June would be a good time for me. Lately I have been a bit crowded due to Dan Walsh's ordination which turned into a ten day fiesta. However, as V. may be pretty crowded himself, I would be happy to have him come whenever he can. If he could manage to spend the day here, fine. Plenty of accommodations etc.

Merton wrote his last letter to Freedgood on the last day of 1967, a poignant letter, since Freedgood died in January 1968.

December 31, 1967

Happy New Year to you and Anne. Bumper crops. Derby winners for Julia. World champion polo for everybody. Swimming cups, Pimms No. 1, five definitive proofs for existence of Santa Claus etc. and world peace is finally assured (after the destruction of Asia).

What I mean is this: how are you, where are you, and indeed ARE you!? I heard you was ill, chap. Me in the dead of the night I wake up also with the pains, you know where so I guess we're all on the skids, but hoopla, like I say, let's win one more Polo Cup or something, after us the Delage, or perhaps the Citroen.

Let there be no more gaps in the ranks of old chums during 68. Slate, Reinhardt, all too big gaps. The mind boggles. [Bob] Lax is back, as you do/don't know. Is of course in Olean. Same old country club, etc.

Now here is something new. I am editing a magazine to be printed by monks (hence no 4-letter words) on offset press here it will be literary with poems and also with texts from Asian relig. etc. Would Anne have any Polish poets waiting around to bust into the prints who meanwhile could appear in the Dittograph Blues of 1968? I do as a matter of fact have a lot of good poets coming in (mostly because Jonathan Williams contacted them) it will maybe turn out a live magazine, all for free, all give away.

Need poets, short proses, Asian relig. texts, African proverbs, short quips by Wizz of Oz etc. Anything you can scare up will be welcomed with shouts. Happy New Year, joy, peace, polo, etc.

To John Howard Griffin

*I can think of nothing I would like more of you than for
you to get yourself good and well.*
MERTON TO GRIFFIN
MARCH 30, 1965

John Howard Griffin (1920–80) first met Merton while on a visit to Gethsemani in the early 1960s. They met thereafter on several occasions when Griffin visited and was on retreat at the monastery, the most notable of these being Jacques

Maritain's visit on October 6 and 7, 1966. Merton had read Griffin's Black Like Me *and the two became good friends, sharing many interests, including, eventually, photography. Griffin coached and helped Merton in his growing enthusiasm for taking pictures. After Merton's death Griffin was appointed his "official biographer," though he was unable, mostly because of his own increasingly poor health, to finish the biography. His* A Hidden Wholeness: The Visual World of Thomas Merton *was published in 1970 and two works on Merton were published posthumously,* The Hermitage Journals: A Diary Kept While Working on the Biography of Thomas Merton *(1981) and* Follow the Ecstasy: Thomas Merton, the Hermitage Years 1965–1968 *(1983).*

October 29, 1963

. . . Jacques [Maritain] cabled me today that he was happy with a preface I had written for Raissa's *Notes sur le Pater.* I have wanted to stop all prefaces, but this one last one for him was, I thought, necessary. He is such a great person and responds with such wonderful warmth to the least glimmer of truth, or friendship, or humanity. I think I owed it to him and Raissa. (When I say "last" preface it is perhaps exaggerated because I can see I am committed to a couple more, but I am going to have to say "no" a lot more often.) . . .

I suppose it is important for you people to stay there in the South— I mean the deep south. We have a young Franciscan priest from Bouras, La. entering here as a novice. He has seen a little of Confederate life in the raw, too. They tried to blow up his school. Who? The parishioners. Take care of yourself. There are limits. There is no virtue in ignoring them consistently.

December 4, 1964

It was good to hear from you again and above all thanks for the fantastic picture of Maritain. It is the best one of him I have ever seen. Splendid. I wish I could have seen him when he was in this country. I presume he is back in France now. Have owed him a letter for a long time, like everyone else. The mail has got beyond my grasp, and next year I am going to stop trying to answer most of it. Chances are that I will be living more in the cottage, am already there much more of the time now, but as a correlative they are asking me to cut out contacts, ecumenical dialogue with seminary students etc., and the mail will probably reach me only after much more sifting than it gets already . . .

I hear of you this way and that, you seem to be covering all points of the compass at once. I just signed up as a sponsor of this tithing thing that Donald Fraser, the Congressman, is getting up. It seems to make some sense. What do you think of it? Certainly we have to begin to find practical ways to do something about housing, besides protesting. By the way do you know anything of this young singer [Robert Laurence Williams]? I forget if I showed you the "Songs" but here they are, and here he is. We don't have a composer unfortunately. Any ideas?

P.S. Some time when you don't have ten million things to do, could you have someone do up three eight-by-elevens of that fine picture of me that first appeared in *Ramparts* with the "White Liberal" piece? The one looking down at the book? It is the one I like best. Fr. Abbot was upset about the one on cover of *Sign*.

March 30, 1965

Good to get your letter and to hear that you are more or less resting. This is just to say you are perfectly welcome to have any one of the drawings but how will you select it? I have some bad pictures of one or two, but the best are not photographed I think, or if they are they do not show up well. Will you be able to get to St. Louis in April? They are at Webster College there for part of the month. Actually none were sold in Milwaukee where the price was a hundred and fifty dollars. Now we are down to a hundred. If you wait until we crawl out of Santa Barbara, Cal. in September they will be ten cents apiece with a sheaf of green coupons into the bargain. I send you two useless photos of unsold pix for you to judge by. These are not the best, but they were photographed by the newsman because they seemed to have some sort of form he could recognize. The best ones would not attract his attention because they are the most nearly "formless".

What can you do for me? I can think of nothing I would like more of you than for you to get yourself good and well, and happily busy with batting out your best book ever. By the way the scholarship worked out beautifully, almost miraculously in a way. Fr. Abbot said the community would back it. Day after that in came a surprise gift of stock, just about the amount of capital needed for the fund. Right after that a little girl in Mississippi applied to Catherine Spalding College: first one ever applied from that state. We have our scholarship and our scholar, in fact it is two half scholarships and two scholars (the other is from Louisville). So everything is just fine.

July 11, 1965

I am delighted to hear that you are getting out a Reader. Splendid . . . But when are they going to stop cutting you up? Do keep well and take care of yourself. I hope the last operation was successful and that you will get a decent rest so that your body can knit itself back into one decent piece for a while. And then don't go tearing it apart again.

I had a trip to the hospital for some unpleasant tests but got away free, with a strong medicine to fight a gut infection. I have no intention of letting those guys carve me if I can bloody well help it . . .

November 16, 1966

Just heard from Jacques [Maritain] today. Marvelous about *Le Paysan* and the Mauriac review and the sales. I am so happy for him . . .

The contact sheets of the photos never came. Or rather I never got them. I don't quite know what happens to mail here but curious things do happen, and I hope the contact sheets were not lost, thrown away or whatever. Were they sent? Were you waiting for some kind of reaction? If they were not sent, then forget it. I just wanted to check, though. I am of course eager to see the pix, and see how my own on the Picasso camera came out!!! . . .

December 12, 1966

Many many thanks for the magnificent root prints. I signed them as you requested and have sent back the ones you want to have there. They are really splendid. I find myself wondering if I took such pictures. You really brought out the beauty of that big curled one. There is no hurry at all about the contacts—and take care of yourself. I hope the doctors are merciful and that you do not have to get too cut up: in fact, take a good rest if you can.

I am going to offer Mass for all your intentions on the 15th. I hope you will have better health or less bad health or whatever one can reasonably hope to have in such a case, and more than that: and above all that you may have the grace to take it with freedom from all care, as you usually seem to. God bless you John and all the family. I shall keep you in mind especially in the Christmas season. You are probably doing more for the world by bearing up with your Job-like afflictions than you did when you could get around and give more talks.

January 10, 1967

Many thanks for the prints of the two groups in the hermitage and of the Mass. Very fine indeed. I will especially need a few more, three say, of the one where I am giving communion to Jacques [Maritain]. But let's wait until the end of the procession for that. About the roll that I shot, why don't you just send the negatives and I can get the brother here to print up a few for me. That will save you the enormous trouble of doing all that: you have plenty of other rolls to work on!!! I liked the one I took of Jacques—a lucky accident as usual. I thought though it was a bit fussy with light and dark. Should have played around with the aperture if I'd known how.

By the way I don't remember if I ever answered you about the idea of sending prints of my roots or etc. to that academy in California. Really John I don't think it would be right. I'm no pro, and there are lots of good pros who are not in that gallery. Just because I happened to press the shutter release accidentally, when the thing was pointing at an interesting object . . . No, honestly, I see no reason why an occasional picture taker like myself, who doesn't even know how to develop a film, can be considered a photographer. So I'll pass. I can't in conscience exhibit in an "academy" or a "hall of fame" or whatever it is, for all your generosity! Thanks anyhow . . .

Doris Dana's visit here was very worthwhile from many points of view, and I profited by it. Many ideas and new leads for work, reading and so on. I really must finally get into the poetry of Gabriela Mistral. I have only read a few anthology pieces before now. There is just so much to tackle. All day in a hermitage does not suffice to even begin. And one does after all want to meditate! . . .

February 18, 1967

Thanks much for the letter and the negatives which arrived safely and are now in the stage of contact sheets. I am really quite happy with some of them, but I guess the real secret, in this case, is this: it is not that you or I are great photographers, only that Jacques [Maritain] is so darned photogenic. He takes a marvelous picture: he has a real face. Some of the others came out nicely too: good ones of Dan [Walsh] and Jack Ford, and one I rather like of Dan with Penn [Jones] behind him looking worried off into the distance of the woods.

Sorry to hear about (but not surprised by) your continued surgery. Keep up the old courage. Don't overdo those French TV documentaries: I don't know where you get the stamina. I am heading for a little surgery myself in a few days. Only bursitis. Pray for me however, I want to get rid of it. Who doesn't want to get rid of something? I will be in St. Joseph's Infirmary, L'ville, from Friday 23rd for five or six days I guess . . .

June 21, 1967

I don't know how you are, but I am hoping you are well enough to read this and the enclosed and to give it a little thought. I am not saying that the translation of *Le Paysan* is bad but I do not really think it comes up to Jacques' [Maritain] standards and he would want to work it over meticulously: and perhaps he shouldn't. I don't know what to do about it. Of course, as I mention in my letter to [Joseph] Cunneen, when I read this in English it becomes for me an embarrassing book. Jacques is not himself in it, he is so upset. His style is involved, but in French something of his tone remains. In English it is just weird. I think they have tried hard to make it natural and smooth. I think Cunneen had worked effectively in that respect, though in doing so he has tended to get away from the original. I think the translation is *passable*, no more, and I think Jacques himself would not be satisfied with it.

Meanwhile I understand also that they have had a shake-up and a change of translators. The new one is perhaps slightly better. Have you any suggestions? I am not writing Jacques about this, at least not yet, and I don't really want to start any trouble for anyone. I do believe though that I have to say that I don't think Jacques would accept this job as it is. He would want to make a lot of changes and I don't think he really ought to plunge into such a work at this time. Yet I cannot in conscience tell him "it is a perfectly satisfactory translation" and leave him to discover it when it is in print. He would be rightly angry with me.

Anne Ford sent me proofs of your reader, and I have so far not been able to get into it very far, but it is a very rich and meaty book. I think it has been well edited too. I wish you all luck with it, though I know from experience that Readers don't go too well. Still, it is satisfying to get all that material between two covers in a way that makes so much sense. That is what is important . . .

July 3, 1967

I hope you have not written to Anne Ford about sending me the galleys of your reader. I am very glad that she did so, and I would not have wanted it to be otherwise. I certainly don't feel obligated to get out a blurb at any cost. I am sufficiently used to this routine to take or leave the things that are sent in and to write something if I happen to have time, can give it some thought, and feel like it. If I can't I don't and I don't push myself to oblige anyone—except in a rare case like the recent Fr. [James Joseph] Kavanagh book [A *Modern Priest Looks at His Out-dated Church*] which has become rather a "cause" and is perhaps more of a "cause" than a book . . .

August 24, 1967

Are you back? I want to get this to you before you undergo more surgery. I hope everything went well at Kolbsheim and do not imagine the work on the book was easy. Hope Jacques [Maritain] is at peace about it anyhow. And that you are feeling relatively well anyway.

John, I wonder if this is a reasonable request: if not, forget it. I know your Gregory is a great man with a camera and in the dark room. Would he want to earn a little pocket money processing some stuff for me? There used to be a brother here who did very nice work but he has gone to Chile to our monastery there. The present brother is also the dentist and optometrist besides being photographer and even if he were interested in my roots, which he supremely isn't—he would not be able to do the work. So he just sends it in to the drugstore and that is fatal. Could Gregory give it a little of his time for a handsome emolument (name it) (suggest it, really no kidding I want to pay him for the work). (Suppose we pay him whatever it is the brother pays the drugstore, that's only fair, no?) . . .

September 2, 1967

Many thanks for your letter and the enclosed pix. The one of Jacques [Maritain] is especially charming. He looks tired, but full of go anyway.

I am glad he was able to thrive on the revisions of that book. I would have just burnt it and turned to something else. Mass for you this morning, quiet, in the hermitage, before my ikons, including the strong Bulgarian one. I am sure she is a healer, I feel very close to her. I hope all goes well with you. Don't forget your insulin!!!!

Five rolls are on their way to Gregory, separately. I know nothing of such mysteries as ASA speeds. Never use a meter. So I presume everything I did was "standard". Most of it is closeup stuff of roots at f,11 or f,22, and mostly around 100 of a sec. If that tells you anything. Much of it may look incomprehensible, it is so close and so abstract. But then again a lot of it may just simply be lousy. I have no idea how it is going to be as I haven't used this camera before. I am immensely grateful to know the negatives will be in the hands of someone who knows. My blessings to Gregory.

And my blessings to you also. Take good care. The weather is marvelous here, just like those wonderful days in October last year when you were here with Jacques. Come back again some time if and when you are in a mood to travel. September is no good (as last year). October is a little booked up I think (Steve Allen may drop by). After that is not so beautiful, except sometimes November is great. But you'll know if and when you want to come this way. Love to see you . . .

September 21, 1967

First, thanks very much for the advice about sales. Actually I have been contemplating only very small scale stuff, such as letting a print go here and there to friends, people like New Directions. But of course I know these things can suddenly get bigger than one planned. I'll keep those ideas in mind. And the stamp.

About ferotyping—it does seem like an overgloss. If the American publishers take ordinary glossy I'll stick with that, unless in some special case you or Gregory think the other is necessary. The regular glossy paper you sent R 11 # 3 is fine. As to the matte that PR 3 is just superb. I also like the RB 118, but they are all very fine. I leave you to judge what you think best in an individual case, if something different is needed. Gregory's weeds make a very fine picture and I am going to get out and hit some of the weeds we have around here, and there are plenty. Fall is a great season for dry gritty woody weeds. Just what we need!! Thanks for all you have done to get this in the air. I hate to think of you being bothered, but I know you enjoy it, and it makes the results all the more valuable to me.

I haven't had time to take anything new since the meter came. I have been rushed to get various things out, having got committed to a lot of little things I should have said no to. I'll send one—a sermon that is going to be recorded but not by me as the management doesn't like that. However, if you'd enjoy having a tape of some of my new stuff, the

Cables for instance, I'll send one. The book is now in galleys and I think it will shape up well—the stuff you remember I read when you and Jacques [Maritain] were here last year. I am thinking of a new title for it: *Cables to the Ace.* There is a longish section in French. I'll put that on the tape too.

Reading back over this: my mind got sidetracked from the stamp to ferotyping. Back to the stamp, yes, of course, very fine indeed. Just the way you have it is ok.

September 29, 1967

This check is for Roll A—and I added a little extra because of the postage. Will take care of the rest when we have all this next bunch in. The work is marvelous and I can't tell you how grateful I am. On the other hand I don't want to make it too big an operation and I note that, in spite of everything, you are the one who has to do a lot of correspondence work, which I had not anticipated. But I am immensely grateful . . .

Still have not had a coherent moment to check with authority on the gift of camera, and really I am hesitating about it because I just can't get that involved in another "career". Maybe it would be better if I thought about it for a while: there is the question of my utterly abstract "poverty" to be considered too . . . ! Can I think about it for a while?

Today I am snowed under with some unbelievably nutty correspondence and am going to drop it all and go out in the woods. It is a nice cold cloudy afternoon with lots of color and life.

October 3, 1967

Dear John and Gregory:

Thanks for the two possibilities for the *Latitudes* covers. Actually I much prefer the big stones: it makes a fine composition for a cover and Gregory has done a marvelous print of it. The other is all right, but I think this has far more life to it. Also, seeing the contacts for the early ones, I think [Robert] Bonazzi might be interested in some of those strong shadows of the roots. But I leave you to work it out with him. I just wanted to cast my vote for the stones, and also to say that I don't think my "signature" really helps that much (as sampled on the other one). They'll say inside who done it. I am as excited as you are. Thanks, Gregory, for having such a good eye!

Thanks also for the roots of E and F (glossies). Very fine. Now I'll tackle the business of selling New Directions on some of them . . .

October 16, 1967

. . . Today I am mailing you a tape. Mysteries of all kinds. On the top side is the new work I am doing, *The Geography of Lograire*, big poem about every thing under the sun. You'll get a section on some

English heretics, the "Ranters", a section on Mexico and the Mayas, some on the South, some on Wales, some on just anyplace. Then on the other side new poems, and selections from the new book now in course of publication, *Cables to the Ace* including the long French bit. Parts of this you heard here last year with Jacques [Maritain]. By all means take copies if you like, the only thing to be careful about is that they don't get away to be used in any public way (radio, recordings), but perfectly ok for small groups "in the home" . . .

Hope you enjoy the tape. It may take some getting used to!! I don't expect this to do much more than bewilder the reader when in print, but myself I do feel there is something going on here. What, God knows.

December 8, 1967

Just time for a brief note, to enclose this check for Greg, before I go down to concelebrate for this feast. Thanks for your *Reader* which has got here safely and is most handsome. The photographs are utterly powerful, some of them overwhelming. I do hope you go on with the project of a whole book of them. It will be a great one. And the *Reader* itself is so rich. I plunged right in the "Work in Progress" part, and it is always powerful, challenging, full of meat. This will give me a chance to get a look at some of your novels, too, which I had not read before.

About the race situation, I could not agree more. I am afraid you are only too right. More about that after tomorrow. I have a man from Chicago who is very involved in it, coming down tomorrow (organized a recent important meeting on it recently) . . .

I just got through a really marvelous new venture: first time a group of cloistered nun-superiors was here for retreat and seminar, fifteen of them, including your "neighbor", Mother Henry of the cloistered Dominicans at Lufkin. We had a really first-rate session, ending with Mass together at the hermitage yesterday, and such a Mass as you never saw: all joined in to give bits of the homily, to utter petitions at the prayer of the people, etc. etc. Really groovy, as they say.

January 5, 1968

At last the Christmas rush is over and I can breathe again. Thanks for your good letter about the tape. I'm glad you liked it and of course Jacques [Maritain] can have a copy—and I'm glad Bob Bonazzi wants one too. I think the book [*The Geography of Lograire*] will shape up. Wish I had shared your wonderful experience with the Indians in Mexico. Must go deeper into this. Hope I can get to some Indians before I die. Wish I could as a gesture take up "nationality" in the Navahos or something and renounce the other nationality of which I am not especially proud at the moment.

We have had some dazzling cold weather and lots of snow. I have three rolls of film on the way there. But unfortunately the old Rolleiflex is just falling apart. I fell on some ice with it and I am afraid it is wrecked and letting in light. Hence I just wasted the third roll, afraid that it would not come out anyhow. I send these rolls in trepidation. I guess the old box is shot.

That reminds me, diffidently I am reminded, of your generous offer of a camera that is likely to stay in one piece for a year or two yet. I think that with the demise of this one, I ought to seriously consider your offer. It is justifiable for me to have a camera, I think, since I do occasionally sell a picture and it is not just diddling. (One must be a producer.) That being the case, let's discuss it. What do you suggest? Any time I've used a Nikon I like it. Don't especially like Kodaks or Leicas. I have liked the Rolleiflex for focusing and composition. What do you suggest? You know the kind of thing I most like to do. Obviously I am not covering the Kentucky Derby etc. But I do like a chance at fast funny out of the way stuff too. The possibility of it in case. But as I see it I am going to be on roots, sides of barns, tall weeds, mudpuddles, and junkpiles until Kingdom come. A built-in exposure meter might be a help.

Cables to the Ace is in the press and should be out in March. Will send a copy as soon as I have one. Pray for our abbatial election Jan. 13, could be critically important. If we get a conservative half the monks will leave and if we get a radical they'll all be on LSD. There is just about one good man and I hope he gets it. Well, two are possibilities. Maybe three. But the others . . . Like I say, I can always join the Navaho if they'll have me. Note that I put myself out of the running by the enclosed facetious document. For me to take such a job would be a betrayal of everything I believe in.

March 27, 1968

Your letter about the camera was one of the most exciting things that ever happened. THE most exciting was the arrival of the camera itself. It is superb. I haven't had a chance to take it out, though we have some nice afternoons: I have had a lot of people here and problems to sweat out. But first chance I get . . . So far I have only read the instructions, procured film and become acquainted with the different gadgets. What a thing to have around! I will take reverent care of it, and any time you want it . . . I will take good care to see that it goes straight back to you if anything happens to me . . .

Monks Pond is going nicely in the sense that the poets themselves seem very happy with it, and others are pouring in good stuff. It is going to be hard to quit in four issues. Impossible in fact to quit in four, but I still don't want to go beyond five or six. But while it lasts it will, I think, be a good little mag. Have some very good stuff in the summer number. Don't forget to send me something—short prose, tirade, picture, anything . . .

I haven't written to Jacques [Maritain] in ages, but will send him a *Monks Pond* soon. Am running short now, but have more pages around and can assemble these when I get a chance.

March 29, 1968

It is fabulous. What a joy of a thing to work with. I am sending the two first rolls and hoping that they are ok, that I haven't done something all wrong: but the camera is the most eager and helpful of beings, all full of happy suggestions: "Try this! Do it that way!" Reminding me of things I have overlooked, and cooperating in the creation of new worlds. So simply. This is a Zen camera. As for the F.100, I tell you, I'm going to blow my mind with it! It is fantastic, at least in the viewfinder. I'll wait and see what the contacts look like . . .

And by the way, Gregory's kitten, in *Latitudes*, is one of the most beautiful pictures I have ever seen. I hope he'll send me something for *Monks Pond*.

Griffin sent Merton a picture of an elongated African wood carving, labeling it a photograph of himself taken after he'd been abused for supporting the Pope's stand on birth control.

August 3, 1968

Gawd, I never saw anyone whose physical appearance was so affected by a Papal Encyclical. I am almost of a mind to rush you six cases of my own homemade special, "Uncle Louie's Hot Farm Triple Bond" but it is a dangerous brew and a notorious aphrodisiac. So I must refrain, and hope you'll build up again on coca cola. Apart from that I can only compliment you on your exemplary motives. We of the clergy, who by our very grace of state understand everything about marriage, are always gratified when the married laity obey their grace of state which is to defer to the clergy in everything. Meanwhile, according to my latest information there are more beds being broken down by Monsignori than at any time since the reign of Pope Alexander VI. At the latest count, lemme see . . . No, those are the wrong statistics. That's a body count from Vietnam. That's the other way we have figured out to take care of the population explosion. The Bomb.

Well, apart from that, all I can say is that we priests will support the Holy Father all the way, at least until he forbids whiskey for the clergy. Can you imagine having to drink wine? He'd better not try. Joking apart, my face is red if not crimson about all those picnic photos. I am so sorry Fr. George went to such trouble for such lousy pictures. Here's a check for him. I'm going to send along something by way of a bonus. Probably not a book—that would be too much like adding insult to injury. But if there's one he'd like . . . Can he survive Trappist cheese? . . .

To Robert Lax

Let there be nothing secret among friends.
MERTON TO LAX
DECEMBER 3, 1962

Robert James Lax (1915–   ), perhaps Merton's closest and most enduring friend from his days at Columbia University, first met Merton when they collaborated on the university "humor magazine," The Columbia Jester. *Lax figures in* The Seven Storey Mountain, *and the two friends were in touch through the years, at times through Sister Therese Lentfoehr. Lax, born a Jew, converted to Catholicism a decade after Merton. He taught for a time at the University of North Carolina, did screenwriting in Hollywood, and was an editor at such magazines as* The New Yorker, Pax, *and* Jubilee. *In 1962 he went into self-imposed exile in the Greek islands. He visited Merton at Gethsemani on at least four occasions— December 1944; May 1949 (at the time of Merton's ordination); May 1959 (with mutual friend Ad Reinhardt); and June 1968. Merton himself collected their correspondence after 1962 and attempted to publish a selection from the exchange during his lifetime. It was published after Merton's death as* A Catch of Anti-Letters *(Sheed, Andrews and McMeel, 1978). The Merton letters included in that compilation are omitted here. Merton tended at times to address Lax by different names and to sign himself by different names, which are given here. Most of the letters, as Brother Patrick Hart has said; are "Anti-letters, fun letters, friends in a playful mood exchanging thoughts on the world." With Lax, Merton often played with language in Joycean fashion, a style which dated from their student days and was greatly increased after* Finnegans Wake *appeared in 1939.*

548a West 114th St., New York
August 11, 1938

Tomorrow summer session [at Columbia] draws to a close and all the happy people go away, some creeping, some hobbling, some rolling, some dragging their ass along close to the good earth back to Iowa, Minnesota, Waukegan, Pilsen, roaring towns every one. It is concluded.

Me I have worked like a dog, ten twelve hours a day, sweating over dirty old books in the graduate house of Carpenter Institute of English and Old Runes. To be precise I have studied William Blake, I have measured him with a ruler, I have sneaked at him with pencils and T squares, I have spied on him from a distance with a small spyglass, I have held him up to mirrors, and will shortly endeavor to prove the prophetic books were all written with lemon juice and must be held in front of a slow fire to be read.

Truthfully I have an enormous obscure subtle thesis that Blake is all full of Indian and Chinese theories of art, for a certainty. That he has read the *Bhagavad Gita*, I have found out, and then found out that others know this well. But they have not gone into this as I intend, and they say nothing of his art anyway, only explain he was tussling with the druids every word he wrote. But I do not up and be a loud roaring fellow and a stupid shit saying how Blake picked up some old Chinese book and writ down all his theories of art and poetry. I say how he knew about the Indian works from books of travel, how he read the *Gita*, how he was anyhow a fine mystic, how he read strange histories about the east all full of half modern ideas about how one race influences another through means of etymology, and the Greeks weren't so smart as to be all holy and full of truth of their own for that they swiped everything from India and Egypt the book states clearly. This Blake read. Anyhow he hated Plato . . .

Summer school has been good. I have made good friends with the department of English, and Mr. [William York] Tindall, who is a fine scholar, invited me to his house and made a big lime rickey in a glass big enough for a lot of goldfish to swim in. And my Oriental work has made me good friends with Dr. Christy, who is an Oriental scholar in the English house, writing a great enormous book of all the Asiatic influences in England that ever were, and he knows more about references to Indian chintz in the diaries of Lady Mary Wortley Montagu than any other man alive. And Mr. [Hoxie Neal] Fairchild is my friend and Mr. [Emery] Neff also. And Dr. Tindall said he would tap me for Campbells' Boys' Club in the fall and now all I got to do is get fat like Milton Crane.

Me I seen [John] Slate the other night, he come to my house and we drank beer and he talked as though he were perplexed, but he goes to work Monday and every Friday they will shovel a fortune into his lap, bring him pails full of nickels so much that he will have to borrow a wagon to take his salary home to his mother. What he says that is perplexed is this: that he will be working and pretty soon forget there was, for instance, the Manichean heresy. Well I say fuck the Manichean heresy, fuck it up and fuck it down, fuck the Manichean heresy in the seven shores and all over the forty-eight states, I say, for so many dollars as Slate will get. Anyway he won't forget. Nor the gnostics, nor Chroust raising, nor anything at all.

Sunday I was to Seymour [Freedgood]'s house, and he sure has got a dog as big as a horse, every front tooth seven feet long, but affable, kindly, bland, mild etc. or so I thought and then I put on my coat, which is so shabby he doubtless thought me a pauper or a beggar or a countryman, and he barked ferocious and would have chewed off my leg had I not thrown aside the coat saying boldly do not be afraid, good fellow, never fear, it is Merton I cried jovially, so carrying the war into the enemy's camp, and he was subdued.

I work very hard taking courses and reading about Blake and a dozen people. I find Thomas Lovell Beddoes to be fine, I find Francis Thompson to be a pretty good poet. I find Joyce to be a remarkable fine poet, and

I have read *Portrait of the Artist* which is certainly a remarkable fine book, and the best thing I have read in a long time, only not so fine as *Ulysses* of course, but that is all written in words of fire.

Then also I have read Keats and Shelley and Matthew Arnold and none of them give furiously to thinking, but I guess I like Keats and Shelley, like "Adonais" and "Epipsychidion" and "Lamia." And I have read pieces of the *Biographia Literaria* which is a fine book, certainly. I think to go and read pieces of Aquinas, and I think to read about Zen Buddhism.

And listen to what happened. I went up to the Music Library having a hangover, and took *Ionisation* and put it on the thing with the earphones, and Chroust Chroust, it poured into my head so that it sounded like it was my brains falling about, the lobes moving from place to place and changing positions and when the fellow comes in that drops all the trays I thought I was dead and ran away screeching. But I went back another time well warned and with no hangover and it was sure very pretty, and my brain did not fall down one bit. But it was nasty the first time when the noises got inside and walked about so merrily . . .

In April 1939 Merton visited Bermuda. He had not been there since he lived there with his father in the early 1920s, yet, as Michael Mott points out in The Seven Mountains of Thomas Merton, *he records no reactions to being there again or to seeing again the scene of his father's entanglement with novelist Evelyn Scott and her ménage.*

On Board "Queen of Bermuda"
[April 1939]

There is on board one Ida Lichfield of Boston Mass. I say to her oh you are of Boston so you know N[ancy] Flagg? Her reply: "Indeed I know N. Flagg, I was at her house for tea last week." However, as a punishment for not being very beautiful, Miss Lichfield was never to Miss Flagg's house but once.

Yesterday I found the bar but for the first four hours it was about as much fun as the Browsing Room. Later on me & these Boston girls & a nurse from P. & S. & some furniture salesman from Syracuse sat & did drink. This morning it is rough & windy & full of big waves & bright sun & warm winds. I have seen a dolphin bearing in his mouth a red flower, politely tropical. But this furniture salesman rushed into the elevator & vomited all over it. Now he's better, now he thinks he'll eat an apple.

The two Boston girls are fine for wit & intelligence & they all the time giggle at the double talk with the furniture salesman, & Ida Lichfield told me once how her father (she is Flagg's friend) won a portable house playing Bingo! Also how, as a child, she would absolutely not take ether for an operation: so her crazy mother said: if I take it will you take it? So she said "yes," so her mother sat down & had the ether, & went out &

she (Ida) was satisfied & took ether too. So her mother slept peacefully all through the operation. I think this to be a fine story. Here mother, there daughter, stretched out side by side, one being operated, the other sleeping for her crazy dumb charity.

I will maybe write some more to this if I get time. Oh Lax such champagnes! These Boston girls are very good fun, such larfing, & such champagne. Some 4 bottles! Now we are almost to Bermuda. I will see it.

Bermuda

[April 1939]

Listen: Bermuda is the place in the world most like the South of France. It is, hear me, splendid! The first thing happened was a horse being scared by a false train.

35 Perry Street, New York

[July 1939]

I never heard no beard so highly praised except by barbers. I find it is not dames who dislike beard, but fellows much more. Here, the fellows don't say nothing though. Ok! Then there's [Bob] Gibney's mother who run back & forth in front of the beard doing a lot of ostrich tricks & lying that she had never seen a beard before.

I rent my fashionable Perry St. apt. to Seymour [Freedgood] who, I guess, gets married but am not sure. He shall have his honeymoon among my books, I am sure! Therefore I am coming to Olean not so much Friday as Saturday. And this time too I will make some kind of N.Y. Central train to Buffalo & then get a bus. The Erie may go then go sulk along by itself. We were 2 hours late coming down & Rice & I who were so smart we had to check our stuff through to Chambers St. had to wait an hour there for it. Admiration for the beards begun among the girls on the train, & continued among the fine ladies of the capital . . .

[Bob] Gibney come to Perry St. Monday night & we sit and draw pictures & play Carol Huxley's records then drive to Port Washington in the Lassalle. July 4 we go to the yacht club all afternoon swimming & drinking Barbados Rum Collinses. That night to World's Fair & we seen Dali's Dream of Venus & it is fine. We also seen Marquita & we also gone on the parachute jump, which did not scare me until I got home in bed, but was actually very pleasant. The ride up is indeed going very high, too high to have dangling feet: the guy when you start gives you instructions "Don't stand up." Then there is a drop & a jerk & then slow coming down & pretty dull. The bounce at the bottom not so bad. This is what I know about the parachute jump.

New York seems to be so full of nice dames, & W[ilma] Reardon certainly look to me the most beautiful thing in the world, but I guess it's all right for a visit & no place to live, New York. So I want to very much get back to Olean & finish the novel. Listen, Seymour wants my apt. for July & August. Can I stay that late? And listen, too: if Benjie & Gladio [Marcus] won't let you have their house for your friends wire me fast right away, at Perry St. if I would get it Thursday night, at Douglaston if I would get it Friday night Douglaston is 50, Rushmore Ave.

And listen again if they say we can't have the house give them some argument for a minute because now Seymour got my house & me have no place to go. Now I go call [Joe] Roberts to clear his stuff out of my place & give me my money, & call Rice to come to Olean. Rice says he hasn't got a car yet. Roberts says he doesn't know when he can come up. Rice says [Bob] Gerdy's coming up. I hope Gerdy has some money, is all I can say . . .

New York
August 21, 1939

It's hot. It is so hot all the fellows as far as I know have sat down. [John] Slate, I talked to on the telephone tonight, has gone out of his office and through a doctor's office and gone home and sat down. Slate got a raise and so they made him work up until midnight every night with this result, that he is tired. The fair worked Wilma Reardon so hard she sat down too. [Bob] Gibney is not in his job but rather out of it altogether, and I was to see him at Port Washington this weekend only it rained so hard Saturday and I got up so late Sunday I stayed in town. Seymour [Freedgood] I don't know anything about except he isn't paying me any money.

Last week I was all full of illuminating thoughts about New York, how it is a good place all right. And I guess if it would only get cool, New York is a good place. Among my gilded thoughts is one that it was pretty on Madison Ave one day last week. Another gilded thought arises out of me and [Ed] Rice getting a lot of good Balinese records. A thought not without tarnish is that for ten minutes it was fun talking to all these beezils in Dillon's one night last week.

I am pleased about the room problem which solved itself with an easy compromise which doesn't save me so much money: I have moved across the hall in this same house, for ten bucks a month less, into a room which, when fixed up, is prettier than the front one though smaller. It has bookcases in the walls, and through one of the windows you see nothing except trees when you wake up in the morning, provided you wake up in a pretty uncomfortable position.

The novel I don't know about yet, naturally. But I was talking to this Peter Munro Jack in his hovel down the street (a pretty frightening place it is too) and he said Farrar (pronounced your way and not mine as it transpires) (neat use of hotweather word) was a sucker for this particular kind of novel with a lot of place names in it: Cannes, Paris, London, and so on.

God knows I don't want any beer anyway but the Latino is closed and Cafe Society is the same old rotten cafe society as it took me no necessary five minutes of investigation to find out, since before I even turned the corner to go there I was aware that the unanimous voice of the angels was to stay the hell out of THAT cellar.

Okay more tinsel thoughts occur to me from yesterday's visit to the Museum of Modern Art. Oh boy some picasso called seated woman oh boy some picasso hoyhoy dancedance hoyhoyhoy. Similar dances for the cezannes and all the other picassos and at least one Juan Gris, and even one chirico and was happied up by the Miros okay, and one stuart davis sure good yeah, fine. That reminds me I seen [Ad] Reinhardt for two minutes one hot afternoon all busy and gay his girl who reminds me on a hot day of Quinn sitting and watching him work, then in come some dry communists with their usual sheaf of tickets (printed on blotting paper) for gay boatrides down the bay on the ss susquehanna one buck, so I gone away again and bought some rubber cement but didn't get so encouraged by that either.

Hey this city won't be so bad once it gets cool. I found out I could read more Provencal than just those lines in Dante, because I got a big Provencal book with convenient French translations handy and it was okay easy that way, and well, I didn't need the translation for EVERY line. It sure is some of the best poetry you would ever hope to look at anyway, some good language, in a lot of ways better than Spanish or Italian for any kind of poems with short lines. Same old bajan gag insulting all your rival poets too.

I found this French guy Valéry Larbaud to be some good guy too. I just got his novel, *Amants Heureux Amants*, it's swell. This very excellent guy got a splendid eye for jailbaits I must say, too, in his novel *Amants Heureux Amants* which I would laughingly translate jailbaits happy jailbaits only I haven't read the part of it that's really called that yet and it is probably about something else. Last night I got some mild amusement from *Gentlemen Prefer Blondes*, that's good. Oh and yesterday I seen again the [avant-garde film] *Crazy Ray* up at the Museum, and it was better, I thought. Besides I noticed one good thing I had not seen before: when the town is all asleep and they have been stealing right and left, they are going home to the Eiffel Tower in four taxis full of large and small stolen objects, from pearls to furniture, and in the last taxi, sticking out of the back window is the Mona Lisa, cut out of its frame. Also I like the fine solemn diagrams of the ray NOT hitting the Eiffel Tower or the aeroplane. Then I got some happiness out of *'Tis Pity She's a Whore* which is certainly some play. I had never read it. I was not quite so happy as I expected with some of Lyly's plays, which I just read maybe too fast and too sweaty and too disgusted. I was near to a movie [theater] which had *Each Dawn I Die*, when I was to Cavanaugh's eating cold cuts and salad and herbs only I didn't go because I came home to play Balinese records and talk to Slate. But me and Gibney saw a good thing called *Clouds over Europe* about a lot of *39 Steps* spies and plenty of good things besides which brings us to the topic of *Clouds over Europe* which I would prefer not to discuss.

Slate says if they ever let him go away from his office he will go to Williamsport and then drive over to Olean and I praised Olean up and it is sure good you got the cabin, he was to of left this week early but it turns out (nice use of the expression turns out) that he will leave this week late. Like for example Thursday.

[Ed] Rice give me a shock with the beard off although I knew it was going to be off even before he come up behind me with it, as they say off. And now I wish the people in the garden outside here, whom I cannot help overhearing in spite of the typewriter and the gay sounds. I scream at the top of my voice, would stop talking about what they so playfully term the "War in Europe." As I say, New York would be ok if only it would freeze up and I could have the windows shut. I haven't written anything except a poem which I am not so sure is any good, and maybe I ought to be writing more because of the merry jangling of the typewriter so fukkit. Maybe I'll write when it comes the cool days I so fondly refer to as I blow drops of sweat off the end of my nose.

And now down in the garden they are telling a story the climax of which is "She escaped finally through China": so I guess I'll mail this letter and go out and buy a pint of ice cream and put it all over my face. Oh, tell Joe [Roberts] he owes me for an electric light bill for the month he was here ninety-three cents . . .

Perry St., New York
October 17, 1939

[Bob] Gibney made a sharp guess you and Seymour [Freedgood] had flew the coop. Some coop. Then I called up Seymour's house, not making any person to person call in order to talk to someone and find out that it were true: well his mother thought Seymour was coming back yesterday, and I kind of larfed. Some mother, she thinks she knows when Seymour is going to do something he says he will. Tell Seymour hello from me, and also Helen.

In newyork they build a brand new house for the slum people: that is, you know, a wpa projec. This projec is large and square and sullen though temporarily white, and it sits under a bridge and mourns for the days when it was decent separated bricks, and not bricks put together into an ugly hous. There the poor do come, however, with their wretched bundles, singing their song which goes:

> Out of the black hole
> And into the white
> Papa was a mole

But mama is a moth
Temper your tears with a show of delight
And go in the hous, or I'll slam you both.

Well, it said in the paper of certain new tenants to the projec, that one of them got out of her truck with a bundle, and took a direct look at the projec and then she affirmed:

"I think this place is going to be something like a ranch."

I got a song for the rich people to sing, mocking the poor who never ever HEARD OF a ranch:

Fair ladies most tender
And nobles most slender
And gentles whose wits be scarce:
Queen Fortune doth come
With her trump and her drum
As it doth appear by my verse.

This is from Geo. Chapman's "Humorous Day's Mirth." Some play. In it a fine fellow declares: "I will be melancholy as a cat, and no more wear a hatband to my hat" . . .

I know of a man in Rhode Island who asserts you should call the war by its right name: the Krieg. This is, of course, because he is a general and thinks Krieg means cake. When I come to reread this line I won't know what it means either.

I made up my mind about the monastery and now the monastery only has to make up its mind about me. The arguments with [Fr. George B.] Ford were something considerable and he does not yet know they have come to an end. It comes to me as stupid that I didn't do this years ago, let alone this time last year. But maybe not. Now anyway is when I want to do it. I keep walking out of church and seeing the bright sun and thinking, ha, this would be some day to get sent to Bona's on the Erie Railroad, in spite of all the dust and smoke.

Also I walk into the [Franciscan] church on 31st st, and all day long there are crowds of people there, for confessions and sermons and benedictions and all kinds of prayer to God: and there is not anything else in New York, not any place, not any office or any bright guy's typewriter or any gay dame's room full of congas or any museum full of El Grecos or any Library, even full of Dante that is as good as that one church where the monks are busy hearing confessions and praying and preaching. Because even Dante only can tell you to go and find the sacraments but the priests administer the sacraments, and these are filled with the actual grace of God, and are the means of increasing His love for us, and sending us out to do good works, as prayer and acts of charity and love and preaching peace for everybody should do God's will. I wish I knew when I was going to begin the Novitiate [with the Franciscans].

Now I won't write so much more. There goes the whistle and I must end my speech. Like I say, I haven't seen Gibney since about a week ago when he was going to Peggy Wells' and I was to the movies with Jinny Burton. But Sunday I went to the Fair because I had forgotten to see the famous paintings, and believe me they were some of the best paintings you ever saw: the best Breughel I ever saw, Fra Angelico, El Greco, and whole lot of Primitives. And I must say I don't think El Greco paints at all good compared to Fra Angelico, who had one picture there I would not believe it was possible it was so perfect, but I mean you could not only not find anything wrong with it, you couldn't find anything in it that wasn't the best thing you ever saw. But not that I don't mean El Greco doesn't paint like an angel, and compared to him Goya is a lazy commercial artist who slipped a quick sketch and filled in three-quarters of the canvas with speedy ease to make shadows and went home. But still Goya is aces compared to plenty of competent guys who are still artists, and below them you have to go through all the guys who are not until you reach Petty and Grant Wood and Benton and so on. So I'm not saying more than you'd be surprised how much better Fra Angelico is even than El Greco: but that is comparing one of the best pictures with some of El Greco's than which I have seen better pictures.

You would modify your opinion that everybody ought to be writing if you seen the things my class handed in: including the spectacled business guy who writes about things "that are excreted orally each day from the public prints" . . .

35 Perry Street, New York
[Late October 1939]

It come to me today to go to the Fair again although it is nearly locked up or rather because it is. It come to me the curious idea to go to see all the educational exhibits I never saw when they was in full gear. What happened was I run through Switzerland where it was a lot of signs that read: Touching is spoiling. Then I went in the Republic of Dominica and Cuba and Ireland and Greece and then I got a firm resolve to run out of the Fair very fast. This resolve was so firm and strengthening that many old ladies, seeing me, clutched on to me for support with the natural blind instinct of the helpless when all around them, especially the buildings, is falling, falling.

A sign in the Netherlands building says: The Netherlands Fights Death Successfully, a pitiful little leer of a mad country which tries to lie that its people are immortal when it knows there is a war and nobody can go there and check up on them. As if we didn't KNOW they can die in Holland, just like ANYWHERE.

Nevertheless one last look at the Fair, perishing beautifully with mustard all over its face, nearly turned me into a pillar of salt on the ramp of the LI station. And now I guess that is as smart as I will ungratefully be at the expense of a nice 600 acre enterprise where I have after all had MANY an interesting experience.

[Bob] Gibney and me have had a REMARKABLE correspondence, (aw quit the uppercase, then) part of which I send to you like he says. It all started one night with a time I thought I had made a German joke on the telephone to Gibney and had hurt his feelings which as it happily turns out was not so.

It is interesting and instructive to teach a class: it is not true that any of them are crazy at all, but nor is it true that many of them can write English. Also it is true that they are beginning to write better than before, once they can write about their families and their summer vacations, which is nevertheless what they started out with. It is much easier to get them to write saying they really want to be blessed than saying they want to be smart, which as a matter of fact they do not so much care about, but were only told to care about in High School. Thus I love my class very much, individually more than in a lump and will in the future make a gesture of biting off my tongue before I talk about crazies or stoopies for one minute, even with the understanding under which it has hitherto seemed all right: that is admitting everything I have just said and then going on with: "This crazy . . . this stoopie."

One of the most extraordinarily difficult things I have ever tried to do is understand St. Thomas' *De Ente et Essentia*. But it's sure fine when I can manage to make something of it.

[Joe] Roberts come and went and we seen not the very best submarine propaganda movie in the world, having in it W[allace] Beery. [Ed] Rice got me passes to two football games which was pretty in the sunlight from the top of the pressbox. Me and J[inny] Burton went to the Latino. There was and maybe still is some Balinese dancers in town, but I guess you was no fool to return to Olean.

In December Merton went to Olean, New York, to Lax's, to spend part of the Christmas–New Year holidays with his friend.

New York
January 9, 1940

Yes it was nice at Olean and I'm sorry I had to go so fast. But I did save money on the train because I come all the way down and had only one meal instead of ten.

This is a business letter: please find the small black Temple Classics book of *The Golden Legend of the Lives of the Saints* which will have been on the little shelf where the telephone used to be in the maids-mine-Peggy's room. It will be there unless Peggy [Wells] was reading it, but I guess she wasn't, because the last time I noticed it was hid under a lot of bobbie pins. When you have found this small bk. please to mail it down to me because it is a library bk.

Right away when I got home I wrote a long letter to [Mahanambrata] Brahmachari.

I am not going into the monastery until August, they said at the monastery yesterday. I am sorry.

I went and saw *Ninotchka* and liked it a lot, especially the commissars and Garbo's scene when she drunk up the champagne and was happy. [Ed] Rice did not go so much to Georgia, but stayed home and went no place but to bed with the grippe. I am sorry for that too . . . I bet you aren't going to be as fired as you are thinking right now you are going to be tomorrow.

Seymour's mother called me up on the telephone last Thursday and accused me of not daring to admit Seymour's car was wrecked in Pennsylvania. I said Seymour was perfectly safe, as his car is incapable of being driven out on any road where it could come to harm. I told her to call you up and see what you'd say. Are the fellows still up there?

Lilly [Reilly]'s new play flopped in Pittsburgh, she ought to be back today or yesterday. Jinny Burton was back when I arrived.

35 Perry St., New York
February 4, 1940

. . . Last week Jinny Burton and Lilly Reilly and me had a big love feast on my birthday, so big I got drunk. Before that me and five guys in my class had a big love feast too for the end of term and the end of me being their teacher. I lost my section of English composition, and they were going to give me a class teaching spelling to old ladies instead, and I declined, saying no thanks for the offer of that stupid spelling class.

To my class for their examination I gave them to write an essay on one of the following three topics: *A Day at the Races*, *A Night at the Opera* and *A Day at the Circus*. They larfed and smiled but what they wrote wasn't any good.

Some exhibition of Paul Klee, is all I have to say. Some pictures. They are going to make a book of his pictures and I will get it and show you. Some pictures. [Ad] Reinhardt has finished a mural for Cafe Society and tomorrow they put it up. It will be all over luminous paint and looks fine in the dark. You will be able to turn around and look at a completely different mural when they turn out the lights for that dull little guy Jack whatever he is called to come out and imitate Rockefeller.

Only I guess I won't be there to turn around so much. No place depresses me so much as a bar or night club: especially where there is always Lionel Stander at the next table, and another new mural besides Reinhardt's was done by Lionel Stander's wife.

Grapes of Wrath is a good picture. The best scenes come right at the beginning, especially [John] Carradine talking to Henry Fonda in a field, telling him how he used to be a preacher but lost the call, and demonstrating how he ran squatting up and down the ridge pole of a barn preaching a sermon. Some scene . . .

I was out to Seymour [Freedgood]'s house and his uncle Harry told me who his (Harry's) favorite movie star was: Alice Faye, sure was Alice Faye. His next favorites are the four Lane sisters of whom he would probably be disappointed to learn there are but three. That washes up present day rabelaisian characters for me. The funny thing is, Alice Faye is really the country's favorite too. I had never suspected that.

They made in Hollywood a very dull movie about the first steamboat: in itself, it was about the worst subject for a movie I had ever seen. So then they said: "Now we have covered the worst possible kind of a subject. Surely there must be something we can do with it." Sure enough they found what they could do with it. Make the same picture with Alice Faye in it. So now Alice Faye come to the Roxy in a movie about De Witt Clinton. I wisht I was in Cienfuegos, Cuba.

> Percy Straight.
> No Walk, said he.
> Fib. xvi. [February 16, 1940]

. . . I am glad you went to see *Groan with the Wound*: right when you said you was off to see it I thought it was going to be fun walking up to the movie for you and fun buying the ticket and maybe after that intolerable. Maybe I forgot how bad the last part of it was when I talked so much about it. Only I sure still think V. Leigh is good and the torn-down house sequence was good and, too, C. Gable was good . . .

I am not particularly concerned about writing two sentences about anything, ever again, at least until it is God's will that I should write things: and when it is I will know. But what I know now is that it seems to be God's will that I should be a priest—or it is: because there is no vocation to the priesthood except from God.

Lax, when you say prayers, pray for me to be a good priest, and pray for all priests to be good, and for the salvation of all people, nuns, business men, Hitler, everybody.

In March 1940 Merton had his appendix removed. The next letter was written to Lax from the hospital.

> St. Elizabeth's Hospital, N.Y.
> I dunno: March 1940

I had a ghastly experience with some doctors.

(1) The Doctors rushed at me in a group & plucked up my appendix like a flower.

(2) The Doctors approached me severally with tinder and burned down my appendix like it was a house.

(3) The Doctors fell upon me like a tower & cracked my appendix like it was a nut.

(4) The Doctors surrounded me like a wheel and rolled off to the village with my appendix.

(5) I was made an urchin's game for interns and they scoured out my appendix with a pointed stick.

(6) The Doctors came about me like lions, and roared until my appendix ran out of its house in fear.

(7) They climbed upon me like Swiss goats & ate up my appendix like grass.

(8) They came with syringes & took my poor appendix like a bird.

(9) And now the nuns and the nurses and orderlies have possessed me with enemas, clysters and mops.

(10) They have bound me to a bed where I plead & beg for the frills of fruits.

(11) They have come with spoons & forks and poured Wheatena all over my chin.

(12) They have transfixed me with thermometers: they have taken wood-alcohol and rubbed me into the ground.

(13) They put me in a ward full of Irishmen who talked incessantly about the late Jay Gould.

(14) But they have let me subside with a semi-private room, as in a nest on the end of a bough . . .

Before I took sick I was out to Seymour [Freedgood]'s & had a peculiarly desultory argument about religion with [Bob] Gibney. I didn't start it either, nor ever will start any other arguments about religion again as long as I live.

The allusions to pain in the psalm are partly true & partly for literary effect. Really there is nothing so terribly bad just about having an appendix out. Now it's pleasant to sit in bed & eat & drink & larf & read & sleep & make jokes with the nuns and some of the nurses. It doesn't even hurt none, only the ether makes you sick as you can be. Really, as to hurting, later.

So as I finished composing this psalm, which will be entitled "Apud Medicos foedissime passus sum" in come on the one hand a nurse with an enema & on the other somebody with a bill for the anaesthetic I took the other day & which made me sicker than I have ever been in my life. I mean the anaesthetic, although I am by no means beyond making that kind of a cheap joke about the bill, too . . .

Yesterday I laid in bed & read the *Paradise* & yelled for orange juice. Today it is twenty-two below zero & they have all the windows open. Presently they will take down the walls of the hospital so that the freezing air can get inside better.

After I get out of here I go to my family on Long Island to be pampered. Then maybe to Cuba or Peru then maybe in May or June to

Olean or on some journey with you & [Ed] Rice to Cuba or Peru before I go to the Novitiate. Really there is a lot of time before that, because I guess my Novitiate doesn't start until nearly the end of August.

Before I was here me & Jinny Burton went to good conga places & became the best conga dancers in New York. Boy, Hopkins is a good poet!

Camaguey, Cuba
April [1940]

what i say about cuba is true it takes about thirty bucks to get to Havana from new york by train to miami and boat from there, and it really is pretty cheap to live here, a lot cheaper than new york, but boy what a place.

in havana i went to the show and what do you suppose: not only a double feature of two spanish pictures full of flamenco sin-ging and interesting pictures and good spanish jokes, but also on the stage the best flamenco singer in the world, that is a guy called Angelillo. And for the first time i was able to understand the words of the songs all the way through and what poems! Baby. Also you never saw such a thing as the audience while the singing was going on, laughing, crying, holding their breath, shouting like crazy after a particularly good trick, and when the song was over stamping and yelling and weeping and larfing to beat hell. As for me I was knocked clean out of my seat about twenty-eight times, and I don't think there has ever in the history of the world been anything except church music to equal flamenco songs. To begin with for their use of popular speech they make artificial attempts like the stuff Wordsworth tried look ridiculous. This stuff has the same good Damon Runyon trick of using big newspaper editorial words all the time and it knocks you on your head, and I remember one line about somebody possessing a little box made out of polychrome silver . . . "de plata polychromada" with plenty of stress on each syllable, that came in the middle of something terrific, like a murder or something of that nature. But it turns out that flamencos is what everybody in Cuba is really craziest about. Congas and rhumbas are primarily for the blacks, not that they don't love the blacks (except they think they are crazy and dirty, and they won't let them hold big dances in the public squares of small towns, which are reserved for band music) but they like sons and boleros better for themselves but best of all like spanish music, and flamenco stuff. You hear it everywhere, especially in the smaller cities.

On the way out here in the bus, we stopped at some little village and a guy with a guitar and a little girl came out and they each took alternating verses, singing what turned out to be impromptu flamenco stuff about each individual passenger. The guy would sing words like: "Now pay strict attention to the words of my daughter, for in her song she will pour out to you the soul of a child of Spain." Then the little kid would sing something wishing to you prosperity, you handsome and noble gentleman, you were very famous, she had heard you were coming, the town would never be the same after you had left, and no funny business or curtseying about it, she would come and stand in front of you and look at you in the eye and sing serious and direct and loud and clear and fine, good flamenco singing for a kid. And no grinning and simpering either, but a good serious kid.

There is this thing about Cuba it is a very happy and friendly place, and furthermore the Cubans are different from what you might think from the ones you see around New York. To begin with when you get here you find a tremendous proportion of Spaniards, who are without any question at all the best guys in the world, along with the French of the south, and they aren't quite so crazy as Cubans who have really been Cuban for a lot of generations. Everywhere you go you get in great conversations and in the town of Matanzas I met the whole group that would rival the Malcy Johnson group in Olean, and they took me riding in their cars and I had a pretty good time and a lot of talk. I had made friends with them before I had been in the town half an hour, by just sitting on a bench in a public square: in a minute they had come up and started a conversation. The second night then I found myself making a great long speech on metaphysics to about twenty of them, in broken Spanish, in the central square.

I have also been into monasteries and made friends with some priests: one wonderful priest in the Carmelite monastery (which was all full of statues of St. John of the Cross and St. Theresa) was a guy who looked like the Pope, and we had a long talk and then I had a conversation with a Marist priest in Matanzas who knew French. As for the churches around Cuba, I must say I have never seen such churches or such things when I was in a church. There is a church here called La Soledad which has in it a miraculous image, and when I walked into the place I was picked up by my feet off the floor and seen not a ring of pure and endless light but rather a great ring of nothing which was absolutely real, indescribable and also a little frightening. It was clearer than if I had seen it with my eyes, but it was simply nothing, and there was no sensible note included in it anywhere, and anyway I was on the edge of it like on the edge of an abyss. Also it come to me in St. Francis church in Havana with a great shock that nearly stopped my breath that right in front of me was the whole entirety of heaven with the big stadium full of saints Dante describes in the last cantos of *Paradise* beholding in their midst the immense light of God. It wasn't anything like seeing anything with your eyes, but it was a sudden apprehension of a clear and absolute truth so completely certain that I went right up clean through the roof of the church like a rocket.

From Camaguey which is a swell town and a sort of a Cuban louse, full of cowboys on small horses, very swarthy and serious fellows with pistols and machetes, I am going on to Santiago, there a fellow may write me where I will be staying at the Hotel Casa Grande. If you was suddenly to pick up a bag full of silver dollars, I can see no better way of spending them than by coming to Cuba. Some other time I will explain in what way this hotel in Camaguey is the best place in the world to write the best novel in the world.

In the summer of 1940 Merton learned that the Franciscans had turned him down and that he would not, as he had thought, be entering their novitiate.

% Virginia Burton
Urbanna, Virginia
July 24 [1940]

No monastery. Maybe look for a job. I don't think Jinny & Lilly [Reilly] come up to Olean. Here it is nice. I'll come to Olean some time.

New York
[August 1940]

Some complicated misery leaving Virginia Burton's mansion in the state of the same name, for it was the best place in the world, what if it was the hottest and the drunkest? Not a minute without laughs and congas, not a minute without its son, bolero, pregon. Me and Jinny and Lilly and Jinny's cousin who I think to be the queen of the earth, although married, lived in this elegant mansion all for our own, drunk for ten days: hoopla. I am only just becoming once more aware that I have a complicated monk sadness that I should have been worrying about too, only didn't have time. As to the weekends, they was not so elegant, for then came Jinny's parents and visitors and Jinny's cousin's husband who will presently assassinate me. But one weekend come Dona [Eaton] and her husband Ralph Bellamy and her baby Noah Beery Jr, which is a good enough baby and didn't yell a yap so I take it back about Noah Beery Jr: I say just Ralph Bellamy Jr. Dona was fine and nursed her baby rather a lot but went away and sent back some good rhymes (bajan) which gave us all to laugh and weep together. Now I think to vote for [Wendell] Willkie and go off and join the draft with a great sigh . . .

Today I come home with a man in the orange business who says Texas is the new frontier and the west is the country of the future thereby anticipating Horace Greeley by 100 years if Horace Greeley was to be born in 2040, or some future time if any . . .

Mr. Somebody of Modernage books say I write good but he don't understand why I wrote that novel. A dame in Virginia said she knew where the rich old lady who used to have the Black Sun Press in Paris was, namely Bowling Green, Virginia. I believed her at the time, and believed it too when she said this old lady was her friend. The agent [Naomi Burton] give my novel to some press I never heard of run by *The*

Atlantic Monthly. I ain't perplexed, but only because nothing perplexes me for I understand nothing at all, let alone special hard things like why should they give my book to *Atlantic Monthly.* I am going to try and get a job at Bonaventure or any place except Columbia, but the only reason that story is not entirely true is that right after I finish this letter I will write to Columbia arsking for my job back. Tell me what everybody does: I believe it to be good at the hut, invite me back, oh please, to write my novils and operas for the month of Sept. before the draft of Oct. I may not write more, for that I am lovesick and very sad.

Merton sought and received a job teaching English at Saint Bonaventure University. He began teaching in September 1940.

March 13 [1941]

Holloy. How youse? Me not so good, what with the draft. Last week I got the questionnaire, this week, fast like a rabbit, notice to get physical examination somehow, somewhere, which means, I guess, Fort Jiggs of evil memory. Sad.

I put in my ten cents worth of conscientious objection, that is all the ten cents worth I could squeeze out of being a Catholic: namely that I would refuse combatant service but not non-combatant service, like medical corps etc. I haven't had any answers on that yet, but either way I'll probably be in, as I say, Fort Jax of evil mummery. I won't know the answers on the conchie questions until after they give me my Wassermann and peel off my clean skin in the places where they want me to wear my moral and mental scabs in the future. I give as much argument as was in me to give why I don't want to be killing people, and as far as I am concerned that is all I worry about: if I get in the medical corps I make no more complaints, nor seem to swear as much as I do now, either, except for the broad universal reasons that they are going to ship us all to Africa and Fujiyama while the shipping is good, and that is no pleasure.

I'll show that Hitler. I'll show that impolite Hitler. I'll show those card-playing Nazis. I'll go up and take them by the collars of their suits, with my little artifical rakes and hoes I'll be armed with, and give them a good *shaking* and let them know they can't come over here like that and molest Don Ameche and Tyrone Power and PM magazine and laugh at our ice cream sodas the way they do, and criticize our mechanical toilets, and point with scorn to our other institutions, and jape Ann Harding. I'll show those shifty little japs they can't get away with insulting whoever it is they have been insulting.

I walked up and down the main street of Olean this morning looking in all the stores individually and scribbled in my twopenny tablets the following intellectual gem: that sooner than defend all this I'd personally set fire to each one of the establishments and then throw a bomb at the fire house to make sure everything burned nice and proper. Tomorrow, as I say, Fort Mix.

One doesn't even know if they give me until June like the wise guys in my class they have drafted . . .

So all I know is I'm certainly going to be in some part of the army, and what then and when and where, and how much beaten up etc I haven't any idea. The only other thing is that a crazy new directions poet but not john honer loggin the xv has taken a lot of new poems I writ for an anthology and others for some tiny crazy magazine. This one is called charles henri ford, and is really, of course, charles *edsel* ford, and I think my poems are going to be embroidered someplace in the upholstery of lincoln zephyrs . . .

St. Bonaventure, New York
[March 1941]

Some printemps. Outside my fusty room it laughs a great drunk tree as if in the heats of middlemost July. Yesterday I started to write a letter to you which explained and developed in bad esperanto the extremely stupid topic of how I was going right then to walk in to Olean by the river road, which I immediately tore up. Then I walked into Olean by the main road. Only because I had to go to O. Not to see the tree squirrels in the street. But le paysage, as we say: very joli . . .

Everytime I run anything through my mind in a good series, it leads up to a dance step Lilly Reilly was supposed to do in the International Casino for the end of a number: first gay like a bird, then coy like a dove in the ballet of the dying dove, then suddenly furious horrible big vulgar gestures in every direction, and finally cakewalk off to buffalo jig jig jig out of sight like mad, with a completely disorganized look: anthology of everything terrible, and very fast, very funny, each one on top of the next. It gives to laff considerable. If you don't remember it ast her she should some time show you. It gives to laugh plenty, on spring evenings or any other evenings . . .

Boy, I looked for six minutes between the pages of that novil I wrote last fall, and it gave to weep copiously. No wonder the agent doesn't really like it, is all I say. I always had a secret fear it was bad, but never thought how bad, and I suppose if I set myself to thinking back how it was writing that book, I will find out how every wrong way of writing feels. For sheer stupidity, that is, believe me, some book. On the other hand I looked at the Cuba travel book and still liked that all right. I can't think of one part in that novel that doesn't embarrass me like a big electric hair. I thought to write another novel. I guess I did that every day since I was six. I thought of writing a journal in Joyce talk and invented esperanto. That makes me feel better than another novel. The other thing is that it is not absolutely necessary to write anything, either.

Gaudeamus igitur, juvenes dum sumus.
Got around his overture, juniper's confused us.
Chowder in the eggy door, Tubal Cains' consumers
No <u>Sir</u>.

I got a new theory: start talking about bad writing and in ten minutes you begin to write bad. That's like the theory horsehair in a cigarette will make you drunk, bicarbonate cocacola and soap will make you sick, earth mud and dung will repel the least fastidious, and other modern superstitions.

Lorca got a nice poem called "Ode to Walt Whitman." Because I always thought walt wigsby was crazy, I never read the poem. Whatever he was, Lorca is one nice guy, and this is one nice poem, and it also happens to be about Wig Wigsby, and not about something else, which you might have thought, from my saying it was a nice poem. Oliver St. John Gogarty I read one of his books nothing but bicycle races bicycle races bicycle races. I was never able to finish it, it was so tedious. In between the bicycle races he would say Joyce was a little blind pauper, too poor to wear anything but tennis shoes, and tell about four or five times he beat Joyce up and made him look ridiculous, and then he returns to the bicycle races, or else dirty jokes about what this intern said to what intern in the operating room in 1902. This is what I remember about Gogarty.

I get up quarter to six in the morning and go to bed at half past ten, and when I don't teach a clars I sit in my room and either write on scraps of paper or read holy books or just look out of the window where the fleurs push in the gazons, bright and shiny like pastilles and candy. I prefer reading the holy books to the writing of the scraps of paper, and looking at the gaudy trim of the dewy gazons is all right for in between, but the best thing of all is to do the same thing every day, and never have to go any place, which it took me longer to find out than any of the fellows.

St. Bonaventure, New York
[March 1941]

the chaff board hath spoke. I got me drop number: 4e. i will not appeal. there is only one more remote class: 4f, lunatics.

this isn't the number i asted for or expected, but i refuse to complain, but will take it like a man. it means there is no army i am qualified for, not even the salvation army. i do not hang my head for this implied rebuff. if they want to put me in the crazy-conchy class to hoe the trees, it's all right with me, too. let them.

i called up the Olean draff bud, and said what is the significance of the clatz 4e? they said "wait, there is no four e, saving in pennsylvania." i said: "no doubt. but what does it mean." "crazy med conchiz" they spok.

"to hoe and tend the trees and shrubs," i leered archly. "perhop," they renounced, "but only in other districts, not this: perhop in pennsylvania." "when?" i countered with a rough clattering of the teeth. "who knows" they shrug, and that is the end of that. in fine, they haven't made the camps yet, and all it sez on the card is: 4e until further notice, meaning, i suppose, indefinitely, come hell, come china, come the shifty japs.

except all the same, supposing come the war in a serious form, i expect i would not hoe the trees and shrubs, but go volunteer for the medical corpz i was asting to be put in the first place. meanwhile, the peace, i will enjoy the fruits of liberty to pray and praise and read my philosophy books and write my verses and harm no germans.

i think my chaff bor must of been confused and perplexed by the close-print pages of argument i give them why i didn't want to kill the leaping italian, the mathematical hun.

as to the medical i had last week, it was very funny. in a sad way, of course. i was picked up for a ride by some arch bubble headed crazy, to whom i say: pretty soon it will be all over, the war. he brightened up like a burning oil tank, and shouted, "o yes: is it not so? for now we have them german on the run: they can't bluff much longer. pretty soon they'll *have* to give in." "for lack of interest in conquering such unimportant countries as the south pole, which is all that will remain in the 'presently' which you so optimistically envisage," was my unspoken comment.

in the medical they peered into my body cavities with flash lights, took me blood and me piss in small flagons, humiliated my naked flesh in a hundred sneakingly polite manners, give me the classification 1b because of having some iron teeth, and robbed me but bound me not, and let me go, having finally placed in me left hand a small pamphlet of the following type: picture of some soldier boys getting on a train: big letters saying: 'So long, boys, take care of yourselves!' and inside it say 'them huers and pimps you will meet in the army life do not love you for yourself, but only for your money. buy your condoms at the post canteen, and you will recognize your first cases of claps and syph by the extreme pain, humiliation, soreness, festering and unpleasantness which you will share with all your fine companions in the army. so long, boys, take care of your clapped up selves.'

thus i walked out into the street weak with enthusiasm to serve my country by staying home in gaol. i still couldn't figure out if the medical would of got me into the 1b which is what i was asting for in the first place . . .

write and say what happens to all the fellows in their respective chaff boards, in which i pray they will all make the same mistake as mine did giving you 4e, to laugh and scribble in the intellectual army of no-legs.

meanwhile with no further let and hindrance for the time being, i think more and more of going to trappist place in Kentucky for before Easter, and after that to new york, where i will therefore be in some time or other.

In April 1941, at the suggestion of Dan Walsh, Merton went on retreat to the Trappist Abbey of Gethsemani in Kentucky, south of Louisville.

Cincinnati
April 5 [1941]

. . . I stop here on my way south to the Trappists. I meet, on their way north, starlings, (one million) and soldiers (equally) on leave. My draft board was full of lies, it turned out. I am really 1B, after all, and not a convict, off to hoe the trees.

St. Bonaventure, New York
June 30, 1941

I have just rushed incontinent to my maquina scribi and penned with the artful mechanical fingers so thoughtfully devised to jam in my most sincere moments, a series of seventy seven penny postcards which I have had distributed to the four winds.

Various personages, (Bosley Crowther, *Variety* magazine) will eventually receive these documents and learn from them that Roger Hilquist believes the movies to have passed forever out of their Golden Age. Not that I bin to no movie, but somebody mentioned Movies in the times, like where mr bosby growler screeches in a sly undertone between his teeth: "why do the publics no more glue their faces to the silver screens of our free democracy?" instantaneously it sprung to my memory my own case, which I felt mr craustark would naturally be interested in hearing about, because after all that's what he's looking for, an answer. I don't pretend that just my own case can answer the *whole problem* but it may help to throw light on it. Lawks, as if that was all a fellow had to live for, throwing light on Bortli Crubbert!

As I look out of my window I perceive that the Pennsylvania railroad is obsessed with mists and danks, and we have all been beset by the heats and swinks for some time.

The other day I was wawking in the wooeds very lithe and spry and watchful, perring through the trees saying to myselven: "Himmel, we must nought become intangled with the cows and bulls, which are reputed very fierce," what do you suppose happened.

So much was every article of my five senses intent upon the possible presence of the fierce cows and savage bulls that I trod upon a large ferocious milksnake and instantly leapt about twenty-five feet, or some four and a half times my own length, which is the world's record for the standing broad jump, although I wouldn't say I was standing on this here object. I had already run two hundred yards after that before the snake had no chance to complain at all in any manner whatever. This snake was very stupefied, and was, at the time, although huge, asleep. Right after that some guy come up to me and say boy you should of seen the big rattler I killed on the golf course two weeks ago by means of my mashie niblicks. "By means of your conversation and speech, rather," I exclaimed, "for you are extremely coarse to speak to me in this manner. What if I had strode upon not a milk but a roddle snake?" I sweat freely at the mere thought of walking in the woods, which no end curtails the delights of the summer season . . .

It also occurs to me there is a Trappist place in Canada near Quebec which one could go to comes August, not for the Canada but for the French, the coolness, and the Trappists . . .

St. Bonaventure, New York
December 6, 1941

Finally has come the time to go to the Trappists and try to get in.

I cannot explain this except to say it in a lot of different ways: time to get out of the subway and go away to the clean woods; or time to get out of the party full of smoke and pray in a clean bedroom, like before sleeping and resting the way it is sweet. It is time to stop arguing with the seven guys who argue inside my own head and be completely quiet in front of the face of Peace.

It is time for the midnight to get very quiet (through me giving to somebody else everything I am thought to be) so that my house may be at rest, and the soul talk in peace and listen to Peace and learn from Peace.

Maybe they won't take me: but anyway the perplexity about my not being able to be a priest is definitely all off. That was a mistake, and such a mistake, and told me in such a crazy definite way that I guess it was meant to do what it did: keep me out of the Franciscans!

However, the army decided to want me again. If they get me, well, then, I guess I will be very sad. But also it is true that one time I opened the Bible and found the sentence "Ecce eris tacens" and got scared: and I wasn't simply being curious, or playing a game.

No, honestly: it is time to stop being sick, (better than before, of course) and really get well. It is time to be full of peace and silence. And if you have a free and real choice between a world that belongs in a book by John O'Hara and one that belongs in a book by St. Theresa of Avila, I guess you have to make the choice in order to be happy, and quit arguing as if the two were even comparable.

Once I can be in the place where I belong entirely to God and not to anyone less than Him, like some writer having my legal name, then I guess problems about writing and everything else will not be much problems any more. Harlem isn't it, for me. Nor is any college. Nor is New York.

Maybe St. Lucy's Day [December 13] I start out for Kentucky, full of prayer. (Next Saturday.) And round His sunny tent like lambs rejoice. Also, there is absolutely no language to say the things there are to say, about this, except language of love: but there He will teach me to use that language like a child and a saint. Until which, I cannot talk about Him, Who is all I want to talk about.

And in Him while I sing in the big church, (I pray on my face He will let me!) in Him will be also: Lax, Gibney, Seymour, Slate, Rice, Gerdy, Knight, Huttlinger; and Van Doren, and the Baroness, and Mary Jerdo and my brother and my uncle and aunt and my father and mother who died and Brahmachari and the whole mystical body of Christ, everybody, Roger, Gil, all people. Jinny, Lilly, All. All people. The living and the dead. All days, all times, all ages, all worlds, all mysteries, all miracles . . .

On December 10, 1941, Merton arrived at Our Lady of Gethsemani monastery in Kentucky, and was accepted as a postulant.

November 21, 1942

I was happy and surprised that *The New Yorker* took the carol, all full of direct references to God, and everything! That is good. I am glad you sent it, and the abbot said it was all right. So thanks. Maybe when I finish this I can put in with it a couple more poems, which there is no danger of anybody buying, but maybe after you are through with them, send them to [Mark] Van Doren. I haven't written much, mostly because right now there is no need to write anything. Thinking and praying takes up all anybody might want to say, and sitting still, right now, seems to make much more sense than anything I could have said. Also I feel a little awkward because the style of these ones I send seems to me too tricky, and all anybody has to say after being here a year is very, very simple, and not tricky at all.

What surprises me is not that I am happy here but that I ever tried to fool myself I was happy anywhere else—except of course, by God's grace, I guess I was always happy everywhere, even when I was a very bad guy.

It is very very good and sweet to be always occupied with God only, and sit simply in His presence and shut up, and be healed by the mere fact that God likes to be in your soul, because you like Him to be there. And in doing this you also love your neighbor as much as you could by any action of your own: because God cannot be in your soul without that fact having an effect on other people, and not necessarily people who have ever heard of you. Because when God is with you, you begin to desire the salvation of distinct individuals you have never heard of—& the desire is to obtain it. And words are not necessary for this, but they are sometimes a great joy. Other times they are a terrific nuisance.

And when I write that this is very good, I might as well write that it is bitter, too, sometimes, because it is hard to see God doing all the good that is in us, & ourselves absolutely incapable of doing anything in return. If I were less aware of my capacity for giving Him evil in return for good, I wouldn't be sad to think that I can do no good. It is plenty, to let Him do all this good; I am not too proud to simply enjoy His Kindness, but I am proud enough to be constantly ungrateful for it, & letting myself become concerned with things that are not His will, or His immense perfection, or His joy.

But I didn't come here to avoid shame at my own weaknesses. My only complaint is that if I were more of a child of God, or good monk, I would really be glad of my weaknesses, because it is this that has led God to want to do good to me: for if I had not been a sinner, He would not have come to save me . . .

It is very good, too, to live with such good monks as all my brothers are. There is, here, just the same proportion of people with faces that frighten you, as there is everywhere else. The men who come here are the same, originally, as the men in the subway & in Life cafeteria. But the difference is, here they have forgotten about being wise guys, and are no longer scared, or hard, or noisy, or argumentative, or mad. The reason for this is the Rule which we live by. One important kind of charity in a monastery is to keep the rule as perfectly as you can, even when it seems silly, because it is the fact of everybody doing things as the rule says that abolishes all arguments, & opinions, & criticism, & fights & conflicts & makes everybody go about quiet and happy, smiling to himself & to other people. The other & more important reason for this joy is the presence of God here in this house, loving to be with His children because they love nothing but for Him to be with them—& with all men.

It is a tremendous thing to have something to do in a Pontifical High Mass—when there are more than fifteen people around the altar with some function or other. At given times, as the Mass progresses, we shift & change from place to place, like a very solemn & complicated drama of angels, with the serious elation of angels, while the words of the Mass fly up terrible and strong as an army in battle, calling to us the infinite kindness of God, for us and all men.

Also, a lot of my brothers are really saints, and it makes you very happy simply to see them walking around full of God. All the joy in this house is Christ, in whose flesh we know God the only way anybody knows Him, (even those who don't believe in Christ see the invisible God only because Christ was made flesh) and all the joy in this house & in the world is in the Love & Truth that are perfect, & are a Person, or rather 3. But we can only see the Father & His Holy Ghost through Christ, who, being man & God, creature & creator, is the fulfilment of the whole of creation, being the bond that unites everything created with God, not in the order of being, but in the order of Love. For all things are united to God in one sense by the fact that He keeps them in being. But creation can only be perfectly united to God in love, through Christ, because it is through Him that the rational creatures are taken up to God, in love, taking with them all the other creatures by their love for them, in God. And when all things are properly ordered among themselves, the lower & the higher, and when the higher are perfectly ordered to God as their final cause (i.e. love Him with their whole heart & mind because he fulfils them, & He only fulfils them) then there is Peace. For peace is the tranquillity of the order of love . . .

All these things I read in St. Augustine: the Commentary on the Psalms, the Book on the Sermons on the Mount, etc. Also another wonderful writer is St. John Chrysostom, whom I read not in Greek however. All the Greek Fathers are translated into Latin. So I also read Dionysius the Areopagete, who is very like St. John of the Cross. Then I read St. Teresa of Avila's *Autobiography*. O boy! This you should read as fast as you can get it! O what a book! Or maybe you already read it? When I talk about writing, all I want to write is what I just wrote now about Christ: I pray, if the Lord wants me to write, it will be all that, in a book about Christ, about what is Faith-Hope-Love according to St. Augustine, and all like that. I feel as if I never read anything before the Fathers of the Church: everything, even Dante, Shakespeare, etc. seem like nothing. Except Blake, though. I don't read him, but I think a lot, how much he knew about the humanity of Christ, & how important.

One good thing, on a more natural level, is being read to us in the refectory. It is nice to listen to books, even bad books, while we eat our black bread & oats etc. Not that the books are all bad or all good. Sometimes very good, like St. Bernard's *Sermons on the Canticle of Canticles*; sometimes very bad like a few I forget, all except silly incidents in one. Sometimes fairly good, like the *Song of Bernadette* which we have now. In parts it is okay, I think. All the monks laugh and smile when he [Franz Werfel] writes about a strict nun, one of the villains of the book, and about how Bernadette was beaten up in the strict convent, especially a line about "Supposing you had to be a Trappist & take a vow of silence?" I think every time the Abbot wants to make us laugh, he gets some book where it says the Trappists take the vow of silence & sleep on nails. Then everybody is very jocose in the refectory.

At the same time, this place is such a paradise of kindness & gentleness & everybody being unselfish, that I find myself listening to the strict-nun stuff, & being scared, & thinking what if I had to be in one of those tough places. This is supposed to be the 'hardest' order in the Church. Actually our 'hard' rules, kept with love, make the life very easy & pleasant, on the whole, & I bet anything it is far easier to live here than in some less strict order where they are allowed to talk all day, & get to sitting around criticizing, then beating each other—like St. Bona's. Please say a prayer & help me thank God for bringing me here, where I belong, & not getting me into any other Order!

Anyway, here is the important thing. The Abbot says, if you want to you may come here for two weeks & sit & do as you like & pray & think, and as for the money for getting here & back, if you write and tell me you are coming, right away I will send you moneys, enough for coming & going. As for staying here, of course, no moneys. So please come. It is nice here. I guess I won't be able to see you, as you are not a relative, & don't be surprised if I don't look up and wave or anything like that. But come. And bring a lot of sweaters, because it is cold in the church in December. The best time is Christmas week. But come anytime you can. I gather from the Olean postmark you are at loose ends: or maybe I am wrong. How about Harlem? How about [Robert] Gibney? [Edward] Rice? Tell Rice there was a soldier from the parachute corps here in the novitiate 2 weeks, on furlough. He made a vow to be a monk after the war's over, so the Abbot lets him spend his furloughs in the community. He is a nice guy, very happy when he is here. How about Seymour [Freedgood]? [Mark] Van Doren? [John] Slate? The Baroness [Catherine de Hueck Doherty]? Everybody? Tell hello to Gladio [Gladys Lax Marcus], Benjie [Marcus], Dick, your father, Mary Davis, everybody in Olean.

My brother [John Paul Merton] was here, & baptized, very happy, in July. Now he is in England, with the Canadian Air Force, & writes good letters. Please come, when you can. And write. And pray for peace, & for us here, & for everybody. The thing that makes the most sense is to be in the presence of God, & live by His will as we live on air & bread, & to ask Him to make us all be with Him forever.

November 23, 1943

. . . What I want to say is to you and to Mark [Van Doren]: soon I make temporary vows if God wills to let me. (I would have made solemn vows the first day I was here, & still would, only more so. But we have to wait.) Then I will have nothing to do, officially now, with property, ms. etc. I told Mark he could have all the stuff I had written & given him. So now I repeat that, but only add that if he wants to get rid of anything he should give it to you, and if you don't want it, give it to Bona's or make hats for the orphans out of it . . .

Even when you can't see your hand in front of your face, spiritually speaking, this life is always very very happy. Even when you are beaten into the ground by the weight of your own pride, which is the only thing that ever caused anybody in the world any real pain or any real sorrow. Everything else is joy—except what separates you from Christ in Himself & in yourself & in other people. Pride is crucifixion because it separates you from yourself, but to know it, & not refuse to remember it all the time, is a crucifixion that heals the separation & brings unity with yourself & with Christ, who is the center of yourself, & with others, who are your other selves,—selves that you cannot do without. Because God is love & if you had no brothers to love you would never have more than a shadow of God, but with them you become *part* of God, because your love for them & theirs for you makes up the Mystical Body of Christ. Write. Come, too. Spring is the best time.

Easter Day [1945]

Dear Bob—& pass it on to Mark [Van Doren]: After my confessor had said no poems, then I was talking to Fr. Abbot [Frederic Dunne] about something completely different & he suddenly said very emphatically I should write poems. That was on the feast of the Conversion of St. Paul (January 25). Who was praying: you or St. Paul? Here are the poems then. I have very little time to write them & none to work on them a lot & make corrections—or type out better copies.

The liturgical book: Fr. Abbot says OK. Now that it is Paschal time & we have more hours work, I can begin to do something about it. So far I have done nothing—busy with finishing the book about the nun [Mother M. Berchmans] & correcting a translation of *The Lives of the Saints*—which Bruce & Co think to print—only after the international situation. But Rev. Father wants me to write a book on the Contemplative Life, as the old Cistercian writers conceived it and that is just what I feel like saying plenty about—so pray that God may give me grace to do it well for His glory & to teach men the ways of His peace.

The last paragraph looks as if I wrote all the time but as a matter of fact it is only for six hours a week or, now, eight. Thank God it is no more. But it no longer bothers me much in choir: since I leave all the decisions to Fr. Abbot I have nothing much to be preoccupied about, & so I can forget the stuff, relatively speaking, & pray a little.

My health is a lot better & I feel all right. Also I am keeping the full rule again—though I only had the complete fasting for the last 4 days of Lent . . . Oh, did you ever send a copy of the poems [*Thirty Poems*] to my grandmother in New Zealand? If there is any hitch about it let me know & tell me what to do . . .

P.S. Today I opened a letter from someone called Raymond E. F. Larsson who sent me a good poem dedicated to me & Bob Lowell, for both being poets & both loving God & His peace . . .

[May 1947]

Thanks for your letter. I am fine. In fact March 19th I made my solemn vows & so everything is all sewed up finally. It is a terrific relief. I go around singing inside about it all day. It is very good even from the angle of having a completely definite juridical status in the Church, because it means that everybody from the Pope & all the Cardinals & the whole Roman Curia & all down to our Abbot & my own spiritual director are there to take care of every possible problem I might have. All I have to do is remember to breathe, and I will become a saint.

That's one angle. Another angle is that for the first time in my life I am convinced that I am no longer 10 years old. Before, I was never sure. All my quick and self-confident decisions were all 50% to bluff—although I didn't know that either. Another angle is I am glad to realize how dumb I am now that it no longer matters, since God is doing my thinking for me. All this comes of being in a definite groove. It leaves you free to follow the Holy Ghost because you are no longer hanging on to the things that are stationary & only corrupt from inside without leading anywhere.

On the other hand I am very aware of a sort of where-do-we-go-from-here angle, as if a new avenue was opened out by profession—I mean in the spiritual order.

For a long time I have been wondering about all the writing I do & asking if that was stopping me from anything. But everybody, including the Abbot General of the whole order [Dom Dominique Nogues] who was here tells me to write, write poems, write everything, especially write about the contemplative life. As at present I have no choice although it feels useless when I am doing it. Still, that is one of the tricks of this life—doing the things you are told rather than the ones that feel safe and excellent.

You complain of being idle. I feel as if I were too busy. It depends what you mean by idle & busy. One thing is true: you don't need to *accomplish* anything in order to please God, and He doesn't need anybody's movement & activity. But He does want your love and my love . . . I hope you will one day get settled in something you will know is definitely God's will and all directed to Him alone. Because that is the necessary thing.

About Hollywood I myself would I think want to get away from it. Ask a good director, but someone who knows you because after all direction depends a lot on that. General answers are not enough—or they are, in an emergency, but not to make everything perfect. If you stay there why don't you write a movie about Charles de Foucauld, since you are all full of research on the Sahara. He was a Trappist, then he was a beggar at the door of a convent in Jerusalem, then he was a hermit in the Sahara & finally the Tuaregs killed him. But the Abbot General says he won't be canonized because really in all this he was just doing what he felt like. We've got books about him here, one full of pictures.

Humble George the colored pilgrim is wiser than you. He shows up here every 6 months or so. In a couple of months we are starting a new monastery in Utah. Mormons won't like it. I don't know if I will be sent there but if I am I won't be doing much writing.

Harcourt Brace is publishing the autobiography [*The Seven Storey Mountain*] & all the fellows are in it, so is Peggy [Wells]. If anybody doesn't want to be in it, let me know quick; I don't say anything unprofitable for anyone—I hope. I intimate that Seymour [Freedgood] was fond of exaggeration. Is this bad? I think he would be pleased for it makes him out to be very sly. It is all straight stuff & no novel . . .

April 1, 1948

You see it's still Gethsemani, not Utah, though the Utah foundation sounds fine. It is at Huntsville, 18 miles from Ogden & where Fr. T[homas] à K[empis] Reilly got the idea I was there is probably the article ["The Trappists Go to Utah"] I wrote about it in *Commonweal*.

[James] Laughlin was going to print the essay in the New Directions anthology, until I remembered canon law says Catholic writers ought to be careful where they appear. That was also the reason why I couldn't write for '47 the magazine of the year. Fr. Abbot saw something in it he didn't like. Otherwise I have been writing a lot for magazines . . .

The autobiography [*The Seven Storey Mountain*] comes along slow. Haven't seen page proofs. Bob Giroux must be very busy. I was reading T. S. Eliot—"East Coker," etc. & this time I liked him a lot. I got those books by Ruysbroeck—in French. He is wonderful. I'd like to do an edition of him for N. Directions. As it is I am going to do John of the Cross' *Dark Night* for them in English & Spanish with notes—using Peers' translation & not doing one of my own. Also I am doing a book of more or less disconnected "thoughts" & aphorisms [*Seeds of Contemplation*] about the interior life also for N. Directions.

A Dominican nun in Erie, Pa. has been writing me fine letters & together we are getting up a leaflet on contemplation. She is a friend of Sister Madaleva who writes the poems & Sr. Madaleva will—it seems— print this leaflet. Sr. M. is running some kind of a theology course for lay people & that is very good.

The B[aroness Catherine de Hueck Doherty]'s book *Friendship House* was read in the refectory & everybody liked it a lot. Tell her if you write to her. And I read *Dear Bishop* & it made me wish I was a bishop.

A long time I thought I would run away & live in the Arizona desert, I guess that's why I want to write that movie about Charles de Foucauld. But I don't want to run away. I just get great yearnings to be all alone in solitude by myself alone but everybody says that is dumb. Anyway I don't know how to cook & I can't eat roots.

Also I keep a Journal. They made me sub-cantor. Am sending a booklet about the Abbey [*Cistercian Contemplatives*]. Did I tell you [James] Laughlin of N. Directions was down here & I like him very much. He is a fine guy & he has a good friend in San Francisco called Kenneth Rexroth you ought to see maybe. I'll give you his address if I find it . . .

F. of St. John of the X.

[November 24, 1948]

Thanks for your beautiful letter. One of the best things I liked about *The Seven Storey Mtn.* was the index which they fixed up at Harcourt Brace and which came to me as a surprise. It made me wish I had mentioned a whole lot more people in the book. It reads like a big party on the night before judgment day, with everybody invited by Providence to be in this book also invited to go to heaven in a big yacht provided by the prayers of the ones who were the biggest saints like Francis, Saint and Blake, William and Michel-de-Cuxa, Saint. It certainly is an interesting party. It certainly includes the ones that are not explicitly mentioned. But I get this wonderful exalted feeling that we are all going to ride into heaven together and that Christ will get great glory in the work of His love that united us all together in ways that we will never understand until then . . .

Anyway it turns out in the end that having written the book was a very good thing to have done and that it would have been silly to wait until I was older and all the bookshops in Louisville are selling it hand over fist and a Presbyterian minister from up the line somewhere said he was broke but he'd awfully like to have a copy so I am sending him one.

Right now very busy trying to fix up a fancy picture book about the Abbey for our centenary [*Gethsemani Magnificat*]. Some very classy photographers from Louisville were out here twice and they are very good. One of them is a kid nineteen, just out of the Marines but he works like [Ed] Rice works, with the same kind of seriousness. He was lying on his back on the floor of the Church with his head resting against a radiator and a graflex on his knee shooting a picture of ceremonies in the sanctuary. I like it a lot and they like the abbey like anything. They flew all around the place in a plane Armistice Day and when they got home they were sick but they had some fine pictures. They all read the book too and say they want to talk about it some time.

Last summer after Dom Frederic [Dunne] died, I went to Louisville for the first time in 7 years with the Vicar General who came from France and wanted an interpreter. We went to the Good Shepherd Sisters who wear blue and white uniforms and are very nice. They rescue fallen girls and I translated a speech of the Vicar General who was, incidentally, in a prison camp during the war and told me a lot of things.

Going to Louisville was a nuisance but not as bad as I thought it might be. It was nice saying office riding fast through the cornfields and the tobacco, and the city looked stupid but the people all looked very interesting, that is to say I felt a whole lot of sympathy for them although they seemed to be pretty balled up, still Louisville is less balled up than most places, because they don't run so fast there and I got the feeling that everybody was of terrific value, immensely precious and bought with a great price and all their souls were like jewels, very rich and ought to be pretty as anything but I was glad to get back and since we were late for supper Fr. Benedict had us something fixed up in the hotel with scrambled eggs and things like that—butter, milk and so on—which were so strange that I got sick. Not that milk is strange, though. We have a new pasteurizer. I definitely strictly honestly do *not* have TB. So there . . .

[James] Laughlin thinks he has got T. S. Eliot to bring out a selected poems of mine in London with Faber and Faber and wants any unpublished early poems to look at. I don't think Gladio [Marcus] has anything worth while that has not been printed already. At Bona's they have only journals in big fat ledgers. I wrote to Clare Boothe Luce (who is very friendly and nice and gave me this typewriter which is smooth and fancy) . . . Anyone who wants to can write. The Laughlin I mentioned is New Directions and you really ought to know him, he is a terribly nice guy and he was down here again. Really you'd like him a lot.

Give my love to everybody, [Bob] Mack, Gladio, Mary Davis, Gib [Robert Gibney] Nancy [Flagg] Ed [Rice] Sy [Freedgood] and everybody. I sent the book to Brahmachari. Holy Christmas. Come down some time. Evelyn Waugh is supposed to be coming down. It was nice working with Bob Giroux and he is doing another book [*The Waters of Siloe*] now, about the Order. Pray that he will take all the beautiful pictures I have got lined up to illustrate it. And here are some drawings.

November 27, 1949

Thanks for the letter and the list of poems and the news of Gib and Nancy [Robert Gibney and Nancy Flagg]. Is Virgin Islands any good for a monastery?

I am not writing, too busy teaching mystical theology and a big orientation course for novices to get into the liturgy. I have suddenly woken up to the fact that somebody needs to be teaching theology the way St. Augustine did and not the way textbooks used in seminaries do. Someone should be able to find the living God in Scripture—and this is His word—and then lead others to find him there, and all theology properly ends in contemplation and love and union with God—not ideas about Him and a set of rules about how to wear your hat. The Mass is the center of everything and in so far as it is Calvary it is the center of Scripture and the key to everything—history, everything. All the trouble going on now.

Anyway pray that the classes may work out. It will certainly do no harm to stop writing now for a while and all this will build up easy into a better book than I ever thought of before. If God wants it that way.

Naomi Burton wants to come down here and persuade me to lie low for a while and she does not believe that this is exactly what I am doing. I have manufactured a private boardwalk out behind the old horsebarn which is half destroyed and there I walk up and down and make up songs that I will never be able to write down, partly King Oliver and partly Stravinsky or somebody and partly Gregorian chant. It is about the only way I can pray but it is mildly pacifying and doesn't disturb the cloud where God is. I say it is the only way I pray—no—there is a big opera started inside me when I get in choir but it is strictly opera and for me *Il Trovatore* isn't prayer and I shrug it off, when I remember . . .

Merton wrote less to Lax in the 1950s than he did before and after. He stayed in touch with him, at least partially, through Sister Therese Lentfoehr, who became a friend of Lax's.

[*Cold War Letter 16*]

[December 1961]

Here is at my side your exceedingly ribald Christmas card in many foreign languages inciting to joy.

Here without feet running in the sand or on the burning deck beneath the ships here amid the wolves we meditate on joyeux noel,

Here with the ship of state already half submerged and with waters up to board standing nobly in the tottering captain's bridge

We Santa Claus salute you.

Jubilee should move to Chile, or to Tierra del Fuego. There is joy, if also hunger and cold, in Tierra del Fuego. There is no need to live in a hole in Tierra del Fuego, though perhaps there also a two week hole would maybe turn out useful. Here I am told on good authority the guys who go down into the holes they will find that while they crank the hand blower the blower will be melted by the heat of the firestorms. Some fallout shelter.

Did you hear about the scientist who built himself a very fine fallout shelter for thirty dollars made out of railroad ties and along came an ordinary everyday grass fire which burned out his house and garage and gutted his scientific shelter. It seems to me that there must be a moral in this somewhere. It seems to me that there must be a moral in a lot of the funny things that people are saying somewhere. But the noise of the announcers leaves no more time or peace to hunt for a moral.

If *Jubilee* moves to Chile and if *Pax* moves to Chile there will be no more purpose in wearing yourselves out putting out a magazine. This also has its advantages as any editor can readily see. You can spend most of your time dancing in the mists, while of course being very careful not to slip off the rocks into the perpetually wintry sea. You may occasionally visit the seals and sealions. You may light your houses with lamps of whale blubber. You may write poems in Fuegian. There will be little reason to do much else. But this at least has its points.

Well let's see what is the news of the monastery? Today on the Feast of the Holy Innocents, Father Innocent got up and preached a sermon all about Sartre and generally quite favorable, whereas he was expected to preach rather on the Holy Innocents. This met with some disfavor and I believe that Fr. Innocent is about to be immolated in one way or another. Of Fr. Innocent a wise Benedictine once said "Nomen est omen", but he didn't know the half of it. Fr. Innocent hasn't read Sartre any more than anybody else around here and kept calling him "Sarter." Anyway it was an interesting sermon and nobody slept. Apart from that all that has happened is a great controversy about this year's Christmas Crib which looks more like the window of Bonwit Tellers than like the window of a third avenue pawnshop.

The guys at the *Catholic Worker* have said nothing about using the bit from Clement of Alexandria to which you now have exclusive rights in English and Fuegian. You have it first and last.

Hoopsa boyaboy hoopsa. Watch out for the fires. Don't look at the fireball. We Santa Claus, up to the snout in ashes, salute you. I hope to miss most of the fun by eating large quantities of fallout celery. Eat your strontium spinach and you will be too weak to look at the fireball. All the Santas salute you. Ding ding. Take cover.

[*Cold War Letter 40*]

[February 1962]

Dear Major Smithfield,

Indeed the poem of Nick the Gosling is a very fine poem, Major. I think you crazy, Major, if you givem this poem to Swami's revista. This very fine poem, sharpie poem, sharpie poem, much knowledge of monk-house. I am amazed, heretic yes, dancer yes yes, I am swept away by this very fine poem of Nick your agent on Sinai. It was on Sinai then he get these black lights? Major, my advice to you is to publish this poem so damn fast they cannot see you for the smokes, O major.

Furthermore since the cries go up incessantly that there is in Pax no variety, then I feel this is a further ragione for publish this magnificent sequels.

What cry? You balk, what variety? What goes? What goes up?

What cry? Cry of "Hola, no variety in papst."

"Helas, helas, my prince, my prince helas."

"My o my, no varieties."

"I am extinguished with weariness from always that same poem in Paps."

What goes? It goes up. The cry goes up. "Always the same damfool poem."

Which way is up? Relativity is up. Astronarts is up. Apes is up. Russians is up.

As regards up, when I look into ces espaces infines, am I afraid? What is space? What is infamous space?

I look into space and I figuratively or otherwise see: stars, apes, Russians.

Who is afraid of apes or Russians, or Mister Powers release shortly after?

Up in air is the all seeing eye of some instrument.

But it makes no variety in Paps. For this reason I commend

the magnanimous poems of Harry O'Garfield your agent from Dublin. (The cry also goes up in Dublin.)

> Yrs in deep thought
> Harvey Cucumerario

Poscraps: We have here entering a fine calypso singer from St. Lucia West Indies but he refuse to bring his guitar.

[*Cold War Letter 78*]

June 4, 1962

Here is an answer to your riposte of the nth. Since that time my dear agent we have been in contact with chiefs and sub chiefs, hostages and proto hostages, crypto chiefs and proto communists, proto pentecosts and crypto baptists, out and out card carrying propter hocs, and pseudo sub rosa investigating pinks. I have momentarily lost my crypto card and I am at a loss for words, plans, programs, hostages, protos and cryptos. But I have seen the man with the portrait under his arm. It is a picture of a crypto you know. It is a photo of a card carrying vestige. It is an image of a void. It is a most impressive card of identity, and all must whip out at a given moment the cards of identity.

Propter hoc ostendat unusquisque faciem suam et judicabitur.

In this amazing liturgy of chiefs I too have exchange the hostage, the ham, the hambone, the smoked trout, the vino rosso. Best hostages you ever saw. We sat in the grass and talked over the plans.

The plans are very simple. Take over the Pentecost.

Wipe out the identity cards and start over with the Holy Coast.

There's gold in them thar. Which? Them. Them.

Now here is a secret poem about my agent in Jodhpurs.

I have been silence. I have been nacht and nebel for my war book [*Peace in the Post-Christian Era*]. I have been put in the calabozo. I have been shut up in a tin can. I have been shrewdly suppressed at the right moment. I have been stood in the corner. I have been made to wear the cap. I have been tried and tested in the holy virtue of humility. I have been found wanting and tested some more. I have been told to shut up about the wars, wars is not for Christians except to support.

The following was omitted from the exchange between Merton and Lax, A Catch of Anti-Letters, *because it referred to his trip to New York in June 1964 to meet with Zen scholar Dr. D. T. Suzuki, a trip which Merton was put under obedience to keep secret.*

July 10, 1964

Dear Smyrnik:

. . . Here on the other hand is many quails which the rustics will all blast in the fall but for the moment was a quail running across the back grass and indeed the zen garden you didn't know we got a zengarden.

There is nothing so pretty as a quail running real fast across a zengarden leaving not a trace.

Now here is also what happened, no connections with the zengarden except fortuitous in the extreme. I was to visit with Suzuki, yes Suzuki, you heard me right. I was to visit with him very old, but secretary young and spry make the tea ceremony and Suzuki with the ear trumpet propose many koans from a Chinese book and in the middle they gang up on me with winks and blinks and all kinds of friendly glances and assurances and they declare with one voice: "Who is the Western writer who understand best the Zen IT IS YOU" they declare. You in this connection means me. It is I in person they have elected to this slot and number of position to be the one in the west. First west in Zen is now my food for thought. What did it ever get me, I ask ruefully. Did it get me to Kalymnos, nah, nor to Japan, ha! Well it did get me a visit with Suzuki. Where you think? You missed: Butler Hall. Yes, I repeat, I no kidding, this not Zen. Like I said first, Butler Hall, man, Hall. Oh you don't believe it you never believe it. It is absolutely true but it is a big secret and don't tell nobody from the gang because I was there [in New York] creeping around sly and hiding with whiskers etc false names, dark glasses, but yes indeed, Butler Hall. The old campus [Columbia University] you wouldn't recognize. I was to the New Asia about the only thing I remember. All the rest is all shot up. What was restaurants is paper books and what was otherwise is restaurants and all around it was gangs with knives and you could hear the Moslems shooting each other down in Harlem my I swow it was some experience. Zip zip out and back in the jets with nobody the wiser not allowed to tell nobody not allowed to tell [Edward] Rice or call *Jubilee* or Naomi Burstong [Naomi Burton] or Bob Gingeroo [Robert Giroux] or *The New Yorker* or nobody not allowed to hunt for Lilly Reilley any more either, but ate in some sly French restaurant drinking Benedictines and making like tourists. All this is sober truth big secret don't ever tell anybody or I end up in the calabozo.

Now for you quiet the imaginary phones there is no phones there is no party there is no riots there is only Orthos and fresh air and all that there is the cells and cells is best there is also the hermit cottage where I wander about and think such thoughts as befits the number one Zen of the west: that is to say not one thought of Zen. But glad to be number one. Besides that what I study is Irish monks and you be surprised they are not all ragging around with that colleen stuff like the Irish you and me remember they are serious monks but a bit quaint.

Like one monk he is walking on the water and he meets another monk in a boat and the one in the boat say what you doing walking on the water and the other one says this is no water this is the meadows and for proof here is a flower so he bends down and picks up a flower and throws it at the guy so the other one says nothing he reaches into the water and picks up a salmon and throws it at the other guy. After that the other guy was called by everybody "Salmon" in memory of this occasion.

Who won?

This I tell Suzuki expecting him to be very happy but all he did was ask where the first one got that flower. Not a wink about salmon, no siree.

Well after that I guess we better close the bar and throw all the guys out and go home.

April 28, 1965

Dear Henry

You telling me mae murray is dead she sure is dead you aint gonna get no laughs out of THAT movie. But anyway I was hesitant to write you in the midst of the Pastrami where you are now found, far from the isles of greece, not knowing whether you were just whipping in and out of the o's of Italy with or without holes man that is some typewriter it is all z's and I don't gather for sure if you like sinister pessoa but it is true, it is true, besides being the visionary of Fatima she is also a square, lackaday, the spirit of full awareness, I will be less aware in the future, with the goings on in the societies I will take some powders and snuffs that do away with all awareness for five thousand years. Pessoa he is an old dog, he should not have been allowed to say he was aware. His village stinks. It does not help you to know that she lacks simplicity. You are right. Divine simplicity bah. Run down the street and see Padre Pio, he has the right dope.

> *Mae Murray is dead, just died, yep.*
> *Wher'd you get so many z's on one typewriter?*
> *Mae Murray died from too much neti neti.*
> *Just now she died of it.*

You should not have seen that round table discussion with henry armetta it caused you to be prejudiced against the full awareness. We in Vietnam are fully aware. We have jumped to our own defence until we have jumped out of our own underwear and we are all sheriffs we are all mad I say mad mad mad. It is not going to go well with all the underwear we have jumped out of in Vietnam I can tell you. Mark my palabras we are in the crap for fair this time . . .

Yes it is true I sleep in the woods, I eat in the woods, I come down to the monastir only to say an occasional fie upon the commandant and to subvert the troops. Or to write five or six novels. In my house in the woods I resist war. I resist everything. That is why the hermit life is called the piece de resistance.

What happened about the collected letters of you and me, is that I collected what I had and chopped out the names of insults and a lady typed up with many a moan and I have sent to Laughlin but have not heard his outcry so far. I will tell you what he thinks, I can send a copy of the prints, you like? No.

July 17, 1965

Hoy:

There I was close to writing the cartolina when I sunk into a supposition and it developed so profound that I was not come up again for a year now I got to write my memoirs of one year in the bathyscaph ["Day of a Stranger"] which is take up all my moments. Never get stuck for twelve months in the bathyschap is all my mottoes. Mark the motto and avoid the scaph.

What else is the news? I cannot fathom all the silly news it is so stoopid. Here everybody change the name, but when the names was changed I was in the bathyscaph and became overlooked, so I came back with the same name. Here is the change the haircut for aggiornamento. They got me and cut my hair when I was not looking I was in a brown study when they cut my hair and after I come out it was no more crown. This is what they have done around here in lieu of aggiornamento. As to taking away the whips not a bit of it man, still the same old whips, just change the haircut in the name of aggiornamento. I cannot fathom such silly news as this.

Here all is forgetfulness of the morals and of the Vietnam, everybody just want to forget issues. The doors slam and people retire to forget the issue and stick their heads all the way into the TV where the issue is befuddled and made comfortable. What do they do in Kalymnos for forgetting the issue? I bet they don't even have an issue to forget. That makes you once again the luckiest boy of the year. I send you however my estimate of the issues and I pull all the bishops away from the TVs and I say you must not forget the issue, put down that damn beer can and listen to the issue you weasels. It is thus that I take up the topic of aggiornamento with our good bishops, every one a mighty fine bishop wearing each his rocket and his parsnips and his zucchetto and his flim-flams. Come away from the beers and listen to an issue I have dreamed up I remark with a sly dig of fun. It will cost me my neck, but I done it. Here is the sly fun for the bishops, which are already back once again to the TVs and have not listen . . .

I go now and think up an issue for the Pope.

I send all these issues in one packet even if it cost the price of the plane.

August 11, 1965

Dear Sam:

All right then tell me this: why didn't the house collapse when we was fighting for [Mahanambrata] Bramachari's turban back in '06?

I got to admit Blackie got the number of those Belgians all right.

Tell all the shooting to stop in Athens Mr. Giroux is coming there (my publishing).

Now about the newsreels of makarios: I am king makarios of crete but out of largesse everyone can have the scallops that accrue from the moveraps. I don't know what anybody got to say on the flipflaps, and since the poem is snatch in any case from the ancient greeks, why should anybody turn even a mild thought to the flipflaps? This is my solution to all the dilemmas. Tell all the dilemmas to cease.

Like I said before on the inst, all your huge books of poems is now swimming the ocean on the way to Kalymnos.

To my mind Macarius and the pony should be the movie of the year and why not radio city? If not radio city it is not the fault of the pony but of the city.

Let the pony be all over the TVs is what I say.

Tell all the dilemmas to stop. Shooting may continue after departs Giroux on the way home with the secrets.

Don't stay in the house if everybody else goes out to fight for the turbans. You be the first to fight for the turbans, even steal the turban the first of all. Then the house come down good riddance.

Germans is worst but Belgians are little vipers with the keen tooth of ingratitude. The United Kingdom is folded up in a small pile ready for disposal. The United States is nervous from too much cocacola. And now to make it worse everybody says you got to be more nervous and belong to the pepsi generation. It has come the pepsi generation and this explains Vietnam. It is the pepsi generation that is tearing all the turbans of Vietnam. Pres Johnson that old fool thinks he is in the pepsi generation. He will discover how wrong an old fool can be.

Nuts to pepsi cola say I.

November 27, 1967

Ho Master Parsnips

You have return, you are back to the prinzip, you is regress to the fonts, you is the oilwells, the Bradford airstrips, the old home, the Olio Hops, the Madison ski jump, everything.

Perhaps you have already been welcome back by the parades. Shall I say more? Not now. Here is merely the spiritual nosegay, the artistics, the panegyrics, the conscript jollities, the corncob poperies, the wits, the announcements.

Thanks for your instructio interscriptio or interscrutabilio. I will study the inscriptio or the instructio. I will fire into the air old rockers of pottery and conscripts of lobo-novo to all the editings you have recalled to mind. I will make small black letters on the papyrus lying face down under a sheet of solid inspiration.

Once again I am in a throe of making up type of all our letters to sell to Random Hops. Too many other editors I could mention are cold to the project, sniff sniff at the project, turn up the naso, look down the probosco. Well say I a fig for the judgments. Of all this more later.

Maybe we get up a congress of roundelays and nachtigalls and you come down with the springes.

Prosper, O Marse!

December 1, 1967

Dear Rugby:

Well, guess who it is comes to meet you and shake the hand as you disembark from the Olium Greyhounds? Ho ho ho noe other than Santa. Yes, here is Santa with his flowing barba twenty-five days in advance. Santa has beat the gun to meet you with Oilums for the New Yips. It is a hidden Santa who wishes to remain locked in the secrets it will do you no good to figure out the signature, this is not he. The writing is other than Santa. The true Santa is Barbara but that is neither here nor there. Who would not have supposed anyhow that Santa was in California.

Thus it is your own personal Guggenheims for the Mars Bar fund and for creativities in the New Years.

Incidentally this is also my day for grinding out over again the jokes for the true Guggenheim, alas my jokes never win for nobody. But while I was jiving around yawning and trying to get away from the jokes I took to leafing through the pamphlets about who was last years Guggy and there did I see the name of Old Reinhardt alas. Died in the year when he got the Googy. Thus the ironies of fate. Well, back to Santa: I speak of nothing else. It will do you no use to decipher the names of the banks etc. This is no clue to the secret Santa who is *watching your work*. Aha, all too few are the secret Santas, but you have one.

With this donation and encouragement you will learn to set all the Mars Bars to music no doubt. In any event do not fritter it away on the slot machines at the golf club, this at least do not do, but spend it on nourishing foods, fruits, medicaments (tried and true home remedies none of them miracle drugs) warm socks, sweaters, etc. I leave you to imagine the rest. While you are doing that I must pursue my labors and write to all the nuns.

Nothing like five hundred dollars to bring back the old bounce into the step. I will send back Prancer with the news to the source that all is well with the monies.

Where's [Edward] Rice?

Keep jiving.

Monks Mop
Wedsnip 28 Feb [1968]

Hoy:

Here is copies of letter sent to Teo Savory, Unicorn Press, Santa Barbara. She is very anxious to see letters, says she might be able to make a small book with help from Santa, 1500 copies. To be paid for by Santa and given to Barbara. Maybe with small emoluments.

But before that why don't you perhaps show to Bob Giroux? Or have you some other illuminations?

Anyway just want you to apprehend the goings of the book to Santa B. In the hands of Teo Savory (peace movement lady). She will send some of the books they have done (pretty) (but all small) (some on the other hand big as posters) (all small printings) I don't mean small letters. Some times huge letters high as the front of a building but ten copies.

Jesuit lady fifth column typist in NY is send you a xerox of the ladders. All behind this book is Jesuits in maskeroo. False glasses, abundant artifical moustarch, big cloaks, violins etc. Destined to at least a success d'estime because of assistance by masked Jesuits. Book already highly esteemed by the masked J's. Surely this is already something. But it is not enough, not enough.

Meanwhile between moving the peace Teo Savory is appreciate the delicate ladders.

I write more about Deans Day in a momentico, stay ready for Dean's Day. Meanwhile however in Lent I make the must retreat, hide in special padded cell etc. I hope, anyhow. Is always bust in too damn many publics. Teo Savory should print for me the biggest billboards to keep out the publics but the bills don't work.

Monks Pond is in a quandary because of everybody publishing liturgies they are all mad for the moment's liturgies and this takes precedence over the poetries for the monks are all in a mad fury of worship.

More in a minute.

Say hellow to the ninciow. I mean the Nuncioe.

Ho ho ho the Nuncio
His house is a communist front
His house is a communist front
Ho ho ho the Nuncio
Is redder than we want, redder than we want
Ho ho ho
The bright Red Nuncio.

March 15, 1968

Ho ho ho.

Jolly undertakers solve population problem. The birth control of the death. The resurrection of the unfittest. The survival of the mummy. The traffic of mobiles. Midnight is the time to view dead friends on the run. All dressed up like Christmas trees. Santa in the window with the stiffs. Hands full of bouquets, diamond horseshoes, etc. "You win Jake." Zip zip zip go the cars of bypassing amigos. "So long ol' Pal" Zip zip zip.

Crash at the red lights etc. Looking at the flowery corpse, forgot the traffics. Bam. Snuff snuff, bye bye, let's have another Budweiser.

Makes you think.

When you come to ol' Kaintuck don't let on you are coming to see me. Frantics are burning my books in L'ville (honest, have writ to papers, "will burn *Seven Storey Mountain*: Merton is commie red atheist contra vietnam war pitznik.") Bad reputations for all. Catlick papers all full of turmoil over your friend.

Ho ho ho turmoils.

Ha ha ha burn the books. I rush into the bushes pursued by jolly undertaskers. "We have the window" they cry "it is all lit up." Zip zip zip go the Louisville populations. But uncle is making whiskey in the bushes, Ol' Bushmills, for the party of friends in Maggio. Ho ho ho the party in Maggio. Set up another whiskeys all round and laugh at the bookfires.

Bypass the jolly undertakers with their lighted whorehouse windows. Atlanta Ga is full of crashes with people busting into the windows of undertakers to be with dead friends.

> Atlanta itself what it is but a dead friend I ask?
> All Georgia is but one big sixfoot window of the dead.
> Evelyn Waugh he didn't even begin to imagine Atlanta.
> Loved one on display is pickled in orchids.

Be careful of Kentucky. All full of Fascisti. Burn books of your freund. Do not admit whom you are visit. Say you are coming to see Gov Happy Chandler and spouse in a six foot window. With forget me nots. Oh the macabre humors of the sixty eight. It makes me laff on the wrong side of the tooth. It gives the toothache all the way down the backbone. It is fully bizarre and no mistakes. I just thought you should see the journals. Consider the Giornale. Addio.

Beppo Zampiglione.

April 13, 1968

Hohohoho.
Hohohohohoh Jenl Biddle.
Hhohohohohohoh Jenl Biddle.
Hohohohoh Genl Beagle.
Hhohohoh Jimminy Boggle.
WIN WIN WIN WIN.
Champchampchampchamp.
Winwinwinwinwinwinwinw.

Now here is the biz. Is come in beautiful from Liutgard Choundras Athens Posctop Shell Building from under all the awhings a most timely eyecatching beauties of a pome Jerusalem. Is my write all at once falling over with glee to Liutgard Choubdras to give me have for Monkpond III 250 pieces of this same Jerusalem for inserts giveaway handouts freecopy plastercramp artifact extras with the shopping stamps of our issue. 250 is the issue. 250 is the inserts. 250 is the joys and the spreading of hymns and enthusiasmos.

Hohohohohohoh Choundras.

More: was comein with the mails also the conscrips of beauty you was send from Olilamps, like the ooooo and the xxxxx XXXXX xxxxx and this is the blackwhite blackwhite which fascinate the ladies. These is all for the lamps of light in MPOND III. Is above mistake, is want from Choundras for MONKPONB II the Jerusalem. Hohohohohohohohoho Choundras.

Hohohohohohohohoho SANTA SANTA SANTA (a prayer for printing the antiletters)

Now here is the bizznips once again. If is all right me get 250 Choundras hohohoho Jerusalem, the ok. If not all right then tell me. If all right tell Choundras. Hohohohoho Choundras. If not all right. Tell Prexy Johnson. Tell Prexy Truman. Tell Prexy Butler etc etc etc. Hohohohohohoh Butler.

I wrote her she should send Airmail the 250 Jerusalem and is paid all by the New Jerusalem that is the eglise. Sursum corda. Viva il Papa.

Is out the dogwoods is up the parsnips is sliding like you said Mrs Finchbottom down the hillside on her back end. Is sprung the spring. Is out the Easter. Is jump over the hotdog the small brown finks. Is winner of the spring equinox General Boggle College (under Prexy Barney Google for ever. Hohohohohohoho for e-e-e-e-eveRRRRRR.)

Long live the top of the postum box. Longlive the wirtswatch and the ring. Long live the vanilla and the peach and Hohohohohoh yhr Good Humor MAAAAAA-NNNNN. Come June, don't wait for no Rouse [Edward Rice]. Unstop the hesychast bottle with no Rouse, he come later with the architect.

Pat and Mike.

Merton left on May 6, 1968, for a trip to California and New Mexico, returning to Gethsemani on May 20. See Woods, Shore, Desert: A Notebook *(Santa Fe: Museum of New Mexico Press, 1982).*

May 4, 1968

Hohohoho

Well is now in the envelope all the friendly skies of United. All little pink papers admit to friendly skies. High above the cloudburst sits friendly stewardess of United on lap of passenger. (Nix, slap in face of fresh priest, renewal set back 10 yrs). Friendly skies baloney. Anyway, off to the Zulus, off to the Pixies and Pigmaps, off to the Easter Island bunnies, off to the modern nuns in secret colloquies and heretical conclaves. What goes on in the conventicles is too Yogic to mention. Tantrisms in the friendly mumps of United. New light on the Hail Mary. Hidden instincts in friendly scribes of Upanishad. Bhagavad Giftshop is raided by vice squad, priest and nuns found eating candy bars. Psychedelic rosary exploded, maiming four.

Nuns college is found in friendly landscape of skies with United. Like Hot Parks Dakota. Off to Hot Parks California. Fly over Dakota in friendly skies (Nix, too far north). Wow all the collages and inscapes from Hot Park Dakota, folders, foldups, foldouts, fixups, mixups, print-cocktails, flap juleps, mint paychecks, lots of ass in Dakota to judge by some of them prints.

Will send postcarps from friendly sidewalks of San Francisco. Hippie priest with friendly United stewardess invades nuns and scrambles doc-trine in mystery retreat.

Mystery Zulu nun remarks friendly skypilot arrive with Velma in fleeing saucy.

Fleeting nun lifts transports ninemile jive inbreezy intuitions of new dogma.

All off ports west Zulu retreat misty nun with bambam encyclicals.
Cardinals in Rome ears burning with distant insights of conventicle.
Turn off the ears and represent unsight.
Today the Derby, tomorrow the prayer, Monday the flight.
Crosscountry priest in flying carpet Ali lights on nun.
Off to mystery retreat among Zulu redwoods in happy park.
Happy is the Park of Hot Dakota with rum.
Was recently send off to Alfred Kopfs (Knofs) (Knopft) (Kropfst) (Knopgy) the ms of antiletters. Was you heard from Garomn?
Next time you hear form from is misty collage with numps.
Viva the concrete. Viva the Abessa. Viva the Nonna. Viva la Donna. La Donna e mobile, la Mobba e dabile, la Vespa e flabile, la Casa e orribile, il Papa e infallibilissime, la Curia e incorrrrrrrruuuupppttttIBILIE.

More info when touchdowns Rosebowl homeflake uptown Novak retreat with Corita mump under palms of McCormick. Mistery moon is Mulling over his insteps. Off to a fishbowl with the avant garde, cries Lefty, Holahola.

On June 8, 1968, Lax arrived at Gethsemani for his first visit with Merton since 1959, when he and Ad Reinhardt had been at the monastery. He stayed until June 13, his visit including a picnic with the O'Callaghans and others.

June 22, [1968]

Ho:

Glad news back in Cattarops but fie on all the cops and robbers which is took place up and down Union St. Bad enough they should push an old chevvy into Lefty's bar and grill but what is much worse is that they have RILFED—repeat: rilfed!—the golf compartment or the gove companion. THIS RILFING IS TOO MUCH. It has to stop. End Rilfs. Flog Rolfs. Catch the rilf in flagrante derilfo. Next thing you know there will be an assassination committed with a RILF. This is the pernicious sournoiserie with which the criminal element is about to get around the gun law. Ordering Rilfs by mail. Not covered by the Law. All clear. Right and left is nothing but rilfs. This country is truly sick. Pot ok, LSD a mere peccadillo, sex license what is worse after all than dog license? Just wear your sex license on the collar, thatssall. Clear it with bishops any time now. But RILFS! Ugh it is too unmentionable to mention.

Here is relative quiets summer sun with not too much swampfrogs or miasmas. Gentle the breeze with only sporadic attacks of the musket fly or the green swatmidget. Mails is from Columbia Prexy with reassuring notes: "They shall not prevail in Fayerweather let alone Havermayer." "Keep sending your alumnus millions etc." For the rest anyhow not read.

Not seen locals for several days. Tommie O Callaghan mother died. Dan Walsh is absent in many jungles of mystery. Brothers is all agog over the tempo. Was here a phalanx of novice masters a big drag an odious passatempo was come to the hermit box for a speech. "You might as well all leave the clericals" I suggested with a wry leer. Was cheered wildly for this.

Now the importants is this messaggio: was come from a fellow in Kansas City (!) some musics he made to be tacked with scotch tapes to two of my poems. Now after the musics took up only ten feet of tape I fill all the rest with quips and homilies. Was read whole long sections of *Lograire* some what was typed and some what was nontyped and some doubletype and other stereotype and many others forged by eccentrics and clupped up with billboards, is a regular parlor of *Lograires* with also and in particular a section of Elmhurst too tedious to be excused but all the same it is all there with also some Mayans and some other bits. Now the catch on this tape is that it is all stereo which is it runs on four legs and has multiple traps and for an ordinary machine sounds merely like a quadruple dogfight amid the Rilfs of Union Suit or Marketplace where they are rilfing the glovebags. It may well be the musics is straight but the rest is all fourcopped in lanes with doubletake and roaring conflictions. Otherwise enjoyable by the whole family particularly if said family happens to be deaf. Must have stereo bopper to dig the trails on this taupe.

Ju1968 [July 9, 1968]

Ho Robster

First is celebrations of natuiraabbhorrett. Wimwaimwum. Second is lemntification of Zapped Garool. Japed his jup and Zapped his Zop. He is the loser.

Third is idmenification of Holp Rampart and Window which has not yet lost the parties. Tell them to hold on they may yet win. Tene quod habes. Habes thesaurum.

Thirs is Al Knopf he to Zapped his Zopp and lost like a fallen cliff.

Tell therefore Holps Ramshott and Wampum to hold on to the partie and lachez pas le tennis.

Do not lose the set, o Holps Rommig and Wappit, you have nearly won it. Why let go and lose millions now? Faugh.

I return all the wampums together with the celebration of natur.

Is make in the works Monkpond iii such beauties as will take away the bad breath of millions.

Return to me Zapped Knopf. His loss is gain of Rampart Winston like a cigarreet would.

Hold Lantern to Piston and win the book.

Greet all the winners with crowns of cannabis.

Naatur Aabhort Kopenhagn.

Everyday in the mailsdrops come weeping tears of Columbia do not stop to give the millions just because the pigeons took over Hamilstrop Hall. It was always theirs as they well knew. Give back Columbia to pigeons.

Is eyeopenner the three identical postcarps of Oleum chipping center. Is not a whit change since the Indian wars.

Not a whit change since the Hillquist pursue that momma through the halls of the O. House for her hats.

Naaturlich Abort Kopenhavist.

August 28 (aw nuts, 18) 1968

Dear Lobsang:

Well it was always topics anyway. From the start it was topics. If he could have got a chance, Mr Bubblethwaite, he would have imposed on our correspondence his topics. Now ten letters about the beauties of the mustarsh. Now to the utility of the mustarsh (subtle change of inflection) now to the cult of the mustarsh (rub in mustards, etc). It would be no end of his mad topics and we would have all been lost. Instead of which a merry jolly correspondence without topic and unintelligible to editors. Tant mieux. Out with the Mussolinis of publishing. Down with Del Pezzo and the lady of the mustarsh with her Vodka modiglianis. Out with all the fascisti of the printing world.

My suggestion is forget the fascisti and go at once to Emil [Antonucci] without vodkas with only beautiful prints, foldups, clipouts, buildins, explosions of printed joy. But on the other hand you is always thinking of the practico: is essential to think of the practico. But mark my words is coming no enormous checks from the fascisti so might as well forget. In this case the practico is Emil. Forget Random Hops. Unless of course vain hope springs up eternal in the human chest. Or nest.

I-d-i-o-s-y-n-c-a-z-y.

Crazy. Casy. Casy Jones, Crazy Stengel. At the Bam. Crazy at the Bam. One up. Twothreefour. Indisyncrazy at the Bam. Crazy India win pennant. Sing crazy. Indio sing like Casey. "Auld Lang Syne" etc.

Thanks pictures. They is no encouragement. Is gone into a slump the old Vietnam commander. Is up against a problem train with the Tet offensive. Is all offended with Tet. In a moment of humor is crazy with Tet to the point of dropping his camera. Bah for the old Vietnam commander in yr photos. But thanks anyhow, we must face the image. Photo is truth. Awful truth. Trappist poem is elected marshall of all the trains.

I stand on the tower and shade the eye to dusty horizon expecting prodigal Ed [Rice] in Volkswagen.

As for you Tangier sounds like a name rung upon stencils in heaven. Anything, anything, anything at all only out of this mad country.

To Sister Therese Lentfoehr, S.D.S.

I do not hesitate to confess that letters from my friends have always and will always mean a great deal to me.
MERTON TO SISTER THERESE LENTFOEHR,
SEPTEMBER 25, 1956

Sister Therese Lentfoehr, S.D.S. (1902–81), had an enduring and unusual friendship with Thomas Merton, expressed through letters. Born in Wisconsin, where she lived most of her life, she was a poet and teacher (Marquette University, Georgetown, Mount Saint Paul College, and elsewhere). She said she first wrote Merton in 1939 to express her admiration for one of his poems, but it was not until 1948 that they began to correspond regularly. Merton had reviewed her collection of Marian poems, I Sing of a Maiden, *and Sister Therese took umbrage at some of his remarks. This began a twenty-year exchange between them. Merton, often embarrassed by her gifts and by her glowing reviews of his books, started sending her as gifts manuscripts and other materials he had written, starting off with one of the three copies of the original script of* The Seven Storey Mountain. *He continued to send her things through the years and she became the holder of the largest private collection of Mertoniana, which she left at her death to Columbia University. She wanted to visit Merton on numerous occasions, even coming unannounced to the Abbey of Gethsemani on August 2, 1951, when she was refused admittance beyond the gatehouse, where she was photographed (probably by the Prior) with Merton. It was not until November 1967 that the two met properly at a picnic at Gethsemani. It was a head-on confrontation between Merton's exuberance and Therese's reticence, yet the friendship continued and they corresponded until Merton's death a year later. In 1979 her study of Merton's poetry,* Words and Silence: On the Poetry of Thomas Merton, *was published by New Directions.*

November 3, 1948

Your literally overwhelming letter has had to wait a week for me to answer, and I apologize not only for the delay but also for the fact that circumstances compel me to reply in my own abominable handwriting. Your remarks about *The Seven Storey Mountain* are so exceedingly generous they leave me inarticulate—no book written by me could possibly be that good! But I am happy that you really liked it and I know your prayers will do a great deal to make it bear fruit among the people for whom it was mainly written—my own uncouth tribe, footloose "intellectuals." I am very happy that I am no longer one of them. I only wish I was more of a monk . . .

P.S. If the review did not convey the idea, I would like to assure you that I was very glad to get that beautiful big book, *I Sing of a Maiden* & the only reason I accepted the job of reviewing it was because I couldn't resist such an acquisition for our library. I am no longer reviewing anything—and incidentally I felt rather cheap after having made the statement reflecting on all Catholic poets in the U.S. *en masse.* I shouldn't have said what I did if I did not believe it—but I wish I could have avoided the subject.

November 18, 1948

It would be inhuman for a person to resist the temptation to answer such a beautiful letter as your last one, and fortunately I have a moment in which to do so and to thank you for the windfall of books. I have already passed one of *I Sing of a Maiden* to our choir-novitiate, where they can do with a little life and color and Marian music to help them along. The other will be for the guest-house. Meanwhile I have been reading *Give Joan a Sword* with the greatest pleasure, and agreeing with the reviewers on the jacket that the poems are delicate, graceful, full of serenity and peace and order which mine are not. Yes, I liked "First Mass in the Catacombs": and envied such a marvelous privilege. I liked the one on Murillo's painting and "Port-of-Call" and all those that brought back to me the atmosphere of the Eternal City. But I thought the very best was "Write it upon the Stars." One thing that intrigues me about your verse has been formulated by you better than I could do it: in the "Poet and Bird" you reflect how "the summits of my song are hung with mist." That is true, mist is not only one of your favorite words, but it is the atmosphere of your verse, and you seem to tell the reason why in "Poet and Bird." I think the delicate impressionism of your technique is something which is demanded by the character of your poetic experiences, which never quite succeed in seizing that "still unuttered line." And that is the torture of all poets. We try and try, and always there is the feeling: "I just missed it again." "I didn't quite make it." At the same time, when a poet succeeds and the poem turns out nicely, he can secretly say: "Well, if I didn't hit the bull's eye, at least I'm on the target." You do that neatly every time. And in the writing of poetry, bull's eyes are the rarest thing in the universe. In fact, perhaps there has never been one, because when I tried to think of an example, I couldn't; so, ultimately, the only solution is: "Some far day we shall win to this ultimate cadence."

Meanwhile the great poets—Dante, Shakespeare—are the ones in which the words come closest to fitting the experience they are talking about. With me, I know what the trouble is: I come upon a situation and the situation seems to require a poem. So I write a poem. But the poem turns out to be not the precise, individual poem which that specific situation had demanded from all eternity, but just "a poem," a generic poem by Thomas Merton that is something like all the other poems by Thomas Merton and which he drags out of his stock to fit on every situation that comes along. That is why *Figures for an Apocalypse* is a whole string of complete misses. All I can say is that the arrows were in the general direction of some target or other, but I'd be hard put to it to connect the firing with the real object that was there to be fired at. I am quite convinced that *Figures for an Apocalypse* is already stone dead.

Your suggestion about sending something to the Holy Father gives me food for thought. It sounds like a very good idea. Father Abbot is not here now, but I'll ask him. Meanwhile, in order to repay your gift of books with a little token—call it a Christmas present, if you like—I thought you might be curious to see a manuscript of the *Mountain*, since it was much cut. So I'll give you the carbon instead of burning it up. It is of no value to anyone, and when you have looked at it you can do whatever you like with it. I only hope it isn't a nuisance. But in case it is, I'll make matters worse by sending you one or two other little things I did for the monastery . . .

December 27, 1948
Feast of St. John

This time it was my turn to faint! I have never had such a marvelous Christmas present. Your generosity in parting with that relic of St. Therese is certainly heroic. I was afraid Father Abbot might insist on putting it with the other relics here, in the Church. But no: he said, with a sigh of relief and an expression that contained a ray of hope: "Frater Louis, you *need* something like that." He insists that I wear it, in the hope that at long last I may start to be a good Cistercian . . .

St. Therese will help me now to be in some way obscure and solitary. My life can never consist in the noise that surrounds the externalization of *The Seven Storey Mountain*, and no matter what happens outside the walls of Gethsemani, I believe she will really help me to be the most insignificant person in this house, and the ambition is consciously selfish in the sense that I hope, by being insignificant, to be left alone for Our Lord. However, if He does not see fit to grant that ambition, I will know that whatever else He may have in store will empty me more of myself and make me even more insignificant than before . . .

January 18, 1949
St. Peters Chair, Rome

... The point you raise about the part played by natural temperament in disposing a soul for contemplation is something that I must investigate, especially since I have embarked on the perhaps presumptuous task of writing a kind of theological study of the contemplative life. If you come across anything that will give me further leads in that direction, I would be grateful for the hint. The question of temperament will come in to a chapter in which I will try to navigate the stormy waters of "the contemplative vocation" without being shot by the Dominicans or torpedoed by the Jesuits. But please pray that I may do this job at least with the prudence and love and care that Jesus wishes of me. One of the essentials is to avoid haste: and that means making room for the work to go on steadily, and therefore discarding non-essentials.

Really, the *Mountain* did need to be cut. Its length was impossible for any publisher. The editor at Harcourt was, is, my old friend Bob Giroux who comes into the book for a line somewhere. He did a very good job. Evelyn Waugh has edited the London edition and tells me he cut a great deal more—mostly for reasons of economy and because what he cut seemed to be more or less "local interest" to Americans. I am perfectly satisfied to see anything go out of a book. It will take a lot to move me to object to what editors want to do with any ms. of mine, because I usually suffer so much from the miserable character the finished work will have anyway. When you hear your works read aloud in a refectory, it makes you wish you had never written a word. Fortunately the *Mountain* was not read here. I would never have had the virtue to face such an ordeal!

Besides, if anything good was cut, and if Jesus wants it to be printed, He will suggest the same idea at the right time somewhere else, in some other connection, either in some work of mine or something by somebody else.

Well, everything cooperates for good to those who love God. The new Father-Cellarer, at the beginning of the year, took over the room where I was working. That left practically nowhere for me except the rare book vault. And now here I am behind a double iron door in what is the closest thing to being soundproof in this silent monastery, and surrounded by twelfth-century manuscripts of St. Bernard. It is simply wonderful. It is a miracle that I do any work at all. The constant temptation is to sit still and taste the beautiful silence. I have permission to come in here in the "interval" after the night office on certain feasts—around four thirty a.m.—and study old liturgical ms, missals, antiphoners, etc. What a meditation! There are many things in the old books which we no longer have in our liturgy—and which we are trying to get back. Anyway, you see, it is a great grace. I attribute it to the good people who read the last chapter of the *Mountain* and said prayers that I would have a little solitude. I know you were one of them . . .

P.S. I am afraid there is no picture available that can be given. In any case, I look stupid.

February 19, 1949

. . . In my own work I have had to scrap fifty pages and start the new book over again on a much simpler plan. My whole attraction is to get away from the psychological approach to mysticism and return to the dogmatic treatment which the Fathers used. Not that this would mean ignoring the experimental side of prayer altogether, but I'd like to situate it in a patristic setting. In fact, what I am dreaming of now is a book on the mystical life, with a solid dogmatic foundation, plenty of material from the Fathers, but communicated to the reader through a scriptural and liturgical medium: take part of the liturgical cycle and work out everything there is in it about the mystical life—and the mystical life as experienced, not only by individuals but also collectively by the Church. That is not for the present however.

I sent the other carbon of the *Mountain* ms. to Fr. Terence Connolly at Boston College and he has put the thing on exhibition in his library, so I want to tell you at once that you must feel free to make use of your copy in any way you please. I give you all rights over it, in so far as I can, with Father Abbot's permission . . . [The top copy of the *Mountain*, the one sent to the printer, Merton gave to his editor, Robert Giroux.]

Well, there goes the bell. Our Lent begins on Ash Wednesday, so you see I can answer you still. Many thanks for your kindness, which I deeply appreciate. Let us remember one another in prayer, and I ask Our Lord to make me, at any rate, very simple and humble: you are already both those things.

April 26, 1949

. . . Thank you also for the card from New York. One thing distresses me: it is the thought that you may have been led to ferret around in the Columbia library until you unearthed some skeleton in the closets of the Columbia of fifteen years or so ago. If you did, then I have no need to assure you that those skeletons are certainly skeletons and there is nothing in those closets to edify a religious. I am only thinking of your own sensibilities. For my own part, I ought at least to be able to accept the humiliation of my past as some kind of penance. After all I ought to do something to make amends.

On the other hand you will be glad to hear that the priesthood is very close now and that they have arranged the ordination for Ascension Day, May 26th. I know your prayers will help me to get ready for this tremendous day. I am trying to immerse myself in the Mass—and the more I do so, the more I feel that that Holy Sacrifice is the purest and most perfect of prayers and that all contemplation is to be found therein. It is the fountain of everything and the short way to the heights. I did not make this discovery until I began associating ceremonies with prayers. I had used a missal for years, of course, but really, the making of gestures and movements in harmony with words and *doing* all the things that are said makes a tremendous difference. Of course it brings your whole being into play, and that has the effect of liberation, psychologically. What will it be when I can actually consecrate! Pray that I may keep my feet on the ground, dear Sister. I am the enemy of all exaltation and I want nothing more than to offer our dear Lord, with His own sacrifice, the sacrifice of a perfectly pure and simple and humble heart.

I was saddened by what you said about [Robert] Lowell. What a terrible thing that such a real poet should be silenced by the devil. After all, he is one who can say that poetry is his vocation, whereas the rest of us have other and far more important things to do than write verse . . .

Maria, May 13, 1949

. . . About the ordination—alas, Father Abbot wants everything to be very, very quiet and simple. Here it cannot be otherwise. We have absolutely no accommodations for lady visitors. One or two friends—the close ones mentioned in the book—will be here, I expect. No, we never go out to say a First Mass. That is strictly forbidden. I know that with the slightest encouragement you would probably be willing to camp in a tree with the Kentucky possums, but you must be content to be here in spirit, and I shall profit greatly by your good prayers. How badly I need them. There is practically nothing of the priest about me. I am still a rough diamond, without any gentleness or tact or charity. Well, the first apostles are my consolation. But pray that I may imitate them as they were *after* Pentecost, not before! It is so important for me to become a good priest. Not for myself. I don't just want the consolation of thinking that *I* say Mass fervently, or anything as trivial as that: not that it is trivial to say Mass fervently, if I can ever do it: but all for Jesus alone! . . .

I am busy trying to learn how to say Mass. My health is all right, except that I have a vile cold at the moment. That poor book is simply on the shelf until after our centenary. I get many little errands to do. A Benedictine in Belgium now has me checking variants in our manuscript of William of St. Thierry's *Golden Epistle*. "Do unto others . . ." I cannot refuse these services. Besides, I have the example of your devoted care in sending me copies of so many valuable notes.

About the Columbia *Jester*, the years 1938 and '39 contain less objectionable material than the years when I was an undergraduate. As for that *Columbian* . . . And those inane pictures. Well, I deserve punishment . . .

June 2, 1949

. . . Now, you will be disappointed to hear, as I was, that Father Abbot will not allow me to keep the relic of the True Cross. As I understand it, only Abbots and Bishops and people like that can really claim the privilege of having such a treasure to themselves. A mere Trappist monk . . . And really I have no earthly or heavenly right to keep such a relic. I have it here with me at the moment, and am blissfully happy to have it too. In fact I owe you untold thanks just for the joy of keeping it near me for a few days and profiting by the graces it brings. But really, if we keep it at all, it ought to go to one of our new foundations, to be the object of *public* adoration. Let me know if that would meet with your approval, or whether you would prefer me to return it to you. I think the latter course is the most just one.

As to the marvelous grace of ordination at last I have found the place in the universe that has been destined for me by the mercy of God. The priestly character, unworthy as I am to receive it, is so much "mine," in the designs of God and Our Blessed Lady, that I feel as if I had at last awakened to discover my true name and my true identity, as if I had never before been a complete person. Even my past sins fit into the picture, throwing into high relief the tremendous mercy of God and the imperturbable calm and unswerving directness with which He has worked out His plan. And the Mass. I suppose I am in danger of spiritual gluttony or something, but I wish I could stand all day at the altar and be, most fully, Christ, and taste the magnificence of His power swimming through my veins for His Father's infinite glory and for the salvation of the world . . .

P.S. Your friend Fr. [Reuben] Moscowitz spoke to me on our centenary day. I was in charge of press relations & more or less at the mercy of everybody who might have been a reporter.

June 17, 1949

. . . I think you must have heard somewhere a rumor that Clare Boothe Luce was coming down here for my ordination. I assure you she was not here and has never been here. I had some friends [Seymour Freedgood, Robert Giroux, James Laughlin, Robert Lax, Edward Rice, and Daniel Walsh] here, of course, and two aunts [Freida "Nanny" Hauck and Elsie Jenkins] who stayed in Bardstown. There were mobs here for the centenary and I don't envy any of them. They were all milling around out there in the sun—so were we, for that matter. We are still picking up the Pepsi-Cola bottles.

And now the iron curtain is coming down again. Very wisely. We have just had our regular visitation by the Abbot General. From now on, it seems likely that I will have less chance to write (letters) and perhaps even to receive letters. I do not know exactly what is being arranged. Of course, for the last year or so I have been far beyond the regular quota allowed the rest of the monks who have been cut down to four times a year even in communicating with their families . . .

July 15, 1949

. . . First of all, the books went off to the Holy Father a month or so ago, and I hope he has them by now. Thank you very kindly indeed for your beautiful review of *Seeds*. How like you it is! You have seen deeply into the book and have been very kind to the author, and have neglected the faults of a brash young writer who is perhaps too bold and too careless . . . I am not surprised that some of the clergy are annoyed at me. There will always be careful and conscientious folk who travel a strictly beaten track who will be upset by people like myself who have too little respect for convention. I do not think they are jealous, they are just temperamentally different. But I have seen a couple of stinging letters written by a priest in New York [Gervase Toelle] about both the *Mountain* and *Seeds*. They were more extremely bitter and savage than any criticism I have ever got from Protestants or unbelievers. However, I am glad to get such things. I ought certainly to make a professional point of rejoicing in them, and I shall certainly not be such a fool as to defend myself. *Jesus autem tacebat* . . .

Poor Sister Madaleva! Don't ask her to write *another* article on the poet Merton: she has done at least four articles and reviews, all of them so generous. Dan Walsh is supposed to have given a talk at Manhattanville with some reference to me, and he might have that lying around as the possible basis of a paper. By all means reprint what you wish from the *Mountain*. Father Abbot has given his permission. I'd like to ask that you soft pedal the mystic note a little, as it gets people too excited. There is certainly nothing extraordinary about a contemplative religious having the beginnings of contemplative prayer: but nevertheless the word "mystic" carries the connotation "unusual" and the best thing I can do is to appear to be very usual, which, in fact, I am. I don't mind about excerpts being reprinted without comment, but perhaps comment would be better . . .

About the missing pages—I have nothing at hand. If they are here, they have been used as scratch paper. I'll look at the back of notes and things, to see if there are any fragments of the *Mountain* lying around. I believe there was at least one section that I tossed out deliberately, and made sure that nothing was left of it in any manuscript. Boston is probably the more complete because it was not worked over at all. The one you have was in the hands of the publisher. For that reason I am happier to have excerpts printed from your copy, because I am not sure everything in the Boston copy ought to be printed.

I am thinking of doing a *Journal*. In fact I am working on one. Not spiritual, so much. Just a *Journal*. If you know of any really unusual and interesting published *Journal* will you please put me on its trail? . . .

Sister Therese sent Merton the first of the "excerpts" which she took from her copy of the manuscript of The Seven Storey Mountain, *published as "First Christmas at Gethsemani" with her introductory comment in* The Catholic World (*170, December 1949, pp. 166–73*).

August 26, 1949

You are too kind to me. The article is restrained and temperate and yet it is rather complimentary isn't it? I approve with all my heart your use of the text and see no reason why you should not state your opinion as to its implications, since you are so moderate about it . . . I marked a couple of changes in the text from the ms. May they stand? On the whole it seems to be rather impossible for me to utter an official "approval" of such a nice article. Of course I approve, most heartily. I love compliments. But it is not quite fitting that I should utter my approval pontifically, so for the others I trust your judgment entirely . . .

F. of St. Augustine
August 28, 1949

There is a tremendous pile of correspondence on hand and I am forced to write in the middle of the week which does not interfere with anything at the moment. I have just sent the corrected edition of *Seeds* to New Directions and am waiting to tackle a third manuscript [*What Are These Wounds?*] which needs going over, before Bruce prints it. It is a life of one of our Cistercian mystics [St. Lutgarde]—a routine life, I am afraid. I cannot handle stigmata very intelligently . . .

When you feel particularly low, and are convinced that you have been abandoned by God because of your weaknesses, remember that He is nearer then than in many an hour of consolation. Console yourself with the thought that it cannot help being that way, because God tries those whom He loves and He is close to them that are in tribulation. Both these thoughts are revealed in Scripture . . .

About prayer: have you a garden or somewhere that you can walk in, by yourself? Take half an hour, or fifteen minutes a day and just walk up and down among the flowerbeds with the intention of offering this walk up as a meditation and a prayer to Our Lord. Do not try to think about anything in particular and when thoughts about work, etc. come to you, do not try to push them out by main force, but see if you can't drop them just by relaxing your mind. Do this because you "are praying" and because Our Lord is with you. But if thoughts about work will not go away, accept them idly and without too much eagerness with the intention of letting Our Lord reveal His will to you through these thoughts. But do not grab at anything that looks like a light. If it is a "light" it will have its effect without your seizing it forcefully . . .

The pictures are returned herewith. They are *all* off the target. Some are Father Placid, some are Father Timothy. I am sending a couple of my ordination and first Mass. They are not very good. Please, please,

please never print them or make them public—show them to special friends if you like but you know what I mean, not in a big exhibition, please! I am sending a copy of a new book, *Waters of Siloe* . . .

October 3 [1949]
Feast of St. Therese

. . . The Cistercian mystic is St. Lutgarde of Aywieres. I like her. But the book is not much good. By the way, in your St. Therese article, are you using the chapter from *Exile Ends in Glory* on the Little Way (Ch. 11, p. 152 ff.) It represents some thoughts I once lined up on St. Therese. I imagine it might help, but if you have not used it, it doesn't matter . . .

I wrote no novels on the *Mountain* material at Gethsemani. Bob [Lax] was talking about the ones written at Olean . . . I remember some sisters taking a picture of me and my aunt. Fr. [Matthew] Hoehn was here but I didn't see him. I suppose I can't stop him from printing the picture but I wish he would not. The monk with the hood up on the Cistercian Literature page of the Gethsemani Magnificat is, I believe, the one you are after. I'll look around for an old snapshot of John Paul [Merton]. By the way Fr. Hoehn never sent me any proofs of the article on me either. Fr. [Terence] Connolly has not yet sent back the Gilson. I told him to keep the Blake. You can get some notebooks I kept from the librarian (Fr. Irenaeus [Herscher]) at St. Bonaventure. Ed Rice, my friend, has some snapshots he took down here and some other old ones perhaps . . .

Most of my own prayers are completely inarticulate. I walk around saying "Love!" Or I just mentally keep slipping the catch that yields my whole soul to Love. You might do that too, one way or another . . .

November 12, 1949

Here I am renovated by a retreat. Monsignor [Fulton J.] Sheen preached it and it was splendid. He took a liking to Gethsemani and with his characteristic generosity poured his whole heart into it, sometimes preaching for an hour and a half and holding us all the time. It was very inspiring. I find him a wonderful and saintly apostle and it was a great lift to me to meet him. However, the fact that the retreat is over does not give me time to do justice to your letter and its requests as we are on the verge of a big house-cleaning. The colony leaves for the new foundation in South Carolina next week and tomorrow most of the officers in the house are to be changed, turning everything upside down. Then I have to start teaching Scripture and Mystical Theology and a sort of orientation course for novices next week. I am in the throes of preparation.

The prologue for *Waters*. I wrote the one that now stands printed, first, then I dropped it in disgust. Then Bob Giroux said the book needed a prologue. I wrote a second one—which you have. Afterwards I thought maybe the first was more appealing and sent it without comment to the editor (who was not Giroux but Thomas O'Conor Sloane who is now with Devin Adair) and he picked the first one.

No that is my uncle [Harold Brewster Jenkins]'s writing on the back of the snapshot [of John Paul Merton]. Many thanks for the information on the Papal pronouncement which I am glad to hear turns out to be a rumor. When our Father Abbot saw the Holy Father last September, the Holy Father was very emphatic in telling us to keep cloistered at Gethsemani and to keep our fingers out of active works, to love our strictly contemplative life etc. I got a nice enough letter from Monsignor Montini [later Pope Paul VI] about *The Seven Storey Mountain* and the *Seeds* which I sent to the Holy Father, and I am enclosing it . . . [George A.] McCauliff certainly wrote a kind review of *Waters*—can you get his address for me and I'll send him the new book of poems. I have already an advance copy of *Tears of the Blind Lions* . . . but not the copies to send to friends yet.

About your manuscript of the *Mountain*, I have only a hazy idea of which one it was. I sent one first to Harcourt and then went over the carbon and sent that. Yours is one of these. If it is a carbon, it is the one I went over, but if it does not have so much editorial work on it from Harcourt's side, it probably in fact is certainly not the one they printed from. They have kept that, I guess. The one I sent to Boston College had not been worked over much at all.

The double ending: first I wrote an ending, when I finished the first draft of the book in October 1946. The present ending was written after my solemn profession (March 19, 1947) and was in fact the result of some lights that came to me in prayer on the Feast of the Sacred Heart, June 1947. I wrote the last pages (the conversation with Our Lord) on the afternoon of that Feast. Most of the other parts of the last section of the epilogue (about the monastery) in the new and printed version were written about that time too, in the days before the feast. But the article on "Active and Contemplative Orders" was slipped in there at the suggestion of Dr. Francis X. Connolly of Fordham.

I think the copy you have was probably the one that was sent to our censor, unless it was the one read by our Fr. Placid who was then Prior (the one in those snapshots). He wrote some remarks here and there. But I think the copy he had went to Boston College . . . I assure you that my health is good: really. In fact it is excellent . . .

January 7, 1950

. . . You worry about my writing. I have been publishing far too much and it is time to be quiet for a little. Preparing classes takes up most of my time anyway, but the material will all go to make a book later on, if God wills it. There is surely no great need for a spate of books from Gethsemani: and it is not our vocation. However, I shall hope to get something on paper once in a while. I still have in mind those jobs on St. Aelred and St. Bernard and I do not mean to drop the *School of the Spirit* entirely. Only to take it up again, from a more thoroughly Scriptural and Patristic viewpoint, later on . . .

The classes are going along well enough but they take a lot of time. In all, you know, I have some seventy students. And I am building up from the ground—trying to develop a spiritual theology that suits a contemplative monastery! And one which gives the proper place to the Fathers and especially to our Cistercians. For the rest I am happy with the moments of solitude Our Lord still gives me—moments in which I am able to forget the temptation to take myself seriously. That is a mercy . . .

P.S. The other day I sent some galleys and bits of manuscripts which you can add to the rest of the things you have there, if you so desire.

February 18, 1950

. . . You asked me about the different journals. I am not quite sure what Fr. Irenaeus [Herscher] sent you. The gap in 1939, Summer, is due to the fact that I was writing a novel (*The Labyrinth*) on the hill at Olean. *The Cuban Journal* is now lost, strayed or something. No, not stolen. I think St. Bonaventure has only two journals, the second one in a big black and red ledger being the better. That is perhaps one of those you had. Maybe he sent you both. If so that is all there is, except what I am trying to write here . . .

Oh, do please pray for poor Raymond Larsson, the poet. I have always rather liked his verse and we have been writing back and forth. He is a bit unbalanced but so is most of the world. Anyway, they have now locked him up in a state insane asylum at Orangeburg, New York and from what I hear he is not being too well treated. He is a very spiritual person and I feel that he is suffering very much. May it bring him closer to God and not be wasted. I wish there were something that could be done about him, but Dan Walsh investigated it and said it was practically hopeless.

Good Dan Walsh. He has been suffering tortures by accepting invitations to talk about me before large gatherings, being, as he is, very shy. I asked him to stop and thank heaven he has promised to stop. I wish my friends would not be burdened with the weight of my own old-man-of-the-sea. But I shall not attempt to discourage you because I know you like the labor of it and that my advice would fall on deaf ears. It is getting to be intensely silly for me to talk about wanting to be ignored and forgotten. I will be soon enough, don't worry. Meanwhile I think I am now as completely reconciled as I have ever been to the will of God. And curiously enough I find much solitude just where it would be least expected: in my *work*. The noise that the books make and all the public reactions have become a very distant murmur. I am glad that I have found contact with many souls who help me with their prayers and it is a joy to pray for them but I have ceased to be much tempted by the thought that I am a public figure because I know that Thomas Merton does not exist.

This is all I can do at the moment. I am far behind in everything. May Jesus dwell ever more and more in your soul. And may you get used to the great simplicity with which He works in you in just the way you think He shouldn't. Be at peace and close your eyes to pious conventions and love Him as you can. It is often a help to forget everything one thinks one knows about prayer and turn to Our Lord as though one were a freshly baptized Zulu who had never yet been told anything much about prayer . . .

Holy Saturday
[April 8, 1950]

Since I am a Trappist, I suppose words *ought to fail* me. But even though I am a most loquacious Trappist, words fail me.

Yesterday afternoon (Good Friday) I was out in the woods. To begin with, Our Lord began by stopping our watch so that I stayed out half an hour longer than I intended and thus had that much more prayer, instead of doing some material business which was better taken care of at another time. So then I wondered if I ought to pick a few daffodils for Our Lady, and decided that it was not sentimental and did so. On getting in, she put your package in my lap. So that was quite a profitable bunch of daffodils, if you ask me. Besides that, some notes on Our Lady in the interior life from Fr. Paul Philippe who teaches Mystical Theol. at the Angelicum. But the relic. Now I have unmasked you. You went and got all those relics together and had the people make a special reliquary!! It is wonderful. You could not have picked them better. They went to Communion with me this morning (Holy Saturday) and I think they must have arrived here with a firm, concerted plan to get me to start doing something towards corresponding to Our Lord's graces. They all started pushing at once, so to speak. I needed it. You who sent them here must incite them, by your prayers, to keep up the good work. Our Lord requires much—everything—of those whom He loves. The trouble is that it takes us too long to figure out what *He* means by everything. He does not mean drama but He does mean business. I am shocked at the amount of time I have wasted in this monastery doing things that seemed to be good. I could have done more for Him by doing what, in the eyes of men, would certainly be judged as "less"—because it would not strike their gaze. Oh well, this is just to say that the relic is a tremendous help. But don't you think I have a full cohort of protectors on me by now? If you send me any more I shall be unable to pray anything but litanies . . .

Sister Therese began in this period to do typing for Merton and for the monastery, especially his notes for his classes. Many of the letters written at this time deal with the mechanics of this typing, and these sections have, for the most part, been omitted from the letters.

April 17, 1950

Many thanks for your Easter Letter and all that went with it—especially the nice enlarged copy of the photograph. About [the magazine] *Renascence*—the story was fine. I would like to use the second version in the revised *Mountain*. Would you also send me any bits of the ms. that you think ought to be considered for the revision. I have absolutely nothing unpublished here, I did not think it would come to this. I am still a bit worried about the idea of printing a lot of pictures. The Russ episode ought to go in, and perhaps some more about the monastery.

About Fr. [Gervase] Toelle—really I thought his article ["Merton: His Problem and a Solution"] was fine. You had me all excited. It is no trouble at all to fall into the hands of the Calced. You are too sensitive. What did the poor man *say* that could account for your strictures? He seemed to me to be shrewd and objective and sharp and clear cut. He was not nasty about my faults and he was nice (more than I deserved) about the rest and the article had precisely the right tone for a magazine like that? Sure he was smart—one *should* be. It shows he has been reading acute criticism and that is good. He is quite all right. I am enclosing a little note to thank him—will you please pass it on to him, or will that place you in an embarrassing position? If so just throw it away and tell him that I liked the article or something. Do whatever suits you best.

Health. No, I am quite all right. No TB. Of course we all had the 'flu and I had it along with the rest. It was a pretty bad epidemic and Father Abbot even had to dispense us from the fast for ten days. It has taken some of us rather a long time to shake it off but everyone is all right thanks to penicillin. You know everything there is to know about my health from the *Renascence* excerpts from the *Mtn.* I have to *watch out for* TB but I haven't got it.

There is no great hurry for the revised *Mtn.* Bob [Giroux] is back from Rome but he hasn't written to me about the next move yet. Perhaps I shall be going ahead with the publication of the Journal next. *What Are These Wounds* is exactly the wrong kind of book to have come out just now. It should have been an anonymous pamphlet as we planned. We tried to snatch it back from Bruce but of course . . . The cover. I racked my brains to try and think of something nice to say about it to the publisher and finally wrote him that it was "growing on me." I did not say in what way. It has now grown on me to such an extent that when I send the book to people in Europe I remove the cover first. However I'm leaving it on the signed copy that goes to you by this evening's mail, since you have seen it already and know the worst. I have earnestly asked Bruce to make important corrections at once—there are so many loose and inane statements in the book. In one spot I find myself (horror!) blandly teaching that there are in effect two ways to perfection and that the mystical way is in effect extraordinary. I must be a complete lunatic to contradict myself so glibly. I wrote the thing five years ago when I thought I knew everything. My comments—the thing is being read in the refectory—completely ruin my appetite. I hope you will give it the review—the panning—it deserves. You must be frank about it.

If you do have time to type some of those excerpts it would be fine. Use your own judgment . . .

May 6, 1950

As usual I have a score of things to thank you for and I am far behind with all of them. Taking the most recent arrival first: your article in the *Catholic World* for this month ["I will be your Monk"] is simply delightful. You have done a superlative job. Needless to say, I wish I could be something of what you make me appear to be on paper! But the very fact that you have written so nicely on the subject has, as before, brought home to me many things I did not realize about my love for Therese. It always helps to see the situation through someone else's eyes: and when they are eyes enlightened by such charity as yours . . . Well, you give me something to work for. Evidently she has never made any objections to my rather fresh (in the slang sense of the term) estimate of her character and sanctity . . .

Did I thank you yet for the wonderful job in *Renascence* ["Todo y Nada: Writing and Contemplation"]? The only thing that irked me was the ineptitude of my own writing—rambling and redundant. I don't think my own notes have said anything like the last word on the situation of a writer in a monastery. Hardly even the beginning. The things that bothered me in those days were mostly extrinsic, after all. And that is only superficial. There are deeper purifications. And that reminds me that I am beginning to see what Dr. Parente means in that significant little sentence in the middle of his letter. About the cruel things to come. I certainly need several spankings. I know it is Our Lord's love and I thank Him and want to accept everything. I have absolutely no desire to be a hero, or to be in any way remarkable, or to notice myself for a moment either suffering or rejoicing. Hence it cannot matter much *what* He sends because in any case I hope to be concerned with Him alone and He is unchanging and eternal and One. My highest ambition is to glorify Him by throwing all care to the winds and living on His love, without the slightest vain solicitude for anything in the universe. That should be your ambition too since you understand it so thoroughly and write about it with such insight. It is my only intention for you as well as for myself . . .

It is good that you are writing to [Robert] Lax and [Edward] Rice so much. I almost never can.

You ask about my health. No I am *not* dying of TB. There is absolutely nothing picturesque about me. I had a bad dose of 'flu during Lent but so did everyone else around here. I certainly will not despise any prayers you say for my health, bodily or spiritual! Thank you for them all, I need them.

Did you review the St. Lutgarde book [*What Are These Wounds?*]? I suppose you were your usual kind self, with a blind eye for all the stupidities in the thing. It is really badly done, this time, and we tried to persuade Bruce at any price not to publish it but it was too late. I believe Our Lord permitted this in order to detach me from any conceit about myself as a writer. The sales of the other books have dropped tremendously since *Wounds* appeared: the book is just wrong for the non-Catholic reader in this country. Our Lord will take care of their souls. And if this puts a rift between me and the public, so much the better. That is just what there should be between a Cistercian and the public.

June 3, 1950

. . . One reason why our letters cross and why anything from you takes a long time to reach me is that Father Prior who screens the mail finds your letters so intensely interesting that he puts them aside to read them at leisure and enjoy them, so that I don't see them for weeks: and that accounts for my delay in answering things. Never be perturbed. Perhaps he has a letter of yours now. That is why I mention this.

There are many other jobs on my neck at the moment, so I must close in haste . . .

July 10, 1950

. . . Bob Giroux was down here and now I am terrifically busy trying to finish a short book on the Psalter [*Bread in the Wilderness*]—an expansion of the *Orate Fratres* articles ["The Psalms and Contemplation"]. That is why I only have a bare minute for this note. Please pray that the job may be well done. The Journal, thank heaven, has been put on the shelf. This is an immense relief to me. It was a terrible burden. The problem is this: pure intention or no pure intention (attention Fr. Toelle!) when a thing is in some sense objectively an obstacle between oneself and God, it is going to remain an obstacle. Perhaps it can be negotiated with more or less difficulty: but it does not cease to be an obstacle until it is *removed*. And there are circumstances when the negotiating of it can definitely slow a man down. This pure intention business can be overdone. For me—my vocation is the hidden life. All right: I have to write. Let it be something objective and impersonal. Bob Giroux agrees—a very broad-minded publisher, I must say.

We have had to choke off a man who wanted to write a whole book about me. I don't know how well he is choked, either. Sy Freedgood is writing a book about me and [Mahanambrata] Bramachari and someone else and we are letting him go ahead, because I know Seymour doesn't

throw idle praise around without a generous admixture of irony and objective observation of failings, not to mention MANY entirely personal
intuitions of an entirely humorous character . . .

July 11, 1950

A photographer was here doing some color work and he wanted
to take a picture of me: so here it is. If you can stand it, you may
have it! . . .

July 31, 1950

By now you ought to be back from your tour. I hope you had a good
time and ever a rest—or recreation and change. I thought often of you
stopping at Ed [Rice]'s place, and I hope you did not get into any mischief
in the Village. I wonder how his magazine is coming along. Did the
lectures go well? I know your generous heart must have put much into
them. I hope you did not put anything into the poet that wasn't there,
but I am afraid this hope is not too solid. Now that you have spoken at
some length about this particular poet, perhaps you will consider dropping
him as a lecture subject. He ought not to be overpublicized. It would be
good for the kingdom of heaven if he were kept a little more on the shelf.
I do hope you are tired of such a topic. You know, I got Dan Walsh to
give up talking about Merton, because he was wearing himself out. If I
find out by my secret service agents that you have in any way suffered
from having written or spoken so much about me I shall get very earnest
about trying to persuade you to go a little slower. The trouble is, I am
getting to know you now and I am beginning to fear that persuasion would
not be much use. But I do think of it, seriously.

Here are the orientation notes. I was going to send you a set of notes
of one of the students but thought better of it and only enclose his report
of the opening talk(s). No time to write more at the moment . . .

P.S. Your card just came in and I didn't tell Ed [Rice] anything about
you, but I shall certainly ask him if you are wearing yourself out!!

August 19, 1950

. . . Then, thanks for the avalanche of pictures. Above all for Angelico
and Giotto. There never was a painter like Giotto. He is my absolute
favorite. Really, he has purity and power. I like his strength more than
the lyricism of Angelico. And incidentally I think he is much stronger
than Michelangelo because he has a little less of Mussolini about him!
And believe me I was happy to get the pictures of Picasso, mistress,
pigeon on his head and all. I hope he gets into heaven, for he is a great
man and you cannot be that great without giving something of the right
kind of glory to God . . .

Thank you, dear Sister, for working on the Orientation Notes. The
title page should read: "Monastic Orientation—Lectures given to the

Choir Novices—Abbey of Gethsemani—1950" or something like that. By the way you should be correcting typing errors, mistakes in spelling, unclear statements, unintelligible expressions, etc. as you go along. These are only my personal notes and it is a miracle if anyone else can decipher them. I'd be eternally grateful if you could do something to bring a little light out of the darkness. In a few days I'll send some more that could be tacked on at the end—on the Desert Fathers. You are wonderful to be so generous. One hundred copies will be fine. Lots of people will be glad to get them.

Your account of your visit to Ed [Rice] fascinated and charmed me. I rarely get any news from him, and it was good to see into his apartment with you! Don't worry, I didn't bat an eyelash at your knocking on the window—except in surprise at the thought you would think I would be surprised. Here are a couple of proofs of sketches that are to go in the *Psalm* book . . .

September 26, 1950

You should have been told a long time ago, but I forgot to mention it in the last letter. Father Abbot gave instructions that any money that came in for your articles about me should now be used to cover expenses for the mimeographing, and if there were a lot left over you could get one or two copies bound up permanently in something solid. Use your own judgment and do so also about the other binders. I will not be adding anything to this set—I mean anything that will need to be slipped in. I would rather have them somehow clamped together, at least some of them. Do not do them all if it would be too much work. And anyway it is late now: your classes began yesterday.

Also: the rumor will get to you so I had better tell you now. I just came back from the hospital. Sit still! I am perfectly all right! Cross my heart. Just went in for a check-up. They found no ulcers or anything like that. But I am being treated for colitis. This means a diet. So many changes in fact that they put me in the infirmary refectory here and I eat MEAT! Wow. There, don't think of me as a St. Jerome any more. Fortunately however the merciful Providence of God has upset me slightly, so that I have never enjoyed anything less according to the flesh than my excursions into the infirm refectory. The very smell of the place nauseates me.

I was trying to keep incognito in the hospital. Went in as Fr. Ludovicus. One or two other monks in there (you'll think we're all falling apart!), but they put me on a different floor. So a nurse goes to one of my brethren downstairs and inquires "Who is that Polish Trappist on third west;—Father Ludoviski." After that my confreres became obstreperous and started calling me Ludowhiskey. We talk in the hospital. Too much, too. I was left more or less alone by everybody except my own doctors. Please don't publicize the name Ludovicus though, because I may want to use it again sometime. Really it is a waste of time, if anyone read the book carefully. But I have to go in for a nose operation when the stomach is cleared up. They try to make me rest in the hospital; I'd like to. Had to run out into the garden to get my office said, most of the time . . .

September 30, 1950

For your feast day I send you first of all my best wishes and the promise of special prayers and then these three scraps of things as a present. Sorry present. But since you are so easily satisfied! They are the sort of thing a monk is allowed to give away. If you wanted something better I could not give you a present.

The little white paper is a note of an orientation talk that wasn't typed. On the *Vidi Aquam* that we chant instead of the *Asperges* in Paschal Time. No need to try and fit it in with the rest especially if everything is finished. The yellow paper is what I used to have as a "schedule" when I was a cleric. Rather cut and dried. Sorry it is torn up. The third is a drawing—just any saint . . .

November 29, 1950
Vig. of St. Andrew.

This is going to be a very laconic note. It is wedged in between the hospital and our annual retreat. Have much to do in the interval. The nose operation was a perfect success. It helped a lot. I really had a rather bad nose. We are taking care of it all right. They have me resting still— this stomach business is a result of strain and overwork. Also I had a bad chest X-ray. But not very bad—just a little shady. No TB. Have to watch things though. And I will, since it is His will. Do not worry.

I did some extra work on the Psalm book in the hospital. Jay [Laughlin] cannot bring it out, because [by contract] Harcourt Brace has right to the next book published. This has to wait for completion of the other one which is rather difficult. But I know it all will go well.

You startle me with your delightful invitation to Milwaukee. Alas. Thanks for the kind thought, anyway. No, we never get that far afield, and perhaps it is just as well. The hospital is far enough. Have you heard [Robert] Speaight's record of the poems (the first of three)? He does a very good job on them . . .

Coming home on the feast of St. Catherine I nearly got killed in a car accident. But there was no accident. We took the train out from town because the roads were terrible, but had to drive from the station to the monastery. About 200 yards from home we had to pass a truck on an icy curve. Just as we pulled over, we skidded, spun clean around missing the truck by inches, and landed in the ditch. If the truck had hit us broadside you would be reciting the *De profundis* for one irreparably damaged poet and one young monk and a Hungarian familiar who is a very gay lad and on the whole a good driver. Well, you were praying. I was saying the rosary at the moment, too. None of us was in the least scared or even surprised—with the presumption of children who know that their Mother takes very good care of them—too good, almost . . .

January 8, 1951

This booklet of poems, the Italian translation of a few of mine. I think it is particularly well done and [Augusto] Guidi's notes are very intelligent. I mean by that that he understands exactly what I mean. I suppose it does not necessarily take intelligence to do this: but anyway it is nice to be understood—on that side of the Atlantic as well as this. Do you know Italian? And do you know German? I sent you the German version of the *Mountain* not, however, expecting you to read it but just as a curiosity to add to the pile of things you delight to accumulate . . . This year we took time to let the graces of Christmas slowly sink in. Fr. Abbot let me loose in the woods. I am a new man as a result. Our woods are rather wild in spots . . .

February 10, 1951

To pour some oil in the wounds—and as a surprise (for I have to write in Lent now, whether convenient or not, so much business)—I am sending you this horrible picture taken for official papers: I am going to become an American citizen some time this year, if I pass the examination! Also—today I finished the book *Fire Cloud and Darkness*. At least the first draft of it. It was your St. John of the Cross relic that did the trick! The book is practically all about his doctrine. From the time I got the new relic, I was so flooded with ideas—especially about transforming union—that the thing went like a breeze. It was when I got the other relic incidentally (of St. John) that the book suddenly began to be all about him—but only on the lower reaches of Mount Carmel . . .

March 1, 1951

Many thanks for the wonderful job on the Journal. I can easily fill in the spaces. You did a heroic job of deciphering. Meanwhile, I have finished the book for Harcourt Brace. The title is now *The Ascent to Light*. I guess I told you I had finished it, last time. They are going right ahead with it anyway . . . My health is okay and if I die the world will be none the worse off and I perhaps will be much the better for it . . .

April 28, 1951

Our "Father Immediate" has just arrived for the regular visitation and as I am secretary for these affairs I will probably not get a chance to answer your letters if I do not do so in a hurry. By letters I mean to cover a whole lot. I do not agree with you that everything should be printed. A lot of it is tripe, but I admit the volume you saw is less bad than the others . . . *Please* don't go overrating them. It makes me awfully nervous to be the object of a cultus, you know. I wish you would find some way of being more nonchalant about my mediocre stuff . . .

James Laughlin sent me the program of the CBS affair with you in a prominent position. He said he meant to get there but as usual he was thousands of miles from the scene of the event, skiing. He is an impassioned skier. As such he is a friend of Arnold Lunn [the English writer]. Lunn likes him a lot. I was surprised at the combination of Lunn–New Directions. But skiers are worse than freemasons. They are an international secret society, but an innocent and healthy influence. Laughlin is much berated because he pays no attention to his business and flies off to wherever there is snow, but to my mind he is the only smart business man I have ever heard of. If I had to be one, I would do the same . . .

May 21, 1951

. . . We had our regular visitation, at which I served as secretary and interpreter. This kept me busy. Then the visitor has cut down on my correspondence. Finally I have been appointed Master of the Students— a new thing here. I have to form the whole scholasticate, so to speak, out of the air. It is a job. You understand that I belong entirely and before all to my charges.

About the poem—I will not beat around the bush. Since I have to be serious and direct, I hope you will forgive me—and don't be hurt— if I ask you not to praise me. Just let me put it like that. I know you will understand. I have said the same thing before in many involved ways that were not clear. Please do not praise me. I esteem your friendship beyond words and this is nothing against it. I owe you more than I can say . . .

If I get time I hope to fix up *What Is Contemplation* with another little thing and make a short book out of the two together. But writing will be pretty scarce around here for a while and this makes me very happy. It is a great relief to get out and work in the fields and do some real Trappist work. Please do not forget to pray for my scholastics. There are nineteen of them—and good ones too . . .

May 26, 1951

This must be your time to do special penance. Our Lady must want to see your heart purified more and more, because here I come, Lady, with another one. After that mean letter I wrote you about your poem (and I hold on to the essentials of that nasty message it contained, namely not to praise me) here is a disillusion. You see, I was not worried in the least by your praise of the voice speaking the lines in the Trappist record [*Laudate Dominum*]. That voice is not mine. In a minute I hope to send an atomic bomb to the nitwit at Columbia Records who would not believe us—or the one who affected not to do so—when we said his use of my name would definitely mislead people. My only commentary is contained in the written notes on the back of the envelope. The voice is that of one of our novices [Richard Loomis], a good holy boy—a lot better than I am, both in elocution and in the practice of the obligations of our state. Really, you are full of illusions about me. Do get rid of them . . .

June 5, 1951

. . . The job [Master of Students] is a necessary one. It is almost entirely spiritual direction—and they certainly can get problems! But the big thing is this. I earnestly beg your prayers because I am just waking up to the infinite depths of my insufficiency for this job . . .

I cannot tell when or how often I may be able to write anything. I have the proofs of the new book (*The Ascent to Truth*) on the table—or at least the first few galleys and I am going at them now. But above all, I have to get out into the fields and give these kids a good example. The whole place might well go to pieces on account of me, if I don't brush up and pull myself together and be a monk for once in my life. And I will never become one by writing a lot of books. Sorry to be so grim, but something simply has got to be done. Do pray for me . . .

July 7, 1951

. . . The heat is upon us but it is not too bad. We are starting a new routine of night watches around here—to guard against fires. We take turns going around the house for two hours while everyone else is asleep. I am on tonight and think it is quite probably going to be fun. I have been out in the fields a lot more too, and since I have the students on my hands I feel like a different person . . . I have nothing at all against being a spiritual director, in fact I quite like it: but every moment of it makes me wish I lived alone in the woods . . . Remember me to Ed [Rice] and Bob [Lax] if you write. I'll never get time.

July 13, 1951

Bob Giroux should be sending proofs of *The Ascent* [*to Truth*] to you soon. He is trying to get the book out in September but that is too soon. Bob Lax sent a beautiful long poem written for Our Lady in Marseilles. You undoubtedly have received a copy. Surely that one deserves a place in *I Sing of a Maiden* if you ever revise it! . . .

Abbot James Fox wrote two letters to Sister Therese in September 1951. The first informed her that "one of the good, beautiful, angelic, contemplative, lost-in-the-cloud novice brothers" had cleaned up his office and burned the notes she had typed for Merton's Journal. He added: "The next thing, dear Sister Therese, is please do not tell good Father Louis what has happened. This is just between you and me, and Jesus." The second letter asked her opinion about Merton's keeping and publishing a journal. Dom James asked: "I was wondering about your personal reaction to Father Louis publishing a journal while he is still living . . . There is so much, necessarily and unavoidably of the I, I, I . . ."

September 25, 1951

. . . Harcourt Brace has not sent me enough copies of the new book [*The Ascent to Truth*] for me to get one to you by the third of October— they only sent me one so far. I have to keep it here as I am filling it with corrections. Under separate cover I am sending back the *Journal of My Escape* which you ask for. I am now set on *not* publishing any of it, so please do not type anything into it on my account. But feel free to copy anything you like for yourself if you are interested. It will most likely never be printed—I hope! There is some amusing writing here and there in it but it never gets anywhere and it would be a mistake to print it. Here too is a new pamphlet. And in the *Escape* I am enclosing a few notes. If you want them for your files, all right. Otherwise destroy them . . .

October 8, 1951

. . . Last week I made a retreat—in fact it lasted nine days. It was the first private retreat I had made here outside the regular ones before professions and ordination. It was a solitary affair from which, thanks be to God, I derived a great deal of benefit . . .

Paul Phillipe was very good—yes, he is a friend of Jacques Maritain. He gave me some good advice too. And told me that I really needed a certain amount of solitude—as much as is compatible with the Cistercian life. That was a comfort. Hence the retreat. My health is okay . . .

God bless you sister in your stubborn generosity and interminable patience with these uncouth Trappists. Thanks for your review [of *The Ascent to Truth*] in [the magazine] *Books on Trial*. Have I thanked you yet for half what you have done?

November 27, 1951

. . . I am *not* dying of TB. I get wonderful letters from people in France who call me "Tommy" & who pushed me around in a baby-carriage they say. I wouldn't deny it and I don't remember!

December 19, 1951

. . . Please do not worry at all about my health. It is fine. I am working on a reforestation project in the woods. No writing. The rest of my time is taken up with direction and conferences. I am getting to know my children and love them more and more—hence they take up more of my time. But who has a better right to it? I suppose I will have to write some more—and no doubt if I can do nothing else I will have to try to make some of the ideas in these notes palatable . . .

January 4, 1952

. . . My spiritual children are discovering more and more problems. I have them more and more in my heart, and in proportion as I do, I find Jesus in them, and live in Him, outside myself. That is another pathway to solitude—compassion. I scarcely have time for anything else, although I try also to prepare conferences and Scripture classes. Pray for me. A week ago today I took four of them who had been working overtime on Christmas mail out into the woods in the wildest and most beautiful spot I could find and it made them, I think, very happy.

The Carmelites everywhere seem to be quite pleased by the book [*The Ascent to Truth*], and Bob [Giroux] tells me it has sold 45,000. I have given up trying to understand why. But I am glad to have the Carmelites with me—I feel I belong more and more to them, even though I belong more and more to my own Cistercians. I pray for your good brother [Fr. Theophane Lentfoehr, S.D.S.] and hope that nothing serious will come of his sickness. I am sure everyone of us in religion can profit by an enforced rest . . .

February 4, 1952

. . . It does not seem certain that I shall be able to help out Ed Rice [with his magazine, *Jubilee*]. I am supposed to have backed out of the magazine field altogether. The Abbot General definitely told me to keep my name off the masthead of any magazine—even as advisor. I'll check and see, writing Ed as soon as I know. But I don't think there is much hope. Of course, he can publish anything of mine that is already written and I will try to shoot some notes along to him here and there, and even sections of books in course of publication.

Many thanks for your article ["Poetry in Education"], I mean your letter, in *Spirit*. I do not quite get the drift of the other side of the argument. My general feeling is one of discomfort because when you put me up close to anyone like Hopkins it is quite evident that I am not much of a poet—although you strenuously insist that I am. Sister, I am just not that important—I wish for your sake that I were, since you think I am . . .

April 25 [1952]

Yes, the little volume of Rilke arrived safely and I am delighted with it. I have always liked Rilke anyway. His poems on Our Lady are really meaningful and I relish them. Some of my scholastics are reading them also. Many thanks. This is just a word—I will write more later on. Busy editing the Journal at present. *Bread in the Wilderness* is scheduled for October. I am still dazed by the beautiful notes you did for the Cistercian theol. course . . .

Merton's April 25 postcard was somehow not stamped at Trappist, but came to Sister Therese postmarked "Milwaukee, Wis., Apr 26 1952," and she immediately inquired if he had been in Milwaukee without letting her know.

May 12, 1952

I am sorry I have no idea how our last card got delayed or how it happened to be post-marked as it was. I cannot check on what happens to the mail—but it doesn't matter as long as it eventually arrives, somehow. If this one is post-marked Buenos Aires—let me know. More when I get time.

July 12, 1952

. . . Bob Giroux was down from New York this week, and we were putting the finishing touches on the Journal [*The Sign of Jonas*] which is going to press now. We were also busy with other things. They are of course eager to start moving with the Journal since it will be more popular than some of the other books. Dan Walsh wrote me a very nice letter to allay my fears about publishing it. I began to worry quite a bit about the propriety of such a book. I feel like a hypocrite, writing about myself again. But the book itself is simple enough . . .

You will be glad to hear that I gave Bob the *Journal of My Escape* and that he is thinking of editing it and bringing it out at last. The whole thing is really not decided, but there is a possibility and I am secretly glad. Of course it will require cutting and rewriting, but I shall not attempt a complete job. We will bring it out in fragmentary form if at all . . .

September 2, 1952

. . . I have been tied up in many large and small jobs, as usual. Proofs for *Jonas* have gone back with a lot of changes. We necessarily *had* to drop some passages, and I changed my mind about many expressions. This book, of all books, needs scrupulous editing. I am very much afraid of doing a bad job with it. It requires such delicate handling, all the more so because I feel that this is really the kind of thing Our Lady wants me to be writing, much as it goes against the monastic grain . . .

September 27, 1952

. . . You worry me a little when you talk about preserving all this stuff for "future scholars." That makes me doubt whether I can in conscience send you things! I send them for *you* not for "future scholars." Who says there will *be* any future scholars, anyway? Forget about preserving these things Sister—it is a vain hope . . .

The letter which follows indicates Merton was unaware that Jacques Maritain, at the request of Robert Giroux, had written the Abbot General protesting the suppression of The Sign of Jonas. *The text had been released by Gethsemani and*

was in galley proofs when Abbot Fox, returning from France, told Giroux the
Abbot General had vetoed its publication. Giroux phoned Maritain at Princeton,
asking his help, and Maritain's letter (in French) reversed the ban. Apparently
Merton was never shown his editor's or his agent's letters explaining Maritain's
successful intervention.

November 6, 1952

. . . To set your mind at rest about *The Sign of Jonas*—it was objected
to by censors and the Abbot General withheld his *imprimi potest*, but
matters had gone so far with the printing and publicizing of the book that
it was deemed advisable to let it finally be published, to avoid a greater
evil. I guess it is, after all, a question of two evils. I cannot deny that I
was a little disappointed, from a human point of view, when he [the Abbot
General] refused permission to publish the thing. Yet I recognize that
there would have been, even humanly, many advantages even in that.
At the moment I do not know what I think about the whole thing, and
as a matter of fact I don't suppose there is any point in my thinking
anything. I am sure the General knew what he was doing, and I am sure
that ultimately there was much wisdom in the decisions of the censors.
The book shows quite frankly that I am not much of a religious—a truth
which I have no desire to conceal—and it also gives a clear insight into
various problems. By a series of accidents, it turns out that God's will is
for the thing to be published. I wonder what will come of it? Please pray
that all may turn out for the best . . .

January 20, 1953

One of the graces of my Christmas and New Year is greater solitude.
Surely St. Agnes had a hand in it. I am trying to take advantage of it
while I can: I mean interiorly above all. I am at last finding the solitude
I do not need to write about. That is the sign that I am arriving where I
belong . . .

Tell me how you like *Jonas*, now that it is in print. It is a big question
mark in my mind, that book. Maybe a big mistake. You will say no—you
always do. Did you see Dom Aelred Graham's article ["Thomas Merton:
A Modern Man in Reverse"]? Whatever you do, do not answer it. He
has some good points in it anyway, and the only thing I regret about it
is that he has done himself more harm than good by writing it, and
publishing it in the *Atlantic*. He doesn't like Trappists. No reason why
he should, either . . .

April 30, 1953

. . . The publishers have ceased to write me letters and I haven't
the faintest idea how *Jonas* is going, what the reviews are, etc. Do not
bother to send me reviews, but if the letter you mentioned, in the *Atlantic*,
is that of Fr. Bruno James, I would like to see *that*. Fr. Bruno is an

English secular priest—rather a character I understand. He was ordained on his own patrimony and proceeded to restore the ancient shrine of Our Lady of Walsingham. I am supposed to be doing a short preface to his new translation of St. Bernard's letters. Perhaps my contact with the correspondence of the great saint will improve my letters to my own correspondents. But I doubt it.

May 20, 1953

Father Abbot has given me permission to write something for Ed [Rice]'s August issue but I have heard nothing from Ed himself. And I can't find his address. Has *Jubilee* started to appear? If so, the copy that may or may not have been sent to me got into the ashcan instead. The only reason why I can write this article ["Bernard of Clairvaux"] is that it will also, and primarily, be destined for some such other collection as "Saints for Now." Pray that I may do a not too disgraceful job. Instead of bringing out a real book about him, I am turning out all these fugitive prefaces. I am glad not to have another book—even though on St. Bernard—appearing now. I feel too much like a writer as it is. After *Bread in the Wilderness* things can rest awhile, unless the publisher gets bitten by more inordinate ambitions . . .

Things are rather busy with the scholastics. All of a sudden a lot of dispensations and a couple of delayed ordinations. Now they are all scared and upset. The things that accompany the development of a religious community—especially one that has reached the special kind of development that is going on here—are matters for deep meditation. It is so like the growth of a living body . . .

This May I got the scholastics to put flowers on the altar where I say their Mass. Usually we are more austere. The flowers made more of a May of it, and I feel much closer to her [Our Lady]. Also Fr. Bernardot's book on her is being read in community, and I like it. You see, we are not very much up to date. Have you read Max Picard? I like his stuff very much and am currently in the *Flight from God* which is very pertinent. But that reminds me that I have not yet read the issue of *Renascence* with your article on Rilke . . .

June 6, 1953

. . . I took the scholastics out into the forest on Corpus Christi afternoon and we scattered all over the knobs and valleys. It was very beautiful and profitable—at least for me. I know it was also fruitful for them, because some of them have told me of their happiness and of the graces they received. I hope Our Lady will be good to you also in the silence of the woods. Silence itself is a greater blessing than many things we used to think of as graces . . .

June 30, 1953

. . . We are reading St. Theresa's letters in the refectory and I am relieved to see how human they are and how she makes little or no effort to be professionally spiritual in them. That is to say that she becomes explicitly spiritual only when something explicitly spiritual is called for, and therefore the implicit spirituality of *everything* in her is all the more evident. I like her more and more. Have you seen the new Encyclical on St. Bernard? At first, when I heard about it in a newspaper clipping, it sounded tame. I never saw anything so strong on the mystical life. It was a great inspiration to me to read the original Latin, when our Procurator General sent me the text from the *Osservatore Romano.*

September 26, 1953

. . . *Bread in the Wilderness* should be coming along any day now. It has been through the weirdest vicissitudes. I finished it three years ago in the hospital. I began it four years ago when I had the 'flu. There has never been more than one complete typewritten copy, and that is a mosaic of bits and pieces and has travelled all over the place. It went first to Harcourt Brace and then they traded with New Directions and took *Jonas.* So then it [*Wilderness*] went to N.D. They wanted to have it set up in England and then printed in offset in America. The first English printer who took it went out of business when the book was in galleys. And lately I hear that all the paste-up proofs and everything which was being sent over to this country got lost. The publisher dictated an excited letter about this into a dead dictaphone, and then the material turned up so I only got the good news . . .

October 21, 1953

. . . Troubles with *Bread in the Wilderness* have not finished. Last week I thought the whole thing was garbled beyond repair when I got another wild letter from the publisher. They are juggling around with pasted-up proofs for photo offset, and apparently they got themselves in a tangle. I could do nothing about it. Then just last night a wire came that there was still trouble with the New York censor—they had forgotten to tell him of one of my changes . . .

December 2, 1953

. . . Advent is upon us, with Our Lady's great feast coming next week. After that I expect to be pretty busy preparing five new subdeacons for their ordination, and one priest, not to mention a few minor orders. It seems as though I am going to be teaching Scripture again, next year, too. So please pray for me. My health is getting along all right. The other day I had a basal metabolism test which showed that I am not burning up as fast as they think . . .

December 19, 1953

Bread in the Wilderness was sent to you yesterday and should be reaching you soon. After all the vicissitudes the book went through, and all our anxieties, the finished work is certainly something of a consolation. I think [Alvin] Lustig's design is very fine. The pictures of the Devot Christ certainly make a book of it. I have not been through the text completely, but have found no serious mistakes. So there is very much to be thankful for. But now the book is so beautiful that I wonder whether or not it is a temptation. No, it doesn't bother me . . .

The Marian year is already bringing great graces. Anything that is any kind of gesture of love for Our Lady seems to do that. It is good to think of her more, read about her more, even though books are never satisfying when they deal with her. Ultimately it is good to be unsatisfied—on this earth . . . May God bless you always, and may the Marian year be a most happy one, even though it may bring one or two rainy days . . .

January 21, 1954

. . . I am a little busy with the course on St. Paul. It has developed into a full fledged Scripture course. The orientation lectures are on Mary, mostly. St. Bernard's Mariology . . .

Meanwhile *The Last of the Fathers* (little book on Bernard, with the Encyclical) is in proof. It ought to turn out neatly. I do not think it amounts to anything. I am already tired of the too-much splendor of *Bread*. Too fancy for a monastery. But if God willed it that way, I shall not complain. Did I tell you I enjoyed your review of *Jonas*? You had good words for all my own secret favorite passages—including the Louisville junk wagon. Thank you for it! . . .

Yes, I heard from [Bob] Lax. I suppose he will be busy with *Jubilee*, but hope he will find his way out here. Again, there is no hurry with *Viewpoints* [i.e. *No Man Is an Island*]. I will be deeply grateful for them (it) whenever they (it) come(s). Is a name like that singular or plural, anyway? . . .

[James] Laughlin sent his [magazine] *Perspective* on India. Did you see it? It had some rather good stories and poems. I am looking around for some good modern literature (decent and not too pious) to give to the scholastics as a change of diet when the spiritual life gets too rough—when they need to break training a little. J. F. Powers would be a case in point. I liked very much his short stories, when someone lent me them in the hospital in '50 . . .

June 19, 1954

. . . I got a copy of *The Last of the Fathers* off to the Holy Father. I hope he will be satisfied with it—I asked Cardinal Fumasoni Biondi to present it, and I have no doubt he will. My Scripture course on St. Paul keeps me busy. I am about half way through. We are dittoing the notes here as I go along, and they are not very elegant—not nearly as smart and clear as your work! But I will get a set together for you to read, at the end of the half, and then again later. My students are giving Marian conferences to the whole community in chapter—and doing very well so far. I like the new *Theology Digest* that is coming out at St. Mary's. It is very useful and I have enjoyed a lot of the articles. Just the other day I had occasion to quote the little De La Taille pamphlet on contemplation—the scary passage you marked, about what happens to contemplatives who do not correspond with grace. I think on the whole (although he is perhaps correct) the passage is too narrow. I would underline the words "God's gifts are without repentance" and if contemplatives fall it is not because of failures in things like "modesty of the eyes" (!) but because they take themselves too seriously and because they forget to believe in God's love for them. And then too I think it matters little whether one is or is not on what he thinks is a pinnacle . . .

July 10, 1954

. . . How is the summer going? With us it is, as usual, both busy and uneventful. It is strange how we can do so much, without ever anything "happening." I have hoed potatoes, and hoed tobacco, and hoed beans, and this week I shall probably have my share of hoeing corn. I finally finished the work on *Viewpoints*, which has a different title: I have called it *No Man Is an Island*—words taken from one of John Donne's "devotions". The reference is to the Mystical Body, every man being not an "island" but a "piece of a continent." I don't know what Harcourt Brace will do with the title. I have never thought up so many titles for any one book as I have for this one . . .

A long letter came here from the Secretary of the Congregation of Rites, about the worldwide movement for secular priests to spend an hour each day in adoration and mental prayer. It was addressed to me, and asked the prayers of Gethsemani for this movement, and I have been thinking about it a lot. Solidarity among priests, charity and union with their superiors, is a tremendously important thing. So too is their union with the One Priest. Pray for us all to be worthy of our calling.

I suppose Bob Lax is back in France by now. I meant to write to him when he was in this country and was sorry he did not get down to Gethsemani. What is new with Ed [Rice]? . . .

September 1, 1954

Have you grown tired of waiting for my reaction to your three poems, sent at the end of July? I can say at once that I am most enthusiastic about the one for Our Lady of Knock. It is really inspired & your very best poem. I like it very much. It has everything, and it comes from the depths, & it is universal. I hope you are not embarrassed to use it when you talk about Marian poetry. It is much purer and more real than anything I have ever been able to say about her. It is funny how one's best poems about her can come from the inspirations of a shrine where she has appeared. The only Marian poem of mine that I like at all is "Our Lady of Cobre." Of course I was fascinated with your "Chipmunk," but I think it would be better if it were shorter . . .

Many thanks for your feastday letter. I am entranced to have a friend—a sister who raises hawks on the roof of her convent! Too bad they left. Maybe they belong to the same family as whippoorwills that shout their heads off in the little wood to the east of our orchard every evening in the summertime. I seldom get to hear them, because at that time I am usually giving direction.

It has been a busy summer, & September, with the tobacco harvest & all our acres of corn, will probably be the busiest of all. I would like nevertheless to get a little work done on a book. It is the students' vacation . . . Well, I only got a card from [Bob] Lax at La Salette. All he says on his cards is "Hoy!" I don't need more than that to know he is happy . . .

November 29, 1954

Your letter was wonderful. I enjoyed every line immensely. Especially the adventures on the second page. Not only do you raise hawks, but you attend the rites of circumcision. It was an amusing description. When the little boy grows up and becomes a fervent rabbi, and learns that his circumcision was attended not only by goyim but by religious goyim, the complexity of his spiritual life ought to be enough to produce something better than the novels of Kafka.

By the way, it is so long since I wrote you, I think I never told you that on the feast of St. Therese, a Sunday, I went for a walk in the woods, and as I was crossing a pasture a beautiful big hawk came skimming past quite low, barely twenty feet above the ground and only a few yards in front of me. I took him to be your envoy, but he did not stay long enough for me to see if he was wearing a Wisconsin license plate . . .

The new book? It is called *Existential Communion*. I know you will like the daring title, but I hope the contents are all correct. Pray that they may be so. The book is simply an attempt to show that whatever is good about existentialism is and has been for a long time part of the Christian mystical tradition. I have not finished it yet, and of course it will take a lot of revision. As for the typing—I knew you were very busy and a friend of Dan Walsh's [Mrs. Anne Skakel] had been asking and asking for something like this to do for us. Father Abbot absolutely wanted to give her something as she has been a good friend of the Abbey, so I have promised to let her type the book. I would not have done so if I had thought you would be eager for it. Still, I feel better in a way because it will be less of a burden for Mrs. Skakel—she has a couple of secretaries to take over when she gets tired. Do you mind? . . . I made a little private retreat, four days, over the F. of St. John of the Cross and Thanksgiving—

actually I got caught up in some work in spite of myself, but I had four afternoons in the woods, and they were wonderful. I see more and more how important it is to live by faith and not by our own plans and our own ideas . . .

December 20, 1954

I have been scrounging around for something to send you this Christmas, and there is little here that is worthy of your attention—or proportionate to my debt to you. However, there is one thing which I treasure and which you also will like. It is an old magazine containing an article on my Father's painting and several reproductions both in color and black and white. It is an old beat-up magazine, and may be in worse shape still by the time it reaches you. But I think you will agree on its worth.

Most of the later pictures were done in places I remember very well. The Marseilles one was the view from a room in a little hotel where we stayed on the Vieux Port, and I remember lying around reading Kipling's *Just-So* stories while Father was painting at the window. Murat was another place where we went at Christmas time—you remember from the *Mountain*. My memories of it are awestruck. The town was undoubtedly under the complete sway of Our Lady, whose enormous statue dominated it from a cliff of basalt.

Did I tell you I was writing some material for a beautiful book of pictures [*Silence in Heaven*] on the monastic life, to be put out by some French Benedictines? That has kept me busy this Advent. I finished last week and sent it off, and now I am thinking of adding more. Wait until you see the book—probably next Fall. The pictures are marvelous. *No Man Is an Island* is on the way to the printers and was scheduled for Lent, but it is too late for that now. If you like the title (as I do) please pray that it may stick. There is opposition to it—not from Bob Giroux, so much as my agent [Naomi Burton Stone] who objects that the Donne text has been mined for titles by other authors (v.g. Hemingway who took *For Whom the Bell Tolls* from a few lines higher up).

Things have been busy here, with ordinations and what not, but I hope to make a little private retreat over Christmas. The community retreat is in January. Pray for me to profit by both . . .

January 18, 1955

. . . I am glad you liked the "Art in N.Z." I thought you would. The picture of father in the clipping was taken when he was pretty young. Probably about the time he was married, I should think. I never remember him as young as that.

Nothing has been happening with *Existential Communion*. I finished two-thirds of it in September and since then it has gathered dust. In December I was working on the picture book (did I tell you about it?

For the monks of La Pierre qui Vire). *No Man Is an Island* is now in proofs and they are rushing it through for Lent. I think they are going to hold on to the title: for which I thank God . . .

February 22, 1955

Didn't you ever hear about my experiment in interior decorating here? The whole house is a dreary green—everywhere. I finally got hold of a room for a conference and classroom, and decided to liven things up a bit. I forget the technical name of the red that I picked for the wall. But anyway it is commonly known here as "The Flamingo Room." I assure you nobody sleeps in it. One other person has approved heartily—a Detroit psychiatrist who comes down here once in a while. He says his office has all kinds of different color waiting rooms for the different kinds of patients. He did not specify which of the Kraeplinian categories liked Flamingo red. After hearing that, you may be astonished that I had the gall to give conferences on sacred art (yes, in that very room) . . .

July 12, 1955

. . . Did you hear of our new California foundation [New Clairvaux]? They went out in style in a private car with roomettes on the City of San Francisco. Perhaps too grand. Some of the other foundations had it much rougher. The chosen Superior [Anselm Steinke] of the new monastery is the one who is taking all the punches. He has been in the hospital with an operation for a disc on his spine and lies in the infirmary while his men go gaily off to start the new venture. A terrible blow, for an eager and energetic young superior. Pray for him.

For the rest, everything is quiet around here. We harvest wax-beans, at the moment. I have seen a new bird book with pictures of all the birds, and in which I bet you will find your hawks. Did they come back? I have been watching birds a bit too, and find I am amazed at the number of species that I did not know were around here—tanagers, yellow throats, swamp thrushes and what not. I can't get close enough to the wild ducks that are attracted by the new lakes we dug. On one of them was seen a blue heron . . .

August 6, 1955

. . . My health is all right, and they are certainly not making me Prior. That is not a job for me. I more or less asked to be considered "out" when all Superiorship was concerned and Father Abbot and even the Abbot General have accepted this from me. What I am hoping for now is to find some real solitude. Things at last seem to shaping up to provide me with some, after all these years. God works slowly and I am not the most prudent man in the world so I suppose it is a very good thing that He works slowly in my own life. Yet now that I think of it, things are moving faster than one would think. But I do think there is some hope of my becoming at least a quasi-hermit. I have been put in full charge of the forest. The state rangers are putting up a fire-lookout post on our highest hill and at the moment I am supposed to take charge of it. And so . . . I don't know how much to plan on, how much to hope for, but I am leaving it all in the hands of God. He can arrange things very much better than I can . . . I made a retreat privately after Christmas (before the famous Bruno Hagspiel week in January). And "Elias" [a poem] is more or less the summation of my private retreat—the conviction of a solitary vocation of some sort. Because solitary vocations do not fit into neat categories. And neither do I. All I know about it is that it is of "some sort." The big development has come since I gave up, myself, trying to fit it into too neat a category—"Carthusian," for instance. This, by the way, is in all confidence.

Anyway, apart from the publication of such odds and ends as still remain, I am not planning to write anything more for publication for several years. And at the end of the year, if all goes well, I will no longer be Master of Scholastics. I will at least be full-time forester and the rest, as I said, will be in God's hands. Consequently this batch of Orientation notes will be the next to last . . .

Have you read a wonderful book called *Pictures from an Institution* by Randall Jarrell? It is perfect, in its way—a beautiful job on the faculty of a "progressive" women's college. You would love it. I also managed to get [Evelyn] Waugh's latest *Officers and Gentlemen* which is slow in parts, but in some spots as good as anything he has ever done—especially a marvelous bleak island off the coast of Scotland, inhabited by a weird laird and a lot of commandos. Maybe you have read it. All this is a kind of a binge I have been having, before diving into the bushes to disappear. But at any cost get hold of the Jarrell book. I wish I could send you the copy I borrowed—but it is borrowed . . .

I must close now, and get ready for Vespers (i.e. grab a shower and try to become half human). But one more thing—on the eighteenth please say a good big prayer for my old New Zealand grandmother who is really OLD. She is going to be a hundred on that day. I hope it doesn't run in the family . . .

September 29, 1955

. . . Dom Gerard [McGinley] died at Cîteaux, the cradle of the Order, surrounded by all the abbots gathered for the General Chapter . . . Dom Gerard was one of the most devoted clients of St. Therese I ever met. He was inexhaustible on her subject. I even remember that, when I made my first retreat here, he gave me a lot of sob stuff about her in confession and, to my anger and humiliation, actually made me weep! I was furious. He not only talked about her but imitated her and I think she must have loved him very much, for he had a lot of her spirit of trust and joy and love: and he had gone through a great deal to get it.

A good holy man and we will all miss him, but I think he will be closer to us now than ever before . . .

For my part I have been very busy in the forest, as the time has come to start marking trees for "selective cutting" for the winter's firewood and for forest improvement. Sounds scientific. I have a Jeep which runs furiously once it gets started and the other day I ran into a post and bashed in the radiator, so that the garage man is mad at me and my face is very red. I must learn to use the brake . . .

October 22, 1955

I was glad to hear Ed [Rice] had sent you the original manuscript of *Babel*—of the version that was printed in *Jubilee*. It was very thoughtful of him, and it is just what I would have wanted him to do. I haven't seen the printed version yet, but please don't send me one of your copies. I am sure he sent me copies, but for some reason they have just not come through yet. I think they will eventually. Only about half the things sent to me ever get through. I finally caught on to why your Christmas present did not reach me: it was the book about the Carthusians at La Val Sainte, "White Paradise." Anything eremitical is considered bad for cenobites, and it is kept outside the iron curtain. But I had read the book in French, and it is excellent. The best chapter, "A Carthusian Speaks" is written actually, (or spoken) by the present Procurator General of the Order—is a record of a conversation the author had with him when he was a young professed monk at La Val Sainte. It is terrific, but he thinks now that the whole thing was too elaborate and complex. His ideas now are even simpler, if you can imagine such a thing. He is a real contemplative . . .

Anything you can do for Frank Dell'Isola will be a work of charity: his wife has cancer and he is crushed by it. He has worked very hard to make his bibliography [*Thomas Merton: A Bibliography* was published in 1956] up into a complete book, and is trying to include all sorts of junk and I am trying to prevent him from doing so (*Jester* cartoons for instance!). If you let him have the contents and pages of the new orientation, that will be fine. He is one of the last people to have seen Dylan Thomas alive. He was in the hospital when D.T. came in. He had met Thomas and conversed with him some time before. Thomas was unconscious in the hospital all the time. That was a tragic business . . .

About the orientation notes—please do not hurry. Take your time and suit your own convenience. This, by the way, will be the *last* series. Not that I am retiring to the woods. I thought for a moment I might be able to do that, but it turns out that I cannot. The abbatial election at the Genesee has lit on one of our fathers [Walter Helmstetter], the novice master, and I am to replace him, so it seems. I thought I was headed for the fire tower and silence, and I find I am moving in the opposite direction . . .

However, I shall still be in charge of the forest and take the novices out to fell trees and to plant in the spring. I am busy marking the timber we are to cut this winter. There is one quiet little valley full of beech trees which I love very much—it was always cool and quiet in the summer, and very beautiful in the fall with the sun coming through the colored foliage. But the beeches have to go. They are beautiful but useless, and they crowd out other more valuable trees with their spreading branches. There is no young growth under the beeches at all—which is one of the reasons why the valley is so pleasant: it is like a park. As forester, I have to be firm. I have to prefer a thick growth of young oaks and pines and hickories, so dense that you can't get through it, until it is thinned . . .

Oh, and by the way, don't bother to type a special copy of the Sacred Art notes for me—please! The mimeographed copies are amply sufficient. They are wonderful. Last night I gave one to Peter Watts, an English sculptor who is here to set up a series of stations of the Cross he did for us. They are very good—pretty much along the lines of Eric Gill, better than Gill's stations in Westminster Cathedral. Watts wrote to John Pick about lecturing at Marquette, but has heard nothing. He would be a good man to get, though. I consider him very promising . . .

December 23, 1955

. . . Things have been very busy here in the novitiate. I have just tried my hand at Christmas tree decorating. It is a very simple bit of decoration—took about half an hour. Most of the time the work is rather more rugged. We have been trying to keep the furnace supplied with logs from the forest and since so many left for foundations we are short of help, so there has been quite a lot of work. But it has been fun sawing down big old oak trees a hundred years old and over. Not to mention a lot of smaller ones.

Cardinal Agagianian who is an expert on sacramental theology wrote a nice preface for the *Living Bread* but unfortunately he was delayed in doing so and the whole thing has nearly been held up. As it is the preface has come in so late that it will not be able to be bound in the first edition but will be inserted, I think, as a separate leaflet.

I wish I could send you one of our monastery Christmas cards but I have not the face to do so—it contains a rather corny bit of verse and the tone of it all is a little commercial. Besides, there is no space for anyone to write a message on. So this picture of the scholastics will have to serve to bring you my best Christmas wishes and prayers . . .

February 21, 1956

Here we are already in the first week of Lent. I must get these notes back to you, or I never will. I have been very busy (this week I sing the High Mass). We have a couple of new postulants, one of whom is a Spanish priest who got here via South America and who does not speak English. I try to give him direction in Spanish. There is another—a Benedictine—

from Brazil who, thanks be to God, knows French. Our third South American cleric is fortunately English and it turns out that his sister lives at a village in Surrey two miles from the home of my aunt [Gwynned Merton Trier], where I used to spend Christmas when I was in school in England. Strange, isn't it?

The rest of my flock are relatively humdrum—denizens of Brooklyn, or Texas, or etc. There are only fifteen now. But they keep me occupied. And then this weekend my agent [Naomi Burton Stone] came down to get me extricated from all the business problems that have accumulated in the last few years, and get me more or less in the clear. It is unbelievable how complicated one's life can become without one's knowing it. The book you refer to (*The Gift of Silence*) is a case in point. I wrote a *preface* for a book of pictures [*Silence in Heaven*] being put out by the Benedictines of La Pierre qui Vire in France. They sold it to a French publisher, and lo the book is now appearing in every language as a new major work by Thomas Merton. My agent is wild, and it does complicate things a little, but I think they are straight now. The book by the way is beautiful— a finer collection of monastic pictures has never been seen . . .

Happy Lent. By the way, don't worry about me. The doctors have told me not to fast and have clapped me into the infirmary refectory. I am not dying, or anything, but they just thought I wasn't getting enough protein which is probably true as I am allergic to milk and cheese and never eat it and that is about our only protein source. For a while I have been getting eggs to help out, though. And now even meat. What a Lent . . .

May 26, 1956

You must think I am dead for sure, this time. Have you said a De Profundis for my soul? However I am alive and busy. That is the trouble. It is planting season and as we read somewhere in the prophets the harvester catches up with the ploughman and the ploughman is on the heels of the harvester. While we plant one crop another is coming in and the valley is full of the sound of machines sucking up the grass into their bellies and doing all sorts of things with it before it lands in the silo. The best afternoon we had was one when we were out picking up some 4000 bales of hay and loading them on trailers. The rest of the time it has been mostly strawberries . . .

Bob Lax was down. It was the first I had seen of him in seven years and he was in good form. It was a happy visit, and I was glad to see him again, though he no longer has a great mane of hair. *Jubilee*, it turns out, is going to print some of the Sacred Art notes, and I am pleased. I know you will be, too. And then too I have been writing a few poems—since *The Tower of Babel* is coming out with other poems at the beginning of '57 if we all live that long. I am sending one of the poems. Lax has another which I have not copied [probably the two were "Wisdom" and "The Sting of Conscience (Letter to Graham Greene)"], and I am hoping to get a copy from him . . .

June 11, 1956

Many thanks for your kind and delightful note for the anniversary of my ordination. You talk about flowers being flown from Hawaii. I have a novice from there, and another one coming (he graduated from Notre Dame), and they threaten to have flowers flown from there next Corpus Christi. I hope they do. This year, being novice master, I was back at making designs with flowers on the cloister floor for the procession, and got more fun out of it than I used to (it used to be a break-neck rush to get an enormous job before High Mass on a day when there was practically no time for anything) . . .

What keeps me on the jump at this particular time is that it is the season for postulants. They all poured in around June 1st, when the schools were out. None of them could enter immediately as I make them all take psychiatric tests (which are slow in getting scored) and some have to go to summer school for Latin, but they will be drifting in between now and September—around ten of them, I hope. Pray that I may always make good decisions. I can't expect to be infallible but still it is such an important affair. So many are desperately anxious to enter and yet one can see they should not come here. But there are many really solid vocations among them. I suppose it is the same everywhere.

Meanwhile, I am cherishing hopes of studying a little psychiatry. In fact I have read a little here and there, but have only scratched the surface. Mainly, I want to learn how to give the Rorschach test myself. And that, really, is fascinating: a wonderful adjunct to spiritual direction! . . .

July 11, 1956

. . . The last days have been cool and glorious, and I hope I can take that as a presage of many graces for you on your double feast. At any rate, cool weather helps one to pray better. We did have it rather hot for a while, and I expect it will be hot again. But after a certain point it doesn't seem to matter much, I suppose. I admit that it is rather difficult at night, when it doesn't get at all cool, and you have to try to sleep . . .

Life for me is busy but uneventful, if you know what I mean. In a few minutes I must go and welcome another postulant. When I say that there are floods of them, I only mean that there are many called but few chosen. For example there was a boy slightly crippled with natal paralysis in the hand and one leg: a very nice boy, but it seems we can't take him for all his good will. I can't see him marching out to the forest at the same clip as my energetic novices! It is a shame to have to turn away someone who wants the life with all his heart. Yet we can't go by our feelings, either. In the long run, it would be cruel rather than kind.

What else? I am working my way through the whole Bible with the novices. I thought I would go fast, but after a month I am still on Cain and Abel. It is only once a week . . .

September 25, 1956

. . . In the last year Father Abbot has requested that I gradually cut off all writing activities. I haven't written anything, or worked on anything except projects in course of being finished and a little Christmas thing [*The Christmas Sermons of Blessed Guerric*] which, I believe, will come out this year. Now that everything is more or less liquidated Father Abbot is curtailing all correspondence. And it is really *all*. Though some mail is still coming in about various jobs not yet published, he is handling it all himself and I have only the vaguest idea what is going on. It is a wonderful chance to practice abandonment!

I take this occasion, then, not only to wish you a very happy and holy feast, from the bottom of my heart, but to tell you how really and how deeply I have appreciated all you have done, and how much I have relished our correspondence. Although I have always put on a show of being very ascetic, I do not hesitate to confess that letters from my friends have always and will always mean a great deal to me . . .

You have probably seen the [Frank] Dell'Isola *Bibliography*. It is certainly complete—there are one or two errors, but I will not try to get permission to tell him about them as I do not feel it is the will of God that I should do so. On the whole it is a fine job, fine enough to be embarrassing to me: because it makes it quite evident that with me writing is less a talent than an addiction. Father Abbot hopes I can be cured of it now, and so do I. Nothing has been said about *never* writing again, but at least everyone wants to see how I get along without writing over a period of several years and I think it is certainly a necessary step to take. I have been at the typewriter since the second year of my novitiate, and it has not all been worthwhile or healthy for me, even though Our Lord has seen fit to bring good out of it for many souls. I am glad of the respite from writing, though I will miss the valuable contacts with so many wonderful people—or rather with the few special ones with whom I was still in contact, like you, and one or two Benedictines in France, and Dom [Jean] Leclercq, and Ed [Rice] and Bob [Lax] and Ad Reinhardt and a few like that.

Your letter from the camp was wonderful. I enjoyed your ride in the night and the dark forest—and everything else. How is the book of poems coming along? I hope that will get through to me at one of the right seasons. I should be inconsolable if I missed it, although I have seen so many of the poems in ms already. *The Tower of Babel* with a lot of new poems should be out next spring. I shall try to get lists to the publishers, so that they can send copies around—of that and *The Silent Life* which will be out this fall God willing, and with some nice pictures . . .

November 8, 1956

Many thanks for the All Saints letter. We have until the octave to answer and I am making the best of my opportunities. Although I got a total of four letters this feast, I haven't been able to make much headway with answering them until now. The others who got through were my agent [Naomi Burton Stone], the Abbot at Mepkin (South Carolina) [Anthony Chassagne], and the Novice Master down there. Bob Lax I know wrote, but there must have been something about the letter that was not acceptable, because he did not get through. I hope that will not discourage him altogether! I think it was just that he was asking me to see someone who was coming down, and I couldn't. Father Abbot will have made that clear, I suppose!

I am not complaining of the new situation, though. In fact one enjoys contacts more when the letters are from one's real friends, and not just a pile of ill-assorted business and other nonsense from complete strangers . . . Publishing a book without knowing what is going on is pretty much like going into the prize ring blindfolded. However, proofs and censors' corrections reach me, at least that!

I do hope Father Abbot will include you as "family" now. I got a card from some more "family" just last evening—the mother of Father John of the Cross [Wasserman] who was one of my students and who is now the undermaster of novices. His family "adopted" me several years back, so I do manage to get in on a few minutes of their annual visit . . .

Now to the main point. Father Abbot will not allow me to write *anything* whatever, still less a preface, because after the one for St. Bernard's letters I was forbidden prefaces before the curtain came down. There is nothing I would like better, but I know you will understand. I even feel guilty for jotting down notes for the novitiate conferences still. But that is all right—they are not for publication. I am not allowed to write poems, keep a journal, anything. This may sound pretty fierce, but actually it is wise. Writing with me was really turning into an addiction and I am glad of the respite. I feel sometimes like a patient in a dope farm or someone sobering up after years of alcoholism, but it is certainly important for me to continue as letter writer later on, but if I am to continue fruitfully it must be in a new way, travelling a new road.

Ed [Rice] told you this was a worldwide move. Yes and no. It is true that the Abbot General is progressively tightening up restrictions and making the censorship tougher and tougher so that writers will be definitely discouraged in the Order. And that too is all right—it is really the spirit of the Order to keep silent!!! However not all the writers have been clamped down on and certainly not everybody has had their mail stopped. Fr. Raymond still circulates around cheerfully and occasionally makes me signs about the troubled gestation of his latest—something on the Mystical Body. His mail has been diminished but not cut off altogether, and certainly I am the only one in the house that has his mail heavily censored and screened, even on the four feasts when letters are allowed for all . . .

As for the bird you saw, I'll bet anything it was a pileated woodpecker. We have a lot of them here, though I believe they are beginning to get quite rare. The markings are definitely those of a pileated woodpecker and the call is unmistakable—I used to be scared when I heard those wild excited clucks out in the remotest parts of the woods. Actually it is a fascinating bird, a very ancient kind of species, I believe. We have some within a hundred yards of the novitiate but they don't come out of the woods very often. They like to hide . . .

January 3, 1957

. . . There was a change of undermasters, and I lost my right-hand man—Fr. John of the Cross [Wasserman], one of those who was closest to me among the students, a very talented and holy young priest. He is now master of the students—and has the vault. I am glad of it—he will be a good one for the job and will make good use of the vault too.

Over the Christmas holidays there is a high school boy in the novitiate just to look it over—about sixteen but he looks much younger. He has a cousin in the laybrothers. Christmas was in some ways quite hectic here. There is a relatively enormous tree in the novitiate library outside my door, and the branches form a kind of hedge that I have to plough through to get in and out. They took over the undermaster's room in entirety for the crib. Next year things will have to be more reserved. There are, after all, limits. But it is good to see all the novices happy. Nothing could possibly be more happy and joyful than a Trappist novitiate at Christmas time. The laybrothers are even more fancy than we are—they have carols and all such things. We do our singing in church, and that is plenty. The Midnight Mass was wonderful. Of course I remembered you most especially in my three Masses . . . My own poems [*The Strange Islands*] are supposed to be coming out for Lent . . .

The story of Hungary is appalling and it makes one's religious life appear in a very serious light. Who knows how much longer we have to live? God knows our failings and understands our limitations, but in the time I have left I want to be above all a monk, and not just a monastic journalist. However I don't insist on any plan of my own. I know well enough that God can change things in the most unexpected manner and I no longer try to pry into His plans before it is time . . .

August 21, 1957

. . . It has been a frightfully busy summer for me. I have never had so much to do, so many different things to do, in my life. Pulled in all directions at once. I suppose it is good training—or good something. I don't mind it too much. I have reached such a stage of crass indifference, I suppose. We got a big batch of postulants in June, and there are over thirty in the novitiate at the moment. I don't mean to say that they come in "classes" but obviously at the end of the school year you get a bunch all at once. We did this year and they are pretty good. More still coming. We have a seminarian from Hungary [Laszlo "Ladislaus" Faludi], one who escaped last November, after the police came looking for him. He has not arrived yet, was here for an interview and will enter in September. A good soul, I think. I have a young Nicaraguan poet [Ernesto Cardenal] who is also a good man, and has an interesting background. Through him I am finding out about Latin America and a lot of interesting people in it. Am in contact with quite a few prospective postulants down there. A Jesuit is on his way here from Colombia, sounds like an interesting fellow—and Colombia sounds absolutely fabulous. My Nicaraguan poet has a Jesuit brother in Ecuador and that sounds wonderful too. An Italian missionary with an abundant beard came from Chile but only lasted a week. He was very sad, a lonesome misfit of a man who will never be happy anywhere. I felt very sorry for him. I could tell how he might feel, thinking he had found El Dorado all of a sudden, and then— We have to look for paradise within ourselves, and in the midst of Purgatory. I almost said hell. But after all, if we can't live with ourselves, we won't find happiness across the seas. And what is inside us can sometimes be a good enough imitation of hell . . .

Yesterday, on the feast, after the sermon and everything, I was just about exhausted, and dropped everything to get out into the farthest part of the woods—a nice little valley with pines and beech trees and oaks. It was very quiet and peaceful, and I had a nice afternoon, soaked in silence. I am going to get out there again if I can . . .

I commend your protection of the rabbits. Here in the novitiate garden the novices sit and watch with beaming kindness while the rabbits devour the flowers. They are so tame (the rabbits) that they practically come right up to you. It is really refreshing to see a rabbit eat a flower, anyway. Aren't rabbits better than flowers? I have seen a lot of new birds this summer—a Mississippi Kite (a southern hawk), and a beautiful green heron. It was also the first time I got a good look at a bobwhite. But I haven't been out much. Lately though the novices have been working on a power and telephone line up to the new fire tower on top of one of the hills. I have been out trying to supervise that intelligently—it has been a hot, rough job, and we kept running into nests of yellow jackets, and all of us have been stung a few times. We had to fell a lot of trees and now they are digging holes for the poles. We will have to set the poles ourselves too, and that is going to be fun.

It is true I was secretly smuggled up to St. Johns's [at Collegeville, Minnesota] last summer. Father Abbot came along to see that I behaved and didn't go anywhere. A call came in from somewhere in Wisconsin (some Premonstratensians I think wanted an article for a magazine) and he took it. I went nowhere except to have dinner with [J. F.] Powers at St. Cloud and that was very pleasant. I am keeping all your intentions in my prayers—thanks so much for the reviews, *Living Bread* and *Silence in Heaven.* Yes, the *Cuban Journal* should be coming along. I think you will like it. It is lively. There is a lot more where that came from (a big ms. at St Bona[venture]'s) . . .

October 12, 1957

You can imagine how busy I have been. The postulants have slacked off a little, and there have been the usual departures. The novitiate is down to twenty-one or -two and things are relatively peaceful. On top of it all I have been writing a postulants' guide, correcting the revised ms. of the French translation of *The Ascent to Truth* (it has been a big headache). The novices are transplanting trees all over the place. We have been trying to put up telephone poles for an electric line to the fire tower and the government has stalled about sending us necessary materials, and here we are in the middle of the fire season . . .

Reading—I try to do some. A fair amount here and there. I love Karl Adams' new book, *The Christ of Faith.* And I ran into the poems of St. John Perse—terrific. Mark Van Doren knows him and likes him. He lives in Washington . . .

March 27, 1958

Here I am at last—on the very eve of Palm Sunday. Months ago I got permission to write and send back the Liturgy notes, but everything has conspired to prevent me. We had a bad siege of 'flu. Since I was full of vitamins I did not get it really badly, was just afflicted with repeated colds, did not have to go to bed. But most of the community was down. They took over the old guest house and turned it into a new pest house. It was a shambles . . .

It has been a wild winter. In fact it has been cold, and one of my tropical postulants is hugging the radiators and weeping for home. Of course it is warming up now. In a day or two I hope to be getting a few thousand tree seedlings and go to work planting them, but we are getting competition from the garden man who is having us plant onions like mad for weeks: never saw so many onions . . .

Many thanks for the books—I especially like Gabriela [Mistral], and am pleased with her translator, with the fact that it is Langston Hughes and with his translations themselves. The other one I lent to Fr. John of the Cross [Wasserman] and haven't got it back yet, but there are in the monastery some Patero fans all right. My publisher sent me one of their books, *The Diary of Helena Morley* [by Alice Dayrell Brant, translated by Elizabeth Bishop], which I have not yet read, but the novices to whom I have lent it all voice their enthusiastic approval . . .

April 18, 1958

. . . About the visit: I am always up the same tree in that regard. Father Abbot is getting stricter and stricter all the time about correspondence and visits, the two things he is really strict about, and I just don't think it is possible that he will ever countenance visits of women who are not close relatives—or enormously wealthy benefactors. You are certainly a benefactor, but he doesn't look at it that way. You know how much I would enjoy talking over so many things: but as it is I am left in no doubt that he thinks I am way over my quota all the time, in these matters. I have to save all my best efforts to get permission to go into town and see a novice in the hospital when one is there, or to get a day or two with [Bob] Lax. He has made it quite clear that this is already more than I rate. So we just have to bear with the situation as it stands.

The wrens are building their nest in the birdhouse we established on the clothesline pole. They are late this year since it has been so cold. We got our tree seedlings and planted them this week—that shoved out everything else. I don't know if I told you about the difficulties in getting *The Secular Journal* through the censors—I am sure I must have. Well, today the good news came through. It is all clear. I am overjoyed, and know Catherine de Hueck [Doherty] will be too. I must get a word off to her about it at once . . .

May 28, 1958

. . . The chipmunk is on display: and there are plenty of live ones around too: more chipmunks than novices, in fact. Well, this is just a note and things are extremely busy. I do hope this reaches you in time. (By the way if you pick up some clippings on the Nixon tour of South America, save them please. I am interested. I think a lot of the trouble was his own fault—wonder what the reactions are.) I hope everything is as beautiful there as it is here. Our Lady's month has been more glorious than ever.

July 14, 1958

It is the 14th of July, French Independence day. Poor France. I haven't heard much of what has been going on but just enough to know she is in trouble as usual. What happens to her happens because of, and perhaps for, the rest of the world. She is still the keystone of Western civilization. Our turn comes later. May God help us. With all the confusion, I think she still faces her difficulties with a very creditable intelligence and discretion—at least relatively. Even in her most trying moments she can give the rest of the world lessons in being civilized. And incidentally—I got hold of Camus' Nobel Prize book, *La Chute*, and it is terrific. What a diagnosis of the pride and angelism of our time. So France remains the conscience of the West. It would be well for us to realize the fact . . .

I suppose I have no right to talk, being involved in my own type of vanity. I am planning a book on Sacred Art [*Art and Worship*], borrowing materials for illustrations, planning the book more or less myself—with a layout man in Louisville to do the real work of course. We are publishing it ourselves and thus I can get my fingers in everything. Do please pray that it comes out all right. I hope it will. It is a lot of fun at the moment, though sometimes it gets me in a whirl. But not as badly as it might. By now I have a certain dexterity at keeping these pancakes in the air, alas. My agent [Naomi Burton Stone] reproached me for the project (while they are still sweating over the *Secular Journal*).

I look forward to your reviews. Dan Walsh wrote me that he had felt obliged to pan *Thoughts in Solitude* and was profusely apologetic about it, as he would be, but I never saw his review. That is a strange book. For a while I was dead against it myself. A lot of people say that they like it almost better than anything else I have done. Mystery. I still do not think it is particularly good: but I suppose it has something to say to a few special people whom God alone knows . . .

September 4, 1958

. . . August was riotous: Father Abbot likes to invite down high school kids who are prospects for the life and they mingle with the novices for a couple of weeks. But they don't worry too much about trifles like silence etc., so the place is a bit wild during their stay. We are always very glad to see them go, the little dears. So they kept things very busy. This summer's new postulants seem to be settling down nicely and they are a good lot, on the whole. Perhaps the best group we have had since I have been on the job. We don't take them all in one "class" of course, but it happens that the summer is normally the time when most vocations arrive, having finished the school year. This year's General Chapter will be discussing the new college course we will demand of all postulants . . .

Have you heard of the new book of the Russian poet Pasternak? *Dr. Zhivago*. It is a tremendous thing and a lot of his poems are published in appendix. The book was not allowed to be published in Russia ("idealist deviation" and doubtless also "rootless cosmopolitanism"), but it actually has a very important basic content of religion and the poems (some of them) are the finest religious poems written *anywhere* in the 20th century. It is fabulous. I think this is one of the most significant events in literature in the whole 20th century and something we all ought to ponder. I'd like to write an article about him. In the refectory they are reading Newman's life by Louis Bouyer, a splendid book . . . I think it is the wisest and most outspoken book about the problems of converts that I have ever seen—it has made me really understand and sympathize with Newman for the first time—and now I am sold on him, I think he was really a saint . . .

I hate and detest commercialism more and more, it poisons every-thing. Naturally the poison has got into my own life, because I am a "best seller." I wish I were not. I think the last books are a bit out of that category anyway. I received wonderfully comforting words from Jacques Maritain about *Thoughts in Solitude*. Many people have not liked it, as

I expected, and I do not mind the fact. The book does not say exactly what I wanted it to say. Nevertheless it is one of the books that really does come from the inner depths, where I most unequivocally mean everything in a very personal and definite way. It is a book in which I speak what is really on my mind, or what was on my mind in 1953. Now I would write quite a different one, because I have other things on my mind . . .

I am very content not to "have to" write. It seems that at least the writing part of my life is getting around to being on a more healthy and sane basis, in which I write less and say what I really want to say. I have no vocation to become a publicist, and in so far as I may have been one I have been untrue to myself and therefore also to God . . .

Father Abbot is away at the General Chapter and will not be back until October. I hope the Chapter stops turning somersaults and lets us all settle down in peace with the modifications of the Rule we have at present. There are elements in this house who want to go on changing and changing like whirling dervishes. I am not ultra-conservative (anything but), but I am absolutely against the whimsicality of all the proposals that are going around now—absolutely superficial and silly ideas. The monastic life has to be at least a *little* serious . . .

February 12, 1959

Not only is it Lent but we are on the eve of our retreat (Friday to Friday—please pray for us) and if I do not get this off, with all the other letters I owe, I will be months behind . . .

The preacher [Michael G. Sheahan] is a Father Sheehan (spelling?) from Los Angeles who, they say, is regarded as a kind of Curé d'Ars out there. He has not arrived yet: as I say we begin tomorrow. I hope it will be a good retreat. Personally I do not like a great series of conferences and they usually end by irritating me more than anything else. But there is always a grace nevertheless: the free time would mean more, if there were a lot of free time. I hope to do some tall work in the woods— cleaning up some Virginia pine to sell for lumber and preparing some land for reseeding—later we will also plant seedlings—the usual spring occupation of the novices . . .

I am enthusiastic about Fidel Castro in Cuba: a terrific person, who against all odds (both the U.S. and the Reds were lined up with Batista against him!) has liberated Cuba for the sake of an ideal and not for political gain. He is a good Catholic, and the Archbishop of Santiago once intervened and saved his life when he was likely to have been killed. Any clippings about him would be very welcome—we are all interested. We need more people like him. (Though he has been pretty tough with the vanquished. I guess he had to be.) . . .

April 3, 1959

. . . I think Fidel Castro got too bad a press. Certainly he went overboard in reprisals, and that was wrong, but people have no idea how bad Batista was, or how criminal is our own negligence in supporting such people. We have no right to kick at all, but ought to be ashamed of ourselves. Do pray for Nicaragua: the situation there is as bad as it was in Cuba, and one of my novices [Ernesto Cardenal] has relatives who have suffered much in prison, and been tortured. They want to throw out their own dictator someday soon and I hope they succeed. I only hope the stupidity of our State Department does not make it difficult for them . . . Our daffodils are out everywhere, and the novices are painting the stairs to the chapel . . .

May 14, 1959

[Bob] Lax was down here with Ad Reinhardt (abstract painter) and we had a good talk. It was a pleasure for which I thank God . . .

July 4, 1959

. . . At the moment, guess what, I am rewriting *What Is Contemplation*. It will be a patchy job. But I have been wanting to do it. I may revise other early material, too. It is all very unsatisfactory to me, in fact a lot of it disgusts me. I was much too superficial and too cerebral at the same time. I seem to have ignored the wholeness and integrity of life, and concentrated on a kind of angelism in contemplation. That was when I was a rip-roaring Trappist, I guess. Now that I am a little less perfect I seem to have a saner perspective. And that too seems to be not according to the manuals, doesn't it? . . .

A lot of novices have left and we are down to thirteen in the novitiate now. It is quite peaceful all right. More are supposed to be coming, but I guess we have to be content with smaller numbers from now on. I am by no means hard to please when it comes to small numbers: I am perfectly satisfied with the present size of the novitiate. One can work better, and keep one's head—more or less . . .

September 29, 1959

This week I am really going to give this room a fall cleaning and if I come across anything more I will send it along. Things have been piling up for a long time now, and it is a very small room, so that it is impossible to move sometimes . . .

I finished a book this summer called *The Inner Experience* which started out to be a simple revision of *What Is Contemplation* but turned into something new, and just about full length. It has to be revised and has been sitting here on the desk, waiting for revision for some time, but I refuse to work around the house as they are blasting around on all sides with jackhammers and other machines and it is impossible to think. The novices have been making a good share of this noise, trying to put in a couple of new showers in our crowded cellar . . .

What did you think of Khrushchev's visit? We could use clippings on *that* and on Ike's return match in Russia. We heard bits and pieces of the news but not enough to form any idea of what was really significant about it, and I am not sure whether Khrushchev was a success here or not. I think secretly people admire him because he has "got places" but they don't want to admit it. That is the trouble with our American pragmatism—it backfires on us. We admire success, period. We don't care too much about how it has been obtained, or for what. What simpletons we have all become. But I do think the old crook had a sense of humor and a kind of dash about him . . .

November 20, 1959

. . . Yes, I did get a letter back from [Luis] Somoza, the dictator of Nicaragua: pained astonishment. What, torture, here in lovely, democratic Nicaragua?? etc. etc. I happen to know relatives of people who have been tortured there. Though more recently they are taking care not to do this as it is bad publicity when it gets out. This whole business of political injustice and inhumanity is a tremendous problem and one to which we cannot blind ourselves. We are all getting more and more deeply involved in collective patterns of injustice without having the faintest realization of it. We are certainly to some extent responsible and implicated in what happens in Nicaragua, since Spellman in person made a big speech down there, boosting Somoza and saying what a fine leader etc. etc. The problems get so vast and so intricate that no one can keep track of them, but still even a contemplative—rather most of all a contemplative—has no right whatever to ignore the issues. It is vitally necessary to find out where we stand and definitely come out against evil, wherever it may appear . . .

Incidentally Fr. Abbot is not here now, and that is why I can write this frankly and warn you to be careful—which he would certainly want me to do anyway. He has been called to Rome. Called: no one knows why. There must be some special questions arising, and I can imagine what one or two of them might be. Whatever they are, I might be closely involved—for instance the college problem. So do pray very hard especially at this time, it may be crucial . . .

The Desert Fathers are coming along—that Zen man, [D. T.] Suzuki, wrote a provoking article and I added another to help explain it. People may be interested, and challenged—and maybe shocked, I don't know. I think the dialogue is lively and interesting, and hope it will have the right effect. Of course, there are always narrow minded people to be taken into account . . .

P.S. One more limitation: do please be a little circumspect about exhibiting letters because of the fact, for one thing, that it might encourage people to write and it is simply impossible to answer . . .

December 11, 1959

I just want to get off my Christmas presents in time—mostly pictures. Myself, [Bob] Lax, and Ad Reinhardt the abstract painter. And one or two shots of the little house my Father built at Saint Antonin, France. The people in the picture are strangers—except that they sent the pictures, which makes them in a way friends . . .

January 18, 1960

Here we are just about to enter into the annual retreat and I have not yet written most of my Christmas letters. I am trying to get them out in a hurry. This is not definitive, then, just a shout in the windstorm to let you know I am still alive and keeping afloat by hanging on to whatever spars float by.

Thank you for the new Qumram book which looks solid and interesting. I hope to enjoy it. At the moment I am ploughing through a heavy reading schedule to get into the clear. One very interesting book is [George Justus] Lawler's volume on the *Catholic Dimension in Higher Education*. It is excellent, and I hope many will read it here as we go into our tentative and sketchy college program which I am rather dubious about. I am so afraid of this amateur project which can so easily do harm to young souls. We do have good men for faculty, of course. But the tensions and contradictions under which the project will be carried out well may be tragic. For one thing, the general temper of the house is strongly anti-study. And the college course tends to be a kind of expedient to placate the bishop rather than an effort to give them a real humanistic formation . . .

Have you read the poems of Brother Antoninus [William Eeverson]? Very very fine. I am most happy with their rugged, austere, monastic quality. Serious and deeply sincere, with a wonderful sense of the ambivalence of life and the reality of sin and of God's mercy. That is the very stuff our life is made of, and modern Catholic devotion tries to escape it with sentiment. There is no escape. It has to be faced squarely. He does this, and I am grateful. I went over some of his poems with the novices over the holidays . . .

May 30, 1960

. . . Do please forgive me for not having written at Easter. I know you do. I have not been ill, though I have been having trouble with my eyes. That is no excuse though, because I have been working right along. But I have had a lot of difficulties and distracting cares. First of all with censors. You have no idea how absurd they have been. I wrote an article on solitude and anyone would think that it was an obscene novel, the way they landed on it. There is in the Order a kind of terror of any mention of the solitary life, no doubt because the tradition in this regard is unpalatable among us: we have decided that the cenobitic life is the ne plus ultra and we have to struggle by main force to keep ourselves convinced of this. Such absurdities arise from the arbitrary fantasies of institutional thought; thinking for the "outfit" rather than in accordance with truth and the full tradition of the Church. But I really got in trouble. I rewrote the thing three times, and these rewritings were further developments of an original version written in 1955 or earlier and published only in French ["Dans le desert de Dieu"] and Italian ["Nel Deserto"]. I never could get that one past the American censors (the others did not give it a second thought!) Finally when I thought I had the whole thing simon pure, the censor declared that I was making "direct attacks on Superiors and the authority of the Church." This was for a sentence which ran something like: "Those who say interior solitude is sufficient do not realize what they are saying." This was interpreted to mean superiors, as if no one else would ever think of saying such a thing. In another sentence, where I said that the principal anguish of the solitary life was that the hermit did not have anyone to guide him and the will of God pressed upon him with immediacy or something like that. Overlooking the fact that I said this was a source of anguish, they picked that up and said I was preaching against authority and spiritual direction and saying that everyone should seek to be guided directly by the Holy Ghost. You never saw such a stupid mess. The Abbot General [Gabriel Sortais] picked this up and flew into one of his rages, which can be very stormy, and I was all but consigned to the nether regions as a contumacious heretic. This is all rather silly and I would not bother you with it unless I thought you would be amused . . .

The book in which these things are to appear is now in galleys. It is very appropriately called *Disputed Questions*. It contains the material about Pasternak who, I hear, is dying. And lots of other things. I got into hot water about the Mount Athos article, which is more understandable. I said some rather cutting things about conventional ideas of monasticism, things which were true and obvious, but one is not supposed to say them. Though of course everybody sees and admits them.

Do not be surprised that Ed [Rice] has not written. He has been wandering around South America. I have not heard from him either, though I sent a couple of long articles to *Jubilee* weeks ago. [Bob] Lax is holding down the fort there, and therefore he does not write. They are always in some kind of quandary . . .

I have lately read some Joseph Conrad and he is always a Master. Did you ever read anything of Richard Hughes, *High Wind in Jamaica*? I used to use him [as an English teacher]. I am interested in the new stuff out of Germany. A finely wrought short story by a lad called Wolf-siegfried Schnurr (what a name!) was in *Encounter* lately, called "The Maneuver." Dostoevsky is always tops. Another of the new Germans is Ernst Muenger, and I am liking what little bits of his I see. I want to see more. For short stories, Bernard Malamud has done some fine things . . .

December 5, 1960

This letter is to cover the little broadside [*The Ox-Mountain Parable of Meng Tzu*] which I am sending you separately. Another Victor Hammer piece, which is superbly done as usual. From Meng Tzu. I like the text very much, and got it up from a literal translation which is an appendix to I. A. Richards' book on Mencius. It has implications for the doctrine of grace, too, in many ways. Under the surface.

Did you mention something about Teilhard de Chardin? I have had some trouble there too. Ed [Rice] sent me a remarkable little book of T de C., the *Divine Milieu*. I liked it very much, and did a review article ["The Universe as Epiphany"] praising it. Of course I wanted to make clear that this was just a review of *his book* and not a general approbation of all T de C.'s work (and in any case I have not yet read the *Phenomenon of Man*). The censors of the order were true to form. They went into a panic, and the General took it up. Gave the article to some professor in Rome. The latter said there was really nothing wrong with the article but that Rome wanted Catholic magazines to keep silence about Teilhard de Chardin right now, and that it would be much better if I did not say anything. So it is not being published . . .

I was happy about the presidential election, but certainly did not vote for Kennedy because of his religion, I assure you. I thought there was not too much to choose between them but that Kennedy is the better man, at least shows promise of much more development . . .

New Directions is coming along with the *Behavior of Titans* which I think you will like. And with the expanded *Desert Fathers* thing. And in the New Directions annual I will be having some translations of Latin American poets and an exchange of ideas with the Zen man, Suzuki . . . Then too I think I may do a rather thorough piece of revision on *Seeds of Contemplation*, a new edition is called for. I thought of this when I got a letter from a man in Pakistan [Abdul Aziz] who is an authority on Sufism and realized I couldn't send him the book because of an utterly stupid remark I had made about the Sufis . . .

February 5, 1961

. . . Fr. [Raymond] Roseliep's Christmas Card: it was a nice poem, but one feels a little embarrassed that a priest could have written it. Maritain has a good footnote about this somewhere. I liked the spread of poems you sent and they have mostly been posted. I was glad [Bob] Lax was in it. I am afraid I have had nothing more to do with Teilhard de C. The General demanded that I read a book about T., an attack on him by a rather second-rate theologian. I read it, and the whole controversy fills me with boredom. If I have to approach it from that angle, then I have thirty better things to do, I don't intend to argue. I'll wait until Teilhard is fully published and not misrepresented on one side or the other and when reading him does not imply joining a movement. I still like him. (*Eppur si muove.*) . . .

Frank Dell'Isola came out with an article ["Thomas Merton: Outlines of Growth"] saying my best work was *No Man Is an Island* and that I haven't done anything good since then: which shows his perspective is all off. Not that I claim to be doing specially good work, but to pick *No Man Is an Island* which is vague and not characteristic, and overlook something like the notes on solitude in *Disputed Questions* which is what I really have to say . . .

May 10, 1961

Here we are on the vigil of the Ascension: and the first nice day for a long time. Occasionally we get a brilliantly beautiful May day, but the rest are rainy and cold. I suppose the rain is what makes the nice ones so glorious. I have been wanting to drop you a line and was going to have time after class today (I am still slugging along with mystical theology) but instead I got caught having to go over a pile of the cards and leaflets we have been putting out here. And giving critical comment. Someone is taking the matter in hand, because we have been putting out some of the most abominable trash in the last ten years or so: everything trite, corny, absurd, and vulgar one can think of. It is true, I have seen even worse elsewhere, but we should have enough sense and enough taste to avoid some of the gross errors we have made. Anyway, I gave my opinion in laconic and I hope charitable terms. But it took some of my time from this letter.

Mostly I am busy with class and with Protestants . . . And the chipmunks? They are lucky to have you as their guardian angel. Our poor little chipmunks don't survive long here: a lot of rangy old cats that aren't regularly fed rove around eating what they can get. One hardly sees a chipmunk behind the novitiate any more. Very sad, they are so gentle and quick.

Ed Rice (from whom I haven't heard in months, though I have sent him two articles) is apparently off to Europe with his family and [Bob] Lax has been in France for some time . . .

September 19, 1961

. . . It seems that my time is more and more consumed, and there are reasons for it, as I am now seeing quite a lot of the various retreatants, particularly Protestants still. Also a wonderful Rabbi from Winnipeg a Hasid [Zalman Schachter]: an orthodox priest, a Negro working on fair labor practices for Negroes, and lots of others like that. They are wonderful people, and have so much. It is very encouraging, except that there does not seem to be much they can do with all the good that is in them, in the face of the evil that threatens everyone. I can still get mad at society, all right. It is such a tragic thing that society as a whole should be so violent, corrupt, wasteful, and absurd . . .

Fr. Illtud Evans, the editor of *Blackfriars*, also stopped by briefly. I had a good visit with him. And Fr. [Jean] Danielou was here earlier in the summer. He is my director, more or less. I need someone who can keep me straight in dealing with Oriental philosophies, and ecumenism. He is one of the best, and a charming person. I have always liked him . . .

In addition to that I have had to write a few articles for a new *Catholic Youth Encyclopedia* which, between you and me and the gatepost, sounds rather useless. But maybe they had a method in their madness, and decided to do something that would have more life in it than the *New Catholic Encyclopedia*. I have a long article to do for them, too, on "Spiritual Direction" . . .

One new poet I am very happy about is Denise Levertov. New Directions has done a book of hers, *With Eyes in the Backs of Their Heads*. I think it is very fine, very spiritual in a broad, Jungian sort of way. She is not Catholic as far as I know, or may be. I think a poem of hers was in *Jubilee*. Ned O'Gorman is very fine too, I like him. Haven't yet read his article on the ascent of Sinai, but will soon. It is all right for you to do some notes on the drawings for Tom McDonnell. I am not too sure what they are, but it all sounds ok. Anyway I am sending you what I just referred to as the Auschwitz poem ["Chant to be used in Processions around a Site with Furnaces"] and also a dark bitter tirade I am sending to a friend in Nicaragua ["Letter to Pablo Antonio Cuadra concerning Giants"]. This all may be a bit black, but don't let it depress you. I am mad at the international situation, though it is not reasonable to get angry over what one can't change. I would like to be able to get up and say something that would help people, but I know nothing can be said, and because of the frustration I speak with bitterness . . . The encyclical *Mater et Magistra* was fine and so was the peace appeal of Pope John: but who listens to such things? . . .

[*Cold War Letter 20*]

January 11, 1962

[*Only the last two paragraphs, marked at the beginning with asterisks, were selected by Merton for the Cold War Letter.*]

. . . I hope the new Abbot of Spencer [Thomas Keating] will be down here one of these days. I look forward to meeting him. Snowmass is something of a symbol in the Order. To the business-minded it is a white elephant, and to the ones who like solitude it is a sign that the Order hasn't abjured solitude entirely, or reduced it to a purely juridical concept. There are all sorts of angles, but certainly the mere physical fact of being in a remote, quiet place, undisturbed, is paramount. The mere non-writing of letters, or staying within walls, does not quite do the trick, though that, too, helps. But in a place like Snowmass I don't suppose they really even need a wall in the same sense that we do here.

Have we snow? Well, we have zero weather. A little snow, which does not melt even in the sun, because everything is so cold. But I did not finish what I was going to say in the previous paragraph . . . I think Spencer is really developing into a place with a rather deep and varied life of prayer and thought, and is shining with more light than Gethsemani (as if such comparisons were relevant). There has always been something of a hidden rivalry between the houses, but this is wearing off. I hope it is, anyway. We are quite different in many ways, and that is to be expected . . . I think Spencer will certainly become, if it has not already become "the" Cistercian Abbey of America. Again, I say these things with detachment and reservations, because I cannot really judge . . .

* As for the "extreme groups": they are going to be a difficult problem for the country and may do much harm. The people are in most cases so sincere, even so naive. The mixture of naivete, outraged innocence, and hidden violence can become terrible though. It is very important that the rest of the country, especially Catholics who have retained some sense of perspective in these matters (there are still some) should not merely execrate them, and not merely accept them with passive indifference. If there is any way in which we can help them, keep communication patiently open with them, get a little truth through, make an occasional effective plea for tolerance and reason, then we should try it. If they get the impression that they have been given up in despair by the rest of the human race then they will complete the rejection of others which they have almost completed anyway, and will become entrenched in their self-righteous conviction that they are permitted in the name of hatred, every form of injustice, every form of cruelty in the name of God and country. This is of course the price we pay for something like the cold war. If it goes on much longer, the price is going to get very much higher. And either the cold war is going to go on, or it is going to turn into something worse.

* My own objective is not to crusade wildly for anything, even for peace, but to try to develop an infinite patience and understanding, even though there is little hope of doing anything once you have them. The stuff I have written so far about peace does not have this tone. Pray that I may be what God wants me to be. St. Francis knew what this was all about. In a certain way I see the utter impossibility of my even attempting to take the road he took, and I do not think of the problem in those terms in any case . . .

June 15, 1962

Your book [a catalogue of her Merton "collection"], for it is really a book, really astonished me. It was quite an "experience" for me, too, and gave me much to reflect on. First of all, of course, the care and perspicacity with which you have handled all that material. What splendid use you have made of every little thing: and I was agreeably surprised to find that long forgotten bits of scraps and poems or even essays I had thought long ago destroyed or lost, all turn up there. It is like the Day of Judgment, and that can be taken two ways, since every idle word is to be judged! But seriously, you have done a marvelous job. I have been through it once, and will now go through it again more carefully and make all the observations you request . . .

There is actually a small book now called *What Is Meditation*, or rather developed out of that first draft. But it is so poor that I hesitate to publish it. It is only a quick rehash of an earlier job which I also hesitated to publish and never did publish. The *What Is Med.* was supposed originally to make a pamphlet sequel to *What Is Contemplation*. Oh, I am wrong though: that is what eventually became the meditation part of *Spiritual Direction and Meditation*. The book I have in ms. that is "poor" and which I hesitate to publish is developed from the little booklet *Balanced Life of Prayer* which you undoubtedly have. But you don't have the ms. for this later version, I am sure . . .

July 17, 1962

With a kind of providential slip of the mind and of the fingers I have dated this letter ten days ahead, the day when we celebrate the Feast of Our Lady of Carmel here in the Cistercian Order . . .

Today Victor Hammer, who has printed those various limited editions, is coming over. He has some more work to finish off the crucifix he did for our novitiate chapel. (I will try to dig up a photo of the chapel for you. It is nothing special as a chapel but this "rood" type crucifix is very fine.) And he has finished Hagia Sophia. I hope to send you a copy soon. He is a great craftsman and a wonderful person. I always enjoy his visits, and he has given talks to some of the young monks too, on art, work, etc.

We are not strong on chipmunks anymore. The cats must get them, which is a great pity, and often one sees a chipmunk running around with no tail which means he must have had a narrow escape. Not that we encourage cats, but the place is full of them, living in various cellars. I suppose they are tolerated on account of the rats.

September 20, 1962

. . . Dan Berrigan's visit was most stimulating. He is a man full of fire, the right kind, and a real Jesuit, of which there are not too many perhaps. He wants to write about the real spirit of Ignatius and I think he would be capable of a good job. He is alive and full of spirit and truth. I think he will do much for the Church in America and so will his brother Phil, the only priest so far to have gone on a Freedom Ride. They will have a hard time, though, and will have to pay for every step forward with their blood.

There were other visits: a Rabbi friend [Zalman Schachter] from Manitoba, a Hasid. Apart from that I was busy with the *Reader*, and with the Peace book [*Peace in the Post-Christian Era*] that could not be published. Did I send you a copy? I think I did. I forget about it. I know you had the [Cold War] Letters. *Breakthrough [to Peace]* is now out. The collection of essays. A mess was made of it in the press, and a few other things went wrong but it is out, and I think it is effective. I am sending that for your feast day also.

[Hans] Kung of course I read as soon as I could get my hands on him. I thought it a noble, straight and courageous book [*The Council, Reunion and Reform*]. The vigor and honesty of the message was tremendous. But such books raise vain hopes, perhaps. The Council cannot possibly measure up to all he suggested. Yet precisely for that reason we must doggedly hope that it will . . .

I finished the new Powers novel [*Morte d'Urban*] which got to me from the publisher, before publication. It is a masterly job, ruthless in the first half, gentler and more merciful in the second. The priest is an "operator," a narcissist of the first water, and there is no let up in his appalling mediocrity until suddenly in the second half he becomes human and, though he remains an operator, he gains a real dignity and comes out with a certain nobility. Something happened to Powers himself in creating his character, a sort of breakthrough of some sort, apparently . . .

November 19, 1962

Breakthrough [to Peace] is getting around, and is generally liked. E. I. Watkin in England said it was the best thing of its kind he had seen. He is a remarkable person, not just for thinking *Breakthrough* good, but for more substantial reasons also. Writes very interesting but illegible letters . . .

Someone reported a deer on the property. I haven't seen it, but a deer doesn't have a chance in this part of the world. The Kentuckians are hopeless madmen with a gun. They shoot everything. It is pathological, really. The wild life around here ain't got it so good. I wish there was something that could be done about it, but not all levels of life in the Commonwealth are completely rational.

Thanks for the clippings too, and for the great reviews in *Renascence*. I told a young Italian girl [Cecilia Corsanego] who is doing some kind of thesis (in Rimini, Italy) to get in contact with you about some of these things.

December 20, 1962

Here I come with a noise out of the woods, something to say for Christmas. It was very cold for a while, now it is like late fall again, as if we had fallen back into November, misty. But the wise men are on the way, and the shepherds, and our own childhood. And it will be Christmas again, with all the invisible grace of His coming, His revolution. We do not understand that this business about the crib is the real revolution that once for all turned everything upside down so that nothing has ever been, or can ever be, the same again. But we try hard to sing the "old song" instead of the new one: the song of war, of money, of power, of success, of having a good time: when it is really all much simpler than that. Life is much more fun when you don't have to have a good time, or force anybody to do anything or put anything across . . .

The Council was tremendous, wasn't it? (Isn't it?) Really Pope John has been a great gift from God to all of us. What a superb Pope, and what a heart. The past few months have made me realize the greatness of the Church as I had never realized it before, not the stuffed shirt pompous greatness that some of the Curia people evidently want it to be, but the charity and the real concern for all men, the *cura pastoralis*. This has been a tremendous experience, I think to all of us. And how providential . . . And yet the Church is facing the same kind of critical juncture in thought that she faced with Galileo, and the fact that we have had enough sense to get vernacular in the liturgy is no guarantee that we are going to automatically sail over this hurdle [the peace issue] without tripping up. Much prayer is needed . . .

You will like this: I was invited to write a short piece for a collection of "testimonios" for a South American writer, Victoria Ocampo, editor of *Sur*, who has published some of my things in Argentina. So I did, naturally. She is a fine person. The book came and I opened it to find myself listed as: Thomas Merton S.J.

February 19, 1963

. . . I am glad you had a good session with the Berrigans. They are both tremendous. Unfortunately their book has been stopped by the S.J. censors. The usual fear of someone speaking out and saying something. Did you hear about the faculty of Catholic U. forbidding the graduate school to invite four dangerous speakers: Courtney Murray, Weigel, a third whom I forgot and, last but not least, Hans Kung . . .

Did I comment on *Ramparts*? I have "Hagia Sophia" coming out in it, the next issue I believe. I am not too sure what I do think about them. Some of the layouts are fine, and they apparently swim in dollars. I guess they have their own rather limited views about poetry and poets. I find them a bit too doggedly classical and perfectionistic. Some of their stuff is not bad, but they are very careful not to be thought beatniks, I can see. Yet I think the beats may have more life. I think of [Lawrence] Ferlinghetti. We have got "Prayers from the Ark" in the novitiate library and, once again, I haven't got around to it yet. (Somebody is trying to drill a hole in the floor right under my foot, from beneath. The drill nearly came through my right foot. I don't know if I will survive until the end of this letter.)

One of the things I did read was a manifesto by the Negro writer James Baldwin on the race situation. It is powerful and great. I even gave the publisher a blurb for it, which may get me hanged some day. But it is a tremendous and stirring document. Called *The Fire Next Time.*

Good job, moving up Ignace Lepp to the front of the shelf in the book mart. I did a review of the book [*The Christian Failure*], under a pseudonym (Benedict Monk) in the January *Catholic Worker* . . .

Jacques Maritain is so pleased that I translated a few of Raissa's poems. He is deeply moved by any sign of response to her wonderful contemplative spirit—and his own. A wonderful person, to whom I feel very close these days. I have never got such letters. He wrote a wonderful one on "Hagia Sophia" too, which just came yesterday. He is spending all his time (besides teaching philosophy to the Little Brothers) editing Raissa's journal. I have seen a copy of it, and some of the material is really great . . .

May 1, 1963

I open Mary's month with a letter to you, much too long delayed. Yours just arrived, and you are unfortunately right: I did not slip a note into the package. I have been much too tied up. Correspondence gets bigger all the time, and things one must answer right away, very often. For instance, this will please you, Dom Aelred Graham and I are now great friends, and I am glad. I reviewed his new book on Zen [*Zen Catholicism*], after first sending him a letter about it, and we agree thoroughly. He even invited me to come up and have a vacation and rest at Portsmouth Priory. Some chance I'd ever have of getting that permission. But I would really enjoy it. However I hope he may stop by here one day. I think we really look at things very much in the same way. The Zen book certainly showed it.

Thanks for your little poem, very appropriate for the season. We finally got a little rain and now everything is green and brilliant. A wonderful spring morning. The birds are happy, and there are even a few chipmunks around, though I don't have the art of training them as you have. It is best they remain wild around here so the cats won't get them. A meadowlark was singing outside the window, in the sun, when I was finishing my Mass, and I thought I would go through the roof, it was so beautiful. Sometimes things are just too good, which reminds us that if we would let them be as God wanted them to be, we would be able to bear it . . .

Have you read John Howard Griffin's books? You ought to get hold of *Black Like Me*. It will floor you. He is a fine writer, I haven't read his novels. There was an interesting bit of an autobiography of his in *Ramparts* a while ago. They did a nice job on "Hagia Sophia" incidentally.

I am being given an honorary LL.D. by the University of Kentucky. Of course it has to be in absentia and Victor Hammer has promised to get it for me. Also some kind of peace prize offered by an organization called New England Political Action for Peace. I am glad of that.

I have received permission to make a little private retreat in June up at the hermitage in the woods. Do pray that it works out well. I won't be able to spend the night up there, which is a pity, but I ought to be able to get practically the whole day. This is marvelous . . .

June 30, 1963

After being up to my neck in business mail for days, I want to get around to a few letters to friends for a change. Though it is hard to know exactly where to begin. When did I last write you? Do I owe you more than one letter? I can't find your last letter, which I think was at Easter . . .

My chief distraction is a big mixup with the publishers, a very unpleasant and unfortunate thing, which came from my presumption in trying to get along without an agent. Without really meaning to, I ended up in violation of one of the contracts . . . This is very unfortunate. I hope I have learned enough from this to keep out of this kind of tangle in the future . . .

I just wrote to [Bob] Lax, who has been in Greece for ages, in fact in the Greek islands. I can't imagine a better place for anyone to be, particularly Lax, though I haven't heard from him in ages, since about Christmas time as far as I can remember. [Ed] Rice wrote the other day, having just returned from Europe . . .

Pope John will, I think, be impossible to equal. No one can replace such a man. As time goes by we will see how extraordinary he really was. I have no doubt he was one of the great saints of our time. Am very happy to have a beautiful signed picture of him over the vesting table in the novitiate chapel. Pope Paul will, however, be good in a different way. Bright, energetic, experienced, and I think holy also. Maritain thought very highly of him years ago when he was in the Secretariat, and whatever slight contacts I have had with him have always impressed me favorably.

J. F. Powers sent a wonderful print of Pope John made by a friend of his: it is really remarkable, it gets the spirit of his simplicity and love in a striking way. I am going to have it framed and put up in the novitiate somewhere—it is quite large. I guess Pope John is, as far as I am concerned, "my Pope." I don't expect to outlive too many more of them . . .

August 9, 1963

. . . I have been extremely busy with visitors and so on. Wrote a piece on Race ["The Black Revolution"] which may be in *Ramparts* if it is allowed. Poem on Birmingham ["And the Children of Birmingham"] was in the *Saturday Review* but I do not yet have a copy. It is a poem I am glad about. Dan Berrigan will be in the big march on Washington I hear. Good for him. Say hello to Bert Sisson and the children for me. I love little Grace but also Clare, and all of them . . .

September 2, 1963
. . . The main purpose of this is to send you this classic work of art: the feast day card the novices did for Aug. 25th. Really clever. They are not afraid to kid about the hermitage, but I *don't* have a pipe or that kind of a hat either, still less a gun. After all, I am a disciple of non-violence. At least theoretically. It is true however that I shave only every three days, and the only reason I can't grow a full beard is that the Rev. Abbot is opposed. As to the accuracy of the card as a character study, well, I am not in a position to say. But novices have good eyes, so I trust their viewpoint. But remain unconverted.

The last month has been exhausting: some visitors, and very good ones, like Dom Bede Griffiths, and an Anglican minister [A. M. Allchin] from Oxford, and some Benedictines from Maredsous, Marialaach etc. All very stimulating, but I haven't got any work done and am months behind with everything. The priests of the diocese are here on retreat for Sept. most of the time so the place should be fairly quiet. Yet it seems that the monastery hardly ever settles down to just a quiet normal pace. I suppose it is quieter than the world, but probably not as much as all that . . .

You should get copies of some of the more recent mimeographed things, like "The Black Revolution" and an article on Anselm. I have been working on Anselm a bit this summer. At the moment I am trying finally to brush up the little book on Sacred Art [*Art and Worship*] I was trying to do four or five years ago. First we intended to publish it here. Then I saw it was going to be too complicated, and tried it on Farrar Straus and though they wanted it, we bogged down over a detail. I hope I can get it out of the way—though that is hardly the way to approach a book, least of all a book on art . . .

October 3, 1963
. . . The reason I have not written is that I just got out of the hospital a few days ago. I have had and still have a cervical disc along with arthritis and other unpleasant things. I am trying to get this disc fixed up without an operation & am therefore still a bit cramped. My left hand is not much good for typing. Things are progressing slowly however & I am optimistic . . .

The weather has been lovely here & I have been intent on getting out in the sun—it does me more good than anything else & I think a few fine days will fix everything, though the sun can't change bones, I know.

I read the *Shoes of the Fisherman* in the hospital & thought it rather naive & after all timid & passive. Pope Paul is really much more energetic than the tense Pope of that novel! The recent pronouncements have been fine. Did I tell you he wrote me a personal letter & sent me an autographed picture? I expect great things from Pope Paul & this session of the Council . . .

November 9, 1963

I thought I would put a couple of the latest things in an envelope for you, and since one is a set of notes referring to this Bellarmine [College] affair ["Concerning the Collection in the Bellarmine College Library"], I had better tell you a word about it. The notes are for Dan Walsh to read tomorrow, when they open an exhibit there. One must distinguish this exhibit (for a week) and the collection (permanent).

My suggestion to them was to ask you if you had something you could lend them for the exhibit, or if you could help them in any way. I would not expect you to give them anything for keeps . . . Involved in this are a couple of friends of mine, notably Dan Walsh, who taught me at Columbia and now is teaching both here and at Bellarmine. Also the dean of Bellarmine, Fr. John Loftus. They are not all Franciscans there, but they have a group of conventuals on the faculty. It is run by the diocese and was founded by Archbishop [John A.] Floersh who ordained me. I naturally feel close to them, they are lively and young (ten years). And the committee that is getting up this collection, though they started late, is as lively and interested as anyone, second only to you. They would probably appreciate some chance to see your catalogue, as it would help them . . .

There is a new magazine starting up at the University of Iowa [*Charlatan*], run by Episcopalians. I don't know how good it is going to be, but I sent them the notes on Julien Green ["To Each His Darkness"] which I enclose. They are perhaps too subtle. The notes, I mean, not the Episcopalians. I liked very much the librarian from Pusey House, Oxford [A. M. Allchin], who was here this summer, and who just sent me a new book of Traherne, whom I love . . . I got Fr. [Raymond] Roseliep's latest, but haven't had a chance to read it thoughtfully. Ned O'Gorman sent some of his new poems in ms and a few are really terrific. I liked your latest in *Commonweal* ["Each Spring the Arbutus"] . . .

February 1, 1964

. . . No, I have not been ill, still less to Europe. Fr. Abbot doesn't take people on trips, least of all me, and it is just as well. I can't imagine anything I would enjoy less than being dragged around various monasteries of the Order and having to perform. It is good of him to spare me this, not that there is any danger of it. I have had the usual trouble with my back, but nothing special. I saw an x-ray of it and my seventh cervical vertabra looks a bit like the cover of *Emblems* [*of a Season of Fury*]. (You have that, I am sure I sent it. Did I?) In other words it is an irreversible thing, unless they operate and graft bone, which I would prefer to avoid . . .

You have the best collection of chipmunks of anyone I know. Here one rarely sees one any more, least of all a black one. I am glad your woods are integrated . . . Don't fear that I will go wild in Lent. At best I am a conservative type of penitent, still in the infirm refectory, but able to fast a little none the less. I have absolutely no intention of becoming very austere, but I could be a little more austere than I am . . .

April 1, 1964

I have your good letters and the little Thomas book (which I will read with joy) and by now you must have back the bibliography which I have returned. It is a tremendous job and I do not know how you have the patience to keep at it. I made a few marks here and there, but wanted to get it back to you and so sent it off. Needless to say I am confused and grateful for all your work . . .

I hope the poetry reading to the Jebbies went off well. They are not as fierce as they claim to be, though I suppose they have to cultivate a professional toughness. Were they difficult? And if so, did it matter? There is certainly great variety from one to another, or at least there are members of the society that stand out as quite different from the others: Dan Berrigan for instance . . . has been having some interesting adventures, in Czechoslovakia, etc. There was incidentally a Protestant theologian from Czechoslovakia here, Jan Lochman, a very fine person, quite young, and we had a very moving quiet conversation one evening after he had heard Compline. He did not have much time, but it was inspiring to meet him. They are the people who really have to be Christians. We have a rather unreal and belligerent idea of what it means to live under Communism. Actually it demands a lot of faith and patience and though there is infinite hardship, it by no means implies the loss of everything. On the contrary. I had the impression of talking to someone out of the Acts of the Apostles.

Spring seems to be getting into Kentucky after our floods and storms. There was snow Easter afternoon, but I need not tell you. Dan Walsh came back from Chicago (he is living here now and teaching philosophy to the clerics) with tales of snow storms, not to mention the earthquake. What a mess! But now it is quiet and pretty here . . .

Time for a class, so I must stop. Later I will write more. There have been a lot of interesting books around, especially one huge big life by [Konstantin] Paustovsky [*The Story of a Life*], a friend of Pasternak (who was completely loyal to Pasternak in all the trouble, one of the only ones) and it has magnificent things in it.

July 12, 1964

A second "good word" for your celebration and the assurance of my prayers in my Mass that day. All kinds of blessings, light, peace, joy, grace. And may your trip East be blessed, fruitful, joyful, all that you wish, all that Our Lord wishes for you. You will be reading poetry at Spencer. I must admit that set me back on my heels. Unheard of things. Our Abbot would never countenance such goings-on (he is away now, at the coast) but I think you know his policies. May those at Spencer be blessed for their liberality . . .

Honest to God is causing a bit of a stir in Protestant circles. He [John A. T. Robinson] gives the impression when he is all over that there is no God left to be honest to. I think that is an exaggeration. He is just catching on to the truth that God cannot be expressed in adequate concepts. He is also strong on the new morality and such things. Good will, sincere, naive I think, earnest about getting through to "the world." The people he rests on are stronger than he is. I am currently reading Dietrich Bonhoeffer, Protestant executed under Hitler: magnificent. Wasn't the _Commonweal_ Los Angeles issue a smasher? I had a letter a couple of months ago from Fr. [William] DuBay incidentally suggesting that he and I form a priests' union. I pointed out that I was not in a very good position to organize unions . . .

September 17, 1964

I don't have a decent sheet of paper, but I know you don't need a letterhead. Let the yellow seem to be gold, and I will make this your feastday letter. I will pray for you fervently on the feast of St. Therese and I hope you will pray for me because I will be needing it. The day after that a big meeting of all the American (and Canadian) abbots and novice masters will be held here. I hope we can accomplish something . . .

This has been a slightly hectic summer, most of it given to a battle with poison ivy, and I am finally going to see a specialist about it tomorrow. The skin has been off my hands for weeks, and there is some weird reaction going on lately in the skin of my face, so I think it is about time something was done. I seem to have suddenly acquired a hypersensitivity to it . . .

God bless you and keep you, with all your friends in the woods, your chipmunks and birds, including Louis Sparrow. You make me think of Skelton's nun with her Philip Sparrow which she took to choir with her. You have not gone that far, but the Lord will reward your Franciscanism. May your feast be blessed, and may your fall days be radiant. I know what you mean about these intuitions of passing time. I have them too.

I am now pushing fifty and realize more and more that every extra day is just a free gift, and so I relax and forget about past and future. The "I" that goes from day to day is not an important "I" and his future matters little. And the deeper "I" is in an eternal present. If a door should one day open from one realm to the other, then "I" (whoever that is) will be glad of it. I have no regrets except for sins that are forgiven in any case, and I forget the past, and don't get too excited about either the present or the future. For the rest, He Who is real will take care of what reality He has shared with us.

December 13, 1964

. . . The end of the Council session was not exactly encouraging. I know it was shattering for Fr. [Bernard] Haring, who wrote about it. He said it was shattering for Pope Paul also. I hear by all accounts that the Pope looks exhausted. His peace proposal at Bombay was impressive, however . . .

You mention Daniel Callahan. I have just got through reading proofs of his book, *Honesty in the Church*. You must absolutely read it. It is really explosive. It strikes directly at the abuses you so often mention, the manipulating and politicking and the system that guarantees that the superiors are never wrong, no matter how they get around the law of the Church or violate the rights of their subjects. It is a book that is very timely, but brutal, and I am afraid that some readers will put it down with everything shattered. Still, it is time for such things to be said. If they are not, there is no hope for a real renewal of the Church. And it becomes repeatedly more clear that renewal begins at the top . . .

March 27, 1965

Thanks for your St. Patrick's Day letter and all its new and good wishes. I am afraid I have been a rather poor correspondent this year, or should I say poorer than ever? I am gradually giving less time to letters, as I have less time to give. And the letters pile up . . .

There is a blessing on every attempt at ecumenism that is simple and sincere, and your desire to do this not for your own sake but for God and the Church and for them, will guarantee that it will be blessed in one way or another. I am not in any ecumenical work this year. Fr. Abbot wanted me to withdraw from it as I am planning more and more to be in the hermitage and perhaps even live there eventually. I must meet his requirements therefore, and am not sorry to.

Meanwhile, there is flu in the monastery and I seem to have a touch of it. That always adds a little pepper to Lent, doesn't it? But I don't try to keep the strict fast when I have a cold or flu: I am entitled to a small breakfast, and that helps things considerably in the morning. Usually I don't need it. (Don't worry about me dying of starvation: being on a special diet, I am in the diet refectory and get plenty to live on, including meat for dinner.) . . .

June 16, 1965

Thanks for sending the list to Naomi Burton [Stone]. This literary trusteeship is something that has become necessary. She and James

Laughlin of New Directions have agreed to take care of everything, with a young Catholic lawyer, and it ought to keep any number of problems from developing, as they tend to. But of course with such an awful lot of published and unpublished material around, it is a very complex job for them. I hope everything can be done to make it simple, and then they can handle it peacefully and easily. I suppose that the main thing is above all to keep track of unpublished material that is around in various collections or in the hands of friends or people I no longer know have it. The big job at the moment is for the trustees to get a good idea where everything is and *what* it is. You are the one who can be of most help in this, because you have the most complete collection and the one in which there are so many notes, sermons, unpublished pieces as well as original mss . . .

My hermitage is dedicated to St. Mary of Carmel, and the time is getting close, (I hope) when I will be there permanently. I am semi-permanent there already. It is wonderful to live so close to birds etc. I want to get the wood around there made into a game sanctuary, but it is a problem to keep hunters out. They don't believe in signs and fences around here, and short of having a sheriff around you can't do anything to protect the place. We have a lot of deer, now, too . . .

August 17, 1965

Many thanks for your note from Georgetown. I am glad you had such a good time. You deserve it, and I am sure it will be very fruitful for you, in your life and in your work. I thought John l'Heureux's book of poems [*Quick as Dandelions*] was first-rate and he sounds like a splendid guy.

If you get a couple of miscellaneous packets of things in the mail, you may find in them things you already have. I have been cleaning house, and this week I officially begin the hermit life (Saturday and Sunday, F. of the Immaculate Heart, will be so to speak the formal beginning). The Council voted favorably on it today, the new novice master is all set to take over, and I am all set to go, except that it seems that I may go over the bumps a bit with my stomach taking everything too hard. But so what, I might as well pay my way, spiritually. But I can use your good prayers. It is quite a step, and something that has not been done this officially in the Order since the Lord knows when, way back in the Middle Ages, when we had a few hermit saints. I hope I will follow in their footsteps (sanely however). Expect to come down daily to the monastery for Mass and one meal, serve on private council etc. So I am not climbing a pillar or being entombed . . .

September 28, 1965

I don't think I answered your last very interesting letter . . . Did I tell you that I had moved out to the woods? I came out over a month ago. Go down only once a day, for Mass and dinner, then come back. I get a little supper for myself and as I don't like to bother with cooking or washing dishes I try to keep it as simple as possible. It is really a wonderful life, a revelation, even much better than I expected. It is so good to get back to plain natural simplicity and the bare essentials, no monkeying around with artificialities and non-essentials. It really gives a wonderful new dimension to one's life. I didn't realize, until I got out here, how tense and frustrated I really was in community, though of course I love the monks. I am afraid that community life has become terribly forced and artificial over the course of centuries, and there is no question that a new approach will have to be found if it is going to continue. So I like being a hermit, and I do have real solitude. There is never anyone around in the woods except an occasional hunter, and we are trying to persuade them to go elsewhere. It is real solitude, and just perfect.

The only trouble, if you can call it trouble, is that there is no news and it gets to be hard to think of something to put in a letter. True, I am trying to finish that book, based on Journal material, but not a Journal [*Conjectures of a Guilty Bystander*]. There was a lot of objection in high places to the idea of a Trappist writing a spiritual Journal (probably because it was a bit too frank about the life as it is) so I am keeping it relatively impersonal and objective. I think the book will not suffer. The little book on Gandhi [*Gandhi on Non-Violence*] came out, at a curious time, now that India is swept with war fever. I am afraid that in the end we will have to admit that non-violence really failed in India, as Gandhi himself saw before he died. It asks very much of men: really, true non-violence cannot be carried out except by real saints. In this country there are indeed some really dedicated men in the non-violent civil rights movement, but a lot of them are anything but saints. This has its effect, and as far as I can see the non-violent movement has been terribly set back by the violence this summer. I think it has in a sense failed here too . . .

You mentioned something about being still in doubt about the "collection" and what would eventually become of it. If you want a suggestion from me, I would say perhaps to divide it between Bellarmine and Marquette. There is much that you have that is also at Bellarmine, on the other hand the Bellarmine collection does not have some of the early material that you have. I would say perhaps a few of the important early mss. and other mimeographed material that is not at B[ellarmine] could go there, so as to make it more complete, but the bulk of your collection could still go to Marquette. Unless of course you yourself would badly want to keep it all in one piece . . .

Sister Therese noted in longhand on this letter: "He was later of the opinion that I should not divide it, but keep it complete as is. He also stressed the point that he thought it would be the best plan for collections to have them in various parts of the country—rather than in one place. Georgetown University he thought a

splendid place for my collection—if I so desired to make such a commitment."
Sister Therese finally, after much thought and vacillation, left her collection to
Merton's alma mater, Columbia University.

[November 12, 1965]

I am putting some photos of the hermitage in an envelope and must
go down to the monastery, where I will mail them . . . I am so glad things
are going well in the seminary: this is a sign that they are waking up,
isn't it? All goes well here. Two new books [*Seasons of Celebration* and
The Way of Chuang Tzu] out at once, which is not a good thing but the
two publishers could not agree, so they are now fighting. Not good for
author, but I guess the books will do ok . . .

December 30, 1965

Here it is happy new year and I have not yet said merry Christmas.
I have hopelessly fallen back with my mail now. I have much less chance
to write as I am taken up with a lot of things that I have to do for myself
now that I do not have a community to provide for them as a matter of
course: cutting wood, sweeping, making supper (I don't say cooking as I
avoid that as far as possible) and making breakfast which is easy: coffee
and toast at the open fire. With a good hot fire I get instant toast and
don't have to wait for any popups. I try to not get dishes dirty so as not
to have to wash any. But with all this household stuff my time is taken
up. Besides that after Dec. 8 I wrote hard on a commentary on the
Constitution of the Church in the World ["The Church and the 'Godless
World' "] and finished it: it is about fifty pages. Burns Oates wanted it
but they got more than they bargained for . . .

I was delighted at the beatification of Charbel Makhlouf. Did you
hear about it? It is wonderful to have a monk hermit beatified just when
I am beginning the life myself. Great lift. Actually, I have a second class
relic of his built in to the foundation of this place: I slipped it in there
with a St. Benedict medal and I forget what else when the hermitage was
being built. And now Sr. Luke [Tobin] brought me a first class relic from
the Council when she returned (the observer, Lorettine). (I did not see
her to talk over the Council, but apparently she was very happy about
it) . . .

On an envelope postmarked September 14, 1966, Sister Therese made the follow-
ing notation about letters she received from Merton in 1966: "Three letters of
this year—were destroyed [*double-underlined*]—*I thought it best, for in them*
Merton had confided to me a personal problem (the nurse, etc.) which I felt
(should something happen to me, would not be 'safe' in the hands of others—
though it is known (I believe) by a discreet group in Louisville)." On February

14, 1966, she sent a hurried and flustered letter telling him that three photographs of him had been released, by mistake, to the Milwaukee Journal *for a story about the exhibit to be held at Marquette University.*

February 16, 1966

This morning I sent my quick note about the photos so I hope that is all taken care of. The only restriction on photos I would make would be please don't permit or *show any of the hermitage.* Of me, no problem. I have just written the note for the exhibit and sent same to Bro. John [Lyons]. Second thing out of the way. Now I owe you a decent answer: and first back to Christmas time: your letter and gift came in a couple of days after I wrote. Everything has been terribly delayed here. I have had letters take a couple of weeks to reach me, and one more than a month. I don't know what's wrong. But anyway, thanks for your little gift: it is really charming in its simplicity and as you say, it is from Nazareth, and that adds something imponderable. On the other hand I have been meaning to say that you should not think you have to find a present for me at Christmas . . .

You mention that Bro. John wants to continue with the bibliography: he certainly sounds like a bibliographer who knows what he is about all right, and it would be a terrific job of work if he makes it as complete as he wants to. My reaction is this: there is no hurry to get this all in print, and it might be a good idea to start on the most obvious work quietly, and see what develops. I may be pushing up the daisies in a few years (for all your ad multos annos) and then will be time enough to publish: or else when I really get settled into this solitude and practically stop publishing, maybe. I know myself well enough not to advance this as a firm possibility. I know Frank Dell'Isola's health has broken down. He is always sick. I doubt if he really intends to continue the work himself, though he has hinted at it once about a year or so ago. As to Bro. John's list: it might be hard to track down sketches and so on ("art") also things like "unpublished poems." I wish I knew where they might be! I know I have two or three unpublished books lying around here (Dan Walsh is working over a couple now, for a conference he has to give on prayer). I will see if I find extra copies I can donate, perhaps . . .

In the poetry ms. collection at the U. of Buffalo there must be quite a few mss. of early poems, or rather poems around the time of *Figures for an Apocalypse.* Since then I have sent them nothing. My correspondence with New Directions and mss. I send to New Directions all go to Harvard, with all their other material.

I know about that draft of *Letter to My Friends,* scribbled in the Guest House on the back of the Scotus mimeograph: but I can't tell you where it is. Either in the library here or at Bellarmine. Incidentally there are quite a few boxes of stuff locked away in the library here, too, and it constitutes a "collection." I have little or nothing myself except some very recent material.

Do you have a carbon of the list you sent to Naomi [Burton Stone], and if so could you spare me a copy? It would be useful to me, I think. But I do not want to put you to any trouble. If necessary I would get it typed here. Returning to the question of all the above collections, it would certainly be otiose for Bro. John to catalogue them all in his bibliography. Perhaps it would be enough to mention that they exist and say what unique things (v.g. a carbon of *Seven Storey Mountain* at Boston Coll.) they possess.

The cold spell (to change the subject) was quite an experience in the hermitage, and your prayers were answered: I had a lot of friendly birds around, and fed them with crackers. The deer are around too. It is fine and silent—and lonely. I have no questions about this being the kind of life for me, and it is certainly nothing to play with. It is hard. You really have to face yourself, and believe me that is quite grim. But at least it has one great consolation: it makes sense. I often had a very hard time convincing myself that the life down in the community did that. I always liked the other monks, but felt that the system itself was a bit artificial and unreal, and it seemed to be chewing so many of them up into hamburger, so to speak. I think of them a lot here and relate my own life to theirs. The relation seems meaningful to me and to them also. We all have a feeling that we are trying to find our way honestly. The official solutions and gestures at aggiornamento are all right, but they don't really get very far, and all the work remains to be done by the monks themselves—and God's grace above all . . .

April 5 [1966]

For the moment only the briefest note. I want to get these Easter gifts off to you before we are suddenly at Pentecost.

The Retreat notes should be kept rather confidential, as there is in it the personal case of a sister of one of our communities. So please don't exhibit it. But of course you can catalogue it etc. Then the letters I got from Evelyn Waugh a few years ago. Of course you will be discreet with these. I am glad you are handling the letters so wisely . . .

April 15, 1966

The reason for my long silence is that I have been in the hospital & had to have an operation on my back. It knocked me out for Easter etc. & I am getting over it slowly hoping it will work—but pray, as there are still possible complications. Nothing bad, but it would be nice if this really cleared things up . . . Sleep in the infirmary but can go to the hermitage in the daytime . . .

June 7, 1966

. . . Evidently I have not told you much about the back. Yes, it was the same disc (I am getting used to the c, but I suppose k is ok also) that I had trouble with three years ago. In fact it is an old injury and the disc has simply deteriorated. Not slipped. Had to be entirely removed and replaced with a bone graft from the hip. They call this fusing the vertebrae. I guess they are fusing all right. I haven't tried any heavy work of course yet, this is verboten, and I miss manual labor. Typing was at first a bit painful but is all right now. I am behind with work but things are picking up. I send you incidentally one of the jobs I had to do recently. Ned O'Gorman is doing a mysterious and complex book for Random House, to which many have been asked to contribute bits and pieces. He asked me to define seven words ["Seven Words" in *Love and Living*]. The definitions had to be "revolutionary" because the book is revolutionary thinking. I don't know how revolutionary I was in the seven words, but anyway here they are. They might throw your retreat into a turmoil. You can make a revolutionary retreat. I should have developed the one on war more, but have written so much on it I was fed up with the subject by the time I got that far. The first one on death is largely Rahner and existentialism and I think it is the best. The one on purity will make a lot of people sit up and some will reach for their anathemas . . .

Our Abbot is away in Chile. Gethsemani is taking over the foundation that Spencer made down there (instead of founding in Norway, which was planned for a while). We will send some men down and merge with those who remain in the present community. Though I know Spanish well I don't suppose I will be sent. The Abbot wants me here, though I am not doing anything much, just giving one conference a week to anyone who wants to come. Right now the series is on "Christianity and the World of Today," a little more extensive than the Council Constitution, details about Marxism etc., may go into Freud and others. It is fun so far. Later I have a lot of notes planned on Sufism. Can one be more all over the lot? I doubt it. But I don't care now. In my old age I don't bother to be consistent . . .

Incidentally the Buddhist from Vietnam, Thich Nhat Hanh, was here—a fine guy altogether, I liked him very much. We made a tape together for Dan Berrigan in which we do everything including sing, he a Buddhist Gatha, I a Cistercian Alleluia. Big deal . . .

July 31, 1966

. . . No I have never taped any of my poems. I thought of it at one point, but I don't have a tape recorder myself and never fool with one. It would become too much of a project involving other people. I find that as soon as I try to do anything like that there is a great murmur goes up "What is a hermit doing *that* for?" so I guess it would be a lot better if I just forgot about it . . .

We have had some nasty weather, very hot, but lately it has been much better. I am going along with work, mainly articles, reviews and so on. Am reviewing Edwin Muir [*The True Legendary Sound: The Poetry and Criticism of Edwin Muir*] for the *Sewanee Review* and I am glad to find out how good he is. If you ever get a chance to read him you would like his poetry very much I think. I am also trying to get his *Autobiography* for background. A rather extraordinary person . . .

September 13, 1966
. . . I have Douglas Bush's new book on Milton and like it. I think I will finally get back to some Milton and give a few talks on him myself. I have been giving one talk a week still to the gang. Lately it has been on modern world, and dialogue with Marxism. Notes will get to you eventually I hope. But I am going back to literature. Last year I talked a lot on Rilke. Never typed that up yet, and probably won't get a chance . . .

I had x-rays of my back the other day and the operation turned out perfect, which is something to be thankful for. I have another bad disk to look out for but with care I hope I can stay off the operating table. My bursitis is better—had trouble with it most of the summer. On the whole there is much to be thankful for and glad about. As usual!!!

March 23, 1967
. . . I thought of you and your work on Marianne Moore the other day when I was reading some excellent stuff on her by William Carlos Williams in his *Selected Essays*. Have you seen his essays on her? Very useful. I am just beginning to realize how valuable a man Doc Williams was: great poet and one who developed a new directness of consciousness which I think very salutary. Also I have been in contact with [Louis] Zukofsky (you saw the review ["Paradise Bugged"] I did of him I think) and here too is a very fine poet who has been ignored . . .

May 12, 1967
. . . It is by no means clear that Catholics and Negroes are somehow fighting shoulder to shoulder for the same things. And also the "Catholic" type minority in literature—what is it anyhow? Not Flannery O'Connor, or Jim Powers, surely. Catholic writers, insofar as they are really good writers, tend to merge into the general picture, don't they? Of course there is the Catholic faith, but in specifically literary work that faith is not propounded as a self-conscious minority position—or is it? It is just our faith, our kind of Christianity in a country that still calls itself Christian. Well, anyway, I know that is not clear but it is still what occurred to me. The Jewishness question as it was discussed a while ago seems to me to have been exaggerated somewhat . . .

June 26, 1967

Yes, you are right: there is something quite satisfying about getting things in order, and it is something we all need. As I say this I have deep guilt feelings, because the hermitage is in an awful mess. I have been waiting three months for some new bookshelves that were promised along with the sink which I am finally supposed to get (well was dug between January and Easter, and at least the *pipes* are in). (Been waiting since Easter for the sink.) But I got a little fun this morning clearing out some brush under some trees in a cool spot where I am planning to do some reading and sitting around. I like this kind of work, and try to do a little when I can, but the back is tricky and I don't want to get it started up again . . .

Bellarmine College has some kind of program in connection with *their* collection: want a speaker and I suggested you would enjoy it (?). Have they written you? They'd die of joy if you brought a few of your items, because you have so much more early material than they. That would be in November. If you get down I'll try to work the Abbot over, in the name of aggiornamento, and see if this time he won't let us have a decent visit, spend the afternoon and all. Friends in Louisville [the O'Callaghans] would be delighted to put you up. But don't let's discuss this in letters until it is assured: I think censorship of mail is starting up again and if the boss thinks you are too enthusiastic he'll say no. So let's play it cool. It is really sickening to have to perpetually go about things like this, knowing that if you start something it may suddenly get cut off and nothing come of it . . .

September 5, 1967

It was good of you to send the little clipping about Ad Reinhardt. I had known nothing about his death. It was a shock. I wrote at once to [Bob] Lax out in Greece. He may or may not have heard about it. I have been rather bad about letters this summer and haven't even written to Lax for a long time. Tomorrow I shall offer Mass for Ad here in the hermitage, where I say Mass very quietly now by myself, early in the morning, finishing about dawn sometimes: after the preface I turn out the light and have nothing but the two candles shining on the ikons. Poor Ad. I had been thinking about him a lot lately, wanting to see him again. Had not seen him for about ten years I think. He was really a stupendous person. One of the very smartest and best, and there was a great deal packed into that painting of blacks on blacks.

Yes, Mertoniana II arrived safely. I am most thankful for all of this. I wish I could get [John H.] Slate, that lawyer, moving on the estate business. With Reinhardt—who seemed the most indestructible of us all—gone, the others could go like that. And Slate and [Seymour] Freedgood are all living rather wildly, burning everything out . . .

Too bad about Marianne Moore, but I was amused at your description of the Gotham Book Mart. It obviously hasn't changed a bit. Health here has not been wonderful. I got a virus infection that has been floating around and it knocked me out just in the middle of a difficult job I had to do. Rome apparently wants a message from contemplatives to the Bishops' Synod and I had to do the main job of the first draft. Others are working it over now. I was a bit embarrassed by it, but just followed an outline of topics given. A lot of it is about this "God is dead" stuff. Maybe the other redactors will pull out whatever teeth it may have left. I was glad to get it off my chest.

Things have been a little rough here. The situation is not altogether healthy. A kind of atmosphere of triumphal pseudo-change. It is bound to backfire when the young ones find out that in spite of appearances there is really nothing happening at all, only a game of musical chairs. I feel it, though I am out of it. There are lots of angles I can't put into a letter (though the mail is supposedly not censored now) . . .

September 26, 1967

The Journal of My Escape, which I got from Ed [Rice], is now being typed up and I will probably submit it for publication next year. I don't know whether anyone will want it (of course there is always someone who would be likely to take it for the wrong reasons) or whether Naomi Burton [Stone] will be amenable: she may feel that it ought not to get into print right now. We'll see. In my opinion this might be the best time for publication. I have been having a hard time getting other work done. Am supposed to be doing a book on Camus but can't stay with it: I get drawn aside by all sorts of small jobs that I should not have accepted in the first place. I'll have to get all that in order, finally, and start refusing, and stick to my business.

. . . I'm looking around for another lawyer. Nothing definite has been done at all. I sent [Bob] Lax a telegram in Greece about Slate and the Western Union people called back to say that Lax had left Kalymnos and there was no forwarding address. I hope *he* is all right! With the nonsense in Greece he might be in jail or something. It was tragic about the way Ed [Rice] was taken over by the Herder people. But he is well out of it now. And off to Asia somewhere.

Pretty fall weather here these days. I am enjoying it. Cool nights, cold mornings and bright hot days. How are you? I do hope you finally get a publisher for your poems. The whole poetry publication business is mysterious in the extreme: a gamble if ever there was one . . .

In October 1967 Merton began the final arrangements for Sister Therese to come to Bellarmine College in Louisville to speak at its Town-and-Gown Week and, finally, to visit him at Gethsemani. He called her in mid-October and she wrote to him on October 16: "You were the last person on earth I could have thought might call me! And there you were—your voice so warm and brotherly. But strange, the day before, I had played your tape . . ." They did meet at a picnic with the O'Callaghans in the Gethsemani woods on November 7, 1967, a meeting which Sister Therese later recalled with fondness.

October 13, 1967

Yes, it was real!! I am probably as surprised as you are. I did not think I would be able to reach you, as I did not know the name of the convent, let alone the phone number. But somehow it got through. Hence, I recapitulate: the Bellarmine people are expecting you down in Louisville to give a talk—afternoon or evening of Nov 4th. They will of course pay your expenses. Mrs. O'Callaghan will take care of accommodations, and will bring you out to Gethsemani for a visit Tuesday. Monday there is some hangup with a dinner in Louisville, I am not sure what, but they'll let you know about Monday.

The occasion: the annual "Town and Gown" week of Bellarmine College, in which they have a lot of talks and always try to feature something in connection with the Merton Room. This year there is a photo exhibit by a friend of mine in Lexington [Ralph Eugene Meatyard]. I guess some will be of me (I am sending along the *Motive* interview with a couple of his pictures). Anyway I look forward to having a good chat with you after all these years. The Abbot is away now, but I am sure he will have no objection, and as I said he is about to retire . . . But it is still impossible for me to go anywhere, although I get all kinds of invitations, even one last August to come to N.Y. and meet Cardinal [Franz] Koenig and discuss his work with atheists, etc.

When you write to Mrs. O'Callaghan ("Tommie"—Thomasina, a Southern name!) send her the necessary biographical and career stuff so she can prepare the way for the talk. They are a lovely family and you will enjoy them. I must close now: just wanted to confirm the essentials anyhow, and reassure you that it was NOT someone putting you on . . .

November 16, 1967

I don't want any more time to go by before I thank you for the will: you did not need to send it here. All that matters is to have it in existence: do not send the final version here because the more copies exist the more complicated things are, legally, when the thing has to be settled. I have only two, one for me and one for the lawyer or wherever it is to be filed.

Tuesday finally we signed the whole Trust agreement and I think it is pretty intelligently worked out so that everything will make sense and will be clear to all. There is yet to be an official policy for the various collections, but the rule of thumb is that what is not yet published has to be restricted (all permissions to copy etc. from the Trust); what has been published can be consulted freely under ordinary library rules; and permissions to quote in print are cleared through the Trust.

Your visit was really historic! I am glad it rectifies the austerity of the previous one [when she was refused admission] which, as you know, was not my idea. Anyway, I enjoyed having you here, and I hope you enjoyed it too . . .

In the winter of 1968 Merton began collecting material for his "little magazine," Monks Pond. *Sister Therese was one poet from whom he solicited a contribution.*

[January 1968]
Many thanks for your letter. Tommie [O'Callaghan] is still in hospital but very well. Have you copies of unpublished poems I could consider for a little mimeographed magazine I'm running? Short ones preferable— but whatever you feel are best.

February 21, 1968
I believe you have not seen this set of "Rules governing the use" which has been drawn up for Bellarmine's collection. The idea would be to follow the same kind of practice in all the collections, especially to get clearance for permissions to copy ms. material. Also the Trust people will have some special gimmicks about copyright registry (for Ph.D.'s quoting unpublished material in their theses etc.). That will come later. They will probably want each library that has an M. collection to make an agreement (with the Trust) on the same lines and follow the same procedure. About the "will" you were going to make—the lawyer was asking about that and was going to contact you about it. I hope you'll be patient with all this red tape. I did not realize there would be such a lot of it. J. Laughlin was down here recently. He will handle all my permission and copyright business (in regard to the collections) and has been doing the same for the estate of William Carlos Williams and for Ezra Pound. So he is very aware of all the problems and has people in his office who know all the ropes. If you have any problems or questions about it, you might write him at New Directions . . .
Journal of My Escape has been submitted for publication—after all these years. I had it mimeographed. Unfortunately the pages were not numbered and the lady in Louisville [Marie Charron] who was typing it got them all mixed up so that chapters are in the wrong order and it is a terrible mess. I am trying to get it all back together again . . .
I am having a little addition put on to the cottage: a chapel—and a replacement for the outhouse where I hope "that bastard" [the black snake] won't be able to get in. Modern in every respect. But when I have the chapel and the workmen are gone, I think I'll dig in for a retreat. I wish I could take the whole of Lent. Probably can't (in fact certainly can't as I have some appointments, mostly ecumenical). Still, I think I can make the best of some parts of Lent. Pray for that, too, please!
Returning to the "Rules"—don't worry about "classified" material. I do not think you have anything classified except perhaps *The Sign of*

Jonas holograph material—some of which may be just silly. I don't know. But most of the classified stuff is letters—people with problems etc. Or some of my own wrangling with the Order, way back, about going elsewhere to be a hermit.

Our new Abbot is very fine, and everyone likes him. It is not that he is wildly radical or progressive, just that he is frank and simple and you know where you stand. And he is willing to go along with anything fairly reasonable. And monastic . . .

March 6, 1968

It is not snowy like this today [he enclosed a picture of the hermitage in the snow]. We have actually had a day or two of what seemed to be spring and the crocuses are finally coming up outside my door. Yet we might get more snow. It looks a little that way. First I want to thank you for your kindness and thoughtfulness in sending your copy of *Journal of My Escape*. I did what I could to get the scrambled mimeograph in shape for Naomi Burton [Stone] to judge by, but I haven't yet gone over the whole thing carefully. Your copy will enable me to do this when the time comes. Many thanks.

. . . I want to use three of your poems, probably in the Fall issue: the one for [Bob] Lax and his islands, which I most especially like. I hope that is all right with you. I have Tommie O'Callaghan's copy of the poems [*Speak to Me Sparrow*]. Mine evidently went to Bellarmine with a batch of my own mss. All part of the family treasury.

I have been swamped with all sorts of things and can't seem to get any work done: one of the problems is that people keep coming for one thing or other . . . *Cables to the Ace* is out and will soon be on the way to you.

July 13, 1968

Hope this reaches you at Georgetown in time for your feast days. I think it should, with the mail moving more normally here now. And I hope Washington is not too hot. We are getting some stuffy weather here. You mention flowers: I am no gardener and all I have are day lilies that garden themselves. And a rose hedge full of birds.

I look forward to seeing the new poems . . . As there is only one more issue [of *Monks Pond*], I'll have to be demanding in the interests of space and may not be able to fit in everything I'd like to. People are urging me to go on with the magazine but I'll stick to the original plan of running only four issues. I have treated my poets very badly, holding on to mss. for months without giving them a sign of a decision one way or the other. They have mostly been quite patient.

Did I tell you Bob Lax was here? We had a fine visit in June. But I was so overvisited at the time that I was tired and I guess untalkative. I find I get more and more that way—and answer letters less too. Tommie [O'Callaghan] came out with all the children to have a picnic with Lax.

Her mother's death was a big shock to her, but she is getting over it . . . I have hopes that *Journal of My Escape* will finally be published. Doubleday has accepted it, though grudgingly, and it should be in the works. I don't expect it to be out until next spring. Or summer, maybe . . .

Sister Therese sent Merton a poem, "A Hill is for Celebration / With Certain Apologies to Juan de la Cruz (for Tommie and Frank)," which described her visit to Merton's hermitage the preceding November.

August 20, 1968

Just a quickie. I've almost stopped writing letters. Not only the intense heat, but everything else. But I want to acknowledge your letter and the poem, which is very lively. I guess I can safely include it in *MPond IV*—after all, the only tinkling is of teacups. It can hardly shock anyone even if they figure out the "action."

The poem for Lax ["You Sing from Islands"] is superb and one of your very best. I'm using it too. I think he is presently going back to Greece. He can't stand it here . . . Now I have to stop and try to answer the usual flood of requests to write every possible kind of triviality. Take care of yourself. Keep cool. I haven't seen Tommie [O'Callaghan] for a few weeks: did you send her the poem?

India, November 21 [1968]

I have been a month in India—over a month—& most of it in the Himalayas. A great experience.

Your letter was forwarded from the monastery. Bro. Patrick [Hart] has been taking care of mail & all business. A mimeo newsletter should give a partial rundown on my "news." I am going on to Ceylon & Indonesia & expect to see many more interesting people. God be with you.

On December 10, 1968, Sister Therese received a telegram signed Abbot of Geth-semani, reading: "We regret to inform you of the death of Father Louis Merton in Bangkok."

To Thomasine O'Callaghan

It is embarrassing to have one's friends to go to so much trouble for such an unworthy cause.
MERTON TO TOMMIE O'CALLAGHAN,
APRIL 5, 1967

Tommie O'Callaghan (née Thomasine Cadden) met Thomas Merton through Dan Walsh, who had been Merton's teacher at Columbia and her teacher at Man-hattanville. Merton became a close friend of hers, her husband Frank E. O'Cal-

laghan III, and their seven children, Kathie, Nancy, Diane, Colleen, Kim, Sarah, and John, in the 1960s. Their home in Louisville became "a kind of way station" for Merton on his regular trips to the doctors and to St. Joseph Infirmary just down Eastern Parkway from the O'Callaghan home. Though she admits she was in awe of Merton the first time he came to lunch, and took care to serve lamb chops ("good meat for this poor guy who never got it"), the friendship soon became comfortable enough for peanut-butter-and-jelly sandwiches. Their relationship became Merton's first experience in many years with any sort of family life. Tommie O'Callaghan has recalled: "Being a busy mother of seven, I didn't have time for Thomas Merton, the serious writer. We often discussed the responsibilities of marriage and the Christian training of young children." He helped the children with their homework, played guitar with them, swung them in his arms, drew pictures and doodles (many of them on his letters to Tommie), often would ride along with Tommie as she did "endless car-pooling" for the children. They called him Uncle Tom and were astonished when they learned that he was a famous man. In his last years Tommie became something of a hostess for Merton, planning, arranging, and preparing picnics at his hermitage for the O'Callaghan family, and for such guests as Robert Lax, Ralph Eugene Meatyard, Sister Therese Lentfoehr, and others. In 1967 Merton asked her if she would serve on the literary trust he was arranging. She agreed, little imagining that he would die slightly more than a year later. In the first letter, Merton refers to a mutual friend in Ecuador, Father Feliciano Delgado, S.J., who had written an essay, "Thomas Merton: Estructura y Análisis."

March 23, 1963

Dan [Walsh] has told me of your illness and I am very sorry to hear it. He seems to think you are going to be in the hospital for quite a while. That is a shame. But he said you had a successful operation, so maybe it will turn out to be more hopeful than anticipated. Meanwhile I am sending you a couple of things to divert you for a moment. It must be hard for Frank and the children to be without you at home.

I haven't heard from Fel [Delgado] and haven't written to him, though I think you told me he was going to Spain soon, rather than staying in S.A. . . . If you write to Fel tell him I certainly liked his essay about my work and thought it was very perceptive. A friend of mine who is starting a new magazine might like to publish a translation of it: but I don't know where I have put my copy of it. Disorganized as usual . . .

Well, keep your chin up (or will that ruin the effects of the operation?). Keep in any position that is comfortable and will help, and trust in the Lord. There must be some good reason why you have to go through all this, and you will surely grow in love for Him, though you probably won't feel like that most of the time. I can't imagine anything more tedious than being in bed for weeks, though I admit that there are days when I think I would like to try it, just to see if I could meet the challenge.

April 5, 1967

Naomi Burton [Stone] is arriving here April 19 and will stay over the 20 and 21st, leaving the 22nd. Hence the 20th and 21st would be good days for you and Fr. John [Loftus] to come out—I suggest a picnic, and hope you could get here around 11 or 11.15?? Let me know what you think. I hope the weather will be nice at that time.

I want to take this opportunity to thank all the speakers who turned out and spoke for the TM room seminars. I am most grateful for the trouble they all took and for the excellent talks they gave. Really it is embarrassing to have one's friends to go to so much trouble for such an unworthy cause, but I am touched by their charity. I promise to keep them all in my prayers and ask God to reward them for what they have done. And you above all, for the work of organizing it.

Naomi Burton Stone, literary agent, also became one of the trustees of the Merton Legacy Trust in 1968. Father John Loftus, O.F.M., was Academic Dean at Bellarmine College in Louisville and the moving force behind Merton's leaving his literary estate to the college and the establishment of the Thomas Merton Studies Center. The first Merton Seminar had been held at Bellarmine that spring with Dan Walsh, Dr. James Wygal, and Dr. E. Glenn Hinson giving talks. In a memorandum for the picnic titled "Burton & Merton," Tommie O'Callaghan noted that guests were Merton, Naomi Burton Stone, Father John Loftus, and Ron Seitz. On May 14, 1967, Merton's old friend Dan Walsh was ordained to the priesthood in Louisville. Merton attended the ordination and the reception, which was held at the O'Callaghan home. Tommie O'Callaghan noted: "Tom's antics in the late afternoon were a riot. The champagne hit him hard."

May 15, 1967

Thanks for a splendid party yesterday. Much enjoyed it, and I know everyone did. Hope I did not ruin everything by holding forth and making speeches at the end, about whatever it is I make speeches about at such times. I think I predicted the ruin of the western world or something. Hope no one was upset.

I am expecting you and the Meatyards Monday the 22nd for a picnic, right? . . . I will be waiting for you all out in the avenue at 12 or 12.15 OK? I forget whether I will be seeing you tomorrow or not, hence this letter. Write and let me know if it is all cockeyed. I think I stayed fairly sober yesterday until the late afternoon, when we were no longer making plans. Or were we?

By the way I do have a rather terrible diet: I can't even eat bread, because it has milk in it. But I can eat crackers that don't have milk in them, like saltines. Chicken is no problem. I can't touch anything that has even the slightest suggestion of milk or cheese hidden in it anywhere . . .

Merton sent Tommie O'Callaghan, then pregnant with her seventh child, a cartoon by Richter depicting a family of bareback riders standing on a galloping horse, with the wife saying: "Darling, I have something to tell you. We're going to need a bigger horse."

June 27, 1967

I thought this work of art might seem appropriate. Boss will be back day after tomorrow and censorship then starts again so beware all references to picnics and mail may not get thru. I'll get a message through when things are propitious for getting together with the gang. Love to all the kids and all of you.

August 31, 1967

Thanks for the letter and the xerox on computers which I will read as soon as I get a chance to go through the piles of articles etc. that has now accumulated. I have a few copies of the *Bulletin of the Atomic Scientists* which Draghi sent. It is one of the best magazines I know of, like it a lot.

I have been thinking a lot about you, expecting news at any moment of the new arrival. In fact I am persuaded it will be plural. Twins at least. Two boys, for self defense against the feminine majority. (If it's two more girls! . . .)

Saw Dan [Walsh] briefly yesterday. Talk about the congress of theologians. He will apparently be at [Bellarmine College] most of the time from now on, only out here Tuesday and Wednesday. I expect to see less of him. I haven't been near town since the Dr. gave me the serum I need. It is fairly ok. But I had a bad bout with the flu over last weekend, still haven't quite pulled out of it.

I hope the kids will like the new school [Louisville Collegiate].

October 17, 1967

This will be a serious letter for a change. About my estate business and so on. On the advice of J. Laughlin I am getting a Kentucky lawyer and bringing the scene of action a little closer to home. Jim Wygal suggested his own attorney, John Ford, so I have had a talk with him, and I think things will perhaps move a little now.

Under Kentucky law, it is not certain that J. Laughlin and Naomi Burton will qualify as the only trustees. It seems necessary to have someone from Kentucky in it also. And besides that, J. and Naomi are about my age, so it would also be wise to have someone younger.

If you would consent to it, I would very much appreciate having you as a co-trustee for my literary estate with J. and Naomi. The responsibilities of the trust will be simply to take care of the publication of unpublished materials and to protect the literary estate, the drawings and so on. The estate will be owner of all materials, including those held as deposit under the custody of places like Bellarmine. And the money will go to the Abbey. I hope you can be on the team. Naturally all the publication work and all that will be handled by J. and Naomi. But it will be good to have someone connected with Bellarmine or with "the Room" involved also.

Another of your most important duties will be to see that the author, during his declining years, is occasionally revived by picnics. And that he has access to suitable sources of creative inspiration from time to time.

Jim Wygal will be named as alternate co-trustee.

This will all be official after I can get the Abbot to agree to it on principle and let me draw up a new will. I don't think he will object. The important thing (the monastery getting the money) will have been included.

Have you heard from Sister Therese [Lentfoehr]? Maybe when she is down here we could clarify the standing of her collection also.

When Sister Therese Lentfoehr read Merton's poetry at Bellarmine, an exhibition of Ralph Eugene Meatyard's photographs of Merton was also mounted at the college. In reference to this, Tommie O'Callaghan wrote Merton: "Gene and Madylyn Meatyard came over Mon. eve . . . We got the series of 20 pictures up and they are great. Even the main subject matter does not detract from the goodness of the photography."

October 30, 1967

Naomi Burton [Stone] will be down in a couple of weeks. I hope very much that we can all get together in town on Nov 14 and get that Trust thing signed, settled and all. (Unless J. Laughlin holds it up in N.Y.). I have written to the lawyer, John Ford, about it. Fr. Abbot is not back yet but I hope to fix it up with him Thursday.

I look forward to seeing you and Sister [Therese Lentfoehr] in a week or so. Hope we will have nice weather—and hope everything is fine with Gene [Meatyard] and the pictures Sunday.

November 3, 1967

Many thanks for the letter: sorry to hear Frank is sick but I hope it will clear up fast. This is going to be a bad winter for flu everyone says. But maybe too much suki-yaki could have a bad effect too.

I will look for you all Tuesday: that day I have to see the lawyer in the late morning, so if you arrive around 11 or 11.15 you will have time to show Sister [Therese Lentfoehr] the Church and whatnot. I'll probably be busy with him until 11.45 or so. It will be a good thing for him to meet Sister. One of the major jobs involved in this thing is to get clear what happens to all these collections, how they are to be used, etc. Where should we do all the signing on the 14th? Would it be ok to meet at your house for a drink or something rather than his office? (Don't plan anything elaborate—when I say just for a drink or something that's what I mean, not a big lunch. Sandwich wouldn't hurt maybe.)

Everything is clear with Fr. Abbot, my making new will etc. I am glad that it is all completely official.

Got a note from Sister [Therese Lentfoehr], she is bubbling over with all kinds of expectation and I am sure will enjoy everything thoroughly: she is very much full of life, and appreciates very much being able to stay with you. I wish I could be there Sunday! But it is of course quite impossible! We will have to make the best of Tuesday, and I hope it won't rain or be cold or anything.

Other day I heard the setting done by John Jacob Niles for three poems of mine and I must say I really liked them very much, though some of my friends and his don't seem enthusiastic. But I think he did a fine job, and is in any case a great person.

Probably too late to mention this, but I hope they don't print any picture of me in connection with Gene's exhibit. Will only cause (minor) trouble with Abbot, especially if it is one of the out of the ordinary ones. Abbots don't understand some things very well.

After the picnic with Sister Therese Lentfoehr at Gethsemani on November 5, 1967, "Trusty Tommie" wrote to Merton on November 8: "Don't think Sister had descended from her cloud even by today. She was a dear, and certainly thinks the most of you and I'm sure that she'll never forget this five day experience."

January 21, 1968

How do you feel?? Is everything ok?

I had hoped to get in and see you but the snow made any trip to town impossible for me (they wouldn't send in the truck just for me). Then when it became possible to get in I had the flu and was too far gone even to write a note. I hope by now you are happily recuperating and all is well.

J. Laughlin says he plans to blow in here from the West this week or next. I don't know exactly when. As soon as I do, I will get on the phone to Valley Rd and find out if it would be possible to meet you—his co-trustee. Would you be well enough? Also he ought to . . . see the Room at the library . . .

You know our new Abbot is Fr. Flavian [Burns]. My candidate, so I am satisfied with the election, and I think he is easily the best for the job at this time. He seems to be starting well, but Dom James [Fox] has not rushed madly into the woods by any means. He is still there and I guess it is necessary for him to be around and show the new man the ropes as far as the business end goes. I hope Fr. Flavian is strong enough to resist learning some of the other ropes that man used. I think he will be much more open and humane.

After Tommie O'Callaghan became one of Merton's trustees, he often asked her to take care of business connected with his literary effects.

[February 1968]

Thought I'd send you this letter from a possible friend [R. Fentener van Vlissigen] in Holland, with my reply. When you have taken note of contents, address etc. perhaps you could pass it on to the Mertroom. I am sure he would be congenial.

March 17 [1968]

Great fun yesterday meeting Mother S. [Kathryn Sullivan, R.S.C.J.]. I like her.

When you come out Thursday for the Blessing: suppose I meet you outside after the Mass? How about a few sandwiches by the lake? And will you do me one favor?

I asked [the Merton Room assistant] to send a Chinese picture to get framed somewhere on Frankfort Ave. She knows, I don't. If you could find out from her where it is and pick up the picture to bring out with you Thursday, it would be great. If they mail it it will probably get broken. It ought to be framed by now, as I asked her some time ago to send it there. I hope they have it and that you can conveniently get it for me.

March 29, 1968

Just after I had talked with you I got a call from a musician, Alexander Peloquin, who is working on the score of some songs I wrote (long time ago). He wants to come down and play them for me on a piano and there ain't no piano at ole Gethsemani. I told him I would be in town April 8th and that you had a piano . . . I don't think this will complicate matters at all except that I might never get to [the doctor]. Would it be ok if he played them over on your piano? He'll probably come in on the morning plane from NY, and we could have lunch some place. I could come direct to your house about 9.30, or could meet him at the airport and come there by cab, or whatever. Maybe the latter would be the easiest. Then if still standing I could go to [the doctor] on his late afternoon shift. Might then be a problem of getting back (NO couldn't possibly stay in, Holy Week).

Is this all a terrible imposition? I haven't got the final word from Peloquin but he's calling this Monday and I could call you after that and give you all the dope.

That isn't all about the songs: there are enormous problems with a Negro singer [Robert Laurence Williams] to whom I donated them and whom Peloquin doesn't want to have sing them . . . Headaches.

Let me know quick if this is no good—any alternatives?

In California, Merton gave a series of conferences to the Trappistine nuns at
Redwoods Monastery in Whitethorn. He wrote to Tommie O'Callaghan from
California using Community Council of San Mateo County / Action Study on
Community Health Services stationery.

May 14, 1968

It's been a really great week out here. The nuns (nothing to do with
letterhead) are tremendous. So is the place. Last two days I made a retreat
out on the shore of the Pacific—absolute solitude. Perfect!

I am going to New Mexico tomorrow. Probably stop off in San Francisco & see Chinatown or something. Will be in New Mexico over the
weekend & will fly back to Kentucky Monday 20th. (Sorry no picnic for
Colleen that day at Gethsemani.) I get in at 10.48 p.m. American airlines
Flight 774. Can I stay overnight at your house?

Can figure out about a ride to Gethsemani the next day. Ron Seitz
could handle it I think.

Anyway, I'll fly in at that time & call from airport—or can stay any
place for the matter!

Really it's been great out here. The nuns are really alive. They even
dance in Church. And it's quite impressive.

Colleen O'Callaghan wished to go on a picnic to Gethsemani for her birthday.
The picnic was eventually held on June 11. Merton's old friend Robert Lax hap-
pened to be visiting at the time. Tommie O'Callaghan noted about the picnic:
"Fun."

[June 1968]

OK for June 12, about 11.30 am?? Just got through a busy week with
group of nuns, and will probably continue like that for a while. Hope to
go into a more retreatlike bit in July. As to your coming here for retreat
I'm sure it would be ok though Fr. Flavian [Burns] got away before I
could talk to him about it. He'll be back, but you can plan on it if you
like. I'll make myself responsible. I'm keeping your mother in prayers.

[June 1968]

I'll expect you around 11.30 Tuesday—OK? Bring an extra sandwich—Bob Lax will be here & will join us . . . Hope your mother made
out ok—we've all been praying.

June 22, 1968

The brothers passed on to me the sad message of your mother's
death. I was quite surprised, though I knew she was gravely ill. I guess
we are so used to thinking that the doctors can do anything they like and
fix everything with a knife. I am really sorry to hear it.

This morning I offered Mass for the repose of her soul, and I shall continue praying for her throughout the day and after that also. It is almost time for the funeral and I will be thinking of you all and asking the Lord to give her eternal rest.

Please convey to all the family the message of my deepest sympathy. It seems we all have to face one sad thing after another. But let us not forget the hope our faith gives us. God is our strength, and no amount of trouble should make us fail to realize it. On the contrary, trouble should help us deepen and confirm our trust. This is an old story, but as far as I am concerned it is the one we always get back to. There is no other.

The Reverend Philip M. Stark, S.J., came to Gethsemani in the summer of 1968 to be "literary secretary" to Merton and to help him put out the last two issues of his "little magazine," Monks Pond. Stark recalled the experience in "A Summer at Gethsemani," Continuum 7 (Summer 1969), pp. 306–12: "Merton's great love of the world found expression in countless other ways, too, from enjoying a can of beer or poking around in a supermarket to discoursing on the evils of nuclear armament." Of the day mentioned in the following letter, Stark recalled: "One day, for instance, he planned to go to Louisville and I was going along. On the way to the garage my idle question, 'Shall I drive?' brought out his burbling chuckle and the instant reply, 'I think you'd better!'—an answer that carried all the hilarity of the famous episode of the jeep in the woods, his first and last attempt to drive."

[August 1968]

I plan to come in Friday with the Jesuit & will call you in case you'd like to meet us for lunch somewhere. If you are busy or have something else planned that's perfectly OK. Pretty hot out here now. Sweating all over everything.

P.S. He doesn't know about Asian trip so I won't be mentioning that.

In late August 1968, Frank O'Callaghan took Merton shopping to buy things for his Asian trip.

[August 1968]

I had a very successful day with Frank yesterday and I guess we pretty well covered the most essential things. Most of the stuff will be delivered at 89 Valley Rd, for security reasons. I hope you don't mind. I hope to be there on Monday the 16th of Sept. to pack up and so on— if not before. I'm not sure whether I'll be in again before then.

While in San Francisco in October 1968, on his way to Asia, Merton sent Tommie O'Callaghan a postcard of Alcatraz Island.

[October 1968]

Fine flight out & a lovely bar in the airport. Makes good rum collins. Here's a picture of where I may be indefinitely—with "the nuns." Just like home.

To Beatrice Olmstead & Family

You really are "my" family in more ways than you can tell.

MERTON TO BEATRICE OLMSTEAD

JUNE 9, 1959

Beatrice Olmstead and her children—Dorothea [Dotty], Brian, Lenore [Norrie], and Terence—became a kind of adopted family for Merton. He often urged them to visit him at Gethsemani. In a letter to Robert E. Daggy she said: "Most of [the letters] were written to me and my children when we were a struggling Catholic family living in a Long Island, N.Y. suburb. My children dearly loved Father Louis and wrote to him about all their school problems, etc. and sent him all kinds of crazy things. As I look back now, I think we all were a terrible trial to poor Father Louis. He really is a saint."

January 12, 1953

If I don't write now, it will be an inexcusable delay in thanking you for the Mass and for the other Christmas presents, especially the Infant of Prague. The way things are, we cannot put the Infant in the Church, but He is in the reading room of the family brothers and postulants—the ones just arriving. He made their Christmas—as well as my own—a wonderful one. They especially rejoiced in His coming since they are a little lonely at first, when they arrive here. They will see that He is not lonely either.

But above all, thanks for the Mass. I offered it last Saturday—the Feast of St. Paul the first hermit. I received many graces. You know the biggest intention I have for myself—to be able to give myself most completely to God and live for Him and with Him alone. I also included you and all the children in a most special way. I feel as if you were all my own relatives, my own flesh and blood. Our prayers and especially the warm-hearted charity of all of you have brought us so close together in the Heart of Jesus. May He bless you always. I think it must have been Brian's potato chips they gave me for collation on Christmas eve. They were a nice surprise for a feast day. Of course I remembered you all at the altar on Christmas morning. There is a new book coming out pretty soon [*The Sign of Jonas*]. I told the publishers to send you one—you may like it better than the others. It is more personal—and shows that I don't amount to very much. I hope it will earn me more prayers on that account . . .

February 16, 1953

I have just a moment to spare in which to thank you for the Mass stipend. What could be a more welcome present? Please thank Dotty also. I said the two Masses last week and remembered you both in them—and all the children.

Please, whatever you do, don't worry about the statue [of the Infant of Prague] and *don't* save up to buy another one. Don't worry about giving us elaborate presents, for heaven's sake! Your prayers are the best thing of all, and if you must send something more tangible—let it be a Mass stipend.

I got a wild idea about writing to the Bishop of Brooklyn [Thomas E. Molloy] to get the pastor to unlock your church but I didn't do it. I don't know if it would help. But anyway, Jesus loves you and sees the desires of your heart. Don't try to do more than you ought to do during Lent. I will keep all of you in my prayers. Thank Dotty for her letter in French. She is really quite good at it—a few faults of spelling here and there, but even the French can't spell. That goes for me, too. French and English both.

February 5, 1955

It has taken me a long time to get around to thanking you again. I was happy to hear about the hideout in the attic but I bet you won't get much use out of it. But that does not matter. What matters is the faith and love that are in the sanctuary of your heart. There God has His hermitage and His resting place, a refuge in a troubled world. The more you abandon yourself to His will, the more He will find His peace and His joy in you. You must believe this more and more. Visit Him when you can, recollect yourself when you are able but it will not always be possible. But you can always love Him. There is great spiritual poverty in a life that is devoted to others and that leaves little time for the consolation of prayer. Thank you for your prayers and your intentions for me. Let us love Him and accept whatever He wills. Love alone matters. Let us speak only to give Him what He wants of us.

I will have a new book [*No Man Is an Island*] out in a few weeks. I am glad to hear all the good news about Brian and the other children, especially Norrie's first communion. Brian sent me a card and spiritual bouquet from Alabama, and I was very glad to hear from him . . .

To Lenore "Norrie" Olmstead

June 3, 1955

I was so happy to get the beautiful picture of you on your first Communion day. I know Jesus is very happy now that He can come to you each day in Holy Communion. He loves to come to souls in secret, and He loves best those who know how to receive Him in the secrecy of faith. He is a God Whom we never see but if we believe it is almost better than seeing. He guides us and helps us always, and I am sure you will faithfully follow Him wherever He leads you. Who knows, perhaps one day He will ask you to give yourself entirely to Him in the cloister. But it is for you to follow the love which the Holy Spirit will inspire in your heart. Love Jesus, love your parents and brothers and sister. I hope you will pray for a very special intention of mine, too.

June 9, 1959

. . . How time flies. Dotty is already out of college, and the youngest, Norrie and Terence, and growing like mad. I was happy to hear from all, and I think often of all of you. You really are "my" family in more ways than you can tell.

The ten years of my priesthood have gone by like a flash. It seems that time moves faster and faster. But it does not matter. We live in another dimension. A hundred years from now no one will remember any of us but we will all be happy in a place "which the eye has not seen nor the ear heard, nor has it entered into the heart of man to conceive." We have to remember such words when we think of heaven. There is no way of picturing or imagining our life in God. That is all the more reason for hope and joy. It is not going to be what we expect, and we don't have to strain our heads expecting it and trying to understand because we just can't. It is going to be "what we don't know" . . .

February 6, 1960

This is to thank all of you for the letters, presents, prayers and good wishes for Christmas and my birthday. I was so happy with everything, especially the cards and spiritual bouquets of the children (I hope you didn't twist their arms to get them to write now, that would never do!) But really it is wonderful to feel some of the warmth and faith that come from the hearth of such a good Christian family, blessed by God. Such a family, with all its responsibilities and headaches, is nevertheless most pleasing to Our Lord, and that is what is so wonderful. To think that though perhaps you yourself do not realize it, you are all giving Him such glory just by being you. It is all much simpler than we think: we always want to make the spiritual life something added on to the rest of life, and so to speak *compensating* for our normal life. What compensation is needed? Our normal life is life "in Christ." It is Jesus who makes the children's eyes shine and their cheeks pink. And that is even in the liturgy for the feast of St. Agnes! The martyr sings "His blood has made my cheeks beautiful."

It is to me a privilege and a grace to hear from time to time a distant echo of that love, and to feel that somehow I can share in it, as if I were one of the uncles or something.

Brian wrote a good note on his card. I'd like to answer everyone in particular but you understand how it is. Why doesn't Brian come down here and make a retreat some time when he has a vacation? I won't try to pull him into the novitiate. I think he would enjoy it. He is always welcome, anyway. Just let me know beforehand, so that I can get permission to see him for a little talk. Who knows, maybe some day you can *all* come down, but that is an enormous project. But you will always be welcome.

I am glad you liked the picture. Don't take it too seriously now—I mean it is not an ikon and I am not yet eligible for public veneration. The way things are going I probably won't be ever. Of course that is not the important thing: what matters is the goodness and charity of friends . . .

June 17, 1961

For several days I have intended to drop you this note and I hope I am not too late with it. I am of course hoping that you will be able to get down here as you say sometime towards the end of the month. To iron out a few details:

a) When you know exactly when you hope to get here, let me know by some means and I will try to make arrangements to say Mass for you all. That would be normally around 7 o'clock in the morning, our time, or perhaps a little earlier. I can leave word with the brother at the gate, or perhaps even speak to you briefly about it the day before if I am free.

b) Also I will try to arrange for you to have at least your dinner at the ladies' guesthouse here though it may be a little late to get you a room there. I guess you will have to stay overnight in a motel: plenty in Bardstown. If Brian comes he can stay in the Guesthouse all right.

c) So let me know when you are getting here and how many of you there will be, if it is possible. As I say I want at least to say Mass for you. Ideally if you came this way in the afternoon I might be able to drop out and see you and make arrangements about the Mass for the next day . . .

To Terence Olmstead

May 24, 1962

Well I am going to get a letter through to you if I bust. I am grateful for your letters and I always like to hear from you. I suppose by now that you are almost through school and I bet you are not sorry. It is good to enjoy a vacation and to play ball and get out in the air.

Here it is really pretty hot, as bad as midsummer. We have a lot of novices, including even one from South Africa and one has just written from the Philippines who wants to come. He looks good too, but he will probably have a hard time getting here. We have one from the West Indies and another who came from Czechoslovakia and got out ten years ago after the Reds took over.

I hope your family is all well. I am glad to have heard from them at my birthday. I want to write your mom a good letter one of these days, but you know how it is with letters. And I have a huge stack of them.

Tell her that I will write soon. I am finishing a book and won't be so busy, I hope, in a couple of weeks.

I haven't got around to seeing how many push-ups I can do. I used to be able to do about twenty-five or thirty, but right now if I start doing push-ups, I will have to push a hundred and eighty pounds and that is a lot of weight. I think I'll wait a little and see if I sweat off a few pounds . . .

June 4, 1962

Thank you for your good letter. I have been thinking of you all, and of course I know you pray for me. I pray for all your dear family and for you too. May God always multiply blessings upon all of you. Especially I am glad to hear Brian is doing well. You do not have to worry too much about him being among non-Catholics. I am sure that after a good college like St. Peter's he is able to handle the situation and to tell the truth we badly need Catholic intellectuals who can just stand on their own feet and hold their own among people of different beliefs and backgrounds. In this way we will develop a better and stronger Catholic laity, and this is most important for the Church today. And if Brian is looking ahead to politics, that is good too. Because after all we need politicians who are honest and upright and maintain traditional philosophies of law and the standards given by God, without which man cannot live happily. In other words we need to do all we can to preserve a Christian order and the traditional standards of civilization, and we can't do this if the politicians aren't interested. That is the trouble today, to a great extent. The general chaos of social and political life due to the corruption of the idea of law and moral responsibility. We have been depending too much on "economic forces" or "science" to do everything for us and solve all our problems.

It would be fine if Brian and Dotty could come down some time. If they ever get a chance, just let them get in touch and I'll see what we can do . . .

To Lenore "Norrie" Olmstead

June 15, 1963

. . . I hope you are all well. I am always happy to hear from all of you. The letters are all good in different ways, and each one has his own individual approach. Norrie writes a real good newsy letter. Terence is in a class by himself. I enjoy hearing from him. In fact I send my love to all, and will keep you all in my prayers. Today is a great and beautiful feast (The Sacred Heart) and I am sure you will all be close to Our Lord. I will remember you at the High Mass which will be in a few minutes.

January 4, 1964

This is a brief note to thank all of you for your Christmas letters and presents. I was especially touched by Terence's gift of a Mass stipend from his paper route earnings. I sent him a fruitcake. Hope it got there all right and fits in with his dietary arrangements.

Things are going all right with me. My shoulder is still a little bad, and I probably won't get rid of the trouble altogether . . .

July 4, 1964

How long can it be since I last wrote you and the family? I have a feeling I owe you all at least a dozen letters when it is all added up. I have enjoyed all the letters and cards, and think of you all often, Brian going on into law, Dotty with her teaching and her trip to Europe, Terence with his various projects and Norrie with her debating: and you, with your wild life, drinking Irish coffee with a bunch of nuns! I had that a long time ago and could do with some more (but don't take that as a hint to send a bucket of it down here, please!)

Anyway thanks for everything. What news have I? You can guess I have been busy. I have a bad back which slows me down a bit. Things are quiet in the novitiate. No ordinations this year, we have extended the study program over more years and slowed down the preparation even before they begin studies, so there will be fewer in the future for a while. The big idea in this life is not so much to make it to the priesthood as to become a really good monk and content with the life. Otherwise some get restless after ordination and want to get out into a diocese. Many have done that in recent years . . .

There has been a lot of trouble and delay over a new book [*Seeds of Destruction*] I am trying to get out. The material on race and war in it is a little too hot for comfort and I have had to do some rewriting. I am still waiting for final approval, and would appreciate an extra prayer that everything can go through without being terribly watered down. The awful thing is that the clergy and bishops are so afraid of offending rich and conservative people that they won't speak up and fail to give the guidance that is urgently necessary in these very serious problems. If the Church were just as strict on war and race as she is on birth control and pornography, we might begin to say what needs to be said. But it would not be very acceptable . . .

June 15, 1966

Thanks very much for your remembrance on my ordination anniversary and for the note written without glasses: it certainly was perfectly written and I would never have known. I appreciate both, and especially the trouble you went to to write to me like that. I am also grateful for Terence's good letter, which was lively and spontaneous. He sounds as though he is doing well.

Probably I never got around to telling you that I had to have an operation on my back in March. It left me laid up for a while, though not in bed for long. Still I have had a hard time getting back to work. Typing was painful for a while and then I got bursitis in an elbow and that slowed down the typing too. I need to get some work done, and it is hard to have to try to spare the elbow all the time, but I think it is getting better now and I will soon be back in the swing of things.

Apart from that everything is ok. They are renovating the church here. The old steeple is gone and many changes are being made. You would hardly recognize it.

May and June have both been very nice here, and so I imagine they must have been on Long Island too . . .

January 1, 1967

Many thanks to you and Norrie and Terence for your letters and for the Masses. And Happy New Year. I am going down to the monastery to concelebrate in a few minutes and I shall be sure to remember you all, and all your needs for the year. The attached letter, mimeographed, will give you the bare essentials of the Christmas news. There is not much to add. I am trying to avoid another back operation this year. Hope I can get out of it. I suppose sooner or later they will catch up with me but I don't want another one so soon, and I definitely hate being in the hospitals.

I hope you all had a good Christmas with Brian there: I bet it was lively and that it fulfilled all your expectations . . .

Really there is nothing much I need. Occasionally I run out of coffee (any good brand, regular grind) but right now I have a good supply.

Beatrice Olmstead wrote in October 1967 telling Merton she had written him and then lost the letter in Woolworth's; she hoped someone had found and mailed it to him. She also reported that her son Brian had returned from a three-week vacation in Ireland and that her daughter Norrie, a student at Fordham, belonged to a peace group and had been shown on television in a peace demonstration.

November 16, 1967

It is already a long time since you sent the coffee and everything. It came right at the best time, I was running out. I am most grateful. Good coffee at 4 a.m. does wonders in the hermit life. Thanks too for the letters, the news, the pictures and all. The family is really growing up fast and they all look great.

The letter you said you lost: no, it never got here. Probably someone picked it up and opened it to see if there was any money in it or something. I envy Brian's vacation in Ireland: there's nothing I'd like to see more than the west coast. In fact I'd like to settle down there in a cottage miles from no place. It would be much quieter than it is here, with all the racket of machines, hunters, guns at Fort Knox etc etc. They don't let you forget that there's a war on: helicopters come batting around here all the time. I tried to get transferred to our place in Chile last summer because Chile can never be a great "military power" with H bombs etc.

But I could not get the permission to go. They have a hermitage there, in the Andes.

How did Norrie make out at the Peace March? I hope she wasn't one of those that got kicked or hit over the head. Lots of people I know were there, including some ex-monks. I think it is smart for her to live at Fordham: that subway ride must be formidable.

I am trying to catch up with mail this afternoon so I will not continue chatting. But I wish you all the best of everything. I have been saying Mass in the hermitage since summer, not every day though, as I still like to have a server once in a while . . . My love to all of you, keep well, keep praying.

To Ad Reinhardt

He was really a stupendous person. One of the very
smartest and best, and there was a great deal packed
into that painting of blacks on blacks.
MERTON TO SISTER THERESE LENTFOEHR
SEPTEMBER 5, 1967

Adolph Frank Reinhardt (1913–67), a friend of Merton's at Columbia, graduated in 1935. He was an artist and sent Merton a "Black-Cross" painting. He visited Merton at Gethsemani in May 1959 (with mutual friend Robert Lax) and they began a sporadic correspondence, Reinhardt's side frequently consisting simply of drawings and doodles. Only three of Merton's letters to him have survived. In 1962 Reinhardt wrote Merton about his recent travels in the Middle East to see the mosques. He told Merton that he was teaching a survey course in Islamic and Coptic art at Hunter and Brooklyn Colleges in the City University of New York.

[*Cold War Letter 45*]

February 1962

Once, twice, often, repeatedly, I have reached out for your letter and for the typewriter. Choked with sobs, or rather more often carried away by the futilities of life, I have desisted. Dear relatives and classmates at tragedies. Ah yes, how true. As life goes on, as we descend more and more into the hebetude of middle age, as the brain coagulates, as the members lose their spring, as the spirit fades, as the mind dims, we come together face to face with one another and with our lamentable errors.

Our lamentable errors. My lamentable errors.

Truly immersed in the five skandhas and plunged in avidya, I have taken the shell for the nut and the nut for the nugget and the nugget for the essence and the essence for the suchness. Form is emptiness and emptiness is form.

You throw the centuries [of the mosques] at me and you are right.

Throw them all. Kneeling, I receive the centuries in a shower cascading all over my head. Weeping and penitent I receive upon the back of the head Jordan (8th cent.) and Damascus (8th cent.) You do not mention Isphahan, or the place where the Blue Dome is and where some Imam whose name I forget is venerated (9th cent?). These are the centuries, indeed they are the centuries. And I, as I look at myself with increasing horror, I remark that I have become a boy of the twenty-first century. Throw then your centuries at me, you are right, the centuries are right, and the twenty-first century has very slim chances of ever existing.

Going further down I see you do mention Isphahan after all but you spell it with an F. Go on throw it, I deserve it with an F also.

I have embraced a bucket of schmaltz. I have accepted the mish mash of kitsch. I have been made public with a mitre of marshmallows upon my dumkopf. This is the price of folly and the wages of middle aged perversity. I thought my friends would never know.

Victor Hammer is coming today. He does not know. If he has come to know about this disgrace, I shall efface myself in a barn someplace and become a sheep. I shall weave rugs out of cornsilk, equivalent in substance to my artistic judgements which I shall eternally regret.

My artistic judgement has contracted the measels. My love of kunst has become mumped. My appreciation of the sacreds hath a great whoreson pox and is reproved by all with good tastings and holy lauds. What would it be if he knew, the Imam? If he knew? Under his blue dome? He would stir, he would stir.

You are pro-iconclast and you are right. You are quietists and you are right. You are non-objectivist and you are right. Down with object. Down with damn subject. Down with matter and form. Down with nanarupa. I mean namarupa. Sometimes get my terms wrong. Terms in general have the weasels.

Now the thing is, I am up to my neck. I am in the wash. I am under the mangle. I am publically identified with all the idols. I am the byword of critics and galleries. I am eaten alive by the art racket. I am threatened with publication of a great book of horrors which I have despised and do recant. Bring the bell book and candle and have me shriven. Lift the ban, dissolve the excommunication, release the golden doves from the high dome, let the bells ring and let me be reconciled with the Moslem Synagogue. Help, help, rescue your old fellow sachem from way back in 1937 or whenever there was sachems. Tell [Bob] Lax, help, help, help.

Reinhardt chided Merton in 1963 for making his "calligraphies" too small. He had also participated in a Freedom March to Washington in which he said he saw no Catholic poets, neither Robert Lax nor Ned O'Gorman, "their being on Greek or Manhattan islands."

October 31, 1963

Well, October has thirty-one and here I am again your friendly old calligrapher always small calligraphies down here, I am the grandfather of the small calligraphy because I don't have a big brush and because I no longer run about the temple barefoot in the frosts. But I am amiable and the smaller they get the more mysterious they are, though in fact it is the irony of art when a calligrapher gets stuck with a whole pile of papers the same size and texture, why don't friends from New York who received all kinds of expensive samples of paper send me samples of exotic and costly materials I invite you to pretend you are about to print a most exotic book and get samples of papers from distant Cathay and all over and then send them to your dusty old correspondent who is very poor and got no papers any more except toilet papers for the calligraphy.

I mean it about the sample. Or scraps that are left over from your large calligraphies (come on, I know you are making large calligraphies in secret and that corners of the huge papyrus are lying around and fed to the mice they should rather be sent down here and to be made into calligraphic minuscules of which I am the grandfather).

Here are some more calligraphic hats for New Years.

And now a jocular thrust: history has sure made your face red, yes? when all the time who was at the parade but Ned O'Gorman the Catholic Poet and you having surveyed a small sea of only two thousand faces mostly non-Catholic have cynically asserted that there was no Catholic poets present, well history gave you the lie because there it was in *Jubilee* not only Catholic poets but also Catholic babes, extremely well fed and furnished by nature with unusual great wads of insulation fit for the pencil of a Rubens. Oh for the pencils of a Rubens. (You don't get the classical reference of this quip it is an 1840 book by some Lord Curzon or other who was in the Greek monasteries and mocked at the monks and when some staretz would creep out of a grotto with a beard this Limey would mock out loud: "Oh for the pencils of a Rembrandt." Well now I a boy of the twentieth century exclaim for the pencils of a Rubens at all the well baptized flesh that was in that parade and you had no eyes for any of it, you were in one of your trances, you were getting into one of those dervish moods of yours, you were hobknobbing with the Muslims and not paying attention to the delights of Christianity, it is pretty easy to see you are no Rubens you big quietist wait till the Jesuits get after you but this is only a jest and not a threat you go ahead be a quietist I am right with you I am a Jansenist also and a Sufi, I am the biggest Sufi in Kentucky though I admit there is not much competition. Anyhow it is when I dance that I make the calligraph.

Lax was very piqued with all your nasty stabs about the parade and he has written me since then fifteen letters about the parades he has been in that you were not in I have no doubt he has treated you to the same. What else I do is make a snapshot of old distilleries. And now enough of art. Take seriously the samples.

Reinhardt wrote late in 1963, beginning: "Tom: Rev. M. Louis Merton, O.C.S.O.—is that still your title, rank status, position, do you get promoted inside there in the monastery as everyone does outside. If one endures long enough in our art world, one becomes a 'dean.' I'll be the 'dean of abstract art' when a few of the older men are no longer alive. Stuart Davis used to be 'dean' but now he's only 'dean of regional art' or is second in line after Hopper, 'dean of American scene art.' Josef Albers, I guess, is 'dean of squares.' Robert Lax is 'dean of the American Catholic poets in the Orthodox islands.' Did you ever see Lax and O'Gorman on the telly (TV) reading their stuff? I'm sure you're the dean of something besides small calligraphy."

January 12, 1964

Yes, as one dean to another, I am frequently promoted as dean, usually by myself as I get little cooperation in this matter from others. However, it is true that with your encouragement and assistance I am already the dean of the small abstract calligraphy. As to the title of Louis which I share with too many bartenders and taxi drivers, I am detached from it and as to OCSO after the Louis I am in a state of torpor with regard to this. Not unappreciative, just torpid as to letters after names which are a Jesuitical trope. I am through with all tropes. I begin to be nothing but a dean. I want all the letters in front of my name only, and after the name just a lot of room to get out of the way when they throw things, not to have to stumble around with orders and degrees. Promotion is what I despise except promotion once in a while as dean.

Now as to your papers you have been most generous with the papers and if I send you some of the small abstract calligraphies it is not in order to plague you and clutter up your flat, but to show you whereof I am the dean, and you should send back whatever would otherwise just clutter up the flat as I intend to get through to the millionaires like all the other deans. But for you I have signed the small abstract clalligropos which I take to be the most lively, for the Dragon Year as a new year card and stay away from feminine dragons in this year especially.

The big fine Italian hand paper I have not yet got to with my fine Italian hand.

Now what do you think of the printing method I have devised as dean in my specialty? I think it makes for very nice small obscure calligraphies and comes out more fine than the great brush. I am nuts about my method, like all the other deans. While you have a free moment from being Dean of Regionals and Folk Art and Dean of the Great Quiet, maybe you tell me which is the most lively method and second how I get to the millionaires with the minimum of delay. (No this about the millionaires is joshing.) If you think they would be good for calendars or [Emil] Antonucci children books or other such, tell me what you think. In any case these pictures are for pleasures of contemplation and if they have this effect I can go back content to my deanery and make a lot more, however not threatening to send you the whole tidal wave which is soon to break.

What is your mind about the great brush? It seems to me that with the great brush goes also a huge pot, as I cannot get the great brush into the small bottle of India ink, it seems to me I should experiment with a slightly larger brush which I have and make prints and see what happens, but all large brushes drink up the whole bottle of ink in one gulp then where are you, I ask myself? What is your counsel in this grave matter? Maybe there is some funny way of making the ink bottle go a long way like putting in half water or something mean like that.

Lax has got out of being dean of Greek Islands for a while. It is he that starts all the wars in Cyprus. You wait, it will all come out. I hide my head from the American hubris that starts and will start wars and violence all over the place. I go back to be dean of the small silent calligraphy and weep for the peace race. Now it's flags in Panama, and I got a friend just through telling me of peaceful Indians in islands around there etc. Bah. Fooey on the pale faces.

To Edward Rice

I would be saying mass all my life for dead priests if
some nice lady did not send me masses for my friends.
MERTON TO RICE,
JULY 20, 1966

Edward Rice (1918–   ), a close friend at Columbia, was Merton's godfather. They remained friends through the years. Rice came to Gethsemani for Merton's ordination in 1949 and visited him on other occasions, the last time in September 1968. Rice was editor of the magazine Jubilee *for fourteen years, until it was acquired by another publisher in 1967. After Merton's death, Rice became his first biographer, with the publication of* The Man in the Sycamore Tree: The Good Times and Hard Life of Thomas Merton *(1970).*

February 28, 1957

I got permission to write to you because perhaps you can put me in touch directly or indirectly with someone who would be able to do a decent statue of the Blessed Mother and Child for the novitiate here. I'll write more and go into details when I am in touch with the artist. At present, it is enough to say we can probably afford four or five hundred dollars, and it ought to be five feet high. We already have a pedestal about two and a half feet high, in the novitiate library. It will be against a white plaster wall. I am open to all kinds of suggestions—it could be stone, wood, polychrome wood, metal, cast stone.

The following remarks will set limits to the possibilities: first as a rule I am pretty cold to the people who have had some fuss made over them in this country, Frances Rich, Charles Umlauf, Janet de Coux, Jean de Marco etc. etc. I don't want them, or people like them. Nor can I say I am exactly crazy about all the disciples of Mestrovic who are floating around. Peter Watts, and the Gill tradition, are all fine but we already have something of that type, and what I am really thinking of is someone like Lambert Ruki or one or other of the Germans, say Barlach or Schwippert. The best would be Ruki, I suppose. Are any of these people around in America? How could I get in touch with them? Maybe the best thing would be to put me in touch with [Maurice] Lavanoux, whose address I once had but no longer have, and he could help me on from there. But I thought first of all you might have some good ideas and know someone really good who is easy to contact and would not want too much money either, and maybe would be able to come down and look the place over and see what he was doing.

When it comes to getting something like a statue the whole situation is so perilous that my stomach begins to do flip-flops, as I reflect that I may be adding one more to the interminable series of abominations that one sees on all sides . . .

How is everybody? Where is [Bob] Lax? Is [Mark] Van Doren's son [Charles Van Doren] still winning everything on that TV quiz? How's *Jubilee* doing? . . .

September 3, 1961

This letter will serve as an introduction for the Rt. Rev. Archimandrite Basil Kazan. Providentially he spent some time here in Kentucky, taking care of the Eastern Orthodox Parish of St. Michael in Louisville where he has done very remarkable work musically. Father Kazan is now leaving Kentucky to take up an important post in his Church in the Eastern United States. It is not yet known what this post will be, but I am convinced that it has something to do with sacred music.

Father Basil Kazan has given us an opportunity to become acquainted not only with the familiar Eastern Rite liturgy but also with some rare and exquisite Arabic hymns of great antiquity and superb quality. These are rendered by Father Basil himself, who has a fine voice, in a very impressive manner. It seems to me that this very unpretentious and unpublicized venture in the restoration and dissemination of the ancient Byzantine sacred music is a rare gift for which we cannot be sufficiently grateful in this country. I would like to see the records cut by Fr. Basil much better known: they are exceptionally fine.

He is bringing you some of these records himself and I know you will enjoy them. Besides singing in Greek, Arabic and English, Fr. Kazan has also rendered some of the chants in their traditional versions in other languages such as Spanish.

I know you will be delighted to enjoy this ancient music of the Eastern

Church. Father Basil Kazan has visited our monastery and I count him as a good friend, and one who is deeply sympathetic to our monastic and religious ideals.

[*Cold War Letter 33*]

February 10, 1962

The article of Fr. Michael Azkoul is quite good, and it touches on the main theme of eastern Christian spirituality, deification. There is nothing strange about this theme, which is in fact common to both the Eastern and the Western Fathers. The fact that he presents it as something that might arouse opposition (and of course it might) tends to provoke opposition, and also to create a kind of uneasiness in the non-theological general reader, as if there "might be something the matter with it, but I'll just go along with it anyway because now we have to be nice to the Eastern Christians." This would do more harm than good probably.

Also he does bring up the question of uncreated energies in a way that might require a lot more introduction. Here you do have something that can be and is disputed, but once again it is presented in an abrupt way, with a whole lot taken for granted, so that the reader has no way of getting properly oriented and once again realizes, rightly this time, that he has picked up a hot potato. There are no instructions about what he is supposed to do next.

On the whole, then, though this is a good article on a good subject, the approach is such that I don't see how you can profitably use it. It will, as it stands, create uneasiness and confusion more than enlightenment. At least that is how it looks to me.

I think you should have an article on this subject from a reputable and well known Catholic theologian sympathetic to the East, and then follow that with some such article, but again I think it should be by an Orthodox theologian of some weight, like probably Ivan Meyendorff. In short I think you ought to arrange a two-part treatment of this theme, showing the basic agreement of east and west regarding deification as the summit of Christian life. And also showing that it does not mean anything wacky either . . .

I have still no news from the censor about that peace article. Probably it got the axe finally. I have a couple of others which are also getting the axe right now. Except that I am getting one censored in England, where it may have more chance.

Sending a poem. I originally sent it to *Catholic Worker* and I suppose they will want it, so it is just a poem for fun, but if you have some special use for it, and can work it out with CW, go ahead. I don't think you will want to use this. Can't print everything twice. Unless Bob [Lax] wants it for *Pax* . . .

October 26, 1963

Long time ago I said I was going to do an article on the Shakers. Here it is. Under separate cover come a few enormous photographs I took of their old buildings and you could line up some wonderful old engravings of them dancing, and also one of their "spiritual" pictures, especially the one of that tree they were always doing. I think it would be worth while . . . Disk bad, got to stop typing.

August 3, 1964

Hold everything. Stop press. Jangle jangle. Terrible mistake. That piece on Gandhi ["The Gentle Revolutionary"] was, I remember, the wrong one. That one was taken months ago by *Ramparts* and is probably coming out right now or sooner. Other longer text on Gandhi is the one being used by New Directions in book of stuff of Gandhi's which I compiled, edited, etc. Long introduction from my goose quill is there, I don't have available copy here but they will let you have some of what they have I am sure. Sorry for mixup.

Here all is hot as blazes and wet as steambath. If I was a Finn or something I could pretend I was in one of those Finnish baths, but from those one can get out and from this no. All I get is letters from nuns crazies and laypeoples crazies since it now turns out I am the Father of all the crazies.

Write soon. Peace to all the cats.

September 3, 1964

I have not ceased to be sorry for my blunder about the Gandhi article. And I suppose New Directions has been difficult about letting you have their only copy of the other ["Gandhi and the One-Eyed Giant"]. Finally I have got a copy back from the censors, and I am sending it on to you. There are numbers for footnotes which you can ignore as I am sure you don't want to fool with footnotes. So here is the material, and you can use whatever you want of it. Or all of it. It is a bit long, but I think you will like it. I don't know where New Directions may be getting with the book of which this is part, but I assume it is still a long way off as I have not yet seen even galleys.

Things about same here. Occasional whack on the head from above for being outspoken. Otherwise peaceful. You know lot of peace stuff coming out with Farrar Straus and *Giroux* (yes) in the new book *Seeds of Destruction*. You might want some of the peace stuff, rewritten from the mimeographed book [*Peace in the Post-Christian Era*] I did a couple of years ago. It finally got through. You can ask [Robert] Giroux. Perhaps I mentioned this before.

I have given up worrying about anything. (Or I wish I had.) Too dumb to worry anyway. Think about Irish art, Celtic monks, will some time write on Celtic monks. How about something on St. Brendan's voyages? Best wishes, blessings, up the rebels, viva *Jubilee*.

July 7, 1965

Here is a piece ["An Open Letter to the American Hierarchy"] which you might be interested in, as an article. I don't know whether it is right to the point or not. It was written on the basis of information that the revised schema 13 contained a blessing of some sort on the bomb. As I have not seen the exact text, the article may be off target. Perhaps you are better informed than I. In any case, you can judge whether the piece is timely and to the point, or simply useless. In any event it is yours to publish if you want it.

August 12, 1965

Now about that TV interview. I think that the project as such is imposs. How can you have a TV interview with a guy who is not present? Besides, there is this new wrinkle in my existence. Next week I am finally getting relieved of the novitiate job with permission to live in the hermitage. This precludes things like TV interviews, I am afraid, even if the monastery itself did not automatically. Guess it is just no go. I know the outfit in New Mexico. One of our monks from Colorado is going there to be a hermit. Hermits are finally blossoming out all over, but this doesn't call for publicity because as a movement it is extremely precarious and there are likely to be far more non-hermits than hermits among them. Last I heard a (former Cistercian) hermit ran away with the lady benefactress who was supporting a colony of them in Arizona. Be better if all those guys stayed in their hutches. But the fashionable thing today is for Cistercians to leave. The cheese biz types are now pulling out of here, not that this means anything. It is just part of a cycle.

Anyway no TV interview. Sorry . . .

January 27, 1966

Got your letter yesterday at end of retreat preached by guess who Bishop Sheen. I am exempt from going to sermons being a hermit and beyond recall or conversion a hopeless case. But I had a couple of talks with him . . .

Thanks for the contact sheets of pictures of that irascible and stupid looking old man: now like an ape, now like Picasso, now like God knows what, Hilaire Belloc maybe. I checked a few: just to keep it simple, for each one I checked would you please send me *two* blowups, a convenient size, not over 8 × 11, and then I can send some on to aunts, some to nuns etc etc. One, with the sweater, I marked showing how it could be good if cropped off, like where the line is. I know I missed my vocation: in some of them I am distinctly an investigator for the NKVD.

Here is the story from the *Courier Journal* [James Morrissey, "Talks with and about Thomas Merton"]. I imagine there will be a lot of picking it up, for *Time* and *Newsweek* have been inquiring about the picture. And I suppose most of them will take just a little bit of the story and slant it some way.

As to *Jubilee*, go ahead, sure I am twenty-five years in the monkhouse about this there is no question, but not until December of 1966. Don't say anything clear about no hermitage. I don't mean you have to wait til December to say I am here 25 yrs. Smityrse . . .

I got a good letter from [Bob] Lax. He doesn't weep about any sicknesses. I hope he is ok. Glad you will see him. Hope you have a good trip . . . Very cold here, am using up all the wood, everything snowed in. Sure come again in May or June. This time let me know and I will see if I can get someone to pick you up at the plane.

March 16, 1966

Thanks for your letter from Iraq. The trip sounds interesting. I wonder if you are going to be back soon. I was glad you wrote about that program. They sent me a script the other day, and while I was not incensed with it or anything like that, I did find that they devoted too much time to trivial and accidental aspects of the subject. This seems to be a common approach unfortunately. It is not for me to complain about it. I am sorry of course that they did not use your own original ideas, but you could not help that. It is a pity.

Seeing that this is the way things usually pan out I think it would be a lot smarter just to avoid all this in the future. There has been a lot of publicity lately, and as far as I am concerned it is enough to last another ten years. I thought the *Jubilee* piece turned out nicely, by the way. Thanks for that. If you see Naomi Burton will you say that I think we ought to try to avoid all this personality feature stuff, and permit only the usual critical studies of my work, going back to a minimum of pictures and the rest. In principle, all stuff about me should be the exception rather than the rule.

Well, I don't suppose you will be bothered by it anyway. But I just thought I might mention it. I will write to Naomi about it some time too. I suppose that with pictures around they are bound to be reproduced and there is no point in trying to prevent that, but let's keep it within limits anyway.

I am just about to go to the hospital for a back operation. There is nothing to worry about. It is really necessary, the Doctor is a prudent slow-moving guy who has held off since 1963 and even I can see that the trouble is otherwise irreversible. Without it I will be really handicapped. Of course I realize that hiring the handicapped is good business. But I'd just as soon be able to move my arms freely.

Things are getting to be nice here, real spring weather. Yet I don't blame you staying away as long as you can. Hope you had a good trip. I liked the Chinese orphans in *Jubilee* by the way. Like to adopt half a dozen, but I guess it doesn't fit into the local plan. Take care of yourself. Did you see [Bob] Lax?

July 20, 1966

Thanks letter. I will tell you fast if *Cross Currents* rejects article ["Buddhism and the Modern World"], or you might call [Joseph] Cunneen yourself if you don't hear from me about it soon. Hey I envy you going to Aran Is. also India of course.

Business about [Bob] Dylan piece. I would like some of his discs to work on. Can you get for free? He has 3 on Columbia I need:

Bringing it all back home
Another side of B Dylan
The times they are a changing

(I have Highway 61)

Also Joan Baez sings some of his stuff I'm not sure where maybe on Vanguard VRS 9112.

I will get his book from New Directions, and other stuff is supposed to be on the way. If you see anything good or new about him tear it out and send it down.

If you can get these things easy any of the good new stuff on discs could come with the D.

Yeah discs what they did was they sliced my throat in the front and reached in and took out a disc that was all chewed up and put in place of it some bone off my hip and fused two vertebrae with that. It is ok, only man I got bursitis now and another bad disc and also a sprained ankle and it will take more than yogurt to fix that. Still, I am all for the sattvic foods. The food problem is beyond reason. For a while I solved it by not eating but now I am hungry again. Lost 20 lbs but have got back about 10 I guess. Not by trying.

Come down here man any time you feel like, just yell ahead so I can prepare, get permission etc.

Right now I got a huge bunch of masses to say for some dead priest, but when I get through that I got some masses I can apply like I want from a nice lady sends me stipends for that. You don't think we believe this about no stipends around here? No sir we cling hard to tradition on that point. I would be saying mass all my life for dead priests if some nice lady did not send me masses for my friends, and I get to say them that way . . .

August 29, 1966

. . . What I was writing about was the records. I have formal permission to receive these if they come, but they will be returned to you. Hence they will be your records. So do not hesitate at once to procure these gems instantly and at no matter what personal sacrifice. If you have them already just lend me the ones you have and one or two others you think would be helpful. This is a one shot expedition into the land of Nod for your old chum. I will be allowed a record player for this once only time in a lifetime to which I will be glued for half a day or so and then pfft. Further I wish to accomplish this spring rite before too long when I am to make profession as a hermit. Hurry then to your nearest drugstore with all possible patience and longanimity and if you can't get this just send me a bucket of LSD.

Dom [Jean] Leclercq is here with all kinds political jazz about monastic renewal you ought to have an article about the psycho monks in Mexico currently being condemned up to the hilt and all imprisoned in dungeons.

I will do you an article on Camus at the drop of a helmet.

WHAT EVER HAPPENED TO THAT PIECE ON THE BUDDHISTS?

With all expedient haste get down to the drugstore and with shaking hand send me a barrel of LSD. Or if you prefer those Dylan records. I am going to be the teen culture king of Trappist Nebraska.

December 9, 1966

. . . The *Sat. Evening Post* has been heckling me to put out an article on monasticism and I have finally turned them down. I can't write their language or talk to their readers, I don't think, and least of all about monasticism, about which at times I can barely talk to myself in a satisfactory manner. All I know is that I like the solitary type of monasticism and am happy in it, and don't have an awful lot to say about it any more.

Another thing is that with the cheese rush at its peak of fervor I cannot get anyone to type stuff for me here.

You mention the Mt. Savior Monastic Studies: so I gather that number ["Orthodoxy and the World"] finally came out??? I haven't seen it yet, and suppose it will gather dust for a while before reaching me.

A letter came in from [Bob] Lax today: it didn't sound bad. He seems to be a lot better, and can get around ok. He sounds cheerful enough and gives out two or three pages of the old Lax, so I don't worry about him overmuch. We are all older than we were and have various ailments I guess: they are to be expected.

Yes, you did say you were going to Vietnam. If you can make any sense out of it you're good . . .

January 13, 1967

. . . I have written [Bob] Lax a couple of letters since Christmas. My biggest pain in the neck is the mail that sometimes gets unreasonably complicated and full of book-length manuscripts that people think I am going to sit down and read and report back on.

The mere fact that things pile up in such quantity everywhere and that there is no escape from mountains of nonsense anywhere makes life miserable and stupid for everyone. We live in a nutty society, and it's just as nutty for monks as it is for laypeople, though we have less excuse . . .

January 30, 1967

. . . Thanks also for the material on [Jean] Bourgoint. I had a letter from him once five or six years ago about the Brothers' question. Jacques Maritain of course talked about him—was his godfather. Maybe writing to Jacques, and to the Cameroon, I could get together a little material and do a short piece on him. If you get Les Enfants— But I think I can get that from a library. I don't promise to get this done because I have so much work now that I can't fit it in for a long time. If you want someone else to do it fast, go ahead. But perhaps eventually I might be able to. Haven't done anything on Dylan either. Want to get that off my chest first and I guess it is useless waiting for his book. Besides I'll soon have to return the Abbot's record player . . .

No use getting sick of everything. It comes up like bile but don't let it affect you if you can help it. Me I get the same about various things too. Just the depression of living under constant absurd attrition. Fortunately I have the woods.

February 4, 1967

. . . Angst is a big mess, can't help being horrible. What is angst anyway it is the result of truth and life getting fouled and bottled up through fictions, obstacles, social forms, plain crap, and personal errors. So what burns you is good, but it is working in such a way that it is against you instead of for you.

First big thing is not to get so damned attached to the angst that all you are able to do is tread the mill and keep it going round and round. Get off treadmill if you can. There is every reason why the life of the Catholic Kirk should induce all forms of neurosis and anxiety and everything else right up the line. The way the Christian faith is lived is so schizophrenic that it is a wonder one can be at the same time a Christian and sane. I mean to say a Christian according to the pattern and the approved forms. You think I got fun here? Man, you think more. You think I no got angst? Man, think again. I got angst up to the eyes . . .

July 7 1967

. . . I just realized you have a couple of folders of my early writing, and I need to get a copy of the *Journal of My Escape from the Nazis*. They would be glad to xerox it over at Dan Berrigan's office, Jesuit Missions, and send me the xerox. Could you please ask them? . . .

I wonder if [Bob] Lax would not be smart to get away from those islands so near to possible trouble. I wrote him about it. Have you been out there in the last few months? I have not heard much from him, but he did say something about thinking of going to Switzerland.

A girl with Lanzo del Vasto—and I suppose that whole group—is trying to organize a seven-day fast for peace in December. But total fast. They want to invite some "American Churchmen" to participate. I can see Spellman in the forefront. They have asked me for suggestions. I can't imagine any American churchman wanting to fast. Maybe some Quakers. But they want someone prominent. If I take a crack at it, and probably will, it won't be for public knowledge. They want someone who will do it publicly: maybe a group. Any ideas?

July 18, 1967

The Journal of My Escape has not got here yet, but I hope it will arrive safely. Expect also the extra copies. I understand the mail is in very crazy shape these days anyhow . . .

Now have an altar in the hermitage and am able to say Mass here. It is much better—though I don't intend to do that all the time, like sometimes I'll concelebrate down there, or say Mass down there for a few visitors, or else just say Mass down there for a change.

[late July 1967]

Thanks for yours of the 20 and for the *Journal of My Escape* which is here and looks pretty fair after all these years. I am certainly happier about it than about a lot of the published stuff that has appeared in between.

[Bob] Lax wrote and sent some new poems which are now stripped down not to one word a line not to syllables but to plain letters. After that, the blank page with punctuation marks . . .

I am glad you are through (are you through?) with Herder and them krauts. They sound like sonsofbitches for real. They will surely make *Jubilee* a pure square as of tomorrow. But don't worry you sure did your bit and more. Amazing it was so good so long. Now the way of all flesh. It will make money and stink.

Sure you do need a trip. This is not necessarily a cool and pleasant place this time of year but it has been pretty good sofar. This week big boss here from Yurrup, laying down the law. Until about Aug 8 or 9. You want to come down some time after that? Around 14, 15 seems ok for me. If you let me know in time maybe I can get this marvelous photographer friend of mine from Lexington [Ralph Eugene Meatyard] over to meet you, real fine guy too. How's your book coming? The monk pictures? Lemme know what is to develop in Aug. Take care, rest and relax and forget krauts.

August 8, 1967

Now about coming here: after Labor Day everything is tied up through September by the local clergy carrying on their spiritual exercises in our retreat house. Only weekends are free. If you come after Labor Day come then on a weekend, like arrive Friday.

My (really the Abbot's) record player can handle stereo. What I'd really like to have would be some Coltrane, and especially *Ascension*. I haven't heard much of his new stuff but I liked v. much what I heard of his a year or two ago.

I'm getting the Journal typed, with a few minor emendations, and will get busy with possible publication. I still think it is a real good book, one of the best I have done. Hope it works out.

Let me know about Sept. or come before if you can.

To Saint Bonaventure Friends

Last but not least [is] my old friend Fr. Irenaeus, who remains my link with Bona's.
MERTON TO ANTHONY L. BANNON
FEBRUARY 12, 1966

To Father Joseph Vann, O.F.M.

Merton met Father Joseph Vann at Columbia University and it was he who arranged for Merton to spend some time at Saint Bonaventure University in the summer of 1940. While Merton taught there, Vann was at Saint Bernardine of Siena College in Loudonville, New York, founded by the Franciscans as an extension of Saint Bonaventure.

St. Bonaventure
September 19, 1940

I guess you probably heard that something turned up that prevented me from going in to the [Franciscan] novitiate. I guess I was just as much surprised as I was disappointed. However, here I am at Saint Bona's, teaching English. I am glad of that. Under the circumstances I had no particular desire to go back to Columbia anyway, and I was a bit fed up with the place myself: I didn't realize it until I began to wonder where I was going to go to work again.

I am thankful that Father Thomas [Plassmann] could fit me in here. I have that sophomore English Lit. course, two sections of it so far and probably one more in the evening: then Fr. Cornelius [Welch] thinks of starting a course in putting on plays and building scenery etc., which I am to have. He doesn't know how funny that is going to be. Any scenery that gets constructed under my direction will probably collapse and break some bones and crack a couple of skulls here and there, because if there is anything I am inept at, it is putting things either up or together. As for directing a play: that will have to be sheer bluffing, and I have publically admitted it to anybody who cared to listen, but Fr. Cornelius doesn't seem to mind that much.

I asked after you a couple of times in New York, but you were still on your vacation. I assume you are now at Siena. I applied there for a job too, but they said no. Under the circumstances, I guess I am better off here.

I hope that perhaps I will have time and ambition to do some work of my own around here. If so, I will take advantage of Father Philotheus [Boehner]'s presence here to try and find out something about the aesthetics of St. Bonaventure, and also of Scotus, and maybe some day I can use that towards a Ph.D. dissertation in English or philosophy or whatever department at whatever university will consider such a topic . . .

My class burst into tears when I told them they were to have a textbook eight hundred pages thick (double columns), costing $4.00. I am using a thing called Snyder and Martin which is big and fat and has a good selection except it has no plays in it. I think it ought to be valuable.

I thought maybe I'd enclose a poem I wrote a couple of months ago, to see what you think of it. I hope the imagery isn't too baroque and surrealistic for you (I have found out that baroque and surrealistic have a lot in common—like Crashaw, for instance) but anyway here it is. The *Catholic World* wrote and said they were accepting an article of mine on A. Huxley ["Huxley's Pantheon"], but there's been no further sound out of them. I also guess I had better get busy and do some more reviews for those stuffy Sunday sections, too, not for money, not for glory: but in order to get some books and in order to keep this typewriter from rusting.

I hope all goes well with you, and that you are flourishing in Siena "sicut platanus plantatus secus decursus aquae" or whatever the line is. Now I can write no more, as a bunch of students are imitating Hitler's fierier speeches outside in the hall . . .

To Father Thomas Plassmann, O.F.M.

Father Thomas Plassmann (1879–1959), president of Saint Bonaventure University from 1920 to 1949, hired Merton to teach English there. He is mentioned in The Seven Storey Mountain *and, according to Michael Mott, was one of the men whom Merton most admired, "even venerated." When he wrote asking Merton to write a textbook on education, the following letter was Merton's reply.*

July 23, 1945

It was indeed a pleasure to get your letter, and to hear from St. Bonaventure where I spent such a happy and profitable year and a half—it seems long ago! About the book: it would, unfortunately, be completely impossible for me to do any work of the sort, as we have absolutely no facilities here. Our library is purely monastic; then, too, it would not quite be in harmony with our Rule. Our General Chapters encourage

works of a more or less spiritual nature, and histories of the Order, etc.—
and the poems I write are tolerated in so far as they are spiritual. But as
education is more or less out of our field, a textbook would be impossible.
However, I shall send you at once, under separate cover, the anthology
I once collected, and beg you to use it as you see fit. May I also suggest
what I think is a happy solution to your problem? Robert Lax, of Olean,
has been doing graduate work and teaching at the U. of North Carolina,
and I think he is just the man you want. You can send a letter to Olean
House and they will forward it. Bob was converted to the Faith a couple
of years ago. Please remember me at the Holy Sacrifice, dear Father,
and commend me to the prayers of all the good Fathers at St. Bona's. I
have you all, always, in mind in our prayers—at least virtually.

To Father Irenaeus Herscher, O.F.M.

*Father Irenaeus Herscher, O.F.M. (1902–80), who insisted on calling Thomas
Merton "Mr. Myrtle" in the pages of* The Seven Storey Mountain, *was librarian
at Saint Bonaventure University from 1937 to 1971. They kept in touch through
the years, with Merton frequently requesting books from the library, which Father
Irenaeus duly sent. Merton left notebooks, poems, journals, and other materials
at Saint Bonaventure when he departed in 1941. Father Irenaeus presided over
these materials and developed them, with later acquisitions, into a "Merton Collection," one which Merton always acknowledged had some significant items. He
visited Merton at Gethsemani in the summer of 1964. His reminiscence, "I In-
troduced Tom to Saint Therese," was included in "Thomas Merton: His Friends
Remember Him,"* St. Anthony Messenger *(December 1978).*

February 12, 1958

How are you? I hope you aren't all down with colds up there. Here
the infirmary is full and people with temperatures are sacking in almost
anywhere. The dormitories are a bit too cold for the sick! However I am
not just writing about the weather, I wonder if you would be able to do
me a favor. I have not forgotten your willingness to go out of your way
to help others.

You remember those manuscripts, the big volumes I left with you,
in longhand, with thick covers? They contain a journal I used to keep.
We are working on publication of part of this material, and I would very
much like to have the originals, as I want to add more material which is
only to be found in those volumes. You realize it is impossible for me to
come up to Bona's (much as I would enjoy doing so!), so I am writing to
ask if you would be kind enough to send the books down here? I have
no other way of getting at what I need. The copy we have been working
on here contains only a very small part of what is in those books.

If you see Bob Lax, tell him I got his most recent letters and am praying for his cousin who has cancer—and that I hope to write at Easter. How are all of you getting along at Bona's? Please remember me to all my old friends and ask them to pray for me and my novices . . .

May 4, 1958

Many thanks for the early history of St. Bona's (*The First Bonaventure Men*) which I was surprised and happy to receive. Also for the giant postcard which shows me for the first time how Bona's has grown since 1941. I was happy to see the new Seminary out where the old tank lots were—I used to walk around out there when it was a wilderness. It all looks very fine.

Thanks also for the photostats of my old Journal. I am returning them under separate cover. We have been able to use a little more material in the book [*The Secular Journal of Thomas Merton*] which will eventually appear, *Deo volente*. I would like to have a good look at the originals some time—in case we use any more, and I think we probably will. In any case, I may be wanting to borrow these again.

This brings me to one rather delicate point. Obviously, things written so long ago, and when I had so little wisdom, often call out loudly for a change here and there. Naturally, one must preserve the original as much as possible but there are some very glaring instances which I do not think either charity or justice would allow to stand. Unfortunately I can't take care of them now, but there is just one place where I think I must ask you to make deletions for me: I feel I have the right and duty to ask you this.

The passage concerned was written January 3rd, 1941. It is in the second paragraph on that page—marked off above and below by three x's. The passage concerns an important personage, now a Catholic. I would like you to render illegible part of the third line and the whole fourth line ("because she herself . . ." down to the end of the 4th line of the paragraph). And also most especially the last three words of the 8th line of this paragraph. To preserve the intelligibility, it would be best also to cut the two words before "by being . . ." and then the rest of the line.

I hope you don't mind my asking you this, and hope also that my request is intelligible in the terms in which I have put it. If there is any problem please send me back p. 53 of the photostat. The passage is evidently on p. 52 of the Journal.

I often think of all of you at St. Bona's and pray for you. I trust also that I am sharing in your own good prayers.

August 24, 1964

Well, it certainly was a pleasure to see you again, as young as ever after all these years. I enjoyed your brief visit very much. Thanks for coming.

You remember I spoke about something for *Cithara*. I would have sent the copy immediately, but it is still not completely ready. What I enclose ["From Pilgrimage to Crusade"] is just something for the editors to get a general idea of it. I am reworking the article somewhat, making corrections and additions, and adding footnotes. It was not originally written for a scholarly publication . . .

You probably have the *Antonianum* there: I wonder if there is a possibility of borrowing a volume or two on interlibrary loan. If there is, I will give Fr. Regis the exact references and all can be done in due form.

To Anthony L. Bannon

Anthony L. Bannon, editorial staff writer at Magnificat, wrote to Merton about a proposed article on his connection with Saint Bonaventure University. The resulting article was "Thomas Merton: A Growing Legend at St. Bonaventure," Magnificat 11 (March 1966), pp. 3–4.

February 12, 1966

First of all if you want material about me, there was an article in the Louisville *Courier-Journal* recently. If I can dig up a copy I will send it, but I know Fr. Irenaeus has several and could lend you one.

I will briefly say a few words about St. Bona's, of which I have the most pleasant memories. It was really a providential step along the road of my vocation. As you know, I first thought of being a Friar, but that did not work out because Fr. Edmund [J. Murphy], down in the provincial's office in N.Y. (he was the provincial's secretary at that time), thought I was still too new a convert and was not yet ready. I had had a rather wild life, certainly wilder than most of the holy postulants who were entering that year at Paterson. However I decided that I wanted to at least live with the Friars, in the atmosphere of a Franciscan college. St. Bonaventure was really ideal. I felt that I was in contact with the authentic simplicity, cordiality and charity of St. Francis. These Friars were good, warm friends. I felt they accepted me and I certainly liked them. I also liked the Sisters of the Immaculate Conception, also Franciscans, who worked in the kitchen and worried about my eating, and packed up box lunches for me when I went off to spend a day alone in the woods. The box lunches they gave me seemed to indicate that they thought I was not one man but a squad.

It was when I was teaching English at Bona's that I first began to write poetry that was half way respectable, and I wrote quite a lot. Living there in that quiet atmosphere, under the same roof with the Blessed Sacrament, I was able to cut out drinking and smoking and with my head clear I was discovering a lot of new things about life—namely, that it could be pretty good if you gave it half a chance.

I remember especially among the Friars Fr. Richard Leo [Heppler], O.F.M., who was teaching English along with me, Fr. Cornelius [Welch] who was my boss, and of course Fr. Tom Plassmann who was the President and a great good friend. Of course there was Fr. Philotheus [Boehner], the expert on Occam, who gave me some tutoring in the philosophy of St. Bonaventure along with one of the seminarians, now Msgr. Richard Fitzgerald of Erie. Fr. Philotheus was the one to whom I went for advice about entering the contemplative life. There were other Friars I knew well, like Fr. Joseph Vann whom I had met at Columbia, but who was at Siena when I was at Bona's. Fr. Juvenal [Lalor] I remember, and of course all those too numerous to mention whom I used to meet and talk with on campus. Of course last but not least was my old friend Fr. Irenaeus, who remains my link with Bona's, as we occasionally correspond about books and other such things. He still lends me books, I have one of them here now.

Naturally there were lots of lay professors and other eminent lay figures such as Griff on campus, whom I will never forget. The lay profs used to eat together and razz each other a lot: Ray Roth, Dick Engel (who was head of the ROTC at that time), Sunny Behm (is that how it was spelled?), and others who lived off campus like Jim Hayes. It was a great bunch and I enjoyed every minute of my time at St. Bona's. If I tried to recall all the students there would be no end, and I still remember a lot of the names.

To sum it all up, St. Bonaventure's represents one of the happiest periods in my life. It was a transition stage. God had something else planned for me, but it was a necessary stage. I will be forever grateful for the hospitality of the Friars, and will always feel that I am still in some secret way a son of St. Francis. There is no saint in the Church whom I admire more than St. Francis.

To John H. Slate

I am happy that the business of my literary testament
brought me back into contact with him.
MERTON TO MARY ELLEN (SAMS) SLATE,
SEPTEMBER 22, 1967

John H. Slate (1913–67) was one of Merton's classmates at Columbia. Though they had not corresponded, they had news of each other through mutual friends for nearly thirty years. Slate was an aviation lawyer and when Merton needed legal help in setting up his literary estate, he turned to his old classmate. Slate contributed several articles in the 1960s to Fortune, The Atlantic Monthly, *and* The Saturday Evening Post.

March 19, 1967

Sy Freedgood has just been here with me for a few days, and we both agreed that it would be a good idea for me to ask your advice in a legal matter. I have two friends [Naomi Burton Stone and James Laughlin] acting as my literary executors, and as yet we have not found a lawyer. I know they have someone in mind but I am not sure anything will come of it. I need a lawyer.

The legal situation as I understand it is this. Under a vow of poverty (recognized apparently by the civil courts in Kentucky) I have no right to any of the income from my writings and in fact this income always goes to the Abbey. It will continue to do so normally after my death. However I do retain proprietorship over my manuscripts, and as proprietor of these I have, with the full consent and approval of the Superior here, turned over these mss. to Bellarmine College, Louisville, where they have a special collection. As I understand it, the college becomes custodian of the mss. What we need now is a lawyer who will help me go about making an intelligent kind of will, and who will undertake to see that after my death the material I leave will not be used against my wishes either by the monastery or by the college or by anybody else. You understand the situation, at least in broad outline. I want to keep the way open for publication of unpublished material and for the study and use of mss. by scholars, free from any unjust limitation or exploitation by others. There may of course be some just limitations. What they are I do not exactly know.

In case my executors have not already found someone, I wonder if you would be willing to take on this job for us? The monastery will take care of the necessary fees and so on. I would like your reaction, and will communicate it to my executors. Naturally I would be delighted to have you on this, as it would provide occasions for you to come down. Sy and I had a very good visit.

Slate responded by telegram that he was "delighted and flattered" by Merton's proposal and planned to come see him as soon as possible.

March 24, 1967

Delighted to get your telegram this morning. Yes, come down as soon as you can. I will be tied up April 1st and 2nd but after that free at least for a week. That first week of April would be very good. Just let me know when you are coming and I will arrange accommodations. For pity's sake don't do like Sy [Freedgood], who hired a Hertz car and ran it into a tree, and sat around here looking exceedingly sinister with bandages all over his face. However the smart thing is to hire a car all right, and drive out the Kentucky turnpike. They'll show you. Just fasten the seat belt, that's all. If that doesn't work, let me know and I may be able to talk someone in Louisville to driving you out. Sy ended travelling in fleets of taxis. Don't emulate him in any respect whatever. I will be very glad to see you, and I will also be glad to make some sense out of my somewhat complicated literary estate.

[Enclosure. Memo concerning literary estate. T. Merton]

Some of the points to be considered are:

1 - Unpublished mss. or material which has been published in periodicals but not yet in book form.

2 - Originals of published work, and also copies of unpublished material held in various college or university library collections.*

3 - Confidential and personal material which should be preserved for possible publication, at some distant date.

4 - Other personal material which should not be published at all.

5 - Drawings, photographs, etc.

6 - Question of earnings from estate (to monastery).

7 - Question of future publication without undue hindrance on part of monastery or Order. Preventing material from destruction by any but author.

8 - Question of protecting material from misuse by well-meaning idiots.

9 - Guaranteeing reasonable use of material to bona fide scholars, etc.

Slate visited Merton at Gethsemani on April 5 and 6, 1967, losing his wallet during the visit. His wife, Mary Ellen, to whom Merton sent some drawings and calligraphies, later wrote: "John glowed with pleasure in his retelling of your reunion and was more than a little relieved to find that you had not, in fact, lifted his wallet."

April 7, 1967

That was a very fine visit. I look forward to your coming back again. Since we have a ladies' guest house you can bring your wife if you like. Though I suppose that would make it necessary for me to speak less colorfully. Anyway thanks for coming.

April 15, 1967

Thanks for yours of the 12th. I enclose a memo showing the sort of thing I want to do when it comes to making my own will regarding the literary estate. I don't know if this is any use. It could be much clearer, but I suppose it is enough to show what I am trying to get straight, partly . . .

Good: come with wife. Sy [Freedgood] coming with wife. All come with wives together and will have congress of wives (I will get myself one with lasso on highway). Come rather with or without Sy but we can plan on it anyhow. Naomi Burton [Stone] here in a few days. No time for any plurals at the moment. Got to run down to the gambling den.

* Collections are in: Bellarmine College Louisville, University of Kentucky, Columbia University, Boston College, Boston University; possession of Sr. Therese SDS, 3516 W. Center St., Milwaukee, she will probably pass it on to Georgetown; St Bonaventure University, and probably others.

[*Enclosure. Memo concerning my will and testament*]

1 - After discussion of the matter with Rt. Rev. Dom James Fox, my Abbot, assured that there is no objection on his part, I leave my literary executors Naomi Burton and James Laughlin the responsibility for my literary estate and for any future publication of my work, subject to the following specifications (It is understood that all income from such publications belongs to the Abbey of Gethsemani, Inc.)

2 - Any drafts of books existing in manuscript and not yet published may be published, with the exception of two books: *The Inner Experience* and *The School of the Spirit*. These are not to be published as books. Excerpts from them may, however, be published.

3 - Essays, poems, and other finished material whether published serially or not may be published in book form (or in magazines or in any other way).

4 - Notebooks and Journals or Diaries in holograph:

a) Journals and Personal Notes, or any notes marked "private" or "not for publication," are to be kept unpublished for at least twenty-five years after my death. These same Journals and personal notes are not to be made available to scholars or others until they have been used by the writer of an official biography or overall study of my work, approved by the literary executors. This biographer may have access to the Journal etc. material. He may quote any material from these Journals etc. in his biography or in other studies. The executors may also permit other scholars in special cases and for special approved studies to have access to this material after the publication of the "official" biography. Journal material that I have put on *tape* to be typed may be published any time.

b) Other confidential material, poems, notes etc. entrusted to J. Laughlin shall be treated as the above, except that their use by scholars in general during the twenty-five year period will be more severely restricted and quotation will only be allowed with great discretion.

c) Non-confidential notes, mimeographed or handwritten notes, reading notes, and other worksheets may be used by scholars in the various libraries according to the usual conditions.

5 - Letters:

a) A *selection* of letters may be printed at the discretion of the literary executors any time after my death (if not published before that).

b) Letters used in this selection may be available in ms. to scholars at any time. But letters *not* used in the selection shall not be available to scholars until after the publication of the official biography or study in 4a.

c) If a *collection* of letters is to be published, it may be published at the same time as the biography or after.

d) Before the final collection of letters, the literary executors may permit isolated letters or groups of letters to be published, even in book

form, if they judge opportune. In which case the mss. of the letters will
also become available to scholars.

6 - Other writings such as juvenilia or other unpublished early works,
or any other writings, may be published or republished at the discretion
of the literary executors. [An inventory of mss. and notebooks followed.]

To Mary Ellen Slate

April 28, 1967

Watch out for that ostrich road-runner type bird. He may look ju-
bilant but he can take any twenty cats and make hamburgers out of them.
But if he sees your handwriting certificate he may calm down. He is in
good company.

The other day a huge box of indigestible religious books started on
its way to Port Washington. I hope you can find a place for them which
will not ruin the scenery. The responsibility for this is John's. As for his
wallet, I thought I had those Kentucky pixies trained to hide the wallets
in behind the back seat. I looked there expecting to find it. How was I
to know they had concealed it under the driver's seat itself? I must go
out right now and rehearse with the pixies what to do about the next
wallet that comes this way in a Hertz car. Maybe they can just make off
with the entire car.

It is true that we allow girls to visit this monastery in a small palatial
all-girls motel which commands a view of our cemetery. You are most
welcome to come down with John any time and if you do it will probably
have a salutary effect upon the kind of language we use. I hope so.

To John H. Slate

May 30, 1967

Records arrived safely, promptly, everything fine. Just the sort of
thing I was looking for. Many thanks. I was just worried that the gnomes
might have got at them.

Naomi Burton was here, I guess I told you about that. She hides in
Maine and is not so easy to see. [James] Laughlin is always off on skis
someplace. It is probably one of the hardest things in biz to get those
two together at lunch.

I have partly recovered from social life due to Dan [Walsh]'s ordination and am once again in a state of unruffled stoicism. Meanwhile,
though you are indeed busy, you are perhaps unaware that this is a purely
temporary condition as all law is about to be abolished by Johnny Montini
and you will find yourself with plenty of time to visit here with your wife.
Be prepared . . .

June 6, 1967

J. Laughlin mentioned in a letter you were thinking perhaps of flying to Rome some day to straighten out things about the estate. That might be a good idea if you see the right people. Perhaps the best person to see would be Archbishop Paul Philippe, basically a good guy and a friend of mine, who is also the head of the Congregation of Religious and my highest superior under the Pope. It would be very important to know him and to have his confidence. French, speaks good English, knows me and this monastery well. Very well disposed towards my work etc. However it would probably be better if we talked about it. Perhaps. I can look up his exact address if you are interested. Or you can find it in the first pages of the Catholic Directory, the ones on the Roman Curia (Congregation of Religious).

This Israel–Arab war sounds very nasty indeed. Things feel like 1939. Hope I am wrong. [Bob] Lax is in Patmos. Should he get out of there? Patmos, Greece, will reach him. Let me know if something specially dramatic happens—I may or may not hear things here. Maybe first thing I will know—I will be going up in a radioactive cloud all mixed up with the Gold of Fort Knox and the fissionable materials treasured there.

Slate died on September 19, 1967, his fifty-fourth birthday, of a heart attack. Merton wrote to his widow three days later.

To Mary Ellen Slate

September 22, 1967

I was shocked and saddened to hear of John's death today when my publisher sent the clipping from the *Times*. Still, I knew John had a bad heart. And with Ad Reinhardt's death just a week or two ago, I had been thinking how all of us are pretty much on the toboggan slide. But certainly John is a great personal loss to me. I am happy that the business of my literary testament brought me back into contact with him recently, and especially happy that I was able to see him again, after so many years, this spring. We certainly had a fine time when he was here, and I shall treasure my final memory of him talking Welsh and reciting Mary Baker Eddy to a group of entranced Franciscans.

Be assured of my deep sympathy in your loss. I share your sorrow. I cabled Bob Lax in Greece today, in case he had not heard the news. I shall offer Mass for John on Sunday and Monday. May he be where peace is. If there is anything I can do for you, do not hesitate to ask. I had hoped John might bring you down and we could meet some day.

To Daniel Clark Walsh

I have no relatives and so close friends count as family.
THOMAS MERTON TO WALSH
FEBRUARY 24, 1949

Daniel Clark Walsh (1907–75) had been Merton's teacher at Columbia University and was the person who first told him of the Abbey of Gethsemani. Merton paid tribute to him in The Seven Storey Mountain. *Walsh followed Merton to Kentucky, teaching at Gethsemani itself and at Bellarmine College in his later years; he was ordained a priest in 1967. On the occasion when Father Terence Connolly, S.J., director of libraries at Boston College, mounted a Merton exhibition in 1949 to showcase the "crown jewel" of their projected Merton Collection—one of the three manuscript copies of* The Seven Storey Mountain—*Dan Walsh lectured on "The Impact of Catholic Thought on Modern Life and Letters." The following letter concerns the exhibition and Walsh's lecture.*

F. of St. Mathias
[February 24, 1949]

Many thanks for your beautiful letter. I am sorry this Boston College exhibition has grown to such proportions as to include such things as speeches, and I apologize for the fact that you have to be disturbed, on top of all the embarrassment I caused you by the book [*The Seven Storey Mountain*]. I know I must have caused you some. I did not know the thing would become the public nuisance that it has. However, I hope Our Lord will use it more and more for His purposes. I don't have to hope: I know He will, and is doing so now.

Jacques Maritain wrote me a beautiful letter about it. And all sorts of people I never heard of have written in, saying that the book makes them want to love God more. This is tremendously inspiring to me. I suppose our Lord wanted me to have this sensible and tangible consolation which He usually denies to members of our Order who are strong enough to walk in darkness. However, it does not make me more sanguine about writing, although I can see that for the time being it seems to be my vocation. I certainly enjoy the work, from a natural point of view: but that is what I am afraid of.

It was good to hear from you again. Today I think of Fr. Mathias Faust; I hear he is in Rome. I have many happy memories of St. Bonas and my Franciscan contacts. Occasionally I get something like a Christmas card from Father Edmund [J. Murphy]. Preparing for the diaconate (March 19th—don't forget to pray!) I meditate on Father Thomas Plassmann's "Priest's Way to God." He sent me a copy and I like it.

Needless to say I owe you much more than I can ever pay by a mention in an ungrammatical book. You are another proof of the fact that when a man simply loves God's Truth Our Lord will use him to draw souls to Him without any special effort, or the pushing and pulling and straining which makes the apostolate sometimes more of a scarecrow than an attraction. Talking about the active apostolate: the *Thomist* got after me for something I said. I felt it was rather flattering, on the whole, for a third year theology student to be refuted by one of the foremost magazines in the country. They got me on a technicality—it concerns the material included in pp. 414 to 419 of the *Mountain*. It seems to me that what I was trying to say was obvious enough: first that no matter what state of life you belong to, one can and should lead a life of close union with God, and even be something of a contemplative, and share the fruits of that contemplation one way or another. And I also wanted to say that it seemed to me that since the preaching Orders were engaged in "active works that by their nature flow from the fulness of contemplation" that they were also committed, *ipso facto*, to contemplation, *Nemo dat quod non habet*. I find the same thing stated much more strongly than I made it in Joret's *Dominican Life* (pp. 82, 83). I mention this so that you can tell anyone where to get off if they say I am a heretic.

I do hope you will come down some time. If you tell Father Abbot who you are I am sure he will let us have a chat. I have no relatives and so close friends count as family—especially where there is some claim to spiritual parentage, and after all you told me where Gethsemani was!

God bless you, Dan. I hope the talk will go off well, and thank you for accepting the chore. Our dear Lord will bring good out of it, although I don't have much faith in shows and exhibitions. But don't let Fr. Connolly know that. He has been very nice and kind and I know his motives are supernatural and holy and that he is doing it all for the love of God.

So let us keep praying for one another. The priesthood is getting pretty close, now. What a wonderful gift. Of all ages in which to be a priest, I cannot think of a better one than this! But pray that I may always be faithful, no matter what may come: *sufficientia nostra ex Deo est.*

August 29, 1951
. . . I do not know if you spoke to Father Abbot about the letter concerning our sponsorship of the ms. about Cardinal Mindszenty from Hungary. He seemed to me very cool toward the project, however, and did not seem to want to take it up at all, so it seems to be out of the question for us. Are you writing to those concerned? If not I can get one of Fr. Abbot's secretaries to handle it. It is a general policy of Fr. Abbot to keep me away from such projects—he wants my name to appear as little as possible in connection with other people's books—in blurbs, prefaces, etc. I think this is a very good idea, even though the cause may itself be excellent. It seems to me that I ought to stay as much as possible out of the main current of public life—or any current at all. That a Trappist should launch and introduce new books and new ideas—other than his

own writing, which is already bad enough—seems to be quite against the monastic spirit.

Bob Giroux is off to England, but says he wants to see you before he leaves. If you sound out Mrs. [Anne] Skakel on the project of mimeographing our class notes, tell her of course she can keep the originals if she is interested in them. I have heard that she might be. In that case I would not feel that I was imposing too much on her kindness, since I could at least make some gesture of remuneration although it is a pretty poor gesture.

It was wonderful to have you here, Dan. I hope you will come again soon when we will have more time to talk. By the way it looks as though a new development will help me to get some of the solitude I seem to need so much. I am being trained as a timber-marker—that is to say, I will have a job out in the woods alone marking trees to be cut this winter. It will not take up much time unfortunately! Perhaps Father Abbot will see fit to give me more such forestry work: I certainly love it! However that is no guarantee that it is the best job in the world for me and I take it with detachment . . .

November 1, 1960

I thought you would want to see this heartbreaking letter from Jacques Maritain. Maybe by now Raissa is among the saints. I shall write to him soon & will be able to say Mass for both of them. I'll remember you in it also & in all other Masses these days.

On November 10, 1963, Dan Walsh helped to inaugurate a second Merton Collection, the one at Bellarmine College in Louisville, Kentucky, which Merton eventually named as the repository for his literary estate. At the ceremony formally opening the Merton Room, Walsh read a statement by Merton, "Concerning the Collection in the Bellarmine College Library."

[November 1963]

A long time ago Rev. Fr. [James Fox] approved Gabriel Marcel coming here, at least in a general way. You can go ahead on the basis of that, and I will speak to him further about it tomorrow.

About the "Collection": anytime that Rev. Fr. gets the sense that there is an exuberant activity going on in connection with it, he is going to feel mad, frustrated, and gloomy. I would suggest that the information sent here be kept to what is really necessary. I think the clause about "national publicity" in the last memo from Fr. John [Loftus] will have made him squirm, and the less squirming he does the better off we will all be. I think the people at Bellarmine should send me *no* routine information (which you can tell me anyway if necessary). Rev. Fr. should get of course all that he is entitled to, but I would suggest restraint in accidentals. One idea that I got, seriously: do you think Bellarmine could offer *him*, Rev. Father, an honorary degree? That might "cement the relationships" and calm some of his anxieties about all this kind of thing. Or am I wrong? If you think the suggestion has some validity, you can act on it.

October 5, 1967

I enjoyed the visit yesterday, and I will be glad to see [you and your friend] next Tuesday. However, in order not to waste the afternoon waiting around, I think we ought to set up a more or less exact time beforehand. Then I can plan accordingly. For me, perhaps the best time would be around two or two-thirty (as I assume she would not be over much earlier than that anyway). But at any time convenient to her before 4, provided you let me know ahead. If you can find out and drop me a note, I'd appreciate it.

While I'm on the subject of visits, conferences, etc. that came up yesterday, I think I'll put down a few thoughts about where I stand. It is quite true that I think Dom J[ames Fox]'s attitude is totally unreasonable. On the other hand, it could easily happen that with a change of situation the opposite problem might arise, and with the removal of barriers I might get involved in much more than I want. I certainly do not want to have things interfere with my other work, and even this year, with the few visits I have had and with the necessity of going to the doctor, etc. my writing has suffered and I have not been able to work on a book as I had hoped.

So, to define comfortable limits: I'd be perfectly willing to devote four afternoons a year to the Bishop's conferences, and perhaps one or two others to the kind referred to yesterday. That would be a maximum of half a dozen a year involving people from Louisville. Obviously it is important to set limits for Louisville, because it is near and one could get swamped. I would then be able to leave a little time for other people, and still be able to get my work done. In any case I don't want to get involved in visits or conferences etc. to the extent of more than two or three afternoons a month, and that includes everything. So in spite of my disagreement with Dom James on the bishop's conferences, I don't want to get mixed up in a whole lot of picnics, visits, meetings and seminars. Only a few exceptional ones. And also I think it would be much better NOT to have any at the hermitage.

I am putting this down because now is the psychological moment, and it is well to have a clear limit in mind. Then I can be protected against my own inclination to say yes in unguarded moments when I don't really want to commit myself. I have got beyond the stage where I think these conferences can really fit into my life: if it had been ten years ago I might have undertaken more, but now I am used to solitude and have a great deal of work of my own that is not getting done, so that when I do have to get mixed up in several days of visits, it is a real disruption. So let's go easy.

V.

To & About Young People

What wonderful children there are around, and most of
them children of my friends!
MERTON TO RAY LIVINGSTON
DECEMBER 11, 1962

To Suzanne Butorovich

Suzanne Butorovich, a sixteen-and-a-half-year-old high-school student from
Campbell, California, wrote to Merton on June 15, 1967, asking him for a con-
tribution for her school's "underground" newspaper, the Clique Courier, *offering*
to "educate" him in pop music, and telling him generally about her life and
concerns. She signed herself "The Nut" or "Disaster" and, taking her cue from
Merton, occasionally addressed him as the "Hippie Hermit." This exchange be-
came Merton's fullest one with a young person and it lasted until just before he
left for Asia in 1968.

June 22, 1967

I don't know if your letter was a disaster: but anyway, if it was, it
was a nice disaster. I suppose I'll begin at the end and work back. I like
underground movements and publications, they are irresistible. So I send
you a piece of my new book, coming out next Spring I think ["Prayer to
the Computer," from *Cables to the Ace*]. It is a mosaic of prose and
poetry, experimental, and pieces of it are being published in U.S., England and Mexico in literary magazines. So now maybe it will fit in to
your underground paper, too. Take what you want: don't take all of this
selection unless you like it all. Maybe you won't like any, but if you listen
to it right you probably will. It is a bit Dylan-like in spots because I love
Bobby D. I have lots of his stuff here and what do you think I am: six
hundred years old or something, that I don't know Paul McCartney is a

Beatle? I have their record of "Revolver"—only one I have. I like them fine.

Go on then educate me in pop music. I don't know much about pop music. I am a confirmed jazzman, but I need to know more about pop also. Like some of those outfits you have out there that I hear such a lot about—Grateful Dead and all those—tell me about them and send me your number on the Monterey thing. I am glad you got a pass you sound very enterprising. And anyway who wouldn't give a pass for that Egyptian nun, I think it is beautiful. Here is a stamp one kid made for me here a few years ago (Fr. Louis is supposed to be my name around here but how many names do you need anyway?)

What kind of pop music do I like? I haven't heard much but on one of the latest Dylan records I like "Obviously Five Believers" for instance (that's in the album "blonde on bl."). That strikes me as inspired, shamanic, and everything. On the Beatles record I like "Taxman" and all the rest too.

Look, it is no use sending letters here certified mail. This post office cheats so bad all the brothers who run it ought to be doing life sentences in the federal pen. The return slip is always signed by anyone who happens to be around and is no indication whatever that the letter reached the right person. May never get it. Twenty-five people are likely to read it on the way through and one of them may just throw it away. This one got through. If you are really anxious to get through and afraid you might not, mark it *conscience matter* and make it look like you are just entering the convent or leaving it or something. (Don't worry about that part, but you know what I mean.)

You are right, you probably don't have to take LSD, you sound real alive without it. I look forward to seeing *Clique C[ourier]*. Keep in touch. I live alone in the woods and borrowed a record player. I am a real sneaky hermit and oh yes I love the hippies and am an underground hippy monk but I don't need LSD to turn on either. The birds turn me on.

July 18, 1967

I refuse to call anybody Susie. (I met a girl in a bar in London who was called Boosie Susie thirty years ago.) As to where Campbell is, you're telling me it is South of Alviso and that is a real big help. Later on however you let the cat out of the bag when you say San Jose Light Opera etc. but I am pretty hazy about San Jose too. Anyway it's in California. Once someone I knew went to California and the following conversation took place between me and the guy who sold papers on our corner.

Me: X went to California.

Him: Yeah? What street?

Honest. I wouldn't lie to you.

I have got a tape recorder but it is so super splendid that it is no good as a means of communication with the rest of the world, because it is stereo and does things on two tracks at the same time and maybe fights other tapes it can't chew right. I don't know. You can always try sending a tape if you want to risk it and I'll see what happens. But it would be better just to send me the titles of the things I really ought to hear. Thanks for the good lyrics from "Sergt. Pepper." I have a secret agent who is going to sneak me the record one of these days then I will hear it all and concentrate on everything.

Yes I know about Gibran. I read a small book of his and liked it—some short meditation things. Tolkien too I know, I read an article about him called "Kicking the Hobbit." O. Henry I read one time when I was stashed away in a strange hotel in Rhode Island over a Labor Day weekend and was distracted by the pixies running up and down the hall. And can you believe it, John Lennon I have never read but I will promote Lennonism if I have to overturn the Vatican to do it. No, I really like the Beatles and their ideas and their ways of doing and saying things. I think they are absolutely all right and make sense and that people who can't figure them out might as well run into the sea and vanish like Lemmings.

Suzuki books: one of the best to start with is a big fancy book called *Zen and Japanese Culture*, and it ought to be easier to get hold of than some of the others. Then there was a selection of his stuff in Anchor Books (paperback) series but I forget what it was called. Maybe just *Zen*. Anything of his you can get, try it out. *Zen and Psychoanalysis* is real good. Another good Zen book is Paul Reps, *Zen Flesh, Zen Bones*.

If I had to rewrite *Seven Storey Mtn.* I'd cut out a lot of the sermons I guess, including the sales pitch for Catholic schools and that. Yes, you can certainly use the Prayer to the Computer.

You mention that they want to shake you down already twenty-five dollars to be in an Underground Press Syndicate. I do not understand this. The Underground is where there is no organization, no status, and consequently no dues. What is the use of being in the Underground if you have to start all over again with status, organization and dues? And will somebody then start telling you what to do and what not to do? The Underground is where you tell everybody else to go jump in the lake and—if you can—charge them twenty-five dollars for doing it. But honestly, it is better to keep the smell of freedom, don't lose the scent or you're lost. Twenty-five dollars smells bad to me.

I understand about Ravi Shankar because I like Indian music (anyway he is on a Beatle record playing that thing, no?). There is some real groovy Indian music with a great beat and everything, some of the traditional stuff, some crazy song about one of the gods getting disguised as a parrot and then escaping and the whole town is out trying to catch this parrot: a wild song, very happy, a whole lot smarter than the God is dead movement.

I'm glad your grandmother fell in love with the tabla player. Our generation doesn't give up easy. As I interpret it, the bit about Ravi

Shankar treating all the reporters from Datebook as impartially as a farmer treats his livestock is pleasant irony. They mill around him like animals and he is cool because he is the farmer. They xist [*sic*] for him and not he for them and they can't fix it so it is the other way round. Yes?

I said Mass for your friend Monday. Here is more reading matter. I forget if I sent you the one about the lepers ["Rites for the Extrusion of a Leper"]. Thanks for the beautiful engraving in red on p. 2 [Suzanne had kissed the page, leaving a red lip mark]. I don't know what to do about that one. Maybe I could give you a footprint of my head.

Lots of love. I look forward with confident joy to the next number of *CC*. How do I come to be called Tob? Does your typewriter have a cold?

Suzanne wrote to Merton on August 28, 1967, telling him of and lamenting the death of Beatles' discoverer and manager Brian Epstein on August 27, 1967.

August 31, 1967

The certified letter came today and by the time you get this you will have got back the little pink card showing the letter was not eaten by weasels. I am terribly sorry to hear about Brian Epstein. I'll say mass for him Sept. 5th. Did I ever tell you that once on a radio program he was asked to name his favorite book and named the *Seven Storey Mtn.*, only with its English title, *Elected Silence*? I always felt closer to him after that—glad, of course, that he brought out the Beatles. Glad they are working on their meditation.

I got the other things too, didn't answer because I wasn't sure when you were going back home. The letter from Biloxi was v. funny. I like all your letters. By the way I'd send the address of *New Left Notes* but I don't have it around. Sooner or later I'll see another copy and then I'll let you know. Here's one from an underground paper in Santa Barbara [*Unicorn Journal*]—and one from a paper in England I write for [*Peace News*].

Also I turned that footprint into a poem and if I can find it I'll enclose it ["Why I Have a Wet Footprint on Top of My Mind"]. I'm happy to hear you have someone to run off *CC*, because if your life is ruled by *CC* and no one can print it, what will happen to you? I was thinking of bullying the people at *Ramparts* into printing it for you in the cellar or something.

Everybody who comes back from Cal. says the hippies make them cry. That's bad. I guess they mean not the real hippies who are sitting in their rooms having visions, but the kids wandering around in the streets barefoot or something at the mercy of every drool with a polaroid camera.

I was sick with flu and it was nice being all alone and making tea and lying around and doing without society, though for one day it was a bit unpleasant. If I ever got really sick I could always go down to the monastery and crawl into the infirmary, but I'd rather be just up here until I got so sick I had to go to a hospital. When I am in a hospital I hate it so much that I get well fast just in order to get out.

If you make a tape, and I hope you will, the only problem I know of is that it is supposed to be quarter-track and not half-track, but you don't have to record all the tracks. I have a Sony stereo and I am making tapes like mad for contemplative nuns: "Sister, are you in a TRAP?" and things like that. Really shattering for the girls.

Now I have to go and cook my kasha (know what that is? If you are ever broke and need food that goes a long way, that's it).

October 7, 1967

I am thinking about you: are your ears burning? My house in the woods, all full of San Francisco sound in the middle of night. Some former retreatant sent the guestmaster a tape of all kinds rock and he passed it on to me. Sounds very nice. Had a good supper of some kind of noodle and chicken deal you get in the supermarket (kind benefactor brought). Life is very content.

The sound I like so far is Jefferson Airplane and Country Joefish but not so much Moby Grape. Haven't got to Grateful Dead, yet they are coming up about fifty feet down the line.

Real happy got a magazine of Zens from Japan and they all say I am America's number one Zen. This is very nice for the Japanese Zen to say about home town boy make good.

Well here's Grateful Dead: Golden Road to unlimited devotion. Pretty good. Very appropriate for the religious life. And the beat is good for the hermit life, which is more to the point.

Maybe I won't be able to get you into the cellars of *Ramparts* because the guy I used to know who used to own it has sold it. But there is a nun writing to me from SF and she talks like she likes poets. Want to know some more nuns?

I have just fixed up for publication a novel I wrote a long time ago about how I escape from the Nazis [*Journal of My Escape from the Nazis*, published as *My Argument with the Gestapo*]. I don't know if it would be good for a Beatle picture. It is mostly in an invented language. The Grateful D's are going great with a thing I like plenty called "Cold Rain and Snow" I guess. This is my kind of sound.

Hey here is a group in Austin Texas called the 13th Floor Elevators. I like this a lot. Do you know them??? They are the best thing yet on this tape.

My book *Cables* is now called *Cables to the Ace* and is on the way to the prints. Will send you one. When is *Clique C.* coming out? It rules your life: better rule *it*.

The 13th Floor Elevators are sure yelling fine right now. They got this real freaky psychedelic sound. Or maybe that is what it is, since I don't take LSD these days. I hear Timothy Leary got 30 yrs. in jail. I think that is a horrible example of legal overkill. Very sorry for the poor guy. I quit now.

December 9, 1967

Sorry for the long delay. I've been very busy. Just had a wonderful time with fifteen cloistered nuns who came here for a sort of retreat and conference deal to study "problems." As they don't generally get out, still less to a place like this, they were all very keyed up and alive and it was a groovy experience: they are smart, too.

Anyway, I wanted to say something about you going to England. I think it is a great idea. You should do everything you can to get there. Only the competition is probably rough. English secondary schools are tougher than ours, and I don't know any way of getting around the matriculation exam except by passing something already harder that they will accept. For instance, I got out of matric. because I had passed Higher Certificate which is already on the college level, and also I got a scholarship and the scholarship exam is much tougher. Unless they have some new kind of exchange system I wouldn't know about, you probably have to face matric. and you might have a tough time with it, but you can get hold of previous exam papers to get an idea what it is like. Where would you go? Lot of new good universities there.

The nuns who were here want me to do a tape on Zen too, but I don't know whether it is possible really to put Zen on tape. I'll think about it. Maybe . . . Thanks for all the peanuts, but I still haven't figured out whether they burned the blanket or only half burned it. If they burned it, I revolt. Now I have to write five million other letters, so bye for now. Have a good Christmas.

February 11, 1968

What did you think? That I thought the Crimble Box was a bomb and jumped in the lake with it? Not at all. I liked it very much and became the largest collector of Beatle relics in Kentucky. Though I don't think that will remain as permanent. What I do have on display is your 1st communion picture, up on the mantelpiece. You look very angelic. Probably have ceased to do so, but anyway, I love it. So many thanks to you and Linda [Macmillan, Suzanne's "little sister"]. I shook out all the papers and got everything I think. Maybe the pictures of the Beatles on TV are the ultimate truth of Zen.

I have been under a tidal wave of mail and also got that flu again, and this time it was an awful drag. Lot of other crazy things too, so I haven't been answering letters that much. I tell you what maybe I'll do is send you a mimeo of a novel I wrote before I entered the monastery. It is called *Journal of My Escape from the Nazis* and maybe you'd like it. Except the girl who typed it for me got the chapters in the wrong order. But maybe I'll be able to figure out how they originally were (original ms. all scrambled up too). Maybe a publisher will take it, but there is a lot of experimental stuff they won't understand. I don't know.

How to cook Kasha: you mix it with an egg, and make a kind of mush. Then you dilute the mush with salt water and cook it in a deep frying pan or saucepan with butter or oil for about fifteen minutes over low heat. Comes out very filling. With one helping you feel like you are full of cement and don't get hungry for a long time. It is what they eat in Russian prison camps. But probably without the egg and with a whole lot more salt water. Anyway it is all on the box. I must go and answer a bunch of guys who are leaving monasteries in all directions. I tell them "Go, buster, go."

June 4, 1968

Don't mind the letterhead, this is just the secret headquarters of my drug pushing outfit (aspirins, etc.) ["Community Council of San Mateo County / Action Study on Community Health Services"].

I was very happy to get your graduation picture. You have grown into a very charming and interesting young woman. Congratulations on the graduation, I was remembering you on Saturday, at Mass etc. Go forth into the wide world and help it, make some kind of sense. Or anyway less nonsense. Graduation present: 2nd issue of *Monks Pond*. Hope you like it. How about getting together some of the stuff your underground paper never put out and sending it to me? I might be able to use some.

To Sister Marialein Lorenz, O.P.

Sister Marialein Lorenz, a Sinsinawa Dominican, taught in Mobile, Alabama, and later in Anaconda, Montana. While teaching at an all-black high school, Heart of Mary, in Mobile in the late 1940s and early 1950s, she had her students write to Merton. They sent Merton an amice and other gifts at the time of his ordination in May 1949.

April, 1949

Thanks for your fine letter—I read it *all* and it made me very happy, especially all you said about the kids in your school down there. Don't worry! I'm writing or trying to. A million things get in the way. Keep it a secret, but I'm to be ordained priest on Ascension Day. Ask all the kids to pray for me & I'll remember them in my first Mass—& after that too. We've got 4 fine colored novices here, one a priest.

May 27, 1949

I used the amice, corporal, purificator & finger towel at Mass (1st) today— Prayed for you all. An Encyclical will follow when I get time to breathe!

June, 1949

I hope this letter isn't too late to reach all the kids. I didn't have a moment before now. Really I loved all their letters and hope God will bless them all and you too, for your generous heart. I remember you and all the Sisters at Mass & send you all my first Blessing—God love you & keep you—& keep praying for me.

To Sister Marialein Lorenz's Class

June 2, 1949

I can see where I owe you people a letter. You have written me letters and Sister Marialein sent the essays you wrote about the Trappists, and then you got together and sent me the ordination present. All these things were swell and you ought to know that I really appreciate them. I have not been able to write to you before now because I was on retreat for ordination; then I had some friends here for a couple of days (which is a very rare thing in the life of a Trappist). After that we had our centenary celebration which kept us all very busy. This is my first chance to write to you.

Your ordination present was fine. When I said my first Mass last Friday May 27th I was wearing the amice you sent, and used the corporal and purificator and the finger towel. I guess you will be happy to know that there was another present along with yours: one of my friends, Dan Walsh, brought a chalice which was consecrated by Cardinal Spellman. You can be sure I prayed for you in that first Mass and have not forgotten you since, either.

One of the main reasons why I am glad to hear from young fellows and girls is that you have all the same problems that I once had and I think that God has shown us all the same way out of it. That is why the will of God has worked around to this writing job for me.

You know, God is a consuming fire. The Holy Ghost gets into your heart and burns you clean and makes you strong. Christ said: "I have overcome the world." He overcomes the world in the souls of each one of us by filling us with faith and with love, and giving us the strength to resist all the appeals of what is below us and unworthy of men made in the image of God.

It is terribly hard for people to find happiness in our time. Everything is mixed up. All the wrong ideas and all the wrong values are on top. Everywhere you go you find the papers and the movies and the radios telling you that happiness consists in stuffing yourself with food and drink, and dancing and making love. All these things are good and necessary, but they are not the whole reason for existing. They are given us as means to an end. The way to be happy is not to love these things for their own sakes, but to use them wisely for the glory of God. And you have to be awfully careful how you use them, because if you use them wrong they will ruin your life and make happiness impossible.

Some medicines are made out of poison. If you put just a little bit of poison in the medicine, it will help to cure a sickness. But if you take too much, it will kill you. That is the way it is with pleasure. Pleasure is like arsenic in a medicine. Just a little bit of it, just the right amount of it will do you a world of good: but if you get an overdose of it it is likely to kill you. And it takes the grace of God, the inspiration of the Holy Ghost in our hearts to really show us what is the right amount of pleasure in created things, and how to use the good things of the world to give glory to God. The only way to really learn all this is by sacrifice and self denial.

Things would be simple if there was plenty of food for everyone and plenty of pleasure for everyone, and all you had to do was be wise, and choose what is good and reject what is bad.

But what makes things so bad is that some people get too much of everything and other people never get enough. Some men have all the food they want, and they eat so much that they get sick and can't have any fun out of anything. Others never get even the food they ought to have for nourishment, and they have to spend their lives worrying where the next meal is coming from. They can't get jobs. They have families, maybe, and they see their children getting thin and sick and they don't know what to do about it. They can't go to the doctor because they haven't any money and they are always worried sick. Their life becomes a hell on earth. Finally they get disgusted, and they will do anything just to forget.

Life in the world is terribly unhappy for many people. They cannot see the way out. They do not know that Christ has overcome the world.

The evil that is in the world is the punishment of the sins and passions of men who have lived easy and luxurious and sinful lives and have taught everybody else to believe that everything consists in having pleasure and satisfying all their passions. They have made people forget that happiness is something that is found *inside* you. Happiness does not come in a bottle or a can. You won't get it out of the radio, because it doesn't come over the air. Happiness comes out of the depth of your soul, and it springs from the union of your soul with God.

God is Life. God is Love. When we can get in contact with Him and when our souls wake up to the presence of the Living God and feel the touch of His fire striking at the roots of our hearts, then we begin to know what happiness really is.

This happiness is not reserved for the monastery or the convent. It also belongs to people in the world, people who have dedicated them-selves to God in work and in family life. Married people can worship God and find God in their love for one another and their children, if they live according to God's will, because God will bless them and make Himself known to them.

You have the privilege of a good Catholic education. You ought to pray to God and beg Christ with tears to send the Holy Ghost into your hearts and burn you up with the tremendous love of God that changes and purifies the world. If God takes possession of your hearts you can become great saints. You can do wonderful things for the world, and you can bring hope and happiness to the people around you in Mobile. Ask God to teach you how to do this. Ask Him to show you what work He wants you to do. Maybe he will inspire you to a new kind of Catholic action that has never been attempted before.

I believe sometimes that God is sick of the rich people and the powerful and wise men of the world and that He is going to look elsewhere and find the underprivileged, those who are poor and have things very hard, even those who find it most difficult to avoid sin: and God is going to come down and walk among the poor people of the earth, among those who are unhappy and sinful and distressed, and raise them up and make them the greatest saints and send them walking all over the universe with the steps of angels and the voices of prophets to bring His light back into the world again. I believe Our Blessed Lady will someday come down and start giving her messages and consolations to people here in America. You know a Chinese monk of our Order came here and told us that Our Lady is appearing everywhere in Red China, just where everything seems to be hopeless, and she is lifting up the poor and the oppressed and those who have been beaten down by the Communists, and she is giving them strength.

Anyway, you pray that all this may come about and I will join my prayers to yours. You can count on me. I am your priest now. My Mass is your Mass and all the infinite treasures and power of the Blood of Christ will be poured out among you and I think we will all begin to go places . . .

To Richard M. Loomis

Richard M. ["Dick"] Loomis had been a monk of Gethsemani under the name "Cuthbert." He narrated the Columbia Records album of Gregorian Chant, "Laudate Dominum," for which Merton wrote the program notes. He now teaches English at Nazareth College in Rochester, New York.

January 4, 1958
. . . The novitiate is all right. Five priests and several older novices, so it does, indeed, go along quietly and relatively sensibly. Occasional flareups of madness, which are always healthy. The usual business nowadays of novices felling trees and bringing them down on one another's heads in the woods, or knocking each other out in the woodshed. My life is a series of continual political intrigues by which I hope, seldom successfully, to get the Jeep for the afternoon work. In the Christmas tree

season, Fr. John of the Cross [Wasserman] and I and two novices and a brother got a truckload of Christmas trees which we decided to take to the nuns at the Bardstown hospital, assuming we had plenty of time, "it is only two-thirty." Returned after dark, laden down with doughnuts and ecclesiastical censures (but no, the nuns had called up meanwhile and told Fr. Prior sweetly that we would be home a little late). Fr. John of the Cross just happened by "chance" to be in the group because he is no longer undermaster, has been Master of Scholastics since last January. My present undermaster is Fr. Tarcisius [Conner], ordained last June, most quiet and holy, a constant consolation.

I am glad to hear of all the additions to the family. May God bless you and them, He knows that family life is not expected to be restful. I will help you with prayers rather than advice, though my psychology book tells me that children are not supposed to be spanked. Real small children have become for me something remote and mysterious which I tend to idealize. The smallest that come my way are a couple of fifteen year olds from Detroit who take their vacations in the novitiate and are very lively. I like to have them around, one does feel more like a father going out to work with one trotting at each side of you and both talking their heads off, while the silent line of novices trails off behind. They scandalize all by an intense interest in wildlife and professional football and no obvious signs whatever of piety. Good solid prospects! They really are very good kids my only moments of annoyance with them are when they insist on shooting tin cans with a twenty-two within earshot of the novitiate. This I cannot brook. They have renounced the twenty-two (I fondly delude myself) after one shamefaced expedition for tin-can shooting at the lake. The rabbits are not hard put to it to avoid such talkative huntsmen.

I still think you and Mary ought to come down for a visit but I know how much easier it is to talk about such trips than to make them. Bring of course the whole family, they can join in the choral singing with improvisations in the tribune. You would see a lot of strange new things around the place.

To Joseph Tjo Tchel-oung

Daniel Bouchez, a professor at Holy Ghost College, a seminary in Seoul, Korea, wrote to tell Merton of the publication of the Korean translation of Seeds of Contemplation *(Myung Sand Eui Ssee). The translation had been done by Joseph Tjo Tchel-oung (also romanized as Jo Chuloong), a seminarian at Holy Ghost.*

April 28, 1961

It is with great satisfaction that I have heard of your translation into Korean of my book *Seeds of Contemplation*. I thank you for the honor that you have thus done to the unworthy author of the book, and I hope that God in His mercy will take this occasion to open the hearts of a people naturally predisposed to contemplation, and fill them with the light of His presence.

It has been my lot, as a writer, to produce several books: among these I value only the few that are worthy of being translated into an Oriental language. This seems to be especially true of the present volume, which is the first of my books to be translated entirely into Chinese and partly into Japanese. This being the case, I can regard the book as a kind of repayment, on my part, of my great debt to the Orient. Even before I became a Christian myself I took a deep interest in Oriental philosophy, and I believe that interest certainly helped to prepare me to understand Christianity which is in many ways alien to the aggressive, materialistic and pragmatic world of the west. We must never forget that Christianity came to the west from the Orient. It is not purely and simply the "religion of the west." The specifically western elements which have come to be identified with Christianity are rather cultural and social elements, the outer garments of the religion, not the religion itself. Christianity, as Dr. John C. H. Wu, of China, has so well observed, is "beyond East and West." Christ is the fulfillment of the latent desires and aspirations of all religions and all philosophies. One must transcend them all to come to Him: yet in Him one finds all that was good and true in every other religion.

Ordinarily the Christian religion presents only its active, apostolic face to the East: the Christian comes as a builder of schools, Churches and hospitals, with a message of mercy and of spiritual development. But the active side of Christianity is nothing without the hidden, passive and contemplative aspect. Indeed, without the secret, interior, lowly, obscure knowledge of God in contemplation, the activity of the apostle is empty and fruitless. Indeed, it is perhaps because the contemplative aspect of Christianity has been to a great extent ignored by so many in the west, that Christianity has been less fruitful than it might have been in the east. It is the union with God in a darkness where nothing is seen or understood, that is the source of the mysterious love which is the life blood of Christianity. It is in the darkness of faith that the soul is united to Christ, and in this darkness the Holy Spirit, like an inexhaustible spring of living water, irrigates the dry wastes of the soul that is exhausted by attachment to the things of sense. This living water revives the soul and makes it capable of a love and compassion which are the most powerful of all spiritual forces because they are the power of God Himself in us: and God is Love.

O Eastern Reader of this book, whoever you are: open the secret ear of your heart to the silence of the Living God present within you. Realize that you are not alone, you are not a lost, isolated fragment of humanity: you are called to be One with all men in Christ. May you, reader, and I the author, be one in the silence and peace of Christ, the Conqueror of evil and division, the Conqueror of death.

To Tashi Tshering

Tashi Tshering, a Tibetan student living in the dormitories at the University of Washington in Seattle, wrote to Merton about his work with other Tibetans in the Tibetan Research Project at the university, where, he said, they were "happy to work together and our culture, religion, history, and language are the basic subjects on which we work." In December 1961 he again wrote Merton, telling him of his studies in "History of USA, Political Science, and English" and of his feeling that he had "the moral responsibility to sacrifice [himself] for the good of the others." The book he sent Merton was Tibet's Great Yogi Milarepa, *edited by W. Y. Evans-Wentz.*

[*Cold War Letter 43*]

February 1962

First of all I want to thank you for the wonderful gift of the *Life of Mila Repa*. This is a splendid volume, and extremely interesting to me. I am absorbed in it, and it gives a wonderful idea of Tibetan Buddhism. It has a character of energy and power which is quite unique. Certainly the Western idea of Buddhism is terribly confused.

You mention the spirit of sacrifice in your letter, and the most notable thing about Mila Repa is the absolute totality of his sacrifice in order to attain liberation. There was no price too high to pay. His will was indomitable. At the same time will alone is not sufficient. This is recognized, in Buddhism, by the idea of karma from a positive or good aspect, and in Christianity by the idea of grace. In any event it is clear that Mila Repa had received a special gift, a power to desire and to thirst for the light.

I believe that this gift is hidden in all of us, and that we should be aware of it, allowing it to awaken in our hearts. To me the Buddhist discipline of meditation and asceticism are very interesting because of the very sure psychological realism they display. I believe that the wisdom of these techniques is not sufficiently appreciated. It is a pity that Christian scholars tend to approach Buddhism with many illusions, believing it to be in some sense a "rival religion". To think this is, in many ways, a complete misunderstanding. The very essence of Buddhism is that it is "non-competitive" because it does not set up barriers and divisions, but rather destroys them, seeking the deepest unity, beyond all oppositions, and seeking it on a philosophical and ascetic plane, rather than by means that would conflict with the Christian sacraments, necessarily. We are dealing with different levels and different ways of approaching the ultimate unity.

In any case, Mila Repa is to me a very significant and fortunate discovery. I especially like his poems about the solitary life and am interested in learning more about the hermit tradition in Buddhism. I am very happy to hear about Prof. Deshong Tuku, there at the Tibetan

Research Center. I am unfortunately not able to come out to Washington, but perhaps some day he may come this way, or we may meet somehow. I am very interested in keeping in touch with you and in hearing more about the research that goes on there. I am you may be sure a sympathetic friend to all that concerns Buddhism, and would like very much to strengthen the points of contact between Buddhist and Christian thought . . .

To Thomas J. Liang

The Reverend Thomas Liang, a Chinese secular priest from the Archdiocese of Tsinan in the province of Shantung, came to the United States as a refugee in 1951. He wrote to Merton from Oakland, California, to tell him of his proposed Christian Unity Corps, which he hoped would offer services "of various kinds and hospitality in American homes to students from foreign countries." He said: "You may not be aware there are approximately 30,000 students from Asia alone studying in the United States and a large number of these are concentrated here in the Bay area in California."

[*Cold War Letter 57*]

March 1962

Your friendly letter has waited about a month for an answer, and I have been taking it very seriously. I do want to help you if I can, in any work involving Asian students. I feel that this is very important and as a matter of fact the Holy Spirit in the last year or so has been multiplying my Asian contacts in a rather striking way.

Your idea of the Christian Unity Corps sounds really fine, and I especially like the last part, about Catholic American families giving hospitality to Asian students. I believe that the Asian, South American and African students are in a way the most important people in the world today. They have magnificent potentialities. They also face tremendous dangers.

So, as I say, I want to help out. Yet at the same time I am afraid I cannot tie myself down to produce a certain definite something at a certain definite time. What would probably be more to the point, if you wish to use such feeble talents as I possess, would be to leave me on a footloose and informal basis, free to bat out a short letter to your bulletin or an observation or something, on spiritual matters. And I could not necessarily guarantee to do it every month. I have too many other commitments. But as I say it would be wonderful to feel that I were part of the group and accepted as a brother and friend by all who belonged to it.

Let me say this: I do not know if I have anything to offer to Asians but I am convinced that I have an immense amount to learn from Asia. One of the things I would like to share with Asians is not only Christ but

Asia itself. I am convinced that a rather superficial Christianity in European dress is not enough for Asia. We have lacked depth. We have lacked the breadth of view to grasp all the wonderful breadth and richness in the ancient Asian traditions, which were given to China, India, Japan, Korea, Burma etc. as preparations for the coming of Christ. I feel that often those who finally brought Christ may have fallen short of the preparation that the Holy Spirit had provided and hence Our Lord was not seen in all His divine splendor.

Yet at the same time I fully realize the complexity of the problem today. The Asians have renounced Asia. They want to be western, sometimes they are frantic about being western. They want to go places. They feel that there have been centuries of inertia and stagnation, and there is a reaction against the humiliations and misunderstandings of colonialism, calling for a defeat of the west at its own technological game. All this is dangerous but inevitable. Christianity of course has a crucial part to play in saving all that is valuable in the east as well as in the west.

To Whom It May Concern

Merton wrote several letters to draft boards in the 1960s about young men who objected to war and the draft. Some of the men he knew, some he didn't. This is the first of these letters on file in the Thomas Merton Studies Center.

May 21, 1962

I have been asked by Mr. James A. Kennedy to offer a statement that objection to nuclear war, or indeed to all war in the context of present-day weapons technology, can be held on moral grounds by a Catholic.

It is certain that a Catholic has every right and even the obligation to follow his conscience in objecting to any given war which he has serious reasons to believe immoral. The Church will always respect the conscience of such a one, in any concrete case, even if some of the clergy might consider that his conscience was in error. In the last analysis a Christian is always obliged to follow his conscience. To act in defiance of the voice of conscience would be a sin. The Church however endeavors to *form* and *guide* the conscience of the faithful. Thus the individual conscience is not left entirely to itself, but judgement must be made in the light of Catholic principles.

What is the present tendency of the teaching Church in forming and guiding the consciences of the faithful? Succinctly as follows:

a) The Church still holds that it is *possible* for there to be a just war of defense even today, but in this just war, with a just cause, purely for defense, just means must be used. If unjust means are resorted to the war becomes unjust and objectionable on moral grounds. Many Catholic theologians state that in the last war, though it began in a just cause, unjust methods were resorted to and the war became immoral. The Atomic bombing of Hiroshima can be called an immoral act and even a crime. Hence it is clear that any war today, even though it may begin with a good motive, can very easily turn into an unjust war that violates the rights of nonparticipants and thus becomes morally unacceptable.

b) The Church holds that in a *just* war of *defense*, in which *only just methods are used*, a Catholic may be called upon to serve his country and cannot rightly refuse that service if it is perfectly clear that *all the conditions for a just war are plainly fulfilled*.

c) However, there are innumerable statements by Pope Pius XII and John XXIII which cast great doubt upon the justice of using nuclear, chemical and biological weapons. Specifically the Popes have said that such methods used on a massive scale would be sinful and criminal. Taking one statement at random, Pope Pius XII in his Christmas Message of 1955, declared that steps to end nuclear testing and to disarm were an *obligation in conscience of nations and their leaders* and this obligation is morally binding. The Pope also said that *insufficient proposals* for disarmament, restrained by fear and suspicion, and showing lack of serious intent to fulfill proposed obligations, would not meet this moral obligation. Pius XII also stated that whenever nuclear weapons are used on a massive scale and without limitation, upon military and civil alike, this could not be justified on moral grounds (1954).

d) In this situation, where there is a very serious probability any war will become an all out nuclear war, which would be plainly immoral, and where there is no guarantee of any moral limitation on the use of the weapons that have been called into question by the highest authority of the Catholic Church, *there is every reason why a Catholic should be prevented by reasons of conscience from serving in the armed forces*.

I do not know Mr. Kennedy and cannot answer for his personal reasons, but he is a member of an international Catholic Peace movement called Pax. As one of the Sponsors of the Pax movement, I declare that the program of the movement included protest against nuclear war. This movement has among its members not only Catholic laymen but also priests and Bishops.

To Elbert R. Sisson

[*Cold War Letter 94*]

August 2, 1962

I was very happy with your letter and above all with the pictures, especially the drawings of the children. I was so moved by Grace (pun) and by her house and her lovely little self that I wrote a poem which I enclose. And as for Clare, even more than Grace, she has just stolen my heart completely and I don't know what to do or say. What a blessing it is to be surrounded with so many images of God and to live in the midst of the loves and sorrows and complications and simplicities that God has given you in them. May He preserve our world a little longer for the likes of such beautiful beings, whom He so loves.

About Cuba, there again I am inarticulate. I got a letter the other day from a poor dear woman [Evora Arca de Sardinia] whose husband went over in the invasion [at the Bay of Pigs] and is now on the Isle of Pines, in prison. She asks me if she ought to raise a hundred thousand dollars to get him out, when he wants to stay. The whole thing makes me utterly furious. Here we, the richest nation that ever existed, make stupid and utterly dishonorable mistakes, out of greed, and out of un-willingness to let a poor and angry neighbor put anything over on us. And for this mistake who pays? The people we self-righteously claim to be "helping" and protecting. These poor ordinary and even heroic people give their blood and then put themselves in hock for a hundred thousand just in order to enjoy a little freedom. Is this how we "free" our friends? When we have used them as cats paws to try out a fire we didn't know was quite so hot?

The next time I hear anything about the iniquity of Castro and the righteousness of the United States I am going to throw a bowl of soup at somebody. I guess I count as a security risk all right. Keep turning on peace, as my beat friends say.

To Donald Fiene

November 22, 1962

I was interested in your letter about your work on [J. D.] Salinger, and I will try to give you some sort of an answer to your inquiry. I am afraid it is not going to amount to much, however, and I suppose the reason is that I am almost the perfectly wrong person to answer a question and give an opinion on Salinger.

First of all, what it amounts to mostly is that I have nothing whatever against him. And secondly I have not really read him. Why should I have anything against a man I have not really read? I am not the sort of person that opens a book and sees a few four letter words and immediately throws it in the wastebasket after purifying the whole place with some kind of deodorant.

What have I read of his? I started *Franny and Zooey*. That is to say, I started Franny, and after that I started Zooey. I thought it was well written. I thought the people were alive, and I could see where one would get deeply absorbed in their concerns, but let me put it this way: I am profoundly engrossed in the 12th century school of Chartres, and in Zen (which I understand comes later in Zooey?) and in Sufism, and in some novices I am supposed to be teaching about the monastic life, and in the peace movement, and in poetry of a sort. My reaction to *Franny and Zooey* was simply that it was keeping me from something else in which I was really interested. I have absolutely nothing against *Franny* or *Zooey*. I am glad they had people who wrote such nice letters to them. But this is what I walked away from twenty years ago and it is just very remote, it doesn't come through any more. I am sorry, this may be a confession that I have drifted away from the human race, though I don't think even Salinger would interpret it that way.

On the other hand one of the young priests in the monastery was floating on a cloud after reading *Franny and Zooey*, and as a matter of fact he was the one who lent me the book. I can see where he perhaps needed the kind of stimulation the book would give, a reminder of what people feel and say to each other and the tangles they get in, because perhaps he did not get a big enough bite of all that before he came in here. I had plenty of big bites of it, I stuffed myself with it, and now I am through. It is like last year's breakfast. And this, I conclude, is a purely subjective judgment which really has no value at all for the purposes of a work like yours. But if you want to quote it for any reason, by all means go ahead.

Let me add this: when I was outside, twenty-two or -three years ago, I used to like Saroyan and I had a girl friend who was in one of his plays, etc. Then this was all very important to me. You see what I mean? I have had it all before. My train has gone way past the station. I am old, well, middle-aged. But let me encourage you with your book and with your writing, because it sounds right for you, and this is what you should do . . .

To Cecilia Corsanego

Cecilia Corsanego was a student from Rome at the Pro Civitate Christiana. She asked Merton's help to write a thesis about his poetry.

April 25, 1963

I will try to answer your questions as best I can. It seems to me that in general you are seizing upon particular allusions, in each of the poems, and taking them to be the theme of the poem itself, which is usually broader.

1) "Song:" (*A Man in the Divided Sea*, p. 24) There is a reference to Psalm 135, because the theme of the poem is exile. But the theme also and especially concerns time and eternity, and the last two lines refer to death not only as temporal but as a spiritual event. The "thieving stars" "stealing our lives" are symbolic of surrender to blind fatalism, whereas the heavens should remind us of God's law and eternity, and keep us watchful so that we may preserve our spiritual liberty.

2) "The Prophet," in *Prophet and Wild Dog*, is *any* kind of economic, philosophical, political, or utopian theorist, whether Marxist or not, whose hopeful slogans are belied by the inexorable course of events. I suppose the wild dog is history itself, or at any rate, what actually comes to pass, destroying the futility of the theory that promised earthly joy and prosperity as a result of material affluence.

3) I dated the *Responsory* 1948 because that was the year in which it was written. I am thinking of all the dead but especially the dead in the wars of our century and of those who may be killed in nuclear war, if it should ever occur, which God forbid. I am, incidentally, very happy indeed about the Holy Father's magnificent encyclical *Pacem in terris* which definitely rules out any serious possibility for Catholics to conceive a "holy war" with nuclear weapons (though some may have been inclined to think that way in the U.S.).

4) *The Rain and the Sun*: This is a poem about a sudden violent shower, and about the vicissitudes and changing illusions of life. The confusion of images is deliberate, creating the impression of a world that has momentarily lost its solidity and its clearly defined outlines (as in the heavy rain) and yet is already illumined with sun while the rain still falls. Basically, I suppose, the poem is about reality itself and our attempts to grasp it. And the implication is that the one unifying factor in the spiritual life is not a theory about reality or a moral or ascetic project, but simply the loving praise of God. The office is not referred to in particular, except by implication. The "noonday dusk" is simply the darkness of the storm at midday when the sun should be brightest (and by implication, spiritual darkness). This poem is deliberately impressionistic, something like a painting by Monet.

5) *Sports without Blood* was addressed to Dylan Thomas and sent to him. I did not know him in England, but this was a letter about England since I assumed that he and I felt the same kind of ambivalence about England. Thomas, as you seem not to know, was a Welshman and was without any doubt one of the most important poets writing in English in the last thirty years. He died tragically in New York some years ago. He was a drunkard, and the last lines of the poem were an appeal to him to consider the uncertainty and the futility of the life he was involved in by publicity hounds and people who exploited him and his talents.

6) *A Man in the Divided Sea*—reference to baptism and the passage through the Red Sea.

Figures for an Apocalypse—sketches for an apocalyptic scene, portraying our modern life which is, as Leon Bloy said, "Au seuil de l'apocalypse".

Tears of the Blind Lions, this is explained by the quotation from Bloy on the title page. I do not recall that there is any special arrangement in these poems.

7) *The Emperor in the Bombarded City* is a stylized figure representing world power.

8) The drops of water in the *Reader* are not Holy Water. There is a ceremonial washing of hands on entering the refectory. The "psalm" is the poem itself.

9) Which of my poems I prefer? Hard to say. I think often that I like the long poem *Elias*, which you may not have seen, as you do not refer to the book *Strange Islands*. This was not a very popular book, but I thought some of the poems in it represented very well what I want to say, though they are perhaps cold and less obviously imaginative than some of the early ones. If you do not have the *Strange Islands*, we can send you a copy. In the early poems, I have a special fondness for *Song for Our Lady of Cobre* because it is an act of homage to Our Lady and is also tropical and simple, and is a souvenir of my pilgrimage to her shrine in Cuba. It also reflects my love for Cuban and Latin American people. I wish you success with your work . . .

To "John"

There are, among Merton's surviving correspondence, several carbons of letters to young people in which no last name or other identification except a first name is given. These letters are included in this section when their content seemed significant.

July 24, 1963

A brief note in immediate response will probably [be] less from the top of my head than a longer one later.

This is the way I look at it.

On one level, there is your LSD experience and various ones of mine, and it seems to me that these are universal, natural and normal: the experience of *being* in the ontological sense, in all its ontological (metaphysical) richness, in its full existential reality, its concreteness, its value, bla bla, whatever words you want to use. It is what we are, what we belong to, what belongs to us, what we are in, the cosmos, full of inexhaustible richness, created (oops, my language now, skip that one) dynamic, and so on.

Into this level of experience the notion of "God" enters either equivocally (as for you) or analogically (as for me). In any case, one can rationalize about God and the relation of the cosmos to Him, or one can so to speak identify this being we experience with His being, and sum the whole thing up as you do with "this is IT". And that is true to a certain extent, it is IT. And yet at the same time and in the same breath it is NOT it. There is a built-in equivocation in this identification of the being we are capable of knowing and experiencing, with God, the Absolute Being. Hence no matter what anybody says, in religious terms, in philosophical terms, whatever terms you like, whenever he talks of being and existence that come within our experience, whether with the help of LSD or not, it is both IT and NOT IT. You are perfectly right in saying that what you attain by LSD is not God: it is you. But you are in the "image of God".

On another level, the level of religion and faith, which nevertheless enters into universal being as we know and experience it, is God Who does not really form part of "being" and is in a sense entirely other than any being we are capable of knowing, so that we can only pass from being to Him by a kind of inexplicable breakthrough. The Zens do it in Satori, we do it by Christian faith, and in neither case is there any point in my trying to justify it to you. You either do or you don't. There *is* a problem of communication but it is not so much the communication that takes place by words as the communion that is effected by love. If one somehow receives the gift to love that being which is accessible to us because we are IT, then one can perhaps pass through the experience to a realization that being is a gift, love is gift, knowledge is gift and the whole shooting match is gift which calls for a gift in return. Treat this as a kind of Ezra Pound poem if you like, all you can do with it is let it sit, and if it doesn't sit comfortably then forget it until the next time. This is in no sense anything I am trying to sell you, I am just telling you how I look at it, and if you can't look at it that way I will look at it that way for you, since we are friends, and whatever good is connected with it in my case will also be imputed to you. I think you ought not to tussle with it. Forget it, and if you need to see it some time, it will get clear. There is much more involved in this than semantics, or religion, or what have you. We live in a welter of verbalism and a confusion of tongues and that is most of the trouble. Got to give a class now . . .

To Anglican Seminarians

November 11, 1963

Sorry I did not see you when you were here. I did not even know you were here, and it all depends on what Fr. Abbot says when Fr. Francis gets on the phone to him. Maybe some other time. I remember the time you were with Sterling Rayburn.

About the poems: *Landscape* is a child's drawing, and plays on the child's view of the world, with all sorts of hidden father-mother business. I suppose you would say the theme of the poem is the awakening of the child's hidden sense that he can choose to make his world, and basically it is a poem about freedom. And about the hazards of freedom, and about attachment to the security of childhood, and so on. Nothing is settled, and the whole thing is left enigmatic. The poem is not a final statement about anything. It just raises possibilities and leaves them hanging in the air.

I don't know what the critics have said, I am delighted that they have said anything at all. I certainly like Dylan Thomas very much, I think he had a great lyrical gift and a powerful inventiveness. I can't point to precise places where he has influenced me consciously, though there are some and they are probably evident enough. Blake of course has been a great influence, Donne to a lesser extent. I have always loved Marvell best of the metaphysicals, as far as vocabulary, imagery and sound are concerned. So many gardens, Bermuda, etc.

My meters are simply those of common speech, I am really most of the time writing prose, deliberately. I like best my poems that are more prosaic. When they get poetic they annoy me. They feel pretentious or something. I place my confidence in a certain poetic quality in the experience itself, but muted and understated. That is why I like the *Strange Islands* more than a book which is mostly very bad indeed, *Figures for an Apocalypse* . . .

To Susan Neer

Susan Neer, a high-school student from Saint Ann, Missouri, wrote to ask if Merton felt the experiences described by John Howard Griffin, particularly the section on "Clyde Canard," in Black Like Me *were basically true.*

December 22, 1963

To the best of my knowledge the story about Clyde Kennard is true, and I believe everyone is more or less aware that things like that *do* happen in some of the Southern states.

When your Father says he has been to Atlanta and met lots of nice cordial people, that also is perfectly true. Southern people are very cordial and charming and have a great deal of kindness and good will. I like Southern people because I live in Kentucky, and the people around here are very pleasant to live with. But even in Kentucky when you get back in the hills or in some areas, the people can sometimes get very mean and act violent. These are not always the "nice" ones that you meet here and there, and I have run into some pretty rugged characters in my dealings with those around this area. Also in the last election the race issue was very strong in this state, which surprised everyone.

I have here in the novitiate a Franciscan priest who was until recently stationed in Louisiana. He has personally told me of the way in which local people, some of them Catholics, bombed the parochial school so that it could not open with Negro students in it. I know for a fact that his statements are perfectly true, and I know other things about the people in that parish which show that they are quite capable of doing the sort of things that were done to Clyde Kennard.

The conclusion of all this: yes, your Father is right in saying you must not believe *everything* uncritically. One must use reason and prudence, and not make hasty judgements. On the other hand, we must frankly admit that all is not roses either in the South or even in the North where this race question is concerned, and unless public opinion is more alert and mature there is going to be some unpleasant travelling over the road that lies ahead. The great thing is for us to try to live up to our American and Christian heritage of independent thought, devotion to justice and truth, fair mindedness, and fair play. We cannot condemn the white Southerners glibly, but we have to admit that they have a very grave problem. The big question: How can we help them solve it, instead of just reproaching them with being mean and violent? That is the problem no one knows how to answer.

To Jim Frost

Jim Frost was a high-school sophomore from Waterloo, Iowa.

January 7, 1964

I don't know how most authors feel about this "write to an author" deal, but my own feelings about it are a bit mixed. However, I must say this, you are very simple about it, you just ask for a note back. Most of the letters I get are usually asking me in some way to write them an essay they have been assigned to write about me. Thus the author writes your homework and saves you the trouble of reading his stuff, which is pretty neat. You however are not doing this to me. But just for kicks I enclose the paper I send them when they do.

So much for that. As for you, you are still waiting for a personal note. What can I tell you? I can tell you that in reality life is good and a wonderful gift, and the more you put into it the better it is. But you must really grow up to be free, and truth loving, and sincere all the way with yourself and others. Don't live on illusions. You don't have to, reality is right there in front of you, and it is better than any illusion. You live probably in the country. I would not live in a city for anything under the sun. I like the woods and the hills. Last evening I was trying to count all the deer that were up at the other end of the field from where I was, but because they were up against some high sage grass and their color blended in to it I could not make them all out, but I counted at least five for sure. It is wonderful to have wild animals for neighbors, and it is a shame that people can't think of anything better than to go and shoot them.

The lesson of that is that we Americans ought to love our land, our forests, our plains, and we ought to do everything we can to preserve it in its richness and beauty, by respect for our natural resources, for water, for land, for wild life. We need men and women of the rising generation to dedicate themselves to this. Well, God bless you Jim. And God bless all your classmates.

To "Jacque" (A Young Girl)

February 6, 1964

First of all don't let anyone push you into a convent. If you don't want to go, it is a sign you don't have a vocation and that God is not asking you to go. If you enter a convent unwillingly it may wreck your whole life, and you must not be thinking that in refusing to do so you are displeasing to God. That puts you in the position of thinking that what really pleases God is displeasing to Him. What He wants of you is to stand up for your rights and follow the light He gives you, and you would not please Him by passively getting pushed into a convent. Only if one sincerely and personally wills to seek God in religion, should she do this. Not because religious life is theoretically the best and so on. It is a fine life, but only for those who want it themselves.

You must learn that life is full of these problems when in the depths of your heart you really know what is right, and your conscience tells you, but at the same time someone else tries to make you believe that they have the right idea and you are wrong. In such cases the court of last appeal is always conscience. You cannot go against it. But at the same time you must know how to listen attentively to good advice and to pay attention to what experienced persons and those in authority may have to say. Certainly you must know how to make sacrifices and give up your own will, even your own ideas. But you cannot give up your conscience. In the last resort, learn to ask of God in sincere prayer and then follow what is the inmost voice of conscience, in faith, and if possible get the backing of someone who knows . . .

To Edward Gerdes

April 18, 1964

The book you refer to is by Ayn Rand, right? I have not read it, but I tried another of hers and was bored to death. Couldn't make it at all. The philosophy is moronic.

The best critique of her thought I have seen is in a magazine called *New University Thought* published in Chicago. I don't have the address. For books that would provide principles which would correct her view, anything by Jacques Maritain, especially on morals.

From my point of view her philosophy is an organized egoism which is based on a completely illusory idea of the "self" and of the "person." This woman just does not know who she is. She strikes me as sick, alienated, and trying to cover up with a lot of brave noise. However the chief argument against following her principles is life itself. Anyone who lives according to her program will soon find out how well it works. Unfortunately there are too many people trying it all the time.

To Silvana Ranzoli

May 31, 1964

. . . I am sorry I was not able to give you the information you needed for your thesis. I hope everything went well in spite of this. As to the book *Disputed Questions*, I think most of your questions are answered by the fact that this is simply a collection of essays written and published separately and then gathered together into a book. The *ratio* behind them is simply that they all consist of views and ideas which were uppermost in my own mind in the years 1956–1959 or thereabouts. I consider the most important essay to be the one on solitude ["Notes for a Philosophy of Solitude"], at least it was the most important to me at the time.

Contemporary American Catholic literature is waking up at last. There are some good fiction writers, chiefly J. F. Powers, and some good poets [Ned] O'Gorman being the one I like best, but also others like Logan, Hazo, Roseliep, and of course Robert Lowell who is not strictly a Catholic. However as I do not read much of the current literature I am not a good judge. There are other excellent fiction writers, one of the best being Flannery O'Connor.

This must suffice, I am afraid. Again, I regret disappointing you. May God bless you and your work. May you be happy and good in the city of Virgil. Recently I dreamed I was in the cathedral of Mantova (which I have never seen) and it was very nice, I mean the dream was. I don't know if it was really the cathedral of Mantova or not.

To Chris McNair

Merton was deeply moved by the incident in Birmingham, Alabama, in September 1963 in which four black children were killed when a bomb was exploded in their Sunday school. Photos of the bombing appeared in Look *and he cut out that of Carole Denise McNair and carefully kept the photograph in his journal. He captioned it: "Carole Denise McNair, one of the four bomb-murdered Negro children, never learned to hate." It inspired him to write his poem "Picture of a Black Child with a White Doll." See* The Collected Poems of Thomas Merton *(1977, pp. 626–27).*

October 12, 1964

This is not exactly an easy letter to write. There is so much to say, and there are no words in which to say it. I will say it as simply as I can, in the hope that you will understand this message from a total stranger. I saw the pictures you took of Carole Denise in *Look* several months ago. One of them meant so much to me that I cut it out, and kept it. It seemed to say so much, principally about goodness, and about the way in which the goodness of the human heart is invincible, and overcomes the evil and wickedness that may sometimes be present in other men.

Being a writer, and a writer of poems, I eventually was moved to write a poem, and now that it has been published I want to send you at least this copy of it. It is a somewhat angry poem, because I think that a little anger is still called for. I hope that love and compassion also come through, for anger is not enough and never will be.

At any rate, I wanted to say what you already know and believe: that the mercy and goodness of the Lord chose Carole Denise to be with Him forever in His love and His light. Nor is she forgotten on the earth. She remains as a witness to innocence and to love, and an inspiration to all of us who remain to face the labor, the difficulty and the heart-break of the struggle for human rights and dignity.

To Charles Cameron

Charles Cameron, a twenty-year-old student reading theology at Christ Church College, Oxford University, wrote asking Merton's views on poetry after having read his essay "Message to Poets" in the April 1964 issue of El Corno Emplumado, *a reading which, he said, left him "a dervish full of ruah." He asked Merton: "How many zany monks are there at large in the church now?"*

November 29, 1964

It is good to get letters like yours but bad because I can't answer them most of the time but thanks for writing. It makes me feel somehow I am in contact with the human race . . . It would seem that the human race is altogether a bad thing to be in contact with, since this prevents one from thinking himself to be an angel but since I have long ago found it difficult to do this and since there has been the Incarnation and since being a gnostic upsets me and since many other things, I will settle for being in contact with the human race. But when it comes to expressing opinions there you have me. I will at great cost to my apparatus produce one opinion about poetry: I like Stevie Smith. This immediately leads to another, that I like very much Peter Levi SJ. The fact that two opinions came out instead of one seems to indicate that liking Stevie Smith agrees with the apparatus.

All I say about being a dervish is ok and I mean it except here you get beaten for being a dervish. I am bruised for this all day long. It is all very well to be a dervish in print in Mexico and yes I imagine you are right about Cuerno if it were in Spain at least. But here in the monastery

334/ THOMAS MERTON

it is best not to be dancing. As to the chant, I cannot even force the beginning of an opinion on that one out of the crevices in my head. I am going to some of it in about ten minutes, I'll tell you that much.

Returning to opinions about poetry I do like the small things that are all over the *Aylesford Review*. Bro. Antoninus was here. He attaches great importance to touching water when he is in a place. When he was here he found water and he touched it, and I have a picture of him doing this. I think it is a very good picture of him, whereas other pictures of him when he is not touching water are obscure and unreal. If he comes to Oxford, will there be something better for him to touch than that unclean river? Perhaps a good pond or something. I was at Oxford in many mists taking an exam and trying to sleep in rooms on High Street as a result of which I went to Cambridge. But I admit that the river at Cambridge is even dirtier and no one I ever knew there was interested in water in any case. I admit I was bullied into rowing in the Clare third boat for a while, in preparation for a longer career in the fourth boat. When I ought to have played rugger, I was a fierce man at rugger. No longer.

Now about politics. A. J. Muste and a lot of good people, mostly from Liberation and so on, were here last week and there was a retreat and we came out with no solution to anything except a hope that is so close to despair that it seems to be one and the same thing. Apart from that I promise you a difficult time with all popery, but with all her wrinkles and spots the eglise is who she is. And I will refrain from any opinion on the end of the third session of the Second Vatican Council, which has persistently been read in our refectory as the Vaticle Council. God bless you, no rejections at all. Welcome if you come here, but write first so I will know about it.

To Roberto Gri

Roberto Gri, a young Italian student, wrote asking Merton how to study. Merton began his letter in Italian and then switched to English.

December 10, 1964

Ho letto tu bellissima lettera e voglio responderti almeno due parole, ma non posso farlo in italiano, poiche ho completamente dimenticato tutto che sapeva. Dunque, si non sai l'inglese, qualch'uno dei tuoi condiscepoli fara la traduzione.

A method of study: it is not easy to tell you this in a few words. There are some things that can only be learned by application and memorizing. But simply memorizing and routine will never help you attain the ends for which you study. The important things are *discipline* (applying yourself at the proper time and not evading what is tiresome and difficult), *order* (taking first things first and relating other matters to what is fundamental), *interest* (some of the things you study will appeal to you and you should investigate them further, going beyond what is strictly required). Do not study merely to pass exams or to please your teachers, but to find truth and to awaken deeper levels of life in yourself . . .

To Antoinette M. Costa

Antoinette Costa, a high-school student from Taunton, Massachusetts, wrote to Merton for help on a research paper; the students were "not required to use footnotes." The paper, titled "Thomas Merton: Poet of Contemplation," is on file in the Thomas Merton Studies Center.

May 13, 1965

About those early critics: it is difficult for me to have any kind of opinion, as no one can judge rightly in his own case. The best thing I can do is say, as objectively as I can, that I felt they were writing about somebody who wasn't there. They had not heard me, they had heard somebody else, and they had not read what I had intended to write. This of course often happens. The whole question of communication is a very difficult one, and most difficult when one writes imaginatively and symbolically as I do. There is a whole class of people who simply react negatively to my kind of thought and my kind of writing. This is not surprising, and it is as it should be. I for my part have absolutely no interest in them either, they seem to me to be prosaic and stupid, and to have very little feeling for what seems to me to be real. They tend to be rationalists, materialists, or else stolid traditionalists of an external type. To these I have nothing to say.

As for [Frank] Dell'Isola's statement ["The Conversion and Growth of Thomas Merton"] that *No Man Is an Island* changed the minds of critics, I don't know. I do know however that one of my early critics, Dom Aelred Graham, did change his mind around that point and what happened was that we both came to see that we really agreed. He is English and I write in tones that some English people get offended at, because it seems to them to be too aggressive ("strident") but since Dom Aelred wrote "Zen Catholicism," which I liked very much, and which I praised [in "Zen: Sense and Sensibility"], we are on very good terms and see that we agree.

Yes, I am writing articles and poems now, and I have a new book on the race question and peace which has also been criticized, *Seeds of Destruction*. I have an article ["Rain and the Rhinoceros"] in the May issue of *Holiday* if you are interested in what is new down this way. God bless you and good luck with your paper.

To Francesca Guli

Francesca Guli sent Merton the ms. of her book on Dante for children, which was published as The Boy and the Stars: A Lyrical Tale of Dante Alighieri, the Boy *(Francestown, New Hampshire: Golden Quill Press, 1965).*

May 19, 1965

. . . Your book on Dante, which I have skimmed over, looks charming and from your description I think it is going to be a fine children's book, but I have not really been able to form a serious judgment. I have read a few of the poems and like them too, and here I am with a positive impression of you as someone I would like to know more of and probably never will. That is the way these things are, because of the sheer volume against which I have developed a rudimentary protection. Do please forgive me for not having more to say and not responding more promptly or more fully. I hope your book will do very well and will bring a lot of children to know Dante so that they will read him later on . . .

To John O'Keefe

John O'Keefe wrote to Merton from Dublin, Ireland, asking what advice he would give to a young, aspiring writer.

November 4, 1965

This will be brief indeed, but in charity I will at least try to send you something. In writing for ordinary people (what other people are there?) I would say do this:

1 - Never write down to anyone.

2 - Never write simply what you think they want.

3 - Write rather what is deepest in your own heart and what you know—as a writer has an instinct by which to know this—is also deep in theirs. In other words, write to elucidate problems that are common and urgent.

4 - Write only after you have thoroughly learned what you want to say—but this has to be qualified. By all means practice. Why not write a novel? Except maybe you have not time. Try a story or two. But don't just write like "a Short Story Writer," or a pro of some sort.

5 - Ireland has great writers, very articulate writers. Read them: I am sure you do. I do not now mean some of my former scandalous favorites like Joyce, but so many others from Yeats and Synge to Brendan Behan (don't be scandalized).

And now you can do me a favor: what is the best bookstore in Dublin for getting source material on Irish monasticism, things perhaps out of print, like the *Rule of Tallaght*, which I need badly? I would be grateful for such information.

To Geraldine McNamara

Geraldine McNamara, a high-school student, wrote asking for information on Trappist life. She later thanked him for his reply, saying: "I read your letter to my Religion and English class. Some of the girls were astonished to hear about the daily menu and the bit about no talking."

November 12, 1965

I am afraid my answer must be quite brief as I have a lot of mail and very little time in which to handle it. But in general I would say don't form too grim a picture of Trappist life. It is not bad at all, and not as hard as one might think.

1) Recreation: personally I get plenty of recreation chopping wood in the woods and doing other things like that. The monks go for walks (alone) in the woods, there is plenty of exercise. There is no formal recreation in which we get together and talk, and thank God for it, I think it would be a terrible bore.

2) We use sign language among ourselves but talking is possible whenever really necessary, with the superiors, or permission may be obtained in exceptional cases.

3) God alone knows how many signs there are. We invent them all the time. There must be three or four hundred in common use. There is also pantomime, for which some have an unusual talent.

4) We get protein out of cheese and milk mostly, also some vegetables and peanut butter have protein in them. Fish is allowed in the Order now as a special dish for those who need more, but we don't get it here much, or ever as far as I know.

5) Typical meal at dinner, oh, soup, spaghetti and a green vegetable, coffee, fruit, bread, maybe some salad etc. We get milk and cheese usually at supper.

6) Why do we pray and work? Because that is the monastic vocation. The monk is not called to the active apostolate, he is called to live alone with God, he is not necessarily a priest at all. The presence of priest monks in the monastery naturally confuses people and sometimes it confuses the monks themselves. There has to be some place for people who want simply to lead lives of prayer and penance. The [Vatican] Council affirms all this in the Constitution on Religious, which you can read for yourself.

7) What led me to become a Catholic? Grace, the mercy of God, the

realization first of God's infinite Being and presence then of Christ as His Son and our Redeemer living and present in His Church.

8) I'll send you a list of books. For you I suggest *The Living Bread, Bread in the Wilderness, The Sign of Jonas* . . .

God bless you and pray for peace, also pray hard that young Catholics do not get too many absurd and crazy ideas about what to do for "peace." They may end up doing the devil's work instead of God's. We must follow the teaching of the Holy Father and the Church and take care not to be deceived by others.

To Jan Boggs

Jan Boggs, a high-school sophomore from Niskayuna, New York, wrote asking for a "definition of a poem" for a poetry unit in English class. He later thanked Merton, adding: "In a world where so many adults have a low opinion of teenagers in general, it means a lot to us when adults treat us like young adults."

February 9, 1966

I received your letter of the 3rd only yesterday. I am afraid this answer will be too late to help you. In any case, I would say that a poem was any piece of writing or spoken utterance which, in symbolic and rhythmic language, seeks to communicate a deep and direct experience of life in some aspect or other. A poem however cannot be confined to mere teaching, nor is it necessarily "inspirational" or even serious. It must however in some way or other strive to be more memorable and more challenging than mere prose. Maybe that will help you. I don't know.

To Mery-Lu Sananes and Jaime Lopez-Sanz

Four Venezuelan students in the Facultad de Humanidades y Educación at the Universidad Central in Caracas—Mery-Lu Sananes, Jaime López-Sanz, Irene Flores, and Ramón Montiel—wrote to inform Merton that their literary group, LAM, had translated his Original Child Bomb *into Spanish. They published it in an illustrated broadside under the title* Niña Bomba Original. *Sananes and López-Sanz were credited with the translation.*

March 7, 1966

After writing an official letter of thanks in bad Spanish to the whole group, I want to say a special word of thanks to you both for your very good job. I often like my own stuff better when it comes out in Spanish. My heart is with you all in Latin America and as I often tell my friends, I am much more close to the Latin American poets than to those of North America, to the point that some North American poets are angry with me about it, and ask me to explain this attitude. It is not a matter of ideology but of temperament and clarity. It seems to me that the North Americans are for the most part bogged down in a kind of emotional viscosity and have no reasons for anything but go into it with blind feeling or blind will—rationalized by technical clichés, or in the case of poets by some sort of pseudo-gnostic aura which justifies everything.

Thus I, an antipoet much of the time, prefer the ring and the bite of a certain ironic clarity and critique. You have caught all this in your translation.

I do not pretend to have answers or theories, but I do hope I will continue to have eyes and to use them. And, in certain situations, having a nose is not always very comfortable. I am grateful for a little fresh air from beyond the Caribbean. I am happy with the warmth of your understanding and your gesture of openness. With all my heart I answer in the same tone. I give you my hand, across the miles that separate us. We are not as far as we seem. Maybe you are closer to me than many who are nearer.

Meanwhile, I live my own form of protest, which is a matter of solitude and irony. My contribution to the affairs of the world is to live in the woods like a Negro and chop trees. And have as little as possible to do with the society which is not without its capacity to tell large lies.

You will find here other poems, which are yours to read and to use if you need them in the magazine which I hope to see soon. Meanwhile if you see Ludovico Silva, tell him I have his letter and am waiting for his explosion to cover this place with fallout and then I will reply. Warm good wishes to all of you and a big *abrazo* for all of you, the boys and the girls.

To A. Philip Randolph

A. Philip Randolph was chairman of the Committee of Conscience Against Apartheid, formed by the American Committee on Africa in cooperation with the National Student Christian Federation. The immediate project, initiated by students at Union Theological Seminary, Jewish Theological Seminary, Columbia University, and Barnard College, was to withdraw money from New York banks in order to withhold economic support from South Africa. Merton's name as sponsor appeared on the group's letterhead as "Rev. Thomas Merton."

July 17, 1966

Many thanks for your letter about the Committee of Conscience Against Apartheid and the interesting material that came with it. I am grateful that you consider it worth while to ask me to be a sponsor of the campaign on the banks which support South Africa financially.

Thinking the matter over, I find one or two small ambiguities in my own position. I am first of all not a New Yorker—or have not been for some twenty-five years now. Second I have no money of my own in any bank. Third, living more or less as a hermit in the woods, I have not been regularly giving my name to campaigns lately.

On the other hand, however, these are small objections in the face of such a monumental and criminal evil as Apartheid and it would be foolish to imagine that such objections could make much difference. On the contrary, this is a welcome opportunity to take a stand on the question, as if everyone could not guess what one's position was. But also I think the campaign sound, like a very effective sort of thing to engage in and it will probably make a big difference.

With all these facts in mind, I accept gladly your invitation to be a sponsor of the campaign. It would be better not to mention my monastery even for purposes of identification, but just list me as: "Thomas Merton, author."

To Mark K. Stone

Mark Stone, a teacher at Olney High School in Philadelphia, had sought and received permission to mimeograph Merton's essay "Red or Dead: the Anatomy of a Cliché" for classroom use. He wrote to ask Merton several questions, including the origin of the phrase.

August 9, 1966

Your letter of Aug. 1 reached me today, via Nyack. I will try to answer your questions as best I can, though I do not have a text of "Red or Dead" handy. By the way, if you would be kind enough to send me four or five of your copies, I would be grateful. I don't seem to have any left.

1. Use of the phrase. I think it is generally used quite loosely. "Red" means here simply "under Communism". But remember that there is a certain mythology behind all this. One of the myths is the diabolical power of the Communists to change your mind for you and "make you" Red when you don't want to be. That is apparently one of the most operative elements in the myth and that is why the idea of being overcome by "them" can appear such an ultimate evil and horror. Once they've got you, you're helpless, you are putty in their hands, etc. etc. Hence any evil is a lesser evil, even nuclear war.

2. I am afraid I forget which "two ideas I attribute to Marx" as I do not have the text here.

3. I am not clear in what "live and act like atheists" presents a difficulty. How does an atheist act? Well, the way you put it, it is quite true that atheists don't necessarily have peculiar ways of acting in so far as they are just people like everyone else. Perhaps I should have qualified

and spoken of those who devote themselves to carrying out a policy of military atheism—and I suppose this is just religion in reverse. But again, as I don't have the text and forget exactly what I said, I can't clarify. All I can say is that I probably had in mind the kind of atheism which draws practical nihilistic conclusions from a somewhat high-powered animosity against the god-image (see Camus' *The Rebel* which explains this very well). This kind of atheism is aggressive, nihilistic, committed to deliberate terror etc. More common in Europe than here. When I think of all my nice warm atheist friends with whom I get along very well, I can see your point.

4. Disarmament: in my opinion a mere sweeping unilateralism in disarmament (getting rid of *everything*) would be unrealistic. But I do think a gradual and realistic plan could be worked out, and such plans have indeed been proposed. If only nations had the courage to accept such plans, and to try to work with them, to risk this or that difficult policy of inspection or whatever it is that is the obstacle . . . I am for gradual reduction of armaments, for international control over the manufacture of armaments and for an international police army (small) to control brushfire wars. All this is Utopian. Yet it should not be impossible some day . . . Wishing you luck with your discussion.

To Gloria Sylvester Bennett

Gloria Sylvester had been one of Sister Marialein Lorenz's black students in Mobile, Alabama, who sent Merton ordination gifts which he used in his first Mass at Gethsemani. She wrote: "Please pray for our dear young friends in the Student Non-Violent Co-ordinating Committee who are daily risking life & limb in my home state." She sent Merton a copy of Confrontation: Black and White *by her husband, Lerone Bennett.*

August 14, 1966

Thanks very much indeed for your note and for the Silver Jubilee Gift. You take me back to the days, already so long ago, when my most prized ordination gift was that which came from your school. The mail bag after the *Life* piece was mixed, as usual. Some fanatics, a lot of mixed-up good people, and a few good people not even mixed up. I think I was happiest of all to get your husband's hard-hitting and very lucid book. I had not heard of it, and I have read through it intently. It is very valuable to me, and a fine book. It gets better and better as it goes on, and by the time I finished I realized I didn't deserve the inscription. My warm thanks to both of you.

You mention your SNCC friends in the South. I haven't heard too much lately, but the little I have heard makes me think a lot about them and about the coming fall. Though ideally non-violence has seemed to be so right and even so effective, this is a time when rightness and effectiveness don't always go together. I wonder how the next step will be, and what will come of it. In any case there is no going back, and there is not much hope of everything making perfect sense. I notice that even in France, people who were strong on non-violence until a year or two ago are swinging to a more violent revolutionary position. I can't claim to understand much of what goes on but one thing is certain: when one is living through a revolution and trying to pretend it isn't there, life is more absurd than it need be. I shall certainly keep Snick in my prayers. And this whole fast asleep country.

I notice Camus is mentioned a lot in the book. I have just finished a study of Camus on violence, and will send a copy along when I have one available. Also a book of mine that is supposed to be out now, when I can get a copy of that. Thanks very much indeed for writing and sending the book. If there is anything you think I need to know about what goes on in the south or in Chicago, please don't hesitate to slip it in the mail. I have a real need for accurate information. And will always be glad to hear from you, and to send you anything of mine that can be of service.

To The New Yorker

Merton read The New Yorker *when he could get a copy. This letter was prompted by his sudden awareness of two young men who had "bucked" the establishment, Lenny Bruce and Bud Powell. Both had died young in 1966. He was obviously unaware that Bruce had frequently quoted Merton in his nightclub routines.*

September 18, 1966

In *The New Yorker* for August 20—which I have just now happened to see—there is a paragraph in "Talk of the Town" about Lenny Bruce and Bud Powell. I was very moved by it. Having been for quite some time in a monastery I had never had any occasion to hear—or even to hear of—either Lenny Bruce or Bud Powell. Powell I can doubtless hear on records some time. What I would like to know is this: how can I now hear what Lenny Bruce was saying, and learn more about the struggle he had to face—doubtless much of it against my Church, or representatives of it. Would it be possible for the writer of that paragraph to get in touch with me and fill me in a little on this situation, and perhaps send me references that I could consult? I would be very grateful. Need I add that my interest is entirely sympathetic to Lenny Bruce and what he was evidently trying to achieve?

November 5, 1966

I hate to keep pestering the "Talk of the Town," but I can't help it. If I am a little late in commenting on the Talk of the Town of Aug. 27, you must realize that a monk gets his *New Yorkers* surreptitiously and at long intervals. I would like to say just this: about the piece on John Lennon, Alotrios, the Beatles and Jesus. This is the first piece of theological writing since the Fathers of the Church that has moved me to tears. Whoever wrote it is my brother. He makes a lot of sense. Most of the official theologians don't. Thank you very much. For this kind of thing I love all of you very much. Keep it up.

To Ivanhoe Donaldson

Ivanhoe Donaldson of the Student Nonviolent Coordinating Committee (SNCC) wrote to Merton asking for a contribution. Merton responded with a contribution, though he claims he does not remember where he got it.

November 13, 1966

I was delighted and surprised to get your letter of the 7th. I am wondering who I could possibly have shook down in order to get that hundred—which I have no recollection of giving you. I am glad I did and I plan to get more as soon as I can work over the right people. It is very hard if not impossible for me to get my hands into the cash box of this flourishing enterprise. I have to resort to a lot of arm twisting, and the boss, whose arm is the one that has to be twisted for significant results, is now absent organizing the campesinos of Chile for better production. The second in command has relayed to him a meek petition of mine for fifty dollars. I have rather a suspicion that SNCC is now less popular in the front office than it was two years ago. Black Power you know. Tsk Tsk.

This letter of mine, therefore, can bring you little more than words and love. It shames me. Of words and love you have more than you need. Especially from the godly (of which I may or may not be one). But I can at least assure you that I will do what I can to get you something more substantial either by begging, by embezzlement or by blackmail. If I can't get anything out of the establishment, I will divert to you the monies resulting from the sale of some poem or article before those monies find their way here. This I can sometimes do.

I am particularly glad you have me on a mailing list. I am surrounded by head shaking misinformation and need to see things like the reprint of Stokely Carmichael's article from *New York Review*—a very clear statement. But of course the whole question of Black Power must be and will remain essentially unclear, and it has to. That is the beauty of it, & its irony—and its singular effect. Behind the whole Black Power concept is a force and a motive drive of purpose and humor—and seriousness—which cannot be grasped except by those who are entirely with it as a revolutionary anti-movement, and to be this one must be black. Singular importance of this!!! It has all my admiration, sympathy, and I will follow the convolutions of it as best I can. I think Black Power will, by getting everybody guessing wrong twenty-four hours a day, accomplish a great work of ground clearing. The day it becomes established and reasonable we will all have gone to the next fruitful irony. Oh man, people are always calling me a pessimist. But I am not so dense that I can't get the ring of the joy that is there and the hope and the undercurrent in your generation. You are a blessed generation, I swear it. You will make it, and make it all the more in that you will, I hope, be careful not to define too clearly what it is you expect to make.

I was moved to get the fine book which I will read religious and cool and intent. And I will report back. Will you keep in touch? I will do what I can when I can, and as I say I will send you money when it becomes possible to get my hands on some. Con un abrazo, amigo!

Donaldson responded with thanks and "un abrazo for you too."

December 4, 1966

I managed by fair and political means to come by the enclosed check which I am sending along a bit late as I had lost your address. I hope it will be of some small help, anyway.

The book *Letters from Mississippi* [edited by Elizabeth Sutherland Martinez] has reached me and I am reading it. Needless to give expression to the deep feelings which it inspires. It is a most important book, and bears witness to a work of courage far greater than can be measured simply by material results. The historic summer project of 1964 will remain an eternal credit to SNCC and to all those who participated in it. Especially those who gave their lives in it.

I think it is a very good thing to get this book circulating these days to remind white people that they haven't been polarized out of the freedom movement, since it is a movement for their freedom too. That point, I think, should not get buried.

Anyway, many thanks, and as I said, do keep in touch. I will gladly be of help in whatever way I can. Under separate cover I am sending along an essay on violence and non-violence in Camus, in which someone might perhaps be interested.

To an Unidentified Friend

January 9, 1967

First let me try to answer your question as it was put: the first name that occurs to me offhand of a "proven homosexual" who probably saved his soul, is Oscar Wilde. The poor man suffered greatly and was certainly sincere. I don't know all the details of his later years but the impression I have is that he went through them with a martyr's nobility. I can think of others who I think did the same though I am not sure if they were Christians so I won't go into that.

In other words, the pitch is this. Homosexuality is not a more "unforgivable" sin than any other and the rules are the same. You do the best you can, you honestly try to fight it, be sorry, try to avoid occasions, all the usual things. You may not always succeed but in this as in anything else, God sees your good will and takes it into account. Trust His mercy and keep trying. And have recourse to all the spiritual aids available. Maybe psychiatric help would be of use.

As I see it, there is a special sort of masochism that gets built into this pattern of inversion. A sort of despair that robs you of any urge to fight back. I'd say that was probably the problem and it is probably psychological in its root. That is what has to be handled, that need to fold up and give up resistance. But why? That is for you to find out. I am not a psychiatric counsellor. All I can say is that God will surely understand your good intentions as well as your weakness, and He is on your side. So have courage and don't give up. And don't waste energy hating yourself. You need that energy for better purposes . . .

To Gloria Sylvester Bennett

January 19, 1967

Thanks for your warm good letter . . . What you say about the children is so maddening to me. That they have to be taught that there is nothing wrong with having a black skin, and that even the nuns don't know enough to help. I have had my own very small share of being beyond the pale in various societies—foreigner in French and English schools and so on—and I have some experience of what it feels like. But I was always able to develop the right accent and the right protective feathers in a few months. Only in nightmares do I really experience it as it must be. You are certainly right that it is terribly important that Negro children should grow up knowing enough to love themselves and be glad that they are themselves. Somehow I have a deep conviction that the Negroes will make out fine, and that God is with them. The really frighteningly God-forsaken people in this country are, it seems to me, the ones in the Redneck ghettoes. The trash. They really spook me. I guess the real heroic thing in this age would be to try to convert them, when they imagine they are the only Christians left. It makes me shudder . . .

To Leilani Bentley

Leilani Bentley, a college freshman from Mulliken, Michigan, wrote to Merton for information for a term paper comparing him with Dag Hammarskjöld "on the thesis of contemplation and peace."

March 20, 1967

Thanks for your nice letter. I will give you what help I can. First of all, I have read *Markings* with great interest and sympathy. One of the greatest bonds between myself and Dag H. is a common interest in Meister Eckhart whom he quotes very frequently. I do not quote Eckhart as much but I use others of the same school, like Tauler, and I get the same sort of material from St. John of the Cross. In my latest book, *Conjectures of a Guilty Bystander* which you can probably get from your library, you may find other material similar to his. I would also suggest *Seeds of Contemplation* and the new edition of same, *New Seeds*.

Another point of comparison would be interest in world peace and unity. Perhaps in this connection you might look up a little book I did on Gandhi [*Gandhi on Non-Violence*]. I think too that Dag Hammarskjöld was quite interested in Oriental thought, as I am, but I do not remember anything specific in this regard.

I have not read the recent biography [Emery Kelen, *Hammarskjöld*]. I was asked to review it but was not able as I did not have time. Finally, I will look around and see if I have any unpublished mimeograph material I can send you that would throw light on your subject. But I don't want to swamp you.

To Tony Boyd

Tony Boyd, a seventh-grader from Ashland, Kentucky, wrote asking Merton to send "all the information about Kentucky music and Ky. facts that you can" for a scrapbook on Kentucky his class was preparing.

March 20, 1967

You are the first person who ever picked me out as an authority on music. I cannot even play a mouth organ properly, though I can play bongo drums, I admit that. All I know is that I like Country Music when I hear it, which is rarely. I like Johnny Cash, but I guess he is not from Kentucky. Here in the monastery we have sung Gregorian chant which is an ancient form of Catholic Church music.

What can I contribute to your scrapbook on Kentucky facts? Maybe you want to know about our monastery. It was founded in 1848 by some monks from France and the building was built by the monks during the Civil War. This ancient building is now being entirely remodelled on the inside. The monks are well known for their dairy farm which produces a special kind of cheese. They keep silence among themselves in order to think more deeply and to keep their minds on God. This is an occupation which other people tend to overlook. I have been in this monastery for over twenty-five years now, which means that I have lived in Kentucky half my life. I like it in Kentucky and I am very glad to be a citizen of this State. Wishing you luck with your scrap book . . .

To Jeanette Yakel

Jeanette Yakel, of Green Island, New York, wrote asking why God permits cruelty to animals; it seemed to her "so unjust and needless."

March 21, 1967

Any question about unjust and useless suffering is difficult to answer, and I must admit that I do not have ready answers to such questions at hand. In the end, I believe the trouble comes from some imperfect way in which we imagine God "willing" or "permitting" these things, as if He were somehow a human being and outside of everything. Who knows? If human suffering has value, it is only from the fact that Christ, God Himself, suffers it in us and with us. Who is to say that He does not in some way Himself suffer in the animals what they suffer? That is a possible answer. God cannot simply look on "objectively" while His creatures suffer. To imagine Him doing so is to imagine something quite other than God. I do not say that the sufferings of animals have a supernatural meritorious value and all that: but perhaps they do have some special meaning that is not clear to us. In any case, from the natural scientific point of view it can be said that the sufferings of animals are radically different from ours in so far as they do not have the same kind of highly developed imagination we have: they do not add the mental suffering that we add on to physical suffering. Note also that the physical organism may benefit in some way by fighting back against pain. We often experience that in ourselves.

These are just suggestions. In any case, human beings who wantonly cause animals to suffer are certainly very much to blame.

To Mario Falsina

March 25, 1967

Thanks for your letter. I am glad you can read English. I will see that some books are sent to you. I will also try to send you some mimeograph conference notes that will be useful in writing your thesis. Now to answer your questions:

1 - My idea of the world: first of all the world as God's good creation. I have the good fortune to live in close contact with nature, how should I not love this world, and love it with passion? I understand the joy of St. Francis amid the creatures! God manifests himself in his creation, and

everything that he has made speaks of him. The Bible tells us to see him in his creatures and the psalms summon creation to praise him with us. Above all man, the summit of God's creation, and the works of man, his civilization, his art, his science, his technology. On the other hand there is a meaning "of the world" in which creation loses its luminosity and ceases to manifest God. The world in itself can never be evil, it always praises God: but man's desires and greed can change his relationship to creatures. When men as individuals or in society seek only to use creation in order to dominate other men, to gain power for themselves, to enrich themselves at the expense of others, then the "world" becomes in some sense the victim of their greed and it takes on the character of those who make use of it in a sinful way. It is the "world" in this sense that the Christian and the monk must liberate himself from. But in reality we liberate ourselves not from created things, but from our own inordinate and wrong desires. The evil is not in the world but in ourselves.

2 - *Marxism*. First of all let me say that I deplore a Christian attitude that seems to equate Christian faith with anti-communism pure and simple. There is much good to be found in Marxism, and a merely negative attitude to it is foolish. Marxism must be taken seriously in the modern world. On the other hand, my experience with Communism, though not very extensive, makes it impossible for me to accept the Communist political line in most things, except where it happens to coincide with my own Christian liberalism. I never actually joined the Communist party, but as a university student in the thirties I was interested in Communism. However I parted company with Communism first of all when I saw that the university Communism of those times was superficial and doctrinaire—a political pose. I became convinced that Communism was not for me when I saw the development of Stalinist absolutism and what seemed to me opportunism (the alliance of Stalin with Hitler). My attitude to Communism has remained substantially the same as that of Albert Camus who saw that Communism is a form of political absolutism that always sacrifices human values to abstract political principles, and depends on force and violence to attain its ends. But incidentally this is not a monopoly of Communism and the western democracies are just as bad. I seriously believe that a radically new form of political life needs to be discovered to fill the needs of twentieth century man.

3 - Reasons for my conversion, besides the grace of God. First of all the discovery of a metaphysical sense of Being, and an intuition of God as *ens a se*, pure actuality. Then the mystical ideas of William Blake, the religious poetry of Gerard Manley Hopkins, and other Catholic literature all of which brought home to me the deep reality of the Christian faith and the emptiness of my own life in the context of a shallow materialism and rationalism in which I could not really be interested: hence a sense of the emptiness and superficiality of a non-Christian existence.

4 - The evils of the world against which Christians must fight.

a) War, especially total war, and the tendency to exalt raison d'etat over the rights of human beings to life and a reasonable existence. The arrogance of military might, and the abstract mentality which destroys human lives by the thousand and even by the million, treating this destruction as no more than a mathematical problem. In a word, militaristic inhumanity.

b) Social injustice, in which wealth is concentrated in the hands of a few while millions starve and do not have any chance to work for a decent living.

c) False social mystiques which elevate political systems to the level of quasi-religious beliefs and absolute systems, in the name of which human values and lives are easily sacrificed. Racism.

The goods to strive for are correlative to these: peace, international harmony and justice, social justice, aid to underdeveloped nations so that all may make progress together. Overcoming race prejudice by understanding and love but first of all by a just sharing of rights and advantages. A decent standard of living for all. Adequate facilities to provide all with medical care, recreation, education etc. Decent housing for all. Land reform in backward countries etc.

5 - Besides Dante, what other Italian writers have influenced or impressed me? Well, among the poets one of the first that springs to my mind is Jacopone da Todi and of course St. Francis was one of the greatest Italian poets. St. Bonaventure is perhaps one of the Italian thinkers who has influenced me most in some ways. Also the mysticism of St. Catherine of Genoa (and to a lesser extent St. Catherine of Siena). But now to speak of modern and secular writers: I have an immense admiration for the poetry of Eugenio Montale, as well as that of Quasimodo and Ungaretti. Pavese too is a great writer of stories who makes the Italian country side very alive. I would not say that these are dominant influences in my life. I add that I am glad to be a friend of La Pira.

European and American thinkers who have influenced me. Religious: St. Thomas Aquinas (well, he is Italian too really), Duns Scotus, St. Augustine, St. Gregory the Great, St. Bernard. Mystics: Tauler, Ruysbroeck, St. John of the Cross, St. Theresa, St. Therese. Modern theological writers: Hans Von Balthasar, De Lubac, Danielou, Bouyer, Dom Leclercq, K. Rahner, Romano Guardini, Jacques Maritain, E. Gilson. Others: Pascal, Shakespeare, Blake, T. S. Eliot, Rilke, Dostoevsky, Berdyaev, Joyce, Camus, Graham Greene, Leon Bloy, René Char, St. John Perse. Americans: Thoreau, Faulkner, William Carlos Williams, Mark Van Doren, Emily Dickinson. Some others: F. García Lorca, César Vallejo, Aldous Huxley. I have obviously forgotten some important ones, but that is the best I can do now.

6 - What counsel would I give to young people today? Make a better world than we have handed on to you. Do not believe yourself obliged to remain within limitations imposed by us. Use your imagination and

your freedom to explore new horizons. Do not forget the past because a mere "loss of memory" will condemn you to repeat the same mistakes that have been made before, but do not be bound to the past, learn to go beyond it. Build a world of peace, or if you fail it will be destroyed. As to the Christian faith, realize that it is not inexorably bound to any particular civilization or culture and the creative power of the Spirit is without limits: hence be open to all that is new and that helps man to be more true to himself and to his vocation as a child of God in freedom. Realize that only the Spirit of Christ can guarantee true freedom that is able to resist the domination of human systems and mystifications.

Thank you for your prayers which you have said you would offer me at Sotto il Monte, the village of our dear Pope John. He was very good to me and I felt that he was personally a Father as he took the trouble to send me good words and do me a kindness that I greatly appreciated. I have a very special love and veneration for Pope John whom I believe to be one of the great saints of the Church. Naturally I also have a filial devotion to our present Holy Father.

To Susan Chapulis

Susan Chapulis, a sixth-grader at Saint Joseph's School in Waterbury, Connect-icut, wrote to Merton for information on "Monks and Monasteries." She added: "I was asked to write to you. I guess you know why."

April 10, 1967

Thanks for your nice letter. You want "any information whatsoever" to help the sixth grade in the study of monasticism. Well, I'll see if I can get the brothers down in the store to send you a little book about the monastery here. That ought to help.

The monastic life goes back a long way. Monks are people who seek to devote all their time to knowing God better and loving Him more. For that reason they leave the cities and go out into lonely places where it is quiet and they can think. As they go on in life they want to find lonelier and lonelier places so they can think even more. In the end people think these monks are really crazy going off by themselves and of course sometimes they are. On the other hand when you are quiet and when you are free from a lot of cares, when you don't have to worry about your car and your house and all that, and when you don't make enough money to pay taxes, and don't have a wife to fight with, and when your heart is quiet, you suddenly realize that everything is extremely beautiful and that just by being quiet you can almost sense that God is right there not only with you but even in you. Then you realize that it is worth the trouble of going away where you don't have to talk and mess around and make a darn fool of yourself in the middle of a lot of people who are running around in circles to no purpose. I suppose that is why monks go off and live in lonely places. Like me now I live alone in the woods with squirrels and rabbits and deer and foxes and a huge owl that comes down by my cabin and makes a spooky noise in the night, but we are friends and it is all ok. A monk who lives all by himself in the woods is called a hermit. There is a Rock 'n Roll outfit called Herman and his Hermits but they are not the same thing.

I do not suppose for a moment that you wish to become a hermit (though now I understand there are some girl hermits in England and they are sort of friends of mine because they are hermits, so I send them stuff about how to be a hermit). But anyway, I suggest that you sometimes be quiet and think how good a thing it is that you are loved by God who is infinite and who wants you to be supremely happy and who in fact is going to make you supremely happy. Isn't that something? It is, my dear, and let us keep praying that it will work out like that for everybody. Good bye now.

To Lisa Bieberman

Merton was interested in the problems of young people in the 1960s, the counter-culture movement, the "hippies," the generation gap, the drug culture, the "community" movement. He wrote to Lisa Bieberman, a young psychologist, after reading her article about LSD, "On Getting the Message," in Innerspace. *She had said: "What would be surprising would be if awareness were possible only to the young, the radical and the rebellious, and not to all people of good will."*

April 15, 1967

I am a monk, poet, priest, and have written a few books on the contemplative life in which I am interested. Which, to some extent, gives us something in common, and that is why I presume to write to you about a very interesting article of yours, "On Getting the Message" in *Innerspace*.

That whole issue of *Innerspace*, the first I've seen, fell into my hands quite by chance (as everything else does I guess). Though I have never taken psychedelics I have been in this business for more than twenty-five years and have been novice master in this monastery for ten. I have had a lot to do with people who get in difficulties with the contemplative life, break down, etc. I have a great deal of respect for what you are doing, and I can see from your article that you are completely on the level and that what is happening with you is like a lot of things that have happened in another way and in another context with me. Therefore, will you let me speak to you frankly and with real concern and love?

The problem of experience and communication, solitude and community, is something I have grappled with for a very long time. It is true one must communicate. But it is most important also not to communicate in words, sometimes, and above all not to be anxious to communicate, not to be anxious to be understood, not to be justified, not to be accepted necessarily. And so on. You know what I mean. I honestly think you people need more than anything else a *disciplina arcani* (like the first Christians—they did not talk about the sacraments). You need to get a good sane group of you underground fast, because with the public emotion and fury about it this whole thing may dissolve fast into something it need not be. You all strike me as lovely innocent people who may suddenly find that all hell has been let loose, and believe me the establishment in this country has developed that to a high pitch of perfection. I know of course this is a sort of charismatic thing like that in the fourteenth century, and no one can keep it underground or even want to. But I think you should have that *too*. I think you really need an element of silence, of loneliness, of non-communication in order to make the whole thing more valid and keep it so. (Incidentally though I think the information in the magazine is most important I am not talking about that.) My impression is that the Indians who used peyote etc. did so under very strict ritual conditions and with a certain secrecy: no? Let me then recommend to you silence, and solitude to some extent, according to your own formulas. I admit that your movement works according to conditions that are not mine and that I do not fully understand, and I don't want to interfere with that. But I do know just what you want, because it is what I want in a different way. If I can be of any help at any time (in this area of inwardness etc.) I will gladly try. This letter is not for publication, but I hope it is of some use and again I hope you don't mind my butting in where I don't belong. But I do feel sympathetic and concerned. Do you know Ibn al'Arabi? Henri Corbin has written on him. You might like the Sufis.

To Grace Sisson

In 1962 Merton had regretted in his poem that Grace Sisson provided no "road" or access to her house. Five years later Grace sent another drawing with a road, which she called The Road to Joy.

May 13, 1967

Of course I remember you and your drawing. If I did not answer in a big hurry, it was because I have a lot of letters to answer and have a difficult time doing that. But I want especially to thank you for your note and for your new drawing which is very significant. I like the way you see all the little creatures tending toward a tree which is a sort of tree of life. I am glad you still draw things with love, and I hope you will never lose that. But I hope you and I together will secretly travel our own road to joy, which is mysteriously revealed to us without our exactly realizing. When I say that, I don't want you to start thinking about it. You already know it without thinking about it.

Well, you must be getting to be a big girl by now. Your handwriting is that of a mature little person and is in fact better than mine. I hope you will write to me again. Say hello to your Dad [Elbert R. Sisson] and to all the family.

To Scott Wright

Scott Wright wrote "The Merton–Mailer Vision," now on file in the Thomas Merton Studies Center, as part of his work for a master's degree in library science at the University of Minnesota, and sent Merton a copy.

May 26, 1967

Thanks for your letter and for your essay on "The Merton–Mailer Vision". I am not surprised at your approach. I have not read a great deal of Mailer but what I have read not only interests me but strikes the right chord, I think. We do have something of the same kind of protest to utter, in our different ways. Besides that, someone [Michele Murray, "Life Viewed Too Facilely"] criticizing *Conjectures* in a Catholic paper, held this against me that I was "like Norman Mailer" (*National Catholic Reporter*, early this year sometime). I'll see if I can dig up a copy of the letter I wrote to the paper ["Thomas Merton Replies to a Perceptive Critic"] accepting this not as a stigma but as something that seemed to be reasonable. Like Mailer, I am not able to agree with a completely square and sociological sort of liberalism which really accepts the suburban and technological thing just as it is, and wants only more of the same. Unfortunately this is what passes for advanced thinking among many Catholics since the Council. They imagine that this is what it means to understand the "modern world." I'll send a copy of an essay that has something to do with this, if I can find it. I am grateful for your thoughtfulness. Did you send a copy to Mailer? In any event, your essay is a reminder for me to go and read those things of his that I have not read (most of his books). I also like James Baldwin, as you know.

To Arthur John Harris

John Harris, a schoolteacher in Devonshire and later in Cornwall, England, had helped Merton in his communication with Boris Pasternak and they corresponded during the last ten years of Merton's life (Merton's letters to Harris are included in the first volume of the Merton letters, The Hidden Ground of Love). *In 1963, Harris sent a picture of his children and Merton responded: "I love those pictures."*

In January 1967, Harris mentioned that his twelve-year-old son, Arthur John, wondered if Merton could send him some stamps for his collection from the mail Merton received. Merton responded with stamps and called Arthur "our trusty secret agent in Cornwall." Merton signed himself X127 and A127, 127 being his laundry number at Gethsemani.

[February 1967]

Since, as you realize, I conduct an immense and sinister traffic in hallucinogenic drugs and Argentinian soccer players and since this traffic has ramifications in five continents and many large and small islands, my secret agents everywhere keep me well provided with STAMPS.

Thus it is not difficult for me to send you from time to time a few of these, some of which are still impregnated with opiates, others scrawled with secret information concerning future interplanetary wars. Please give my kind regards to your estimable father whom we in the transcontinental dope ring regard as a most deadly sleuth.

Sincerely yours,
X127
(alias Thomas Merton)

[June 1967]

Dear Agent:

A dangerous man to be watched is a certain Duke William, so-called "conqueror." Blow him up if he gets near Hastings. He may give you some trouble.

Yours for an independent Cornwall,
A127

To John Wu, Jr.

John Wu, son of Merton's friend Dr. John C. H. Wu [Merton's letters to the elder Wu are included in the first volume of the Merton letters, The Hidden Ground of Love]*, and a student at Seton Hall in New Jersey, wrote to Merton about his conscientious objection to the Vietnam War.*

June 9, 1967

The letters I really like to answer get pushed aside because I prefer to think a little before answering them, and then they get lost . . . And first, I know what you mean about Coltrane, because I have heard him and admire him: also I like very much Ornette Coleman and especially Jackie McLean. I haven't heard the Coltrane–Ellington duo. I admit though that I am still more inclined to the old jazz of my own day, not because it is better but because I hear it better.

I am very glad that the draft board was reasonable with you. Not all of them are the same, it is pretty much a matter of roulette. Of course the thing about conscientious objection, in my mind, is that simply to object to war and not to all the other things that go with it, does not make all the sense in the world. It is part of a whole attitude, and what matters is the whole attitude. There is a lot of fuss around now among progressive Catholics about objection to the unjust war but not to other wars. Well, all right, fine. But I can also well understand the military objecting to this kind of objection. One's choice narrows down to a fine little point, that one unjust war: and for the rest, one goes along with everybody else in everything, the secular city is the New Jerusalem, etc. etc. One can drown in martinis if one wants, and make a million dollars into the bargain. It seems to me that we are asked to be a little more revolutionary than that, and one thing I do like about the world these days is that your generation is protesting louder and better and more intelligently than most of the others have so far. So good luck, and keep on going . . .

I am worried about your father. I haven't heard from him, and I think he must be suffering a bit, perhaps in ways he himself does not understand. I must write to him, just to show a sign of life, but I am so snowed under with mail requiring that fast stupid answer . . . Anyway, let's pray for him. I really do not envy his position at all. I think the people he is with are hopelessly wrong in many ways, and yet I can see where he would feel he had to go along with them, and I am sure he is not totally at peace with it. I admire his fidelity and understand his silence, and in the long run I know his integrity is the kind that matters, especially because it is the kind you cannot easily explain. I hope Michael Hodder made out all right with the board. My best wishes to both of you.

To Jon Allen

Jon Allen, a twenty-three-year-old soldier in Vietnam, wrote asking Merton to pray for him and the thousands of others involved in the war. He said in closing: "You might think it strange to receive a letter such as this, but it is a letter I must write . . . It is my confession, the confessions of all mankind. I hope I have not offended you by writing to you, if so, you are justified, you do not know me, and I am not Catholic, I am though, a man, full of fears, and much anxiety, God forgive me."

July 10, 1967

I want to write a few words to thank you for your letter and to encourage you to stick to the good ideas that have come to you. I know things must be very tough out there. War brings you face to face with death and the devil, with the evil that is in man and with some of the possibilities of good. It shows you that your destiny is something that demands great acts of courage and decision, not in killing others but in finding the truth of your own existence and being faithful to it. I shall pray that you may be faithful. Pray for me too. God bless you and all your buddies.

To Meg Shore

Meg Shore, a student at Vassar College in Poughkeepsie, New York, sent a form letter to Merton which began: "Denise Levertov, who taught at Vassar this past year, has suggested that you might be so kind as to give us a holograph copy of one of your poems for the benefit of a Peace Information Room which we are setting up at Vassar . . . The money will go towards the purchase of current books on Vietnam, pacifism, and related topics."

August 3, 1967

Thanks for your letter. I am sending along a poem—in holograph, or kakography, or just plain a-graph: a piece of non-writing. If anybody is mad enough to buy it then they can have it. If you want to know what the poem is, I have enclosed a typescript for your convenience and theirs ["A Round and a Hope for Smith Girls"]. Another possible misfortune is that it is a poem for Smith, and here it goes to Vassar. I mean, do not take this to be an expression of aggressive loyalty to Smith. I love Vassar too, but I happen to have more friends at Smith at the moment. Though maybe by now they are all flown away . . .

To Robert Barton

Robert Barton, a lecturer at Rutgers University, was completing his doctoral dissertation on the Middle English poem Sir Gawain and the Green Knight. *He wrote to ask why Merton had used the phrase "green-bearded Arthur" and why, in fact, he had chosen Arthur at all in his poem "Fall '66," which had appeared in* New York Review of Books.

August 11, 1967

Thanks for your letter. Yes, I think there are probably unconscious resonances of the whole kind of attitude represented by Gawain, which has always been one of my favorite poems—and its wonderful deflation of feudal pomposity. I will try to answer your questions succinctly.

The Arturumque etiam . . . is from one of Milton's Latin poems ["Mansus"]. I do not have Milton at hand and cannot look up where the line actually came from. But it is a reflection of Milton's own interest in an Arthuriad. So the plot thickens! Remember Milton planned first to write an epic on Arthur, and gradually abandoned it for various reasons.

I bet there are still traces of Arthur in Satan . . . I don't know, there was not enough of Arthur around to go by.

The "underground" image is in the Milton poem. Arthur and his knights are still warring in the land of the dead which is also the land of dreams, the unconscious, and Milton's own creative imagination. The warlike Father in our spook collections is always struggling to get out and invade the land of the living. The Washington people are obviously driven on by a cheap mythology—the second-hand chivalry which rescues a maiden Asian nation (inferior nations are maidens) in distress, attacked by dragon etc.

I don't know if the green beard is in the Milton poem or if I thought it up, but in either case it comes quite naturally from the general store of "green man" images (dead-underground-fertility-spring-resurrection-eros-thanatos). In my own making or finding of the poem, the green beard went with the bushes and with coming up out of the underground into the light. In the end of the poem the living green dead become frozen in the zombie statue of Patria. This could use a lot of explication maybe: how the life force begins to be a death force and death wish, when it is pushed away and seen as object, as old man, as Father, as dead hero coming back again (preventing growth—the axe of the green castrating knight the destroyer). I do not mean to be too garrulous, but you see the connections. I wish you all luck with your thesis, which sounds like a good one.

September 25, 1967

One thing I have been meaning to say: if you don't know the poetic work of David Jones, you must get to it. His two big poems are now available in Viking Paperbacks, and there is a recent issue of *Agenda* devoted to him. Now that all my fellow Catholics are falling over themselves to push every last relic of the middle ages out the sacristy window, it is comforting to read a Welsh Catholic in whom that whole tradition is still alive and fresh and real.

You question me about "spook collections." What I meant was that all our father troubles and all our dealings with satan-arthurs and larger than life good-bad warrior loomers out from underground goes back to the primitive heritage of everybody—the old days when we all wanted to make sure that the dead stayed dead, that they went to the realm of the dead and became protectors and crop givers, not hanging around the back yard as ghosts. This occupation of quieting the ancestors has provided us with our inordinately large gallery of badfaces and Green Knights and shades we have to cope with, now in ourselves and now projected outward. And about Milton's Satan, I think really everybody was right, both those who saw Satan as Milton the Boy Buck Rogers and Satan the self-defeating puritan but also Satan as the force that bursts into the land of the living out of hell and the realm of death. Calvinism set Milton up for all possible ambivalences.

Acedia as noonday demon is a favorite monastic trope, from Cassian and the desert. Bernard in his commentary on Psalm 90 has good stuff on it. Two kinds of noonday: one the ordinary noon time of day when you are very hungry because you won't eat until None or Vespers. Other kind, the *demonium meridianum* of Psalm 90 or the devil as angel of light. The hungry one makes the monk look down the road, hoping a visitor will come so he can break his fast and eat earlier. The other makes him do terrible things under the guise of virtue. Both could apply to the Pentagon! . . . Best luck with your thesis.

To Betsi Baeten

Betsi Baeten, an eighth-grader from West De Pere, Wisconsin, wrote to Merton about a panel on civil rights which her class was to present to their parents at a P.T.A. meeting. Since her teacher had said that Merton's writings on the subject were "the most dynamic she had ever seen in print," Betsi asked Merton to "please write a few paragraphs, in language that an American teen-ager could understand, on just why people vent their hatred on the colored man."

October 2, 1967

It is almost impossible for me to give you in a few words the reasons for race prejudice. I refer you to the book *Seeds of Destruction* and will mail a mimeographed paper written recently ["The Hot Summer of Sixty-Seven"].

In general, let's consider only the psychological mechanism. People have a way of selecting the traits in themselves and in others and sorting them out according to likes and dislikes. They instinctively censor their own ideas of themselves and others: the traits they *like*, they tend to see in themselves and in their friends. The traits they don't like they see in strangers, aliens, and those who are different from themselves. Then they feel they can punish these other people for being different, bad, wrong, etc. Instead of having to admit evil in themselves, and having to live with it, they project it on to others. Thus ideas of dirt, evil living, animality, etc., which are all quite present in the unconscious fantasies of white people, tend to be projected on to Negroes and hated in Negroes. That is a real convenient way of handling it, and it is made easy by the fact that Negroes are poor, can't get decent jobs, have to live in slums, and are therefore forced to conform to the ideas others have of them. It is a vicious circle.

The Gospel teaches us to love others as ourselves, and to see in the enemy the same amount of good and evil as we find in ourselves. There is good in all of us and evil in all of us. We have all come to admit this theoretically, but there is a deeply ingrained fear of Negroes and suspicion of them which white people have not learned to overcome. This causes trouble.

To Barbara Ann Braveman

Barbara Ann Braveman, editorial assistant for the student magazine Freelance *at Washington University, thanked Merton for allowing them to use the poem "Newscast" and apologized for their printer's having presented him with a "nom de plume," his name having been printed as "Thomas Inman." She later wrote inviting Merton to speak at Washington University.*

October 19, 1967

Thanks for *Freelance*: a pleasant surprise and a good alive magazine. I have read most of the poetry with pleasure and am planning to get into the Allen Ginsberg interview later. Glad you could use "Newscast", and am interested to find that I have a possible new name. Maybe when I go underground I'll do so as Will Inman's brother . . .

November 6, 1967

Thanks for the extra copies, for the feedback on the poem and all. For many reasons I am happy that people like it: it augurs well for the whole book and for a whole new mood of my own. I was interested in Howard Nemerov's reaction and the account of his visit! It must have been an open and enjoyable experience for all of you, and I wish I could some time have the same chance. That is why I am gratified at your invitation.

Though I would really love to be there and to meet all of you, the rules here do not permit it. It would be useless for me even to think of asking for clearance from the superiors. But also, I have given this a lot of thought recently: supposing the rules were to relax somewhat, I still don't think that in my case it would be the right thing to do. I have made a choice beyond the normal monastic life and am living as a hermit now, partly as a kind of protest against the kind of society we have. For me to come out of the woods for public appearances would tend to neutralize that protest (even though I could perhaps make other and more effective noises outside). Also it is necessary for me to be alone for long periods simply to keep the peculiar kind of perspective that I have. In a word, one can't have both solitude and a great deal of communication. Having chosen the one, I have to do without the other. I really would like to meet all of you and I know that in a way I would profit very much by it. But there does not seem to be a way of fitting it in, though perhaps if you are coming by this way some time and write me well ahead I might be able to keep a couple of hours free for you and a small group some afternoon. Even that is not always possible . . .

To Michael J. Looby

Michael Looby, a student at Le Moyne College in Syracuse, New York, wrote asking: "As a man of conviction, as a man of deep thought, and as a patriotic American citizen, would you please, if it is at all possible, explain your stance on the Viet Nam question to me, a perplexed student?"

November 24 1967

I wish I had time to write you a detailed letter. That is not possible. I send a couple of enclosures, including a letter of mine that I mimeographed last year and it deals partly with this question.

The Vietnam question, the way you present it, is deceptively simple. IF it were a cut-and-dried issue like that, opposition to the war would indeed be hard to understand. IF we were defending the people of Vietnam, instead of destroying them . . . IF we were really working in favor of our own interests, instead of making ourselves hated and mistrusted everywhere. IF we were holding back communism, instead of making it inevitable, after this war which cannot be won in our terms at all . . . My contention is that the government, through stupidity or something else, is deceived by its own myths and is passing on this mythology to the country: but there are not that many fools around. I also think that what the war-people want is war with China, and I think that would be a criminal absurdity. I hope I am wrong in my guess that they want this, and that they are preparing it. In any event, the death of thousands of helpless civilians in Vietnam is justified by no real gains of any kind whatever, and I am afraid God will judge this nation severely for its callousness. Again, I hope I am wrong. But I am very concerned about all those dead people. They have been made to suffer unpardonable and stupid cruelties which they will never forget and more and more Vietnamese are being pushed into the arms of the VC because they are sick of the puppet government we are supporting. And sick of us. That way lies no "victory." Only disgrace.

I certainly admit that some of the anti-war protest has been somewhat strange—and able to be made to seem stranger still. But what surprises me is that it has not been far more wild than it is. Whatever the ultimate truth may be, let us certainly hope that something can be salvaged from all this, that there may eventually be real peace and order, and that useless killing may stop. And that worse things may not come of it.

To Nancy Fly Bredenberg

Fly Bredenberg, who was at Vassar College and studying "verse writing" under David Ignatow, told Merton of her assignment to write a critical study of an American poet ("Of course I chose to write about you"). She asked for his advice and for information about influences on his writing.

December 11, 1967

Denise Levertov was here yesterday and in our good visit together I was reminded of Vassar and thought of your letter. I'd better try to answer it while it is still in my mind. I can't really give you a lot of details, but anyhow I'll try to say something.

First, I am glad you like my poems. It is always nice to have readers who are attuned to what you are trying to say. I don't write in a pure void, and though I am not very much concerned about stature publishing, I am glad to reach readers and especially young ones. I guess most of the readers of my poetry are young. At least they are the ones who seem to respond most. I am happy about that.

I would say that I don't belong with any of the groups or schools, and am certainly not involved in the petty orthodoxies of this and that school.

What poets do I like? I am very fond of some Spanish and Latin American poetry, more than what is written in the States. But of North American poets, well, my favorite is Zukofsky. I do like Bill Williams but I find I don't read a great deal of him. Pound I respect and don't read. Duncan I like. Oppen I have quoted some. Creely etc. ok. I wouldn't say any of these had influenced me. Denise Levertov I respond to very much as a poet and a person. But myself I think I am more subject to European and Latin American influences. Vallejo is perhaps the twentieth century poet who means most to me. And Lorca did a long time ago, still does I guess. Rilke. Eliot. Dylan Thomas. One of the most exciting poets writing today in my opinion is Peter Levi. And in French, René Char: great, great stuff. And I like Neruda. Octavio Paz, etc.

Writing means a great deal to me but I am, as I say, rather out of the literary world, at least the orthodox and competitive literary world. But I have friends in it here and there and all around. Oh, another American poet I like very much and really admire, is Ronald Johnson. Very fine! I'm not nuts about Olson, so like Jackson McLow etc. I could just write a lot of etc's after that. Some magazines I do see sometimes, others never. Criticism: I don't see much of it and I don't get the impression that I come in for much attention one way or the other. Some of the criticism of my stuff seems to me huffy and square: the thing that gets people most mad at me is a certain world-denying protest against the super-market culture, but this is silly and it is only one aspect of my work anyhow. Probably too my Christian and eschatological bent bothers a certain type of academic: but I am certainly not a regular "Catholic poet" in any establishment sense. Far from it! The Catlicks too regard me as something of a maverick, except in the early "spiritual writing." Well, I'll slip a few papers in this that may help, as I have to stop now. Best wishes to you, and I hope your paper comes out all right.

To Gerald P. Roucoulet

Gerald Roucoulet, a twenty-one-year-old student at Christ the King Seminary in Saint Bonaventure, New York, wrote asking Merton's advice and suggestions about his entering the monastic life.

January 28, 1968

Not an awful lot I can tell you. Perhaps the best thing would be to acquire some monastic experience of one sort or other, in an informal way. For instance you might find some monastery where you could work around the place and have some share in the liturgy etc. Try that for a year or two and see what it is all about. Visit one or two of the new experiments (the Belleville Trappists, Weston Benedictines in Vermont, Taize group in Chicago, Little Brothers of Jesus in Detroit. Also the Holy Mother of God monastery in Oxford, North Carolina). Meet some of these people, get advice, work with some group, get a foundation of your own ideas and experience and then see.

To Geoffrey Hewitt

Geof Hewitt (one "f" is correct, as Merton later pointed out to the readers of Monks Pond*), a twenty-four-year-old poet from Iowa, was founder, editor, and sole employee of Kumquat Press. At the suggestion of Jonathan Williams, he sent some of his poems and Merton used four in the second issue of* Monks Pond.

February 1, 1968

Thanks for the new poems. I'm keeping two for the second or third issue of *Monks Pond*. And returning the one for Jonathan [Williams], though I like it. You sense my problem: in detail, it is this: the devout young monk who runs the offset machine for me can cause trouble for me and all my pomps and works by simply refusing to cooperate, denouncing me to authorities etc. Now I am sure he thinks rubbers are something that go on your feet and has not sufficient experience of the world to wonder how they could cost so little. But he does know that bullshit is dirty and I guess he has heard of cock. And then there are all the other old mamas around too. However no one can change the fact that Jim Beam [whiskey] is distilled down the road a ways and so is every other brand I can think of. I would not even think of a brand that was distilled more than fifty miles from here. This is the navel of the universe . . . Send more, poems or short prose . . . observations, proverbs, etc. all welcome.

To John Wu, Jr.

*John Wu, Jr., wrote to tell Merton of his impending marriage to Teresa ("Terry")
Wong of Richmond, Virginia, which was to take place on June 15, 1968. John
and Terry eventually did visit Gethsemani on their honeymoon.*

February 26, 1968

I was happy to receive your letter and to hear you are soon to be married. Also I am glad that you and Terry want to come down with your Father and new "mother." I would be really delighted to have you all here. So let us think about concrete plans.

As things are with me now I am fairly well tied up until after May and I presume you are too. June can be very hot and July worse, but still I'd say those are the best times, being vacation months. If you go into a council with your Father and decide, then one of you can let me know what would be good dates for you. I can arrange for the ladies to stay in the ladies' guest house (which takes more arranging because of limited space). Also Sundays are days off for the staff there. Hence a visit during the week for three days or so can easily be set up if I know fairly well in advance. We can all be together during the days, sit in the woods or something, and enjoy ourselves.

I am glad Terry is Chinese. American women are all right, I suppose, but . . . Congratulations.

What you say about the inner voice is all very true and shows you are working your way through the real problems of development. You are not wasting your time. You are on the right track.

Please tell your Father that I have received the *Golden Age* [of Zen] and will thank him for it as soon as I get a chance to write [Merton wrote the introduction, "A Christian Looks at Zen"].

To Ronald Anthony Punnett

*Ron Punnett, a twenty-two-year-old black poet born in Trinidad, was a British
citizen serving in the American Army. He sent Merton four poems for* Monks
Pond, *three of which Merton used in the second issue.*

March 20, 1968

Sorry to have held up so long in answering. The poems get all piled up, mixed up, lost, found, built into pyramids, birds nests, catacombs, dugouts, temples. Yours got mixed in with the ones possible for *MP iii*, whereas I really want them for *MP ii*, (but for one I return). I am very glad to have them. And I'm sending you a copy of the first issue. The second will be better. There will be another three issues I think. So keep me in mind. I'm glad Keith Wilson urged you to send something. Take care of yourself. Keep in touch.

To Mary Declan Martin

Mary Declan Martin, an education student at Brescia College in Owensboro, Kentucky, was writing a paper for her Philosophy of Education course and asked Merton for his views on education. She said: "I chose Thomas Merton because, ever since high school, you have amazed me."

April 1, 1968

I get such a quantity of letters that it is not possible to answer even half of them. When it comes to requests like yours, the best I can do is try to send material for you to look over. Unfortunately I cannot find a copy of an essay that has something about education in it. All I can send is a sheet with some dates about my life. In the section of *The Seven Storey Mountain* about my days at Columbia you may find some reflections on education, and also in a recent anthology edited by Morris Ernst, *The Teacher*, I have a chapter ["On Remembering Monsieur Delmas"]. But you may not be able to locate the book.

My grandmother was one of the first school teachers out in New Zealand and in the 1860's and many of my family have been teachers. I have taught College English and since being in the monastery have been novice master and have taught other courses. I believe education means more than just imparting "knowledge." It means the formation of the whole person.

To Thomas J. O'Brien

Tom O'Brien, teacher of religion to sophomores and juniors at Brother Rice High School in Chicago, was taking graduate education courses and had chosen for a course in Contemporary Issues in American Education the topic "Catholic Church Non-Involvement in Ghetto Areas, and Consequent Adverse Effect on Negro Acculturation." He asked for Merton's thoughts and comments.

April 9, 1968

Well, since your letter, we have seen some tragic new developments in the area of race relations in this country. The death of Martin Luther King has been a great sign which may or may not finally stir the conscience of the country. But it comes too late to really have the kind of effect it should have on us, this stirring of conscience. What it really shows is that Christians should have awakened to the gravity of the situation ten years ago. Now it is too late for non-violence. What we will have to face is violence. The Church's obligation now is to try to prevent the country from sinking into a kind of police state in its reaction against the violence that is inevitable.

Of course, the Catholic community has on the whole been better on race than it has on war. There has been some real response. But it has still been largely symbolic (nuns at Selma, etc). And always too late.

I think you are right when you say that Catholic spirituality has been too individualistic. That is just another way of saying that it has been the product of a middle-class environment. Carl Amery's book _Capitulation_ has plenty to say about this kind of "milieu Catholicism" in Nazi Germany. We are about to have the same problems here. Though perhaps not quite in the same way. Unfortunately, I am not sure that a more revolutionary Catholicism cast in the mold of a socialist society is going to be much help either. We can't just go on fitting into somebody else's mold.

To Barrie Peterson

Barrie Peterson wrote to Merton that a number of students at Princeton Theological Seminary were "interested in thinking through the possibilities and limitations of forming a radical community or commune." He asked for Merton's suggestions and advice about literature in this area.

April 9, 1968

Sorry for having neglected your questions for so long. I have far too much mail. Besides which your questions are a little harder than they might at first seem, since you are thinking of radical and (I presume) eschatological type communities rather than the current familiar monastic type of community—even those which are experimental. As to these latter, you should probably get in touch with them anyhow. For instance Taize has a group in Chicago. Then there is Emmaus House in East Harlem. Of course Koinonia in Georgia. Catholic Worker Farm, Tivoli, N.Y. Also the Bruderhof—Community of Brothers—Rifton, N.Y. Their founder, Eberhard Arnold, has done good writing on this kind of community.

I won't go into the standard literature on American utopian societies. You can get all that in your library. And of course you know to what extent there is a ferment of eschatological community life among hippies, diggers, etc, and how much there is about this in underground newspapers like the San Francisco *Oracle*.

One Catholic lay theologian you might contact and who can probably help is Mrs. Rosemary Ruether who teaches at Howard University . . . Needless to say I think you have a very good idea and I hope something will come of it.

To Philip J. Cascia

Philip Cascia, a high-school junior at Saint Thomas Seminary in Bloomfield, Connecticut, wrote to Merton about his term paper on ecumenism.

April 10, 1968

I am sorry I was not able to answer your letter before. And I am afraid I just cannot go into details on those questions. In a general way, I'd say that the ecumenical movement is certainly an excellent thing, and it has meant new life for all Christians. Of course it is something of a fad in some places, and it gets the usual distorted kind of publicity. But basically it is a good thing.

People are less dependent on the clergy and nuns, let's put it that way. Doubtless there will be a much more important part for lay people to play, including perhaps married deacons etc. There is no reason why there should not be a married clergy, except that people attach so much importance to the idea of a celibate priest. But celibacy is a charism— we in the religious life appreciate that more I think.

Good folk music at Mass can be a big help, but bad singing and trifling hymns are not much help. But so is bad Gregorian an obstacle rather than a help. I think what counts is life and fervor in the celebration of the liturgy, and whatever helps that in the right way is good.

I have had an opportunity to offer Mass in a home and this is a fine thing, I believe. Undoubtedly there will be more changes, but let's hope they will be really useful ones. Change for the sake of change is useless. I think a lot of progressive Catholics in this country don't really know where they want to go—but will take anything as long as it is different— and gets good publicity.

To Joseph and Karen Mulloy

Merton had corresponded with Joe and Karen Mulloy for some years and had counseled Joe in his objection to the Vietnam War. Joe Mulloy wrote to Alfred D. Pooler, C.P., then director of the Thomas Merton Studies Center, in 1971: "I have enjoyed an intellectual and a personal relationship with Fr. Merton thru his writings for nearly 9 years, beginning when I was 18 years old. Needless to say his thought, insight and strength had a tremendous effect upon the course of my life and my daily work. In Feb. of 1968, thru a mutual friend, I had the good fortune of spending about an hour walking the hills of Gethsemani with him. I had come to seek his advice about the war in Indo-China, my attempts to seek CO status with my local draft board in Louisville, and if he were me, would he risk a prison term. I knew that he was opposed to the war but he surprised me when he said this country was not worth prison. He then offhandedly suggested that a revolution was brewing in Bolivia and that that's where he would go if in my shoes. We discussed the poverty in Appalachia and the life and death control that the coal operators have over people's lives. He wished me luck and then wrote a letter to my draft board . . . I have also enclosed a letter received by my wife in April. By this time I was already in jail."

April 14, 1968
Easter Sunday

This is to thank you for your letters and to say that this morning I will offer Mass for you. I thought Joe's statement to the court was excellent, courageous, straight to the point. He will obviously have a real impact on a lot of people and the fact that he got a dirty deal will only add to it. I hope you will get the help you need to get Joe out of jail if possible and to appeal the case—if possible.

Meanwhile it is hard to say if the war situation is going to get better or what. Perhaps the future is in some respects hopeful, but one can never tell. The death of Martin Luther King is another sign of the times, but again it has spoken eloquently to a lot of people.

It is with hope and affection that I send you these Easter wishes, and encourage you to go on with your struggle.

To George Lewis Fields

George Fields had corresponded with Merton and spent time on retreat at Gethsemani in 1963. As a medical student at the University of Kentucky in Lexington, he wrote to Merton in 1968 extending an invitation on behalf of one of his professors, Dr. Joseph Engleberg, for Merton to conduct a seminar on nonviolence.

April 28, 1968

It was a pleasant surprise to get your letter. I infer from it and the contents that you are using your time well in Med. School. As a future doctor, you have an obligation to be on the side of the forces of life, and against the massive death wish that is gradually gaining possession of a very sick society . . .

With the new developments in the Church I have naturally had to give a lot of thought to the question whether or not I would eventually go out and talk in various places. The rules of the Order have not yet been changed, but I guess it is quite likely that I could slip out to someplace like Lexington. On the other hand my new Abbot [Flavian Burns], though not being like the old one, would not be very much in favor. And I agree with him. Because if I once started to say "yes" it would be impossible to say "no"—or to do so consistently. And I am afraid that not all invitations would turn out to be worthwhile. In fact, I'd end up just going around talking perhaps rather irresponsibly, and not doing the thing I am really meant to do.

From the point of view of non-violence, there is some basis for a special witness of silence, non-presence, non-imposition of one's own views and personality, etc. True, if one writes it is already ambiguous. But there is definitely in my life a partial element of wanting *not* to "be somebody", not to be there talking and making an impression. I know there are all kinds of arguments against this.

On the other hand, as you rightly say, it is crucially important for people to carry on the ideals and work of Dr. King. I have many friends who were close to him (he was even thinking of coming to Gethsemani for a retreat about the time he went to Memphis instead!) and I certainly want to do my part to keep alive an understanding of non-violence when, in a deteriorated situation, the whole thing may just blow up. If you like, I can send some sort of statement. Dan Walsh or Wendell Berry (a good friend of mine) might read it or report on it. Something on the *ramifications* of violence (for instance in the destruction of ecological balance). Perhaps even a small group of you might want to come down here and spend a couple of hours some afternoon and discuss it *here*. (But May is not possible, perhaps during Summer School or the Fall term) . . .

To Adria Marconi

Adria Marconi, a twenty-four-year-old student of foreign languages at the University of Milan (she had studied in the United States on a Fulbright scholarship at the University of Colorado), wrote to Merton that, in order to graduate, she had to write a thesis on an American or English writer. She chose Merton because his books "often helped us to go on and believe everyone can become a saint."

May 3, 1968

Thanks for your kind letter of April 21. I am honored that you wish to write a thesis on my work. My suggestion is that you concentrate on that aspect of the work which interests you most. For my part, I can send you some material that has not been published, or has appeared only in small magazines here and there. Also some new books which you perhaps do not know.

Recently my work has taken some new directions: an interest in Oriental religion, more literary work in the fields of poetry and criticism, and also some material on the problems of renewal in the Church and in monastic life.

Two American Ph.D. candidates [James Thomas Baker and Dennis Quentin McInerny] are now at work on aspects of my social thought, about war, race relations and so on. I could put you in touch with them if you like.

There has not been a great deal published on me by critics, and once again most attention seems to have been focused on my response to social problems. The early books are still more widely read than the more recent work. Perhaps an obvious subject might be the development and change of my ideas from *The Seven Storey Mountain* to the present.

Please feel free to ask any questions you like. I have an immense correspondence which I cannot adequately answer, but I will do my best to help in some small way or other, at least by sending things you would not otherwise have. I hope you do not find your subject too tedious!

To John B. Brown

John Brown, a student at Union Seminary in New York, wrote about his thesis on race relations in the United States, saying: "I am rather ashamed to admit that you are the first R. Catholic writer that I have read seriously, and then only on the recommendation of C. S. Lewis, who in a letter not long before he died, stated that he had just discovered your writing, and found it quite the best spiritual writing he had come across in a long time."

August 7, 1968

Thanks for your kind letter. I am certainly happy to think that so sound a judge as C. S. Lewis found something to like in my writings!

Regarding your thesis at Union: yes, I do think that consciously or otherwise there is a great deal of provocation or of self-fulfilling prophecy on the part of white racists precipitating violence. I think there is much of that on both sides and do believe we are already practically becoming a kind of apartheid police state, or may do so soon.

One person who holds strongly to your idea that there is deliberate provocation, is John Howard Griffin. He has a new book on this coming out [*The Church and the Black Man*]. I have no doubt that if you wrote to him, he would share with you some ideas . . .

Index

Ursuline College (Louisville), 43
Utopianism, 365–66

Vallejo, Cesar, 349, 361
Van Der Post, Laurens, 82
Van Doren, Charles, 3, 25, 26, 30–31, 35–39, 41, 44, 284
Van Doren, Dorothy, 3, 25, 26, 30, 33, 35, 52
Van Doren, John, 3, 25, 26, 35
Van Doren, Mark, 3–55, 164, 167, 168, 229, 284, 349; Alexander Hamilton Medal (Columbia), 33; Algonquin Hotel dinner, 18–19; *Autobiography of Mark Van Doren*, 27–28; *Collected & New Poems*, 45–46; *Liberal Education*, 31–32; "Merton's Woods," 53; *Narrative Poems*, 49; "Prophet," 44; *Selected Poems*, 26; *Spring Birth & Other Poems*, 24; *Winter Diary*, 26
Van Vlissigen, R. Fentener, 269
Vann, Joseph, OFM, 293–94, 298
Vatican II, 91, 334, 353
Venezuela, 338–39
Vergil, 332
Vietnam, 64, 72, 73, 91, 93, 100, 107, 116, 117, 128, 177, 290, 355–56, 360, 366–67
Virginia (state), 8, 157
Von Balthasar, Hans Urs, 349
Von Selle, Margaret, 93
Voznesensky, Andrei, 126, 130–31

Waddell, Helen, 18
Walsh, Daniel Clark, 102, 124, 131, 135, 185, 193, 194, 198, 203, 211, 217, 231, 247, 248, 254, 263, 264, 265, 266, 302, 304–7, 315
Wasserman, John of the Cross, OCSO, 226, 227, 229, 318

Watkin, E. I., 242
Watts, Peter, 222, 284
Waugh, Evelyn, 172, 182, 190, 220, 255
Weber, Max, 125
Weigel, Gustave, 243
Weiss, Gaspard, 61
Welch, Cornelius, OFM, 293, 294, 298
Wells, Peggy, 150, 151, 169
Wentz, Walter Yeeling Evans, 320
Werfel, Franz, 166
Whitman, Walt, 160
Wilde, Oscar, 344–45
William of St.-Thierry, 192
Williams, Jonathan, 362
Williams, Robert Laurence, 62, 132–33, 269
Williams, William Carlos, 257, 261, 349, 361
Willkie, Wendell, 157
Wilson, Keith, 364
Winandy, Jacques, 103
Wood, Grant, 150
Wordsworth, William, 155
Wright, Scott, 353
Wu, John C. H., 70, 319, 354, 355, 363
Wu, John, Jr., 354–55, 363
Wulff, Augustine, OCSO, 74, 78, 80
Wulff, Louis, 74, 78, 80
Wygal, James, 265, 266, 267

Yakel, Jeannette, 347
Yeats, William Butler, 336
Yevtushenko, Yevgeny, 126
Yoga, 124
Yungblut, June J., 113–14

Zen Buddhism, 29, 83, 114–15, 119, 144, 176, 234, 244, 310, 312, 313, 324
Zilboorg, Dr. Gregory, 29, 30
Zukofsky, Louis, 257, 361